Tax Efficient Retireme

Tax Efficient Retirement Planning

Third Edition

Alec Ure

Bloomsbury Professional

Bloomsbury Professional Ltd, Maxwelton House, 41–43 Boltro Road, Haywards Heath, West Sussex, RH16 1BJ

© Bloomsbury Professional Ltd 2014

Bloomsbury Professional, an imprint of Bloomsbury Publishing Plc

All rights reserved. No part of this publication may be reproduced in any material form (including photocopying or storing it in any medium by electronic means and whether or not transiently or incidentally to some other use of this publication) without the written permission of the copyright owner except in accordance with the provisions of the Copyright, Designs and Patents Act 1988 or under the terms of a licence issued by the Copyright Licensing Agency Ltd, Saffron House, 6–10 Kirby Street, London EC1N 8TS. Applications for the copyright owner's written permission to reproduce any part of this publication should be addressed to the publisher.

While every care has been taken to ensure the accuracy of this work, no responsibility for loss or damage occasioned to any person acting or refraining from action as a result of any statement in it can be accepted by the authors, editors or publishers.

Warning: The doing of an unauthorised act in relation to a copyright work may result in both a civil claim for damages and criminal prosecution.

Crown copyright material is reproduced with the permission of the Controller of HMSO and the Queen's Printer for Scotland. Any European material in this work which has been reproduced from EUR-lex, the official European Communities legislation website, is European Communities copyright.

A CIP Catalogue record for this book is available from the British Library.

ISBN: 978 1 78043 674 6

Typeset by Phoenix Photosetting, Chatham, Kent
Printed and bound in Great Britain by CPI Group (UK) Ltd, Croydon, CR0 4YY

Preface

The world of UK pension provision is undergoing continuous change. The austerity cuts of recent years have had a somewhat diminishing effect on attractive pension provision for the future. A welter of legislation and regulation has been introduced into an ever-increasingly complex system. More than ever it is becoming necessary to put in place sophisticated training processes for professional advisers and managers, and effective compliance management systems and record-keeping tools.

The far-reaching changes mean that the focus of this book has changed from previous editions. The tax reliefs and exemptions which remain ensure that pension provision is still a highly attractive means of saving for retirement within the newly laid-down parameters. There are new freedoms to access funds held in money purchase schemes, with some startling (and perhaps worrying) proposals for the future from government. However, there have been further severe cut-backs in the annual allowance and lifetime allowance tax-free thresholds. In addition, HMRC has been given wide-ranging powers of investigation and access to information. Significant extensions have been made to the reporting requirements for both UK registered pension schemes and qualifying recognised overseas pension schemes. Even non-registered schemes, such as employer-financed retirement benefit schemes, have not escaped extra rules and regulation. There have been extensions to the disclosure of tax avoidance schemes which could affect certain pension schemes. The United Kingdom's first general anti-abuse rule has been introduced, and the government is increasing its vigilance on overseas matters which affect UK citizens and property.

In the Preface to the previous edition of this book reference was made to the 'stupidly complicated system of protections' from various tax charges and cuts to tax-relievable allowances. Unfortunately, there are now an increased number of complex protections which border on the unfathomable, with more to come. As before, it is not necessary to have to cover them in the kind of detail required of a book on retirement planning, although they are described in an accessible format where it is appropriate to do so.

On 16 April 2014, the Pensions Minister called for changes to the tax treatment of pensions savings which would include a flat-rate of 30% tax relief and the abolition of the lifetime allowance. On 22 April 2014 the Centre for Policy Studies published a report containing eight specific proposals on the tax treatment of pensions savings. These include replacing tax relief by a Treasury contribution of 50% for every £1.00 saved and scrapping tax-free cash.

Clearly, additional/alternative forms of retirement saving on a tax-efficient basis need to be explored, both within the UK, and overseas, as encouraged by

Preface

the EU Treaty and Directives on pension provision, portability and individual freedoms.

In order to accommodate all the above changes, this book is now comprised of six parts. Part One contains the ever-changing UK registered pension scheme tax rules. Part Two describes the tax charges for UK registered pension schemes. Part Three is given over to matters affecting high earners in registered pension schemes. Part Four is concerned with the increasingly important overseas considerations. Part Five considers other forms of retirement savings. Part Six explains the rules which apply to the disclosure of tax avoidance schemes, and anti-avoidance rules.

I hope that this book will serve as a useful guide to the tax laws surrounding pensions and related matters and will be of assistance to those advisers engaged in the field of individual and corporate retirement planning.

Alec Ure
Alec Ure & Associates

Contents

Preface	*v*
Table of statutes	*xiii*
Table of statutory instruments	*xxi*
Abbreviations	*xxvii*

Part One – The registered pension scheme tax rules		**1**
1	**Introduction**	**3**
	Background to the current regime	4
	The main legislation	5
	Summary of the current tax regime	9
2	**Registration, providers and membership**	**14**
	The main procedure	14
	Core information	15
	Scheme administrator	16
	Scheme practitioner	17
	Applying for registration	17
	Other forms and completion notes required for ongoing maintenance and reporting	19
	Registration rejected	20
	Opting out of registration	20
	Schemes that do not apply for registration	20
	Registration withdrawn	20
	Schemes which lost approval before 6 April 2006	20
	Registering a non-UK based pension scheme	21
	Scheme documentation	21
	Modification powers	21
	Notifying HMRC of changes since registration	26
	Providers	26
	Membership	27
3	**Tax reliefs on contributions and assets**	**29**
	Introduction	29
	Member contributions	30
	Life assurance premiums, pension term assurance	33
	Methods of giving tax relief on contributions	34
	Public service pension schemes	37
	Compensation payments	37
	Reduced annual allowance	38
	Pension input periods	43
	Changing input period end dates	44
	Transitional input periods	46
	Pension input amounts	47
	Carry-forward provisions	51
	Employer contributions	55

vii

Contents

	The spreading rules	58
	Deficiency payments	59
	Levy payments	59
	In specie contributions	59
	Restrictions on tax relief	60
	Reduced lifetime allowance	60
	Scheme administrator responsibilities	63
	Fund assets and yield	66
	Annual allowance charge	67
	Special annual allowance charge	69
	Lifetime allowance charge	69
	The pensions regulator	75
	VAT	75
	Refunds to the employer	82
4	**Benefit rules**	**84**
	Introduction	84
	Pension rules	85
	Easing of fund access rules, drawdown	88
	Lump sum rules	99
	Pension ages	116
	Pension death benefit rules	119
	Lump sum death benefit rules	121
	Pension sharing	127
	Benefit crystallisation events	129
	Collective defined contribution schemes	130
5	**Investment rules**	**133**
	Introduction	133
	The main rules which apply to all registered pension schemes	134
6	**Transfers**	**145**
	Introduction	145
	Permitted transfers	145
	Transfers between registered pension schemes	146
	Transfers from registered pension schemes to non-registered schemes	147
	Transfers from non-registered schemes to registered pension schemes	148
	Loss of protection	148
	Transfer of rights in payment	149
	Must a scheme receive a transfer?	149
	Reporting to HMRC	149
	HMRC response time to a request for confirmation of status of receiving scheme	150
7	**Reporting rules**	**152**
	Introduction	152
	Event reports	155
	Record keeping	159
	Self-assessment	163

	Reporting employer-financed retirement benefit schemes	164
	Tax avoidance	168
Part Two – General taxation and tax planning considerations for individuals and employers		**169**
8	**Tax considerations**	**171**
	Introduction	171
	Other specialist matters	174
9	**Transitional protection**	**175**
	Introduction	175
	Valuing pre A-Day rights for primary or enhanced protection	177
	Primary protection	181
	Enhanced protection	186
	Relevant benefit accrual	191
	Fixed and individual protections	194
	Payment of protected lump sum	202
10	**Tax planning**	**221**
	Introduction	221
	Payment of cash, and alternatives	221
	Inheritance tax	223
	Recycling tax-free lump sums	224
	Hancock annuities and EFPOS	226
	Scheme pensions	226
	Increases in benefits	226
	Loans	226
	Scheme administration payments	226
	Re-allocations of funds or entitlements to benefits	227
	Master trusts	227
	Contract-based schemes	227
Part Three – High earners of registered pension schemes		**229**
11	**High earners of registered pension schemes**	**231**
	Introduction	231
	Employer-financed retirement schemes and EBTs	232
	Pre A-Day rules	234
	Unfunded schemes	242
	Bonus waivers	243
	Flexible drawdown	244
12	**Investment-regulated pension schemes**	**247**
	Introduction	247
Part Four – Overseas considerations		**257**
13	**Overseas considerations**	**259**
	Introduction	259
	Tax and pension rules post A-Day	260
	The main UK tax law for overseas schemes	261
	Other relevant UK legislation	264

IORPs Directive and Portability Directive	270
Migrant member relief	272
Residency and unauthorised payments	280
Principal reporting regulations	281
Transfers	284
Tax charges, penalties and sanctions	288
Residence and domicile – non-resident trusts	291
Summaries of the key recent changes to HMRC policy with regard to QROPS	292
Forms	297
Foreign pensions of UK residents and anti-avoidance	299

Part Five – Other forms of tax efficient provision for high earners and employers   303

14 Other forms of tax efficient provision for high earners and employers   305

Introduction	305
Excepted group life policies	309
In specie payments	312
New individual savings account	313

Part Six – Tax charges, penalties and disclosure of tax avoidance schemes   317

15 Tax charges, penalties and disclosure of tax avoidance schemes   319

Introduction	319
Sources of tax charges and penalties	319
Subject list of tax charges and penalties	320
Accounting for tax by scheme administrator	320
Protections from the standard lifetime allowance	321
General penalties for non-compliance by registered pension schemes	322
Scheme de-registration	326
General anti-abuse rule	327
Disclosure of tax avoidance schemes (DOTAS)	327
Penalties for non-compliance	332
Disclosure forms	333
Non-disclosure	334
HMRC visits and audits	334
Authorised payments, and chargeable events	335
Authorised member payments	335
Authorised employer payments	336
Investment-regulated pension schemes	347
Employer-financed retirement benefits schemes and EBTs	347
The scheme de-registration charge	347
The tax charge on benefits in kind	348
Employer asset-backed pension contributions	349
Tax charges for overseas schemes	349

Appendix 1	Benefit crystallisation events	351
Appendix 2	Glossary of terms	359
Appendix 3	The main features of the pre A-Day tax regime	373
Appendix 4	Overseas transfers of pension savings	381
Appendix 5	Registered Pension and Overseas Pension Schemes (Miscellaneous Amendments) Regulations 2012	404
Appendix 6	Annotated copy showing revisions to SI 2006/206	413
Index		419

Contents

Table of statutes

[*References are to paragraph numbers appendices.*]

B	
Building Society Act 1986	App 2
C	
Capital Allowances Act 2001	1.5
s 472(5)	3.3
Sch 3	
para 100	3.3
Corporation Tax Act 2009	1.5
Pt 16 Ch 2 (ss 1219–1231)	3.26
Corporation Tax Act 2010	1.5; App 2
s 1122	5.19; 12.4, 12.5
1139	14.6
E	
Equality Act 2010	9.41; App 2
Employment Rights Act 1996	App 2
F	
Finance Act 1970	
s 20	9.45
Finance Act 1973	App 2
Finance Act 1981	
s 32	2.5; 9.14
Finance (No 2) Act 1987	App 3
Finance Act 1989	2.14;11.5; App 3
s 76	11.19
(2)(b)	11.19
Finance Act 1999	
Sch 10	App 2
Finance Act 2000	14.3
Finance Act 2001	
s 74	3.45
Finance Act 2003	
Sch 24	App 2
Finance Act 2004	1.1; 1.2, 1.4, 1.6, 1.7, 1.17, 1.18, 1.19; 2.13, 2.14; 3.4, 3.28; 4.1, 4.15, 4.37, 4.50; 5.1, 5.22, 5.27; 7.1; 9.1, 9.3, 9.45; 12.1, 12.6; 13.1, 13.2, 13.3, 13.6, 13.20, 13.28, 13.38; 15.2, 15.27, 15.28, 15.32, 15.45; App 2

Finance Act 2004 – *contd*	
s 29A	App 2
Pt 4 (ss 149–284)	9.34; 12.6, 15.4
s 149	1.4
150	1.4
(1)	13.17; App 2
(2), (3)	App 2
(5), (6)	App 2
(7), (8)	App 2, App 4, App 6
151	1.4
(1)–(3)	App 2
152	1.4
(1)–(4)	App 2
(5), (6)	9.43; App 2
(7), (8)	App 2
153	1.4; 2.1, 2.8; App 2
154	1.4; 2.5
155	1.4
156	1.4; 2.7
157	1.4; 15.13; App 2
158	1.4; 15.13; App 2
(2)–(4)	15.54
159	1.4; App 2
160	1.4; 15.30
(2), (4)	App 2
(4A), (4B)	15.49
(5)	App 2
161	1.4; App 2
(2)–(4)	15.31
162	1.4; App 2
163	1.4; App 2
(4)	5.7
164	1.4; 4.1; App 2
(1)(f)	4.31
(2)	15.28
165	1.4; 4.1, 4.10; 13.17, 13.18, 13.19; 15.28; App 1, App 2, App 4
(2), (3)	App 2
(3A)	11.26; App 2
(3B)	11.26
166	1.4; 4.1; 15.28
(2)	App 2

Table of statutes

Finance Act 2004 – *contd*
s 167 .... 1.4; 4.1; 15.28;
                                                        App 2
   (2A) .... 11.26; App 2
   (2B) 11.26
168 .... 1.4; 15.28
   (1), (2) .... App 2
169 .... 1.4; 4.1; 6.2; 13.8;
                                  15.28; App 2, App 4
   (1B)–(1E) 13.28
   (2), (3) .... App 2
   (5) .... App 4
170 .... 1.4; 4.1
171 .... 1.4; 4.1; 15.28;
                                                        App 2
172 .... 1.4; 13.25; 15.33;
                                                        App 4
172A 9.21; 15.34
172B, 172BA 15.35
172C .... App 2
172D 15.36
173 .... 1.4; 13.25; 15.37,
                                               15.47; App 4
174 .... 1.4; 13.25; 15.38;
                                                App 2, App 4
174A 12.2; 13.25; 15.52;
                                                        App 4
175 .... 1.4; 15.29
176 .... 1.4; 15.29; App 2
177 .... 1.4; 15.29, 15.51;
                                                        App 2
178 .... 1.4; 15.29, 15.47;
                                                        App 2
179 .... 1.4; 5.5; 12.10,
                                              15.29; App 2
180 .... 1.4; 15.29; App 2
181 .... 1.4; 15.38; App 2
181A 15.46
182 .... 1.4; App 2
   (2), (3) 5.7
183 .... 1.4; 15.46
   (2) 5.7
183A, 183F 15.46
184 .... 1.4
   (2) 5.7
185 .... 1.4; 15.46
   (2) 5.7
185A 12.2; 15.52
185B 12.2; 15.52
   (3) .... App 2
185C–185I 12.2; 15.52
186 .... 1.4; 3.38
   (1)(b) 3.38
   (3) .... 3.38; App 2

Finance Act 2004 – *contd*
s 186(4) .... App 2
187 .... 1.4
188 .... 1.4; 13.14
   (2), (3) .... App 2
   (4) .... 3.2; App 2
   (5) .... App 2
   (6) .... 3.2; App 2
189 .... 1.4; App 2
   (2) .... App 2
190 .... 1.4
191 .... 1.4
   (9) .... App 2
192 .... 1.4; 3.8; App 2
193 .... 1.4; 3.9
194 .... 1.4
195 .... 1.4; 3.2; App 2
196 .... 1.4; 13.21
   (2)–(6) 13.14
196A 3.13
197, 198 .... 1.4; 3.28
199A 11.6
199 .... 1.4
200 .... 1.4; 13.14
201–203 .... 1.4
204 .... 1.4; App 2
205 .... 1.4; 4.29
   (1) .... App 2
206 .... 1.4
   (1) .... App 2
207 .... 1.4; 15.51
208 .... 1.4; 15.40; App 2,
                                                        App 4
   (1) .... App 2
209 .... 1.4; 15.41; App 4
   (1) .... App 2
210 .... 1.4; 15.41
   (3) 15.42
211 .... 1.4; 15.41
212 .... 1.4; 9.21; 15.41
213 .... 1.4; 15.41
   (3) 15.42
214 .... 1.4
   (1), (5) .... App 2
215 .... 1.4; App 2
216 .... 1.4; 4.44; App 1,
                                                        App 2
217 .... 1.4; App 2
218 .... 1.4; App 2
   (2), (3), (5) .... App 2
219 .... 1.4; App 2
220 .... 1.4; 9.33
221 .... 1.4; App 2
   (3)–(5) .... App 2

Table of statutes

Finance Act 2004 – *contd*
 s 222 .... 1.4; 9.33; App 2
  223 .... 1.4; 9.33; App 2
  224 .... 1.4; 9.33
   (2), (3), (7), (8) .... App 2
  225, 226 .... 1.4
  227 .... 1.4; 3.13
   (1) .... App 2
  228–230 .... 1.4; App 2
  231, 232 .... 1.4
  233, 234 .... 1.4; App 2
  235, 236 .... 1.4
  237 .... 1.4
  238 .... 1.4; App 2
  239 .... 1.4; 15.45
   (1) .... App 2
  240 .... 1.4; 5.7
  241 .... 1.4; 15.13, 15.46, 15.47; App 2
  242 .... 1.4; 15.13; 15.54; App 2
 Pt 4 Ch 6 (ss 243–249) 13.3
 s 243 .... 1.4; App 2
  244 .... 1.4
  245 .... 1.4; 11.2, 11.3, 11.9; App 2
   (5) 13.3
  246 .... 1.4; 11.2, 11.3, 11.9
 ss 247, 248 .... 1.4; 11.2
 s 249 .... 1.4; 11.2
   (3) 13.3
  250 .... 1.4; 7.14; 15.8; App 2
  251 .... 1.4; 7.1; App 2
   (1)(a), (b) 15.8
   (4) 15.8
  252, 253 .... 1.4; 7.1
 ss 254, 255 .... 1.4
 s 255A .... App 2
  256 .... 1.4
   (2) .... App 2
  257 .... 1.4
   (1), (2), (4) 15.8
  258 .... 1.4; 15.8
   (2) 15.8
  259 .... 1.4
   (1), (4) 15.9
  260 .... 1.4; 15.4; App 2
   (6) 15.4
  261 .... 1.4; 15.4, 15.5; App 2
   (3) 15.8
  262 .... 1.4; 15.5, 15.8; App 2
  263 .... 1.4; 15.5; App 2

Finance Act 2004 – *contd*
 s 263(2) 15.8
  264 .... 1.4
   (1), (2) 15.7, 15.8
  265 .... 1.4; 15.11
   (3) 15.8
  266 .... 1.4; 15.10, 15.12, 15.49
   (2) 15.8
  266B 15.48
  267 .... 1.4; 7.21; 15.43; App 2
  268 .... 1.4; 15.43; App 2
  269 .... 1.4
  270 .... 1.4; 2.5; App 2
  271 .... 1.4; 15.50; App 2
  272 .... 1.4; App 2
  273 .... 1.4; App 2
  273ZA 12.2
  274 .... 1.4; App 2
  274A .... App 2
  275 .... 1.4; App 2
  276 .... 1.4; 9.45; App 2
  277 .... 1.4; 9.38; App 2
  278 .... 1.4; App 2
  279 .... 1.4
   (1)–(3) .... App 2
  280–284 .... 1.4
 Pt 7 (ss 306–319) 15.17
 s 306 .... 15.17
  306A 15.21
  307 .... 15.17, 15.20
  308 .... 15.17, 15.18, 15.21
  309 .... 15.17, 15.21
  310 .... 15.17, 15.18, 15.21
  311 .... 15.17
  312 .... 15.17, 15.18, 15.21
  312A 15.18
  313, 314 .... 15.17
  314A 15.18, 15.21
  315–319 .... 15.17
 Sch 2
   para 25 .... App 2
 Sch 16 .... 15.35
 Sch 18 .... 3.6
 Sch 28 .... 1.4; App 2
   para 1 .... 4.8; App 2
    2 .... App 2
    (1) 4.6
    2A .... 13.25; App 4
    3 .... 4.5; App 2
    (1)(d) 4.5
    6, 8–13, 15 .... App 2
    16 .... App 2

Table of statutes

Finance Act 2004 – *contd*	
Sch 28 – *contd*	
para 16B(3), (4)	App 2
16C(3), (5), (7)	App 2
(13), (15)	App 2
17, 20, 22, 23	App 2
24	App 2
(8A)	App 2
24C–24G	App 2
Sch 29	1.4
para 1	App 2
(1)(c)	4.16
(2)	15.47
2	App 2
3	App 2
(4A), (8)	App 2
3A	13.25; 15.55; App 2, App 4
4	4.30; App 2
(1)(a)	App 4
5, 7–11, 13–17	App 2
19–21, 26	App 2
27	15.47; App 2
29	15.47
Sch 29A	12.1, 12.2; 15.52; 12.52
para 1(3)	App 2
2, 3, 5, 6	App 2
7(1), (2)	App 2
8–15	App 2
16	12.11; App 2
(1)–(4)	App 2
17–19	12.11
20	12.5
(2)–(4)	App 2
27–29	App 2
Sch 30	1.4; App 2
Sch 31	1.4, App 2
Sch 32	1.4, 4.44, App 2
para 11	App 2
17	11.28
Sch 33	1.4, 11.3, 11.13
para 3, 4	App 2
Sch 34	1.4, 10.23, 11.26, 11.28, 11.29, App 4
para 1–3	App 2
4	App 2
(2)	App 4
5	App 2
8–11	11.32
13–19	11.32
Sch 35	1.4
Sch 36	1.4, 10.22
para 2	App 2

Finance Act 2004 – *contd*	
Sch 36 – *contd*	
para 3	1.6
7	App 2
8, 9	4.22, App 2
10–11	App 2
12	App 2
13	9.45, App 2
14	9.42, App 2
15–17	App 2
22	App 2
23	App 2
(5)	App 2
25	4.22
(7)	4.22
28	12.47
29(2)	9.45
31–34	4.21, 4.27
56	App 4
(2)	11.26
57, 58	11.26, App 4
Finance Act 2005	
s 101, 102	1.4
Sch 10	1.4, 4.6
para 38	9.21
Sch 32	1.4, 4.6
para 1	App 2
10, 11	App 2
15, 16	App 2
Finance (No 2) Act 2005	1.4
Finance Act 2006	1.4, 5.1
s 158	12.1, 12.13
Sch 21	12.1, 12.13
Finance Act 2007	1.4; 2.16; 3.6; 9.31; 14.10, 14.11
s 57	12.6
Sch 17	12.6
Sch 18	App 2
Sch 19	App 2
para 13	15.35
Sch 20	
para 2	2.5
5	15.49
Sch 24	15.8
Finance Act 2008	1.4; 4.25; 9.42; 10.6
s 90	3.28; 11.6
901	15.35
Sch 3	13.36
Sch 28	15.35
Sch 29	12.4
para 1	15.28
18	10.6

Table of statutes

Finance Act 2008 – *contd*	
Sch 36	7.2; 13.36
para 7	13.36
12	15.8
Finance Act 2009	1.4
s 72	App 2
Sch 35	App 2
Sch 55	15.8
Sch 56	15.8
Finance Act 2010	15.19, 15.21
s 56	15.19
Sch 17	15.19
Finance Act 2011	1.4, 1.17; 3.13, 3.16, 3.17; 4.10, 4.25, 4.42; 9.38, 9.42; 11.9; 14.6
s 67	9.32
72	13.38
Sch 2	3.42; 11.10; 15.53; App 2
Sch 16	4.10; 10.6; 11.23; 15.35
para 1	App 2
2–5	App 1, App 2
6–9	App 2
10	11.26; App 2
11–19	App 2
20	11.26; App 2
21–39	App 2
Sch 17	3.13, 3.34
Sch 18	3.34; 9.32
para 14	App 2
(11)	9.43
Finance Act 2012	1.4
s 48	15.57
Sch 13	15.57
Finance Act 2013	1.4; 7.2; 13.3, 13.36
s 48	3.34; 9.44
49	3.13
50	4.13
52	13.36
53	13.24, 13.36
Pt 5 (ss 206–215)	15.16; App 2
s 223	15.19
Sch 6	9.44
Sch 22	9.44
Pt 1 (paras 1–4)	3.34; 9.44
para 8(4)	4.31
Sch 43	App 2
Finance Act 2014	1.4; 4.14, 4.50; App 2
Pt 1 Ch 2 (ss 11–25)	12.13
s 41	1.4; 11.25, 11.26

Finance Act 2014 – *contd*	
s 42	1.4; 4.31
45	13.36
48	App 2
49	14.2
234–283	15.19
284	15.20
Sch 5	1.4; 4.16
Sch 6	1.4
Sch 7	1.4; 7.2
Sch 8	14.2
Sch 22	
Pt 1 (paras 1, 2)	App 2
Finance (No 2) Act 2005	1.4
Finance (No 2) Act 2010	
s 6	4.7
Sch 3	4.7
Finance (No 3) Bill 2010	11.10
Financial Services Act 1986	App 2
Financial Services and Markets Act 2000	2.16
Pt 4 (ss 40–55)	App 2
s 235	App 2
236	12.11
237(1)	12.11
262	App 2
Sch 3	App 2
Sch 4	App 2
Sch 15	App 2

I

Income and Corporation Taxes Act 1970	
s 208	9.11, 9.14
226	9.14
Income and Corporation Taxes Act 1988	
s 18 Sch D	13.21
Case I	3.25
Case II	3.25
Case III	4.29
Case IV	8.5
Case VI	11.19
32	4.21
56	3.38
74	11.5, 11.19
(1)(a)	3.24
75	3.24
76	3.27
(7)	3.27
208	4.21
416	12.11
Pt XIV (ss 590–659E)	4.44

Table of statutes

Income and Corporation Taxes Act 1988 – *contd*
Pt XIV Ch I (ss 590–612) .... 2.5; 4.21; 9.11, 9.14; App 2
s 591 .... 9.45
592(1)(h)............................ App 2
595 .... 11.19
615 .... 13.33, 13.38
Pt XIV Ch IV (ss 630–655) ... 2.5
s 660A 11.5
611 .... 7.3
611A 9.11
615 .... 13.3
(3) 13.3
657(2)(d)............................... 11.19
661 .... 2.5
716 .... App 2
788 .... 13.18
832(1) .... App 2
834(1) .... App 2
835 .... App 2
839 .... 5.19; App 2
840A(1)(b)........................... App 2
840ZA 14.6
842B .... App 2
Income Tax Act 2007 .... 1.5
Income Tax (Earnings and Pensions) Act 2003 .... 1.5; 4.2, 4.50; 13.3; 15.37; App 2
Pt 2 (ss 3–61J) 3.11
s 7(2) .... App 2
15(2) 11.21
18 .... 11.21
28 .... 3.3
62 .... 3.42
63(4) 15.37
68 .... 15.37
307 .... 13.29
386(1) 11.5
390 .... 11.18
393 .... 11.19; App 2
(2) 11.5
393B 11.9
394 .... 11.3, 11.9, 11.19
(2), (4)............................... 11.19
395(3), (4)............................. 11.5
396(1) 11.19
398(2) 7.19; 11.4
399A .... 7.19; 11.4; App 2
480–482 .... 14.6
Pt 7 Ch 6 (ss 488–515)............ 14.2

Income Tax (Earnings and Pensions) Act 2003 – *contd*
Pt 7A (ss 554A–554Z21) .... 11.10, 11.15, 11.18; 15.20; App 2
s 554A, 554B 11.18
554Z1............................ 11.19; 15.31, 15.35, 15.36
Pt 9 (ss 565–654) 11.3, 15.28
s 579A, 579D 4.43
636A 4.44
647–654 .... 13.3, 13.33, 13.38
683 .... 4.43
721 .... 15.37
Sch 2..................................... 14.2
Sch 4..................................... 14.3
Sch 5..................................... 14.3
Income Tax (Trading and Other Income) Act 2005 .... 1.5; 3.25; 13.21
Pt 2 (ss 3–259) 3.3
s 34 .... 3.24
Pt 3 (ss 260–364) 3.3
369 .... 4.29
392–396, 405 .... 14.2
579, 587, 593 .... 3.3
707 .... 14.2
Inheritance Tax Act 1984 .... 8.6
s 3(1) .... 13.26; App 4
5.. 11.19
58 .... 10.6
86 .... App 2
271A 13.3
272 .... 13.26; App 4
International Organisations Act 1968
s 1 .... 13.19; App 4, App 6

K

Kiwisaver Act 2006 (New Zealand) .... 13.36; App 4
s 4(1) .... App 4, App 6

N

National Insurance Contributions Act 2014............................ 15.16
s 10, 11 .... 15.16
National Health Service Acts 3.11

P

Pensions Act 1995............. 4.3; 5.6; 9.21; 13.4; App 2
s 35 .... 5.6; 13.4
37 .... 15.51

Table of statutes

Pensions Act 1995 – *contd*	
s 40(2)	5.6
67	2.14
75	3.30
76	15.51
Pensions Act 2004	5.6; 9.26, 9.28; 13.2; 13.4; 13.6; App 2
Pt 2 (ss 107–220)	3.31, 3.45
s 252(2)	2.5; 13.5
255	9.40
(1)	13.5
Pt 7 (ss 287–295)	13.7
Pensions Act 2007	1.4; 2.2
s 67	2.2
Pensions Act 2008	1.4; 2.2
Pension Schemes Act 1993	App 2
s 8(3)	3.2
9(2B)	App 2
Pt III (ss 7–68)	13.28
Pt IV (ss 69–101AI)	13.28
s 159	13.28
Pension Schemes (Northern Ireland) Act 1993	
s 4(3)	3.2

S

Social Security Act 1973	9.45
Social Security Pensions Act 1975	App 2

T

Taxation of Chargeable Gains Act 1992	App 2
s 44	5.25
271	3.38
Pt 8 (ss 272–291)	14.3
s 272	5.20

Taxes Management Act 1970	11.3, 11.4; 15.2
s 95	15.8
98	15.8
(1)(b)(i), (ii)	15.8
(2)	15.8
98C	15.21
(1)	15.21
(b)	15.21
(2B)	15.18
309–319	App 2
Taxation (International and Other Provisions) Act 2010	1.5
s 2(1)	3.3

W

Welfare Reform and Pensions Act 1999	
s 28(1)	App 2
279(1)	App 2

AUSTRALIA

Income Tax Assessment Act 1997 (Australia)	App 6
s 995–1	App 4
Retirement Savings Accounts Act 1997 (Australia)	App 6
Superannuation Industry (Supervision) Act 1993 (Australia):	App 6
Tax Law amendment Act (Simplified Superannuation) Act 2007 (Australia)	App 6

GUERNSEY

Income Tax (Guernsey) Law 1975	App 6
s 157E	13.18

Table of statutory instruments

[References are to paragraph numbers and appendices.]

C

Contracting-out, Protected Rights and Safeguarded Rights (Transfer Payment) Amendment Regulations 2005, SI 2005/555 .... 13.8

E

Employer-Financed Retirement Benefits (Excluded Benefits for Tax Purposes) (Amendment) Regulations 2011, SI 2011/2281 .... 11.2

Employer-Financed Retirement Benefits (Excluded Benefits for Tax Purposes) Regulations 2006, SI 2006/210 .... 11.2

Employer-Financed Retirement Benefits (Excluded Benefits for Tax Purposes) Regulations 2007, SI 2007/3537 .... 11.2

Employer-Financed Retirement Benefits Schemes (Provision of Information) Regulations 2005, SI 2005/3453 .... 7.19, 7.24; 11.2, 11.4; App 2

Employment Equality (Age) Regulations 2006, SI 2006/1031 .... 14.4

Employment Equality (Repeal of Retirement Age Provisions) Regulations 2011, SI 2011/1069 .... 14.4

Employment Income Provided Through Third Parties (Excluded Relevant Steps) Regulations 2011, SI 2011/2696 .... 11.17, 11.18

F

Finance Act 2010, Schedule 17 (Appointed Day) Order 2010, SI 2010/3019 .... 15.18

Financial Services and Markets Act 2000 (Regulated Activities) (Amendment) Order 2006, SI 2006/1969.. 2.16

I

Income Tax (Pay as You Earn) Regulations 2003, SI 2003/2682 .... 1.5; 4.43; App 2

Inheritance Tax (Qualifying Non-UK Pension Schemes) Regulations 2010, SI 2010/51 .... 13.3, 13.17

Investment-regulated Pension Schemes (Exception of Tangible Moveable Property) Order 2006, SI 2006/1959 ... 12.5

M

Manufactured Payments and Transfer of Securities (Tax Relief) Regulations 1995, SI 1995/3036 .... 3.38

N

National Insurance Contributions (Application of Part 7 of the Finance Act 2004) (Amendment) Regulations 2010, SI 2010/2927 .... 15.18

National Insurance Contributions (Application of Part 7 of the Finance Act 2004) Regulations 2012, SI 2012/1868 .... 15.18

O

Occupational and Personal Pension Schemes (Disclosure of Information) Regulations 2013, SI 2013/2734 .... 7.23

Occupational and Personal Pension Schemes (Miscellaneous Amendments) Regulations 2007, SI 2007/814 .... 13.7

Table of statutory instruments

Occupational Pension Schemes (Assignment, Forfeiture, Bankruptcy etc) Regulations 1997, SI 1997/785 .... 9.21
Occupational Pension Schemes (Cross-border Activities) (Amendment) Regulations 2006, SI 2006/925 .... 13.7
Occupational Pension Schemes (Cross-border Activities) Regulations 2005, SI 2005/3381 .... 13.7
Occupational Pension Schemes (Investment) (Amendment) Regulations 2010, SI 2010/2161 .... 5.6; 13.4
Occupational Pension Schemes (Investment of Scheme's Resources) Regulations 1992, SI 1992/246 .... 5.5, 5.6
  reg 5(2)(d) 5.6
Occupational Pension Schemes (Investment) Regulations 1996, SI 1996/3127 .... 5.5, 5.6; 13.4
Occupational Pension Schemes (Investment) Regulations 2005, SI 2005/3378 .... 5.2, 5.6; 13.4
  reg 2–5 .... 5.6
Occupational Pension Schemes (Modification of Schemes) Regulations 2006, SI 2006/759 .... 2.14; 9.44
  reg 11 .... 11.4
Occupational Pension Schemes (Preservation of Benefit) (No2) Regulations 1973, SI 1973/1784
  reg 5 .... 9.45
Occupational Pension Schemes (Trust and Retirement Benefits Exemption) Regulations 2005, SI 2005/2360 .. 2.5; 13.5
Open-Ended Investment Company Regulations 2001, SI 2001/1228 .... App 2

P

Pension Protection Fund (Tax) Regulations 2006, SI 2006/575 .... 3.31
Pensions Act 2004 (Codes of Practice) (Reporting Late Payment of Contributions) Appointed Day Order 2013, SI 2013/2316 .... 3.43

Pensions Act 2007 (Abolition of Contracting-out for Defined Contribution Pension Schemes) (Consequential Amendments) Regulations 2011, SI 2011/1245 .... 11.8
Pensions Act 2008 (Abolition of Protected Rights) (Consequential Amendments) Order 2011, SI 2011/1246 .... 11.8
Pension Schemes (Categories of Country and Requirements for Overseas Pension Schemes and Recognised Overseas Pension Schemes) (Amendment) Regulations 2006, SI 2006/1221 .... 13.3, 13.36
Pension Schemes (Categories of Country and Requirements for Overseas Pension Schemes and Recognised Overseas Pension Schemes) (Amendment) Regulations 2007, SI 2007/1600 .... 13.3, 11.19
  Schedule 11.19
Pension Schemes (Categories of Country and Requirements for Overseas Pension Schemes and Recognised Overseas Pension Schemes) Regulations 2006, SI 2006/206 .... 13.3, 13.36, 11.17, 11.36; App 2; App 4, App 6
  reg 2 .... 11.36; App 4
  Primary Condition 1 .... 11.18
  Primary Condition 2 ..... 11.3, 11.18
  reg 3 .... 11.36; App 4
  4 .... 11.36
  8, 9 .... 11.36
  11, 12, 13 .... 11.36
  15 .... 11.36
Pension Schemes (Information Requirements – Qualifying Overseas Pension Schemes, Qualifying Recognised Overseas Pension Schemes and Corresponding Relief) Regulations 2006, SI 2006/208 .... 13.3, 13.22, 13.36; App 2, App 4
  reg 3(3) 11.20

Table of statutory instruments

Pension Schemes (Modification of Rules of Existing Schemes) Regulations 2006, SI 2006/364....... 1.6; 2.14; 4.1; 9.43
Pension Schemes (Prescribed Interest Rates for Authorised Employer Loans) Regulations 2005, SI 2005/3449............... 5.5; App 2
Pension Schemes (Relevant Migrant Members) Regulations 2006, SI 2006/212..... 13.3
Pensions Schemes (Application of UK Provisions to Relevant Non-UK Schemes) (Amendment) Regulations 2012, SI 2012/1795............ 13.3
Pensions Schemes (Application of UK Provisions to Relevant Non-UK Schemes) Regulations 2006, SI 2006/207...................... 13.3, 13.30, 13.31
Personal and Occupational Pension Schemes (Amendment) Regulations 2008, SI 2008/1979...................... 11.8
reg 2 .... 11.8
Protected Rights (Transfer Payment) (Amendment) Regulations 2005, SI 2005/2906................................... 11.8
Protected Rights (Transfer Payment) Regulations 1996, SI 1996/1461...................... 11.8
reg 12(11)............................... 11.8

R

Registered Pension Scheme (Accounting and Assessment) Regulations 2005, SI 2005/3454..................... 7.16
Registered Pension Schemes and Employer-Financed Retirement Benefits (Information) (Prescribed Descriptions of Persons) Regulations 2005, SI 2005/3455...................... App 2
Registered Pension Schemes and Overseas Pension Schemes (Electronic Communication of Returns and Information) Regulations 2006, SI 2006/570......................... 7.1, 7.24; 13.3, 11.36
Registered Pensions Schemes and Overseas Pension Schemes (Miscellaneous Amendments) Regulations 2012, SI 2012/884............. 7.2; 13.3, 13.15, 13.36; App 5
reg 4(6)................................. 13.36
Registered Pension Schemes and Overseas Pension Schemes (Miscellaneous Amendments) Regulations 2013, SI 2013/2259.......... 7.2; 13.3, 13.36
Registered Pension Schemes and Relieved Non-UK Pension Schemes (Lifetime Allowance Transitional Protection) (Notification) Regulations 2013, SI 2013/1741................... 7.2
Registered Pension Scheme (Audited Accounts) (Specified Persons) Regulations 2005, SI 2005/3456............ 7.16
Registered Pension Schemes (Authorised Member Payments) (No 2) Regulations 2006, SI 2006/571............... 15.28
Registered Pension Schemes (Authorised Member Payments) Regulations 2006, SI 2006/137......................... 15.28
Registered Pension Schemes (Authorised Member Payments) Regulations 2007, SI 2007/3532..................... 15.28
Registered Pension Schemes (Authorised Payments) (Amendment) Regulations 2012, SI 2012/522............... 15.28
Registered Pension Schemes (Authorised Payments) (Amendment) Regulations 2013, SI 2013/1818............ 7.22; 15.28
Registered Pension Schemes (Authorised Payments – Arrears of Pension) Regulations 2006, SI 2006/614..... 15.28
Registered Pension Schemes (Authorised Payments) Regulations 2006, SI 2006/209...................... 15.28

xxiii

Table of statutory instruments

Registered Pension Schemes (Authorised Payments) Regulations 2009, SI 2009/1171 ... 15.28
  reg 10 .... 4.31
  13 .... 7.22
  16 .... App 1
Registered Pension Schemes (Authorised Payments) (Transfers to the Pension Protection Fund) Regulations 2006, SI 2006/134 ..... 15.28
Registered Pension Schemes (Authorised Surplus Payments) Regulations 2006, SI 2006/574 .... 9.21; 10.16; App 2
  reg 2, 3 .... 10.16
Registered Pension Schemes (Discharge of Liabilities under Sections 267 and 268 of the Finance Act 2004) Regulations 2005, SI 2005/3452 .... 13.31; 15.43, 15.48
Registered Pension Schemes (Enhanced Lifetime Allowance) Regulations 2006, SI 2006/131 .... 9.15, 9.22; 15.8
Registered Pension Schemes etc (Information) (Prescribed Descriptions of Persons) Regulations 2010, SI 2010/650 .... 13.3
Registered Pension Schemes (Extension of Migrant Member Relief) Regulations 2006, SI 2006/1957 .... 13.3, 13.15
Registered Pension Schemes (Meaning of Pension Commencement Lump Sum) Regulations 2006, SI 2006/135 .... 15.28; App 2
Registered Pension Schemes (Minimum Contributions) Regulations 2005, 2005/3450 .... App 2
Registered Pension Schemes (Prescribed Requirements of Flexible Drawdown Declaration) Regulations 2011, SI 2011/1792 .... 11.26
  reg 2, 3 .... 11.26
Registered Pension Schemes (Prescribed Schemes and Occupations) Regulations 2005, SI 2005/3451 .... 4.34; App 2
  reg 3 .... 4.34

Registered Pension Schemes (Provision of Information) (Amendment) Regulations 2011, SI 2011/301 .... 7.2
Registered Pension Schemes (Provision of Information) (Amendment) Regulations 2013, SI 2013/1742 .... 7.2, 7.15; 13.3, 13.36
Registered Pension Schemes (Provision of Information) Regulations 2006, SI 2006/567 .... 7.1, 7.2, 7.24; 13.36; 15.44; App 2
Registered Pension Schemes (Relevant Annuities) Regulations 2006, SI 2006/129 .. App 2
Registered Pension Schemes (Relief at Source) Regulations 2005, SI 2005/3448 ... 3.8
Registered Pension Schemes (Restriction of Employer's Relief) Regulations 2005, SI 2005/3458 .... 3.33; 11.6
Registered Pension Schemes (Splitting of Schemes) Regulations 2006, SI 2006/569 .... App 2
Registered Pension Schemes (Surrender of Relevant Excess) Regulations 2006, SI 2006/211 .... 9.21
Registered Pension Schemes (Transfer of Sums and Assets) (Amendment) Regulations 2014, SI 2014/1449 .... 6.7
Registered Pension Schemes (Transfer of Sums and Assets) Regulations 2006, SI 2006/499 .... 13.28
Registered Pension Schemes (Unauthorised Payments by Existing Schemes) Regulations 2006, SI 2006/365 .... 15.47
Registered Pension Schemes (Uprating Percentages for Defined Benefits Arrangements and Enhanced Protection) Regulations 2006, SI 2006/130 .... 9.45

Table of statutory instruments

Retirement Benefits Schemes (Information Powers) Regulations 1995, SI 1995/3103.................................. 7.1

S

Social Security (Contributions) Regulations 2001, SI 2001/1004.................................. 10.8
Special Annual Allowance Charge (Application to Members of Currently-Relieved Non-UK Pension Schemes) Order 2009, SI 2009/2031.................................. 13.3

T

Tax Avoidance Schemes (Information) (Amendment) (No 2) Regulations 2007, SI 2007/3103.............. 15.21, 12.21
Tax Avoidance Schemes (Information) (Amendment) (No 2) Regulations 2010, SI 2010/2928...................... 12.17
Tax Avoidance Schemes (Information) (Amendment) Regulations 2006, SI 2006/1544.................................. 15.18
Tax Avoidance Schemes (Information) (Amendment) Regulations 2008, SI 2008/1947.................................. 15.18
Tax Avoidance Schemes (Information) (Amendment) Regulations 2011, SI 2011/171.................................... 12.20
Tax Avoidance Schemes (Information) Regulations 2004, SI 2004/1864
 reg 4 .... 15.18
 8B.................................... 15.18
Tax Avoidance Schemes (Information) Regulations 2012, SI 2012/1836...................... 15.18
Tax Avoidance Schemes (Penalty) (Amendment) Regulations 2010, SI 2010/2743...... 15.18, 15.21
Tax Avoidance Schemes (Penalty) Regulations 2007, SI 2007/3104...................... 15.21
Tax Avoidance Schemes (Prescribed Descriptions of Arrangements) (Amendment) Regulations 2004, SI 2004/2429 .... 15.18
Tax Avoidance Schemes (Prescribed Descriptions of Arrangements) (Amendment) Regulations 2009, SI 2009/2033 .... 15.18
Tax Avoidance Schemes (Prescribed Descriptions of Arrangements) Regulations 2004, SI 2004/1863............ 15.18
Tax Avoidance Schemes (Prescribed Descriptions of Arrangements) Regulations 2006, SI 2006/1543............ 15.18
Tax Avoidance Schemes (Prescribed Descriptions of Arrangements) Regulations 2010, SI 2010/2834..... 15.18, 12.19
Tax Avoidance Schemes (Prescribed Descriptions of Arrangements) Regulations 2011, SI 2011/170.............. 15.18
Tax Avoidance Schemes (Promoters and Prescribed Circumstances) Regulations 2004, SI 2004/1865............ 15.18
 reg 4(1)–(4) 15.20
Taxation of Pension Schemes (Transitional Provisions) (Amendment No 2) Order 2006, SI 2006/2004............ 4.26; App 2
Taxation of Pension Schemes (Transitional Provisions) Order 2006, SI 2006/572.... 4.44; 15.28; App 2
 reg 9–11 .... 9.7, 9.14
Transfer of Tribunal Functions and Revenue and Customs Appeals Order 2009, SI 2009/56 .... 7.20

W

Welfare Reform and Pensions (Northern Ireland) Order 1999, SI 1999/3147............ App 2

Abbreviations

AA	=	annual allowance
ABI	=	Association of British Insurers
ACA	=	Association of Consulting Actuaries
A-Day	=	6 April 2006
AFT	=	accounting for tax
APPS	=	appropriate personal pension scheme
ASP	=	alternatively secured pension
AVC	=	additional voluntary contribution
BCE	=	benefit crystallisation event
BIM	=	HMRC Business Income Manual
BSP	=	basic state pension
CAA 2001	=	Capital Allowances Act 2001
CDCs	=	Collective defined contribution schemes
CEIOPS	=	Committee of European Insurance and Occupational Pension Supervisors
CGT	=	capital gains tax
COP	=	code of practice
CPI	=	consumer prices index
CSOP	=	company share option plan
CT	=	corporation tax
CTA 2009	=	Corporation Tax Act 2009
CTA 2010	=	Corporation Tax Act 2010
DABs	=	defined ambition schemes
DB	=	defined benefit
DC	=	defined contribution
DCA	=	Department of Constitutional Affairs
DOTAS	=	disclosure of tax avoidance schemes
DRA	=	default retirement age
DTA	=	double taxation agreement
DTRM	=	HMRC Double Taxation Relief Manual
DWP	=	Department for Work and Pensions
EA 2007	=	Enforcement Act 2007
EA 2010	=	Equality Act 2010
EBT	=	employee benefit trust
EC	=	European Commission
ECJ	=	European Court of Justice

Abbreviations

EEA	=	European Economic Area
EFRBS	=	employer-financed retirement benefits scheme
EGLP	=	excepted group life policy
EIM	=	HMRC Employment Income Manual
EMI	=	enterprise management incentives
EP	=	enhanced protection
ERSM	=	HMRC Employment Related Securities Manual
ESC	=	extra-statutory concession
ESSUM	=	HMRC Employee Share Schemes User Manual
ETV	=	enhanced transfer value
EU	=	European Union
FA	=	Finance Act
FAS	=	Financial Assistance Scheme
FCA	=	Financial Conduct Authority – which, with the PRA, replaced the FSA in 2013
FP 2012	=	fixed protection 2012
FP 2014	=	fixed protection 2014
FSA	=	Financial Services Authority, replaced by the FCA and PRA in 2013, under the auspices of the Bank of England
FSCS	=	Financial Services Compensation Scheme
FSMA 2000	=	Financial Services and Markets Act 2000
FURBS	=	funded unapproved retirement benefit schemes
GAAR	=	general anti-abuse rule
GAD	=	Government Actuary's Department
GMP	=	guaranteed minimum pension
GPP	=	group personal pension
GRA 2004	=	Gender Recognition Act 2004
HIERC	=	high income excess relief charge
HMRC	=	Her Majesty's Revenue and Customs
HMRC PSS	=	HMRC Pension Scheme Services
ICAEW	=	The Institute of Chartered Accountants in England and Wales
ICTA 1988	=	Income and Corporation Taxes Act 1988
IHT	=	inheritance tax
IHT	=	HMRC inheritance tax manual
IM	=	Inspector's Manual
IORP	=	institution for occupational retirement provision
IORPS Directive	=	Directive 2003/41/EC of the European Parliament and the Council on the activities and supervision of institutions for occupational retirement provision
IP 2014	=	Individual protection 2014

Abbreviations

IPTM	=	HMRC Insurance Policyholder Taxation Manual
IRPS	=	investment-regulated pension scheme
ISA	=	individual savings account
ITA	=	Income Tax Act
ITA 2007	=	Income Tax Act 2007
ITEPA 2003	=	Income Tax (Earnings and Pensions) Act 2003
ITTOIA 2005	=	Income Tax (Trading and Other Income) Act 2005
LTA	=	lifetime allowance
LAM	=	HMRC Life Assurance Manual
LEL	=	lower earnings limit
LLP	=	limited liability partnership
NAO	=	National Audit Office
NAPF	=	National Association of Pension Funds
NEST	=	National Employment Savings Trust
NI	=	National Insurance
NIC	=	National Insurance Contribution
NICA 2013	=	National Insurance Contributions Act 2013
NICO	=	National Insurance Contributions Office
NIM	=	HMRC National Insurance Manual
NISA	=	new individual savings account
NRD	=	normal retirement date
OEIC	=	open-ended investment company
ONS	=	Office for National Statistics
OPS	=	oversea pension scheme
PA	=	Pension Act
PAYE	=	Pay As You Earn
PCLS	=	pension commencement lump sum
PP	=	personal pension
PPF	=	Pension Protection Fund
PRA	=	Prudential Regulation Authority which, with the FCA, replaced the FSA in 2013
PSA 1993	=	Pension Schemes Act 1993
PSTR	=	Pension Scheme Tax Reference
QNUPS	=	Qualifying Non-UK Pension Scheme
QOPS	=	Qualifying Overseas Pension Scheme
QROPS	=	Qualifying Recognised Overseas Pension Scheme
RAC	=	retirement annuity contract
RAS	=	relief at source
REIT	=	Real Estate Investment Trust
RNUKS	=	relevant non-UK scheme
ROPS	=	Recognised Overseas Pension Scheme
RPI	=	retail prices index

Abbreviations

RPSM	=	HMRC Registered Pension Schemes Manual
RTI	=	PAYE recording in real time under HMRC rules (Real Time Information, launched on 6 April 2013)
SAAC	=	Special annual allowance charge
S2P	=	state second pension
SAYE	=	Save As You Earn
SCO	=	HMRC Special Compliance Office
SDLT	=	Stamp duty land tax
SERPS	=	state earnings-related pension scheme
SIPPS	=	self-invested personal pension scheme
SPA	=	state pension age
SRN	=	scheme reference number
SSAS	=	small self-administered scheme
SSCBA	=	Social Security Contributions and Benefits Act 1992
SSCB(NI)A 1992	=	Social Security Contributions and Benefits (Northern Ireland) Act 1992
TCGA 1992	=	Taxation of Chargeable Gains Act 1992
TMA 1970	=	Taxes Management Act 1970
TIOPA 2010	=	Taxation (International and Other Provisions) Act 2010
TSEM	=	HMRC Trusts, Settlements and Estates Manual
TUPE	=	Transfer of Undertakings (Protection of Employment) Regulations 2006 (SI 2006/246)
UAP	=	upper accrual point
UEL	=	upper earnings limit
UURBS	=	unfunded unapproved retirement benefit scheme
VAT	=	value added tax
WRPA 1999	=	Welfare Reform and Pensions Act 1999

Part One

The registered pension scheme tax rules

Chapter 1

> **SIGNPOSTS**
>
> - There have been major cuts to the annual allowance and lifetime allowance
> - HMRC, Whitehall and the Pensions Regulator have been given increased powers to counter tax avoidance, including overseas matters
> - Access to pension fund rules is increasing greatly for defined contribution schemes
> - The HMRC website contains the comprehensive registered pension scheme manual

Introduction

1.1 This book is the Third Edition of *Tax Efficient Retirement Planning*.

Part One (which described the main tax rules applying to all registered pension schemes) and Part Two (which described the main considerations for high net worth individuals) of the previous edition have been replaced by the following Parts:

- Part One: The Registered Pension Scheme Tax Rules;
- Part Two: General Taxation and Tax Planning for Individuals and Employers;
- Part Three: High Earners of Registered Pension Schemes;
- Part Four: Overseas Considerations;
- Part Five: Other Forms of Tax Efficient Provision for High Earners and Employers; and
- Part Six: Tax Charges, Penalties and Disclosure of Tax Avoidance Schemes.

Her Majesty's Revenue and Customs (HMRC's) discretionary powers were removed by *FA 2004*, which came into effect on 6 April 2006 (A-Day). They were replaced by direct statute law and secondary legislation combined with published guidance.

Sadly, the concept of a simplified pension tax regime continues to be seriously eroded by further changes in addition to those described in the previous edition HMRC'S powers of investigation, the pension scheme reporting requirements and the attaching penalties for failures to meet the new rules have all been

1.2 Introduction

greatly extended. There have been swingeing cuts to the annual allowance (AA) and lifetime allowance (LTA), accompanied by astonishingly complex methods and rules for protections from the various cuts in the standard LTA. Another major target has been offshore investment and transfers, in particular with regard to qualifying recognised overseas pension schemes (QROPSs). As before, some of these changes affect all members of registered pension schemes, and others are of greater importance to high earners. The introduction of investment-regulated pension schemes (IRPSs) and taxable property charges had already had a major impact on high earners, and there has been a concerted attack on employer-financed retirement benefit schemes (EFRBS) in the form of disguised remuneration PAYE and NIC charges.

New powers have been conferred on HMRC, Whitehall and the Pensions Regulator in an endeavour to counter tax avoidance. The disclosure of tax avoidance schemes (DOTAS) rules have been extended and a new general anti-abuse rule (GAAR) has been introduced.

On a more positive note, there have been easements to the access of pension fund rules, but these are confined to defined contribution (DC) schemes and are not without their own problems.

The above matters are addressed in the following chapters, which include guidance on the current rules and how to make effective pension provision within the new parameters. Where it is helpful to do so, worked examples have been provided to assist the reader.

BACKGROUND TO THE CURRENT REGIME

1.2 The problems which arose under the pre A-Day system of eight different benefit regimes were highlighted in the previous edition of this book.

Whereas those tax regimes were repealed and replaced by a single regime under *FA 2004* rules, the new world of simplicity was short-lived. In fact, *FA 2006* eroded some of the good work that had been done by the HMRC and HM Treasury team, and the single tax regime had already begun to disappear at its inception.

First moves for change

1.3 Although the landmark moves for change are by now largely historic, the ongoing reforms continue to make reference to the aims and aspirations of past committees and reports. The most significant events are summarised below:

- 1993: the Goode Report, by Professor Roy Goode, was published by the Pension Law Committee in September 1993. It identified the significant problems associated with the multiplicity of tax regimes, and contained some early plans for change.

- 2000: Paul Myners published his Government-commissioned report into institutional investment on 16 May 2000. The report called for the removal of (approximately) 50 existing barriers to investment growth, and recommended greater familiarity with investment issues, independent custody and shareholder activism. The report is constantly under review and remains a key source of reference.

- 2002: the Pickering Report was published on 11 July 2002 for the DWP. The review had involved a wide consultative process into UK pension provision. The report supported pensions simplification, although it contained some indication of ongoing complexities, particularly in the field of contracting out.

- 2002: the HMRC/Treasury Simplification Team published its first report entitled *Simplifying the Taxation of Pensions: Increasing Choice and Flexibility for All* on 17 December 2002. It published a successor report entitled *Simplifying the Taxation of Pensions: The Government's Proposals* on 10 December 2003. The document contained the main structure of the post A-Day tax regime. The originally proposed LTA of £1.4m as at A-Day was raised to £1.5m for the tax year 2006/2007.

THE MAIN LEGISLATION

Finance Acts

1.4 The key statute is *FA 2004*. The relevant sections of the Act are *ss 149–284*, and the relevant Schedules are *Schs 28–36*. The *Act* has undergone various amendments and extensions since it came into effect (see **1.1** above for a summary). The main amending statutes are:

- *FA 2005, ss 101* and *102*, and *Sch 10*, and *F(No 2)A 2005*, which restored some of the provisions of the original Finance Bill 2005 and contained rules on the disposal of assets overseas by residents and non-residents;

- *FA 2006*, which:
    - contained amendments in respect of tax-free cash lump sums;
    - imposed a charge to IHT on certain death benefits;
    - imposed investment restrictions and taxable property charges on IRPS, being schemes or arrangements in which there is an element of direct or indirect member control over investment activity;

- *FA 2007*, which:
    - abolished tax relief on premiums paid on personal fixed term life assurance policies provided via personal or occupational pension schemes where the only benefit payable is a lump sum on death or critical illness;
    - imposed restrictions on pension schemes which invest in UK real estate investment trusts (UK-REITS);
    - relaxed the timing of the payment of lump sums;

1.4 *Introduction*

- introduced changes to ASPs;
- introduced changes to the categories of persons who can establish and register a pension scheme;

- *FA 2008*, which:
  - contained amendments in respect of tax-free cash lump sums;
  - imposed a charge on tax-relieved pension savings which are diverted into IHT using scheme pensions and lifetime annuities in other circumstances than ASP;
  - contained further amendments to the rules which apply to residential property held by SSAS and SIPPS, and a relaxation of the definition of an IRPS;
  - permitted regulations to be made to provide for the commutation of small stranded pots of less than £2,000 in occupational pension schemes;
  - provided for IHT relief from A-Day in respect of certain overseas schemes, in line with the exemptions which apply to UK registered schemes;
  - prevented the avoidance of spreading contributions for tax relief purposes by means of interposing a new company and financing it to pay the contribution;
  - required contributions to be physically alienated from the employer, in the relevant accounting period in which they are paid;

- *FA 2009*, which:
  - imposed a £20,000 special annual allowance (SAAC) on anyone with relevant income of £150,000 or more;

- *FA 2011*, which:
  - reduced the AA and LTA;
  - removed most of the age 75 restrictions;
  - repealed ASP and introduced capped drawdown rules, flexible drawdown that allows funds to be drawn as taxable lump sums if a minimum income threshold is met;
  - introduced disguised remuneration tax charges;
  - increased the lump sum death benefit charge from 35% to 55%, except for benefits which become payable on death before age 75 in respect of an individual who had not taken a pension (which are tax free);
  - limited the tax relief for employers when they make asset-backed contributions to their defined benefit pension schemes;

Introduction **1.4**

- abolished life assurance premium relief in relation to payments by employers to EFRBS from 2012;
- extended DOTAS;
- imposed major restrictions on QROPS, mainly from 6 April 2012.

- *FA 2012*, which:
  - permitted individuals, in personal pensions or similar vehicles, aged over 60 to commute pension funds of £2,000 or less into lump sums without the need to take into account other pension savings, with a maximum of two commutations in a lifetime;
  - announced an increase to the limit on the amount of pension an individual may take each year under capped drawdown;
  - provided for the monitoring of the use of unfunded pension arrangements to ensure that that they are not used to circumvent the restriction of pensions tax relief and the disguised remuneration requirements;
  - further limited the tax reliefs which apply to asset-backed pension contributions with effect from 29 November 2011;
  - proposed a tax charge on income on transfers of assets abroad which are sheltered in 'overseas envelopes';
  - provided for reviews of QROPS, to exclude them from any jurisdiction that makes legislation or otherwise creates or uses a pension scheme to provide tax advantages which UK tax and pensions legislation does not intend;
  - confirmed a reduction in the top rate of tax from 50% to 45% from 2013, increased age-related allowances and BSP;
  - confirmed the future introduction of a single tier flat-rate pension to replace BSP and S2P.

- *FA 2013*, which:
  - reduced the AA to £40,000 for the tax year 2014/15 onwards;
  - reduced the standard LTA to £1.25m from the tax year 2014/15 onwards, subject to a protection known as 'fixed protection 2014' (FP 2014), and proposed an additional form of individual protection (IP 2014);
  - made further relaxations to trivial commutations and small pension pots;
  - envisaged a state single-tier pension from April 2016, confirmed the 'triple lock guarantee' on state pension and accommodated the removal of S2P through a DC scheme from 6 April 2012;
  - announced awards for individuals with a pre-1992 Equitable Life with profit annuity;

1.4 *Introduction*

- introduced the UK's first GAAR;
- changed to the rules for bridging pensions;
- required QROPS to re-notify HMRC every five years that they continue to meet the requirements to be QROPS; and
- introduced 'family pensions'.

- *FA 2014* which brought in the following changes:
  - an increase in the capped drawdown pension limit and pension death benefit limit from 120% to 150% (*s 41* with effect from 27 March 2014);
  - a reduction in the amount of minimum income requirement for flexible drawdown from £20,000 to £12,000 (*s 41* with effect from 27 March 2014);
  - an increase in the aggregate amount of commutation limit for purposes of trivial commutation lump sum from £18,000 to £30,000 (*s 42*, with effect from 27 March 2014);
  - an increase in the trivial commutation lump sum limit of £2,000 to £10,000 (*s 42*, with effect from 27 March 2014);
  - the necessary further provision in connection with the increased pension flexibility (*Sch 5*);
  - transitional provision in relation to the new standard LTA for the tax year 2014–15 etc (*Sch 6*);
  - extensive new HMRC powers under *Sch 7* (see **7.2** below).

HMRC's Pensions Newsletter 61, March 2014, was published on HMRC's website on 14 April 2014 as at *http://www.hmrc.gov.uk/pensionschemes/newsletter61.pdf*. It covered the 'Finance Bill 2014' and 'later Finance Bill'.

Employers will need to take into account the auto-enrolment staging dates if they do not provide their employees membership of a scheme which meets at least the minimum requirements the *Pensions Act 2007* and *Pensions Act 2008*, as amended. The staging dates to comply with auto-enrolment are:

- for employers with more than 250 employees, October 2012–February 2014;
- for employers with between 50 and 249 employees, 1 April 2014–1 April 2015;
- for new employers setting up business from 1 April 2012–30 September 2017, 1 May 2017 and 1 February 2018.

There will be an exclusion for employers with fewer than 50 employees from legislation until next parliament.

Statutes under tax law rewrites

1.5 The following Tax Law Rewrites have been completed. Many have highlighted, amongst other things, the multitude of taxation legislation which applied to tax-advantaged pension schemes:

- the *Capital Allowances Act 2001* (CAA 2001) – effective from April 2001;
- the *Income Tax (Earnings and Pensions) Act 2003* – effective from April 2003 (ITEPA 2003). This *Act* included the important repeal of Schedule E by way of a grouping of employment income, pensions and social security income within 'earnings';
- the *Income Tax (Pay as You Earn) Regulations 2003 (SI 2003/2682)* – effective from April 2004;
- the *Income Tax (Trading and Other Income) Act 2005* (ITTOIA 2005) – effective from April 2005;
- the *Income Tax Act 2007* (ITA 2007) – effective from April 2007; and
- the *Corporation Tax Act 2009* (CTA 2009) – effective from April 2009,
- the *Corporation Tax Act 2010* (CTA 2010) – effective from March 2010, and
- the *Taxation (International and Other Provisions) Act 2010* (TIOPA 2010).

SUMMARY OF THE CURRENT TAX REGIME

1.6 The main features of the current tax regime are summarised below, and cross-references are provided to the detailed explanations of the subject matter which is contained in the chapters of this book.

The pre A-Day legislation is of diminishing importance. However, the transitional protections which are described in **Chapter 9** still apply to protected persons as can any outstanding actions or enquiries which apply to pre A-Day events. Accordingly, **Appendix 3**, which contains tables which summarise the main pension tax rules which applied before A-Day, has been retained.

The timescale of the modification powers under *FA 2004* for the purpose of providing transitional protection for schemes if their documentation had not been amended to comply with the new tax rules was later extended, as described in **2.14** below. *Regulations* overrode existing scheme documentation. The *Regulations* included, amongst other things, a rule of construction and they gave trustees discretion over whether or not to make a payment which would otherwise fall to be treated as an unauthorised payment. The statutory period by which schemes had to be amended in order to comply with the current legislation ended on 6 April 2011 (*FA 2004, Sch 36, Pt 1, para 3*). Trustees, scheme managers and employers should have ensured the desired changes were made to scheme rules before that date. Failure to do so could expose a scheme to additional liability.

1.7 *Introduction*

The main features of the current tax regime are given below.

Eligibility

1.7 *FA 2004* provided much greater access to registered pension scheme membership than under earlier regimes for tax-advantaged schemes. Not only may members include the employed and self-employed, but there is also an opportunity for non-UK residents and non-UK workers to become members. Individuals may also concurrently be members of any type or any number of schemes (for example, occupational pension schemes and personal pension schemes). Details are given in **Chapter 2**.

Tax-relievable allowances

1.8 The pre A-Day limits regime was replaced by a limit on the aggregate amount of contributions/fund growth on which tax relief will be given on an annual basis (AA), and by a limit on the aggregate amount of lifetime savings on which tax relief will be given (LTA). The allowances are described in detail in **Chapter 3**.

The government intent was that the relatively generous level of the LTA would prove to be an incentive to pension saving for individuals who were previously restricted by short service to small benefit provision. The full impact of change is not yet known, but there has been a clear increase in the number of new money purchase (defined contribution, or DC) schemes and in the number of defined benefit (DB) schemes which have converted to DC schemes. The number of closures of DB schemes has also increased, partly due to the tight statutory regime which applies to such schemes under DWP rules and related legislation.

Tax-relievable contributions

1.9 Until 2011 tax-relievable contributions could be paid at much higher levels than pre A-Day limits by most members and employers, and scheme income and gains continued to be generally tax-free. However, there have been very severe cut-backs in the levels of tax-relievable contributions and assets in recent years.

Further information is given in **Chapters 3** and **5** respectively.

Benefit style

1.10 The sponsor and/or provider shall determine the nature and structure of benefits to be provided. Multiple-employer schemes are permitted, whether or not those employers are associated. The main aim is to provide greater member mobility and more flexible benefit provision. To some extent the relaxations were driven by the need to comply with the IORPS Directive (see **Chapter 13** below). Its objective is to allow pension funds to benefit from the internal market principles of free movement of capital and free provision of services.

There is flexible provision to take pensions, including whilst remaining in service. For DC schemes, pensions may be taken as secured lifetime annuities, as capped drawdown or as flexible drawdown. There are ongoing changes to the drawdown rules, as described in **Chapter 4** and an extension of flexibility to access funds.is being considered for DB schemes.

Transferability of member rights

1.11 Transfers may be made freely between registered pension schemes, and also from registered pension schemes to overseas schemes which are regulated as pension funds in their country of establishment (if they undertake to comply with information-reporting requirements). Again, the changes were partly driven by the need to comply with the IORPS Directive.

Further information about these significant relaxations concerning transfers and overseas considerations is provided in **Chapters 6** and **13** respectively.

Investments

1.12 Many of the restrictions which applied to the investments that could be made by tax-advantaged schemes before A-Day, including the removal of the bar on investment in residential property for most schemes, were removed. However, special rules apply to IRPS (see **Chapter 15**). Otherwise, the current legislation generally relies on the 'prudent man principle' to be applied by investment managers, trustees and scheme managers, in keeping with EU guidelines.

Further information about the investment rules, and IRPS, is given in **Chapter 5**.

Transitional protection

1.13 An important facility, which chiefly benefits high earners, is the provision of transitional protection for their pre A-Day rights and entitlements. Further high earner protections have been introduced following the ongoing reductions to the LTA. Detailed information about the transitional protection rules is contained in **Chapter 9**.

Focus

- Transitional protection for pre A-Day rights remains important
- There have been further important protections from the LTA cutbacks
- Detailed information about the transitional protection rules is contained in **Chapter 9**

1.14 Introduction

Registration

1.14 The rules which apply to scheme registration are described in **Chapter 2**. Most actions must be conducted online.

Reporting and self-assessment

1.15 A codified system exists for reporting various events, and for self-assessment. Again, most actions must be conducted online. The rules which apply to reporting and self-assessment are described in **Chapter 7**.

Compliance, and unauthorised member payments

1.16 There must be strict compliance with legislative requirements and published codes of practice and guidelines. Tax charges, penalties, sanctions and unauthorised member payment charges may be incurred in the event of non-compliance. The compliance requirements extend to trustees, managers, administrators, fund managers, pension scheme promoters and scheme advisers, as appropriate.

Further information concerning compliance and unauthorised member payments is provided in **Chapters 7** and **15**.

Focus

- It is essential to meet the extended compliance requirements in order to avoid prohibitive charges
- Further information concerning compliance and unauthorised member payments is provided in **Chapters 7** and **15**.

Non-registered schemes – EFRBS

1.17 Under the legislation which prevailed before A-Day, funded or unfunded schemes which were not approved (FURBS and UURBS) received certain tax and NI concessionary treatment. The current legislation effectively removed these tax advantages, with some transitional protection for accrued rights as at A-Day. Legislation limiting the use of these schemes was contained in *FA 2004,* and *FA 2011* (see **Chapter 11**). Additionally, HMRC is vigilant in checking unfunded schemes which may be used for purposes of tax avoidance.

Non-registered funded schemes are known as employer-financed retirement benefit schemes (EFRBS) under *FA 2004.*

Further information concerning these schemes is provided in **Chapter 7** (the reporting rules) and **Chapter 11**.

Overseas issues

1.18 *FA 2004* brought in many changes concerning overseas matters. The main impact was that transfers can now generally be made from UK registered pension schemes to overseas schemes, and migrants who come to the UK will receive tax reliefs on their contributions in place of the former corresponding relief provisions.

Further information about overseas matters is provided in **Chapter 13**.

HMRC Registered Pension Schemes Manual (RPSM)

1.19 The HMRC website contains the comprehensive RPSM. This manual is published in six volumes covering technical pages, member pages, scheme administrator pages, employer pages, international regime and a glossary. It is a very large document, only available online, with a significant number of links. The RPSM can be accessed at: *http://www.hmrc.gov.uk/manuals/rpsmmanual/index.htm*.

CHECKLIST

- There have been swingeing cuts to the annual allowance and lifetime allowance
- A major target has been offshore investment and transfers, in particular with regard to qualifying recognised overseas pension schemes
- New powers have been conferred on HMRC, Whitehall and the Pensions Regulator in an endeavour to counter tax avoidance
- There have been easements to the access of pension fund rules, but these primarily are confined to defined contribution schemes
- *FA 2004* provided wide access to registered pension scheme membership
- Several Tax Law Rewrites have been completed
- Non-registered schemes are governed by changing legislation and practice
- The HMRC website contains the comprehensive registered pension scheme manual

Chapter 2

> **SIGNPOSTS**
>
> - New schemes must be registered with HMRC to receive tax reliefs
> - Core information must be provided. A Pension Scheme Tax Reference will be allocated
> - HMRC can withdraw registration
> - An overseas scheme may register as a registered non-UK scheme
> - A scheme must be an occupational pension scheme or established by a person with permission under the *Financial Services and Markets Act 2000*

Registration, providers and membership

THE MAIN PROCEDURE

2.1 All new schemes must be registered with HMRC PSS once they have been established if they are to receive the tax reliefs on contributions, investments and lump sums (see *FA 2004, s 153*, and **Chapters 3**, **4** and **5** respectively below) which are available for registered pension schemes. The application process must be completed online by the scheme administrator who may not devolve that duty. The procedures are described in HMRC's RPSM (see **1.19**). They are summarised in this **Chapter** and are available with detailed links on the HMRC website. The main forms and maintenance procedures are described in **Chapter 7**.

The scheme administrator may arrange for a scheme practitioner to be appointed (see **2.4**).

HMRC's Pensions Newsletter 62 (see *http://www.hmrc.gov.uk/pensionschemes/newsletter62.pdf*) was published in May 2014. It refers to the latest changes to the registration procedure, and states that more information can be found in the Online User Guide. The relevant document in the Guide is entitled '*A Guide to Using the Online Service for Scheme Administrators and Practitioners.*'

Online applications are processed instantly, and tax relief will be available on contributions from the date on which HMRC acknowledge the registration of the scheme. The scheme administrator will receive a success message which includes the Pension Scheme Tax Reference (PSTR) consisting of 8 digits and 2 letters – see RPSM02306020. HMRC's acknowledgement of the registration will be placed on the scheme administrator's Pensions Notice

Registration, providers and membership **2.2**

board within Pension Schemes Online. Changes to details concerning scheme administrators and practitioners should be reported by using the Pension Schemes Online service. The PSTR must be quoted in all correspondence with HMRC concerning the scheme.

Elections to contract-out of S2P must also be made online to HMRC, although contracting-out is being repealed in the future and has already ceased for DC schemes (see **1.4** above). The Pensions Regulator maintains a register (see **2.5** below), and details are contained on the Regulator's website.

EFRBS must provide certain information to HMRC before 31 January of the year following the year in which the scheme came into operation (see **Chapter 7** below).

Focus
- Core information is listed below, to accompany an application for registration

---

CORE INFORMATION

2.2 The registration procedure requires core information to be provided to HMRC PSS. HMRC has twelve months from registration date in which to raise any queries.

The core information requirements are:

- the legal structure of the scheme (a trust is not essential);
- the size of scheme membership in bands of 0, 1–10, 11–50, 51–10,000 and over 10,000 (HMRC consider that small schemes may carry more risk than large ones);
- the establisher of the scheme (HMRC consider that schemes which are established by a connected employer may carry more risk than 'off-the-shelf' products);
- details of the administrator;
- the degree of member control over assets;
- registration for relief at source (RAS), where applicable;
- registration with the Pensions Regulator, where there is more than one member;
- election to contract out of the state second pension (S2P), where required;

Following the application process, registration of a scheme will appear online and the administrator will be able to authorise a practitioner or practitioners to carry out administrative tasks if he so wishes.

An application may only be made if the scheme is an occupational pension scheme or is established in the UK by a body authorised by the Financial Conduct Authority (FCA).

2.3 *Registration, providers and membership*

The National Employment Savings Trust (NEST) can register as an occupational pension scheme by virtue of *PA 2007, s 67*, as amended. Employers with any employees who have not been offered membership of a scheme which meets at least the minimum requirements of *PA 2007* and *PA 2008* must make certain they meet their enrolment dates. The staging processes are:

- for employers with more than 250 employees, October 2012–February 2014;
- for employers with between 50 and 249 employees, 1 April 2014–1 April 2015;
- for new employers setting up business from 1 April 2012–30 September 2017, 1 May 2017 and 1 February 2018.

The staging dates exclude employers with fewer than 50 employees from legislation until next parliament.

SCHEME ADMINISTRATOR

2.3 The main responsibilities of the scheme administrator concerning scheme registration are described in RPSM02101010. The administrator should register to use Pension Schemes Online by first obtaining an activation token and ID online. He must submit to HMRC a fully completed application in the form specified by HMRC. In practice, this will all be one online form. Applications may not be made before the scheme has been established. The relevant maintenance forms and completion notes are listed in **2.6**.

The scheme administrator must be resident in:

- the UK;
- another EU member state; or
- another state in the EEA (ie Liechtenstein, Iceland or Norway).

If more than one person is appointed as the scheme administrator, each is jointly and severally liable for any tax charges on the scheme administrator.

For deferred annuity contracts and assigned policies, the scheme administrator must be resident as stated above. If no scheme administrator has been formally appointed, HMRC regards the person who controls the management of the pension scheme (policy or contract) as the scheme administrator of that scheme.

Once the scheme has been registered, the scheme administrator can authorise HMRC to deal with one or more practitioners acting on their behalf (see **2.4** and RPSM02307000).

HMRC requires that the administrator understands the responsibilities and functions imposed upon him by the legislation, and further requires him to declare that he will discharge those functions at all times. This is a far-reaching commitment as it applies whether the administrator is resident in the UK or overseas. The main information contained in the declaration is that:

- the scheme is fully compliant with the legislation in its application to a registered pension scheme;
- the information provided by the administrator during the application process is correct and complete; and
- the administrator is aware that any false statements are likely to lead to penalties and/or prosecution.

SCHEME PRACTITIONER

2.4 The main responsibilities of the scheme practitioner will be those which are covered in his letter of appointment and list of services which is given to the scheme administrator or trustees. He can register to use Pension Schemes Online by first obtaining an activation token and ID online. He can conduct most activities, other than scheme registration, on behalf of the scheme administrator.

APPLYING FOR REGISTRATION

2.5 The Pensions Regulator maintains a register. The relevant application forms and completion notes are provided on the HMRC website in PDF format. The main forms and completion notes can be found at Pension Schemes Online. Some functions cannot be carried out online and must be in paper form. These are:

- relief at source repayment claims;
- submitting form SA970;
- reclaiming tax paid on investment income;
- registering a pension scheme; or
- changing the scheme administrator.

Any persons regulated by the PRA (previously the FSA – see **11.10**) are able to establish a registered pension scheme other than an occupational pension scheme (*FA 2004, s 154*, as amended by *FA 2007, Sch 20, para 2*).

A scheme may be established by different methods, for example, by:

- a trust
- a contract
- a board's resolution
- a deed poll.

However, under *PA 2004, s 252 (2)*, and the *Occupational Pension Schemes (Trust and Retirement Benefits Exemption) Regulations 2005 (SI 2005/2360)*, an occupational pension scheme with its main administration in the UK must not accept funding payments unless it is set up under irrevocable trusts. The following are exempt from this requirement:

2.5 Registration, providers and membership

An occupational pension scheme which is:

(a) a public service pension scheme;

(b) an occupational pension scheme with fewer than two members; or

(c) an occupational pension scheme which:

    (i) has fewer than 100 members;

    (ii) provides relevant benefits; and

    (iii) is neither:

        (aa) an approved scheme;

        (bb) a relevant statutory scheme; nor

        (cc) a registered scheme.

In addition to the registration and notification forms for registered pension schemes listed below, it is also necessary to register buy-out policies, *section 32* contracts (*FA 1981, s 32*) and assigned policies. Buy-out policies and *section 32* contracts are deferred annuities (ie they will provide an annuity to the member at some time in the future). Individual policies which are already held under a registered pension scheme and are earmarked for the provision of a member's benefits may be assigned to the member and will fall within the category of deferred annuity contracts (see RPSM02104010).

In the case of deferred annuities, the scheme administrator does not have to complete the entire registration application process online, but he must make the required declarations (*FA 2004, s 270*). Further details are given in RPSM02306150.

Focus

- A list of the prescribed forms to be submitted to HMRC is provided below.

The main registration and notification forms to be submitted online are listed below:

Form Number	Description
APSS 100	Pension Scheme Tax Registration
APSS 100 Notes	Completion Notes for APSS100
APSS 101	Election to contract out
APSS 101 Notes	Completion Notes for APSS101
APSS 102	Election for industry-wide money purchase schemes to contract out
APSS 102 Notes	Completion Notes for APSS102
APSS 103	Relief at Source details

Registration, providers and membership **2.6**

APSS 103 Notes	Completion Notes for APSS103
APSS 103A	Relief at Source details – specimen signatures
APSS 105	Relief at Source Interim Claim
APSS 106	Relief at Source Annual Claim
APSS 107	Relief at Source Annual Statistical Return
APSS 108	Declaration as a Scheme Administrator of a deferred annuity contract scheme
APSS 109	Notification of succession to a 'split' scheme
APSS 109 (Insert)	Supplementary page for Question 3
APSS 110	Notification of succession to a sub-scheme

Approved and exempt-approved schemes as at A-Day were automatically treated as registered pension schemes unless they opted-out of such status. This applied to:

- schemes formerly approved under *ICTA 1988, Ch 1, Pt XIV*, being approved retirement benefit schemes and additional voluntary contribution schemes;

- personal pension schemes formerly approved under *ICTA 1988, Ch IV, Pt XIV*, being approved personal pension schemes, approved stakeholder schemes and approved group personal pension schemes;

- retirement annuity contracts or retirement annuity trust schemes approved before 1 July 1988 under *ICTA 1988, Ch III, Pt XIV*, being insurance contracts for the self-employed or employees who did not qualify for approved scheme membership;

- public sector schemes, being relevant statutory schemes for members of the public service, Parliament and national assemblies;

- schemes with split approval under *ICTA 1988, s 661*, but only in respect of the part of the scheme formerly approved under *ICTA 1988, Ch I, Pt XIV*;

- old code schemes, being schemes which were formally approved superannuation funds before 1970 with frozen contributions since 5 April 1980; and

- deferred annuity contracts of a specified nature.

This applies in all cases unless the scheme has its registration withdrawn (see **2.10** below).

OTHER FORMS AND COMPLETION NOTES REQUIRED FOR ONGOING MAINTENANCE AND REPORTING

2.6 The relevant maintenance forms and completion notes are also provided online. They are listed, together with the reporting forms, in **7.15** below.

REGISTRATION REJECTED

2.7 If an application is rejected (see RPSM02101030), HMRC will give the reason for the decision. The scheme will be treated as an EFRBS (see **Chapter 11** and **Chapter 15** below). The scheme administrator has the right of appeal to a tribunal against that decision within 30 days (*FA 2004, s 156*, and **7.20** below).

OPTING OUT OF REGISTRATION

2.8 Under the provisions of *FA 2004, s 153*, a scheme could opt out of automatic registration. If a scheme did not opt out before A-Day, it would have been treated as a registered pension scheme. If it did opt out, a 40% charge would have been applied on the market value of the fund (which means the assets and/or other sums which were held for the purpose of the scheme as at A-Day). Opting out would also have negated the pensions business status of any life assurance provision under the scheme at the beginning of the company's period of account in which the opt-out took place.

The scheme administrator was responsible for payment of the 40% charge; and, where more than one person acts as the scheme administrator, each person is jointly and severally liable for the tax payment. Thereafter, the scheme would have been treated as an EFRBS (see **Chapter 11** below).

SCHEMES THAT DO NOT APPLY FOR REGISTRATION

2.9 Where an occupational pension scheme does not wish to be registered (see RPSM02101040), it will not qualify for the tax reliefs shown in **Chapter 3**. It is likely to be treated as an EFRBS (see **Chapter 11** below).

REGISTRATION WITHDRAWN

2.10 The effect of HMRC withdrawing the registration of a scheme is described in **Chapter 15**, below. The administrator may appeal against such a decision (see **7.20** below). Registration may only be withdrawn by HMRC; there is no provision for voluntary de-registration. Registration can only be withdrawn from an entire pension scheme, not from an arrangement or arrangements within the scheme (see RPSM02105010).

SCHEMES WHICH LOST APPROVAL BEFORE 6 APRIL 2006

2.11 Any scheme which had lost approval before A-Day could seek to become a registered pension scheme at any time from that date onwards if its scheme administrator applies for registration for the scheme and satisfies the registration conditions.

REGISTERING A NON-UK BASED PENSION SCHEME

2.12 A pension scheme which is set up outside the UK may register as a RNUK with HMRC (RPSM02102050). The same conditions apply as for a UK-based scheme, including the residence of the scheme administrator. The scheme administrator must make the same declarations as apply for a UK-based scheme, as described in **2.3** above.

SCHEME DOCUMENTATION

2.13 The governing scheme documentation will need to be in place before registration can be sought. There are no requirements under the *FA 2004* for HMRC to be provided with documents which govern the scheme provisions, except where HMRC determine that they need to have sight of documentation for a specific purpose. There is also wide freedom in the choice of scheme design, and schemes can be set up by one or more written instruments or agreements (see **2.5** above).

Focus
- Pre A-Day limits can still apply is the scheme provisions are not modified
- A flowchart is provided to assist with the process

MODIFICATION POWERS

2.14 *FA 2004* contained modification powers (see **1.6** above) which largely preserved the way in which the scheme rules were applied before A-Day, in conjunction with the tax approval rules that applied before that date. Much had been made of the fact that removal of the existing HMRC benefit restrictions on A-Day, especially the *FA 1989* earnings cap, could leave scheme sponsors exposed to a significant increase in liability. Phrases such as '... *as will not prejudice the tax approval of the scheme* ...' are scattered throughout occupational pension scheme rules concerning payment of benefits or certain other duties or discretions conferred on trustees.

Furthermore, scheme rules may even compel trustees to make a payment which would be unauthorised under the new current regime. To address these issues, HMRC published the *Pension Schemes (Modification of Rules of Existing Schemes) Regulations 2006 (SI 2006/364)*. They provided transitional protection for schemes whose documentation had not been amended to comply with the post A-Day tax rules. The protection applied up to 5 April 2011. The general effect of the protection up until that date is explained in the following:

(a) If the rules of a scheme would require the trustees to make what would be an unauthorised payment, the trustees have discretion whether or not to make that payment. If, before A-Day, the consent of the sponsoring employer was required before making the payment in question, that

2.14 *Registration, providers and membership*

consent is still required. Where such payment is made, that part of it relating to pre A-Day rights will not be a scheme chargeable payment.

(b) If any scheme rule limits benefit by reference to the earnings cap (in whatever terms), that rule should continue to be construed as limiting the benefit post A-Day as if the earnings cap legislation had not been repealed.

(c) If the rules provide for a certain pension to be paid and mention that a greater payment may be made subject to not prejudicing approval, then post A-Day the trustees can pay up to the HMRC maximum benefit as if pre A-Day limits were still in place, but they are prohibited from paying a sum greater than the pre A-Day maximum benefit. If, before A-Day, the consent of the sponsoring employer was required before making the augmentation, then it is still required post A-Day.

(d) If the rules provide for any payment to be made of such amount as would not prejudice approval, then post A-Day the trustees are prohibited from making a payment which would be greater than HMRC maximum benefits calculated as if pre A-Day limits were still in place.

(e) If the rules do not permit the trustees to recover from a member any lifetime allowance charge for which the trustees are liable, then post A-Day the trustees are able to reduce the member's benefits to reflect the amount of tax paid, and such reduction is to be determined in accordance with 'normal actuarial practice'.

(f) Transfers may be made only to the extent that the payments would have been authorised by the rules immediately before the coming into force of the *Regulations*, and subject to not prejudicing the scheme's approval.

(g) If the consent of HMRC is expressed in the rules as being required, the rules are to be read as if HMRC consent is not required.

HMRC Pensions Newsletter No 45 contained a reminder that the transitional period introduced in the *Registered Pension Schemes (Modification of the Rules of Existing Schemes) Regulations 2006 (SI 2006/364)*, as amended, would end on 5 April 2011. Scheme trustees could disapply any particular modification earlier by making an appropriate amendment to the relevant scheme rule.

In addition to these HMRC regulations, the *Occupational Pension Schemes (Modification of Schemes) Regulations 2006 (SI 2006/759)* gave scheme trustees the power to make a permanent modification to their rules by resolution to give effect to most of the above (if they did not already have the power) and to exempt certain modifications from *PA 1995, s 67*, by disapplication. Trustees had to adopt these modifications, if they wanted them, by 5 April 2011.

Consideration must also be given to the requirements of *PA 1995, s 67*, in respect of any amendments to scheme documentation. The Pensions Regulator's Code of Practice dated 24 January 2007 remains extant and provides guidance on the modification of subsisting rights. Employers are required to consult before making certain changes to:

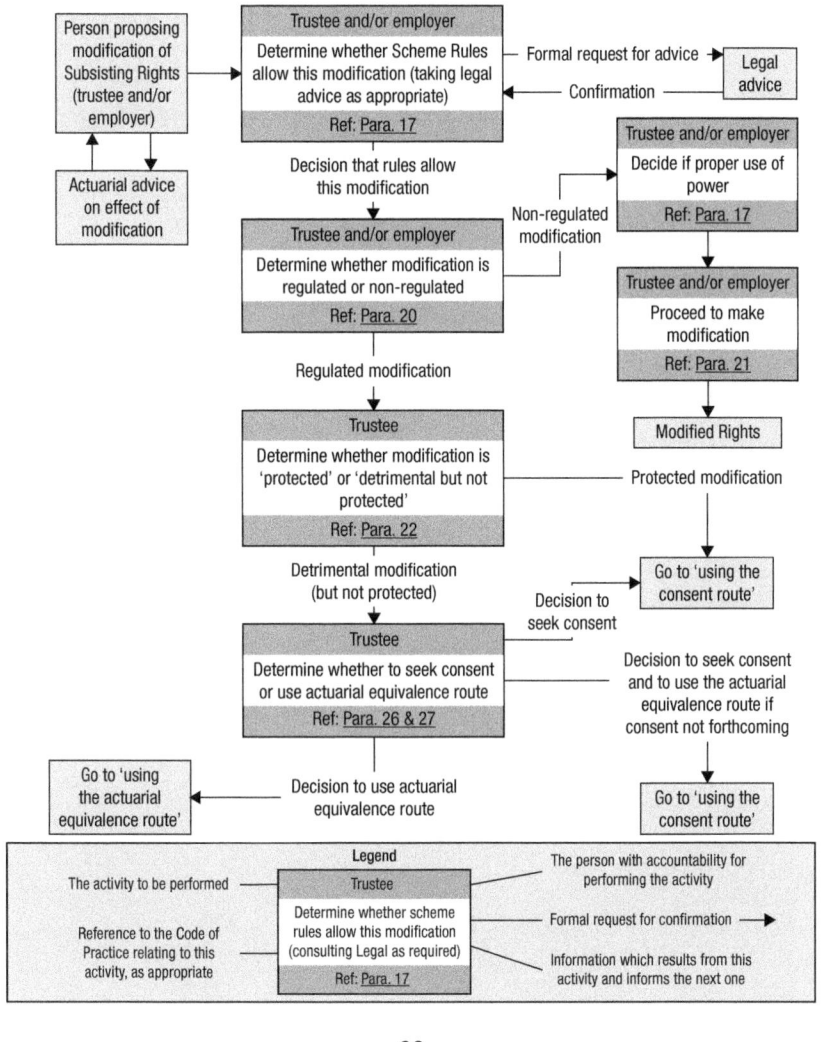

Registration, providers and membership **2.14**

- benefit accrual;
- defined contributions levels of payment to occupational pension schemes; or
- changing the level of contributions to personal pension schemes.

The Code also applies to anyone seeking to modify an occupational pension scheme, and to the trustees of such a scheme. The parties will normally need to obtain the informed consent to any protected or detrimental modification of the benefits of the members affected.

A flowchart is provided within the Code, which cross-refers to the paragraphs thereunder. It is reproduced below.

Activities when seeking to modify subsisting rights

[Flowchart: Activities when seeking to modify subsisting rights]

- Person proposing modification of Subsisting Rights (trustee and/or employer)
- Actuarial advice on effect of modification
- Trustee and/or employer: Determine whether Scheme Rules allow this modification (taking legal advice as appropriate) — Ref: Para. 17
  - Formal request for advice → Legal advice → Confirmation
- Decision that rules allow this modification
- Trustee and/or employer: Determine whether modification is regulated or non-regulated — Ref: Para. 20
  - Non-regulated modification → Trustee and/or employer: Decide if proper use of power — Ref: Para. 17 → Trustee and/or employer: Proceed to make modification — Ref: Para. 21 → Modified Rights
- Regulated modification
- Trustee: Determine whether modification is 'protected' or 'detrimental but not protected' — Ref: Para. 22
  - Protected modification → Go to 'using the consent route'
- Detrimental modification (but not protected)
- Decision to seek consent
- Trustee: Determine whether to seek consent or use actuarial equivalence route — Ref: Para. 26 & 27
  - Decision to seek consent and to use the actuarial equivalence route if consent not forthcoming → Go to 'using the consent route'
- Decision to use actuarial equivalence route → Go to 'using the actuarial equivalence route'

Legend
- The activity to be performed — Trustee: Determine whether scheme rules allow this modification (consulting Legal as required) — Ref: Para. 17
- The person with accountability for performing the activity
- Reference to the Code of Practice relating to this activity, as appropriate
- Formal request for confirmation →
- Information which results from this activity and informs the next one

2.14 Registration, providers and membership

Using the consent route

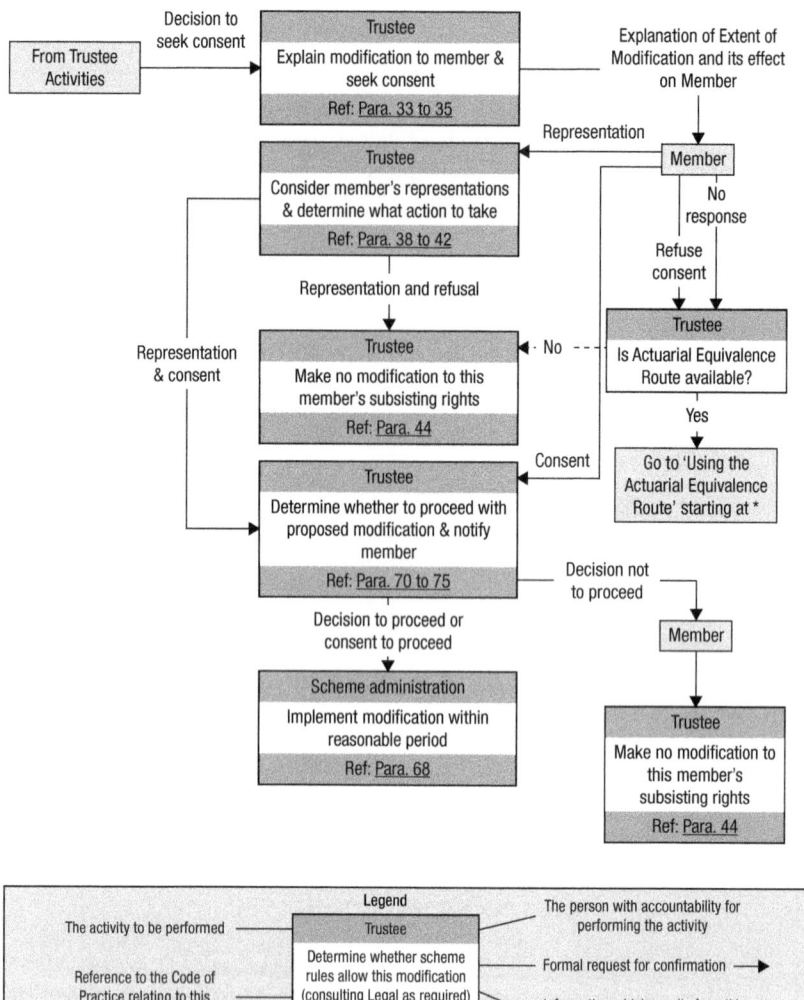

From Trustee Activities → Decision to seek consent →

Trustee
Explain modification to member & seek consent
Ref: Para. 33 to 35

→ Explanation of Extent of Modification and its effect on Member → **Member**

Member paths:
- Representation →
- No response →
- Refuse consent →

Trustee
Consider member's representations & determine what action to take
Ref: Para. 38 to 42

Representation and refusal ↓

Trustee
Make no modification to this member's subsisting rights
Ref: Para. 44

← No --- **Trustee**
Is Actuarial Equivalence Route available?

- Yes → Go to 'Using the Actuarial Equivalence Route' starting at *
- Consent ↓

Trustee
Determine whether to proceed with proposed modification & notify member
Ref: Para. 70 to 75

- Representation & consent (loop back)
- Decision not to proceed → **Member** → **Trustee** Make no modification to this member's subsisting rights — Ref: Para. 44
- Decision to proceed or consent to proceed ↓

Scheme administration
Implement modification within reasonable period
Ref: Para. 68

Legend

- The activity to be performed — **Trustee**
- Reference to the Code of Practice relating to this activity, as appropriate — Determine whether scheme rules allow this modification (consulting Legal as required) — Ref: Para. 17
- The person with accountability for performing the activity
- Formal request for confirmation →
- Information which results from this activity and informs the next one

Registration, providers and membership **2.14**

Using the actuarial equivalence route

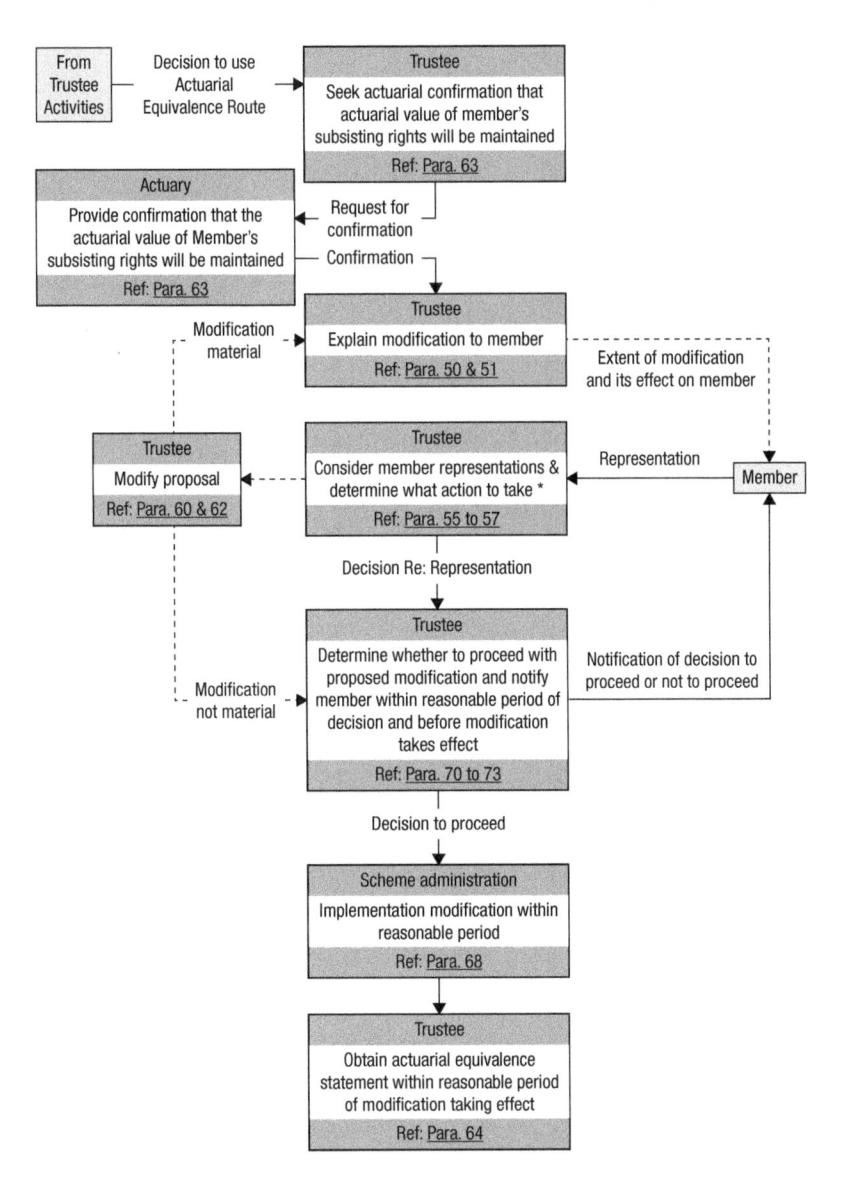

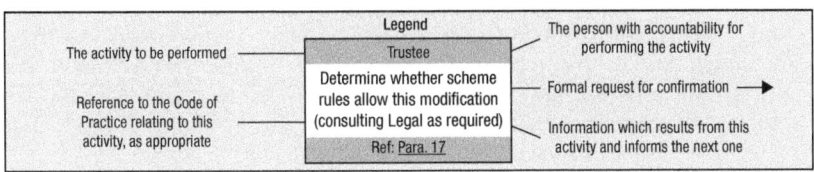

```
┌─────────────┐                          ┌──────────────────────────┐
│    From     │   Decision to use        │         Trustee          │
│   Trustee   │───Actuarial─────────────▶│ Seek actuarial confirma- │
│  Activities │   Equivalence Route      │ tion that actuarial value│
└─────────────┘                          │ of member's subsisting   │
                                         │ rights will be maintained│
┌──────────────────────────┐             │      Ref: Para. 63       │
│         Actuary          │             └──────────────────────────┘
│ Provide confirmation that│   Request for         │
│ the actuarial value of   │◀──confirmation────────│
│ Member's subsisting      │                       │
│ rights will be maintained│───Confirmation───────▶│
│      Ref: Para. 63       │                       ▼
└──────────────────────────┘             ┌──────────────────────────┐
            │     Modification            │         Trustee          │
            │     material                │ Explain modification to  │
            │ ┄┄┄┄┄┄┄┄┄┄┄┄┄┄┄┄┄┄┄┄┄┄┄┄┄┄┄│         member           │┄┄ Extent of modification
            │                             │    Ref: Para. 50 & 51    │   and its effect on member
            │                             └──────────────────────────┘                │
            ▼                                        │                                 │
┌──────────────────┐     ┌──────────────────────────┐                                  │
│     Trustee      │     │         Trustee          │   Representation      ┌──────────┴──┐
│  Modify proposal │◀┄┄┄┄│ Consider member          │◀──────────────────────│   Member    │
│ Ref: Para. 60 & 62│    │ representations &        │                       └─────────────┘
└──────────────────┘     │ determine what action    │                              ▲
                         │ to take *                │                              │
                         │   Ref: Para. 55 to 57    │                              │
                         └──────────────────────────┘                              │
                                     │                                             │
                                     │ Decision Re: Representation                 │
                                     ▼                                             │
                         ┌──────────────────────────┐                              │
                         │         Trustee          │                              │
                         │ Determine whether to     │   Notification of decision   │
            Modification │ proceed with proposed    │───to proceed or not to ──────┘
            not material │ modification and notify  │   proceed
         ┄┄┄┄┄┄┄┄┄┄┄┄┄┄┄▶│ member within reasonable │
                         │ period of decision and   │
                         │ before modification      │
                         │ takes effect             │
                         │   Ref: Para. 70 to 73    │
                         └──────────────────────────┘
                                     │
                                     │ Decision to proceed
                                     ▼
                         ┌──────────────────────────┐
                         │   Scheme administration  │
                         │ Implementation modifica- │
                         │ tion within reasonable   │
                         │ period                   │
                         │      Ref: Para. 68       │
                         └──────────────────────────┘
                                     │
                                     ▼
                         ┌──────────────────────────┐
                         │         Trustee          │
                         │ Obtain actuarial equiva- │
                         │ lence statement within   │
                         │ reasonable period of     │
                         │ modification taking effect│
                         │      Ref: Para. 64       │
                         └──────────────────────────┘
```

Legend

The activity to be performed	**Trustee**	The person with accountability for performing the activity
Reference to the Code of Practice relating to this activity, as appropriate	Determine whether scheme rules allow this modification (consulting Legal as required) Ref: Para. 17	Formal request for confirmation ⟶
		Information which results from this activity and informs the next one

25

2.15 *Registration, providers and membership*

The above regulations:

- allowed schemes to continue to apply the pre A-Day limits to benefits and contributions without a change to the scheme rules; and
- overrode pension scheme rules requiring HMRC approval.

Any registered pension scheme which relied on this transitional period to apply the pre A-Day limits, or because their scheme rules required HMRC approval for any changes, needed to ensure they had amended their scheme rules accordingly by 5 April 2011.

NOTIFYING HMRC OF CHANGES SINCE REGISTRATION

2.15 HMRC must be notified if certain changes are made to the documentation and/or structure of registered pension schemes (see **Chapter 7** below). These include:

- where the scheme changed its rules and it was previously treated as more than one scheme before A-Day (this will include schemes which were split approved prior to A-Day);
- where the legal structure of the scheme changed from one to another of the following categories:
    - a single trust under which all of the assets of the scheme are held for the benefit of all members of the scheme;
    - an annuity contract – two-party contract between scheme establisher and member;
    - a body corporate – eg a registered company;
    - other – eg deed poll;
- a change in the number of members so that they now fall into a different band (see **2.2**);
- a change in the country or territory in which it is established; and
- where the scheme become, or ceased to be, an occupational pension scheme.

PROVIDERS

2.16 A scheme must be an occupational pension scheme or, with effect from 6 April 2007 (*FA 2007*; *Financial Services and Markets Act 2000 (Regulated Activities) (Amendment) Order 2006 (SI 2006/1969)*), established by a person with permission under the FSMA 2000 to establish in the UK a registered pension scheme (see **2.2** above). Before 6 April 2007, non-occupational pension schemes had to be established by:

- an insurance company;

Registration, providers and membership **2.17**

- a unit trust scheme manager;
- an operator, trustee or depositary of a recognised EEA collective investment scheme;
- an authorised open-ended investment company (OEIC);
- a building society;
- a bank; or
- an EEA investment portfolio manager.

An occupational pension scheme may be established by:

- an employer (if membership of the scheme is open to its own or any other employees – such a scheme is an occupational pension scheme, even if other people may also join the scheme);
- more than one employer (if the membership of the scheme is open to their own or any other employees – such a scheme is an occupational pension scheme, even if other people may also join the scheme); or
- government departments or ministers and UK parliamentary bodies (such a scheme will be a public service pension scheme).

An employer will be recognised as a sponsoring employer where one or more of its employees are members and the scheme benefits for those members are directly related to their employment with the employers in question.

MEMBERSHIP

2.17 Registered pension schemes (depending on their own rules) may be open to all, whatever the employment (including self-employment and temporarily non-employment) or the residence status of the individual concerned. Spouses and partners may also be invited to join.

Anyone may concurrently be a member of any type or any number of schemes (for example, occupational pension schemes and personal pension schemes). Employers do not have to be associated and so administrative savings can be made by industry-wide employers or on grounds of common geographical location. There are no longer any HMRC requirements about the way that any employer is allowed, under the scheme rules, to participate in an occupational pension scheme. Accordingly, there is opportunity to design schemes for a wide class of individuals, both in the UK and overseas.

Member earnings can include patent income, share options treated as employment income. The taxable element of a golden handshake over £30,000, and earnings of directors and members of their families who are employees of private investment or property companies can be included.

2.17 *Registration, providers and membership*

CHECKLIST

- All new schemes must be registered with HMRC PSS once they have been established if they are to receive the tax reliefs which are available

- The scheme administrator will receive a success message which includes the Pension Scheme Tax Reference

- The registration will be placed on the scheme administrator's Pensions Notice board within Pension Schemes Online

- The registration procedure requires core information to be provided to HMRC PSS

- The scheme practitioner can register to use Pension Schemes Online by first obtaining an activation token and ID online

- The main registration and notification forms to be submitted online are listed above

- HMRC can reject an application

- A scheme can opt out of automatic registration

- HMRC can withdrawing the registration of a scheme

- A pension scheme which is set up outside the UK may register as a registered non-UK scheme

- The modification powers must be followed, where appropriate

- A scheme must be an occupational pension scheme or established by a person with permission under the *Financial Services and Markets Act 2000*

Chapter 3

> **SIGNPOSTS**
> - The assets of a registered pension scheme accumulate almost entirely tax-free
> - There are limits on the amount of member contributions that may be paid, only on the tax-relievable amount.
> - Contributions can be made in specie
> - The reductions to the annual allowance and the carry-forward facility are explained.
> - The reductions to the lifetime allowance are explained
> - Pension input periods and amounts are described
> - VAT can be an important consideration for some funded schemes

Tax reliefs on contributions and assets

INTRODUCTION

3.1 The tax reliefs and exemptions that are given to registered pension schemes and arrangements traditionally made them an attractive means of saving for retirement for members and their dependants and other beneficiaries. The post A-Day regime had transformed the tax reliefs that are available on aggregated member and employer contributions and the lifetime savings of scheme members. These matters are dealt with in this **Chapter**. Despite the major policy changes by recent governments which have attacked tax-efficient pension provision for savers, the accumulated fund of a registered pension scheme in respect of income and gains remains almost entirely tax-free. These matters are dealt with in **Chapter 5** below.

The tax charges that may be incurred in certain circumstances are described in **Chapters 8** and **14** below.

HMRC's RPSM at RPSM02103010 provides an 'at a glance' list of the main reliefs and exemptions as follows:

- contributions by members and payments made on behalf of members (except employer payments) up to the higher of £3,600 and 100% of earnings;
- increase in pension benefits promised in DB arrangements within the AA;
- employer contributions;

3.2 *Tax reliefs on contributions and assets*

- investment income – free of income tax;
- investment gains – free of CGT;
- lump sum benefits, in specified circumstances, are free of income tax;
- pension business – such of a company's life assurance business as is referable to contracts entered into for the purposes of a registered pension scheme, or is the re-insurance of such business.

Unfortunately, there have been severe cuts in the levels of the AA and the LTA. Any pension provision in circumstances where those limits are exceeded is not generally tax-efficient in view of the charges which fall on excessive payments (see **3.39–3.41** below). Accordingly, high earners and, as a result of further recent cuts, moderate earners, are seeking to bolster their pensions through non-registered schemes (see **Chapter 11** below) alternative savings vehicles or other means of reward (see **Chapter 14** below) or, where appropriate, overseas schemes and arrangements (see **Chapter 13** below).

MEMBER CONTRIBUTIONS

General principles

3.2 There are no formal limits on the amount of member contributions that may be paid by a member or other person in respect of a member, only on the amount on which the member may enjoy tax relief. Full relief is available on member contributions up to a level of 100% of the individual's relevant UK earnings or £3,600 if higher. However, any contributions to a DC scheme (or accrual in a DB scheme) that exceed the AA will result in a tax charge (see **3.39** below) which generally negates the effect of tax relief above that level.

Contributions may also be made by third parties (see **3.23**) in respect of a person who has no earnings (for example, a minor or a spouse who is not working), and *in specie* (see **3.4**).

Additionally, the following qualify as contributions made by or on behalf of a member (*FA 2004, ss 188(4), (6), 195*):

- Pension credit rights from a non-registered pension scheme. These are rights which have been derived from a pension sharing order or provision following divorce or dissolution of a civil partnership. They increase a member's rights under a registered pension scheme. As they will not have previously received tax relief, they can be treated as a contribution on behalf of the member. The member can claim relief on them up to the annual limit on relief.

- Up to 5 April 2012, an amount recovered from a member by his employer in respect of minimum payments made to a registered pension scheme (in accordance with *PSA 1993, s 8(3)* or *PSA (NI) A 1993, s 4(3)*). (Contracting out on a money purchase basis ceased on 6 April 2012.)

Tax reliefs on contributions and assets **3.3**

- Transfers of certain shares in a SAYE option scheme or SIP (see **14.2** below). The maximum permitted timescales for transferring the shares are:
    - for shares in a SAYE option scheme, 90 days after the member exercised their right to acquire the shares, and
    - for shares in a SIP, 90 days after the member directed the trustees of the SIP to transfer ownership of the shares to the member.

The value given to the contribution for tax relief purposes is the market value of the shares at the date they were transferred to the pension scheme.

Transfers-in and pension credit rights from a registered pension scheme are not regarded as member contributions.

The following examples explain how tax reliefs on personal contributions are calculated, and the charges that may be incurred:

Example 1

John had UK earnings in 2013/14 of £35,000. He paid a contribution of £10,000 to his registered pension scheme in 2013/14. John qualifies for tax relief on £35,000 (100% of UK earnings), but is limited to tax relief on his contribution of £10,000.

Example 2

Jim also had UK earnings in 2013/14 of £35,000, but he paid a contribution of £40,000 to his registered pension scheme in 2013/14. Jim qualifies for tax relief on £35,000 of the contribution (100% of UK earnings), but the excess contribution of £5,000 does not attract tax relief. It is not however liable to the AA charge unless, together with the qualifying contribution of £35,000 and the benefit of fund value accrual, the AA (then £50,000) is exceeded. Any tax deducted from the excess contribution of £5,000 (ie by RAS) must be refunded.

Example 3

Joyce had UK earnings in 2013/14 of £170,000. She paid a contribution of £65,000 to her registered money purchase pension scheme in 2013/14. Joyce qualifies for tax relief on £65,000 in 2013/14 (100% of UK earnings), but the excess contribution of £15,000 (£65,000 less the AA of £50,000) together with any further increase in the value of her pension fund in the pension input period ended in 2013/14 is subject to the AA tax charge on Joyce.

Tax-relievable contributions

3.3 In order to qualify for tax relief on relievable pension contributions, the individual must be an active member of a registered pension scheme, and a relevant UK individual in the tax year in which the contribution is paid.

3.4 *Tax reliefs on contributions and assets*

A relevant UK individual for a tax year is a person who:

- has relevant UK earnings chargeable to income tax for that tax year;
- is resident in the UK at some time during that tax year;
- was resident in the UK at some time during the five tax years immediately before the tax year in question and was also resident in the UK when he joined the pension scheme; or
- has, for that tax year, general earnings from overseas Crown employment subject to UK tax, or is the spouse or civil partner of an individual who has, for the tax year, general earnings from overseas Crown employment subject to UK tax (both as defined by *ITEPA 2003, s 28*).

Relevant UK earnings are:

- employment income such as salary, wages, bonus, overtime, commission which is chargeable to tax under *ITEPA 2003, s 7(2)*;
- income chargeable under *ITTOIA 2005, Pt 2*; that is, income derived from the carrying on or exercise of a trade, profession or vocation (whether individually or as a partner acting personally in a partnership);
- income chargeable under *ITTOIA 2005, Pt 3*, derived from the carrying on of a UK or EEA furnished holiday lettings business (whether individually or as a partner acting personally in a partnership);
- patent income charged to tax under *ITTOIA 2005, ss 579, 587* or *593* or under *CAA 2001, s 472(5)* or *Sch 3, para 100*, to that *Act*;
- general earnings from an overseas Crown employment which are subject to tax in accordance with *ITEPA 2003, s 28*.

UK earnings which are not taxable in the UK under double taxation agreements (by virtue of the *TIOPA 2010, s 2(1)*) do not count for tax relief purposes.

HMRC's Pension Newsletter No. 61 dated March 2014 as at *http://www.hmrc.gov.uk/pensionschemes/newsletter61.pdf* stated:

> 'The Government will explore with interested parties whether those tax rules that prevent individuals aged 75 and over from claiming tax relief on their pension contributions should be amended or abolished.'

In specie contributions

3.4 Contributions are required to be expressed as cash sums under *FA 2004*; and, in the vast majority of cases, contributions are paid as cash, deducted from salary or from bank accounts. However, *FA 2004* does allow shares acquired under a SIP or SAYE scheme to be treated as contributions if they are transferred to a registered pension scheme.

While contributions must be expressed as cash, it is possible for members to agree to pay a monetary contribution and transfer an asset in settlement of that debt. Such *in specie* contributions have become less popular since HMRC clamped down on their use in 2007. Nonetheless, if actioned correctly, *in specie* contributions may still be made. See **14.7** for further information.

> **Focus**
> - Member contributions after age 75 are not, at present, tax-relievable

Non-relievable contributions

3.5 The following contributions are not tax-relievable on the individual:

- contributions paid after age 75 (but see **3.4** above);
- employer contributions; and
- life assurance premiums (see **3.6** below).

LIFE ASSURANCE PREMIUMS, PENSION TERM ASSURANCE

3.6 Under *FA 2004, Sch 18*, tax relief was removed from member contributions to personal life assurance policies which were set up as pensions (which are sometimes referred to as 'pension term assurance'). The Act contained a measure of protection for existing policies:

- A policy may continue if it was issued in respect of insurance made before 6 December 2006.

- A policy issued in respect of insurance made before 1 August 2007 may continue as long as the proposal was received before 14 December 2006 or, if the scheme included pension rights, before 13 April 2007. There are slightly different dates which apply in respect of an occupational pension scheme in the unlikely event that this restriction would apply to such a scheme.

Any variations to a protected policy so as to increase its term or benefits will invalidate any protection.

The withdrawal of relief does not apply to life assurance premiums paid by members under an occupational pension scheme as long as the life assurance was a group policy and the other members covered by the policy are not connected with the individual paying the premiums (ie a spouse, relative or civil partner). AVCs made to group schemes to buy extra life assurance cover should still attract tax relief.

Under *FA 2007* there was a change to the rules which apply to pension term assurance policies. The tax relief on pension contributions which are paid as premiums to such policies was withdrawn. Pre 6 December 2006 applications could continue to benefit from tax relief, as could applications which had been sent to the insurance company on or before that date and receipt recorded by that insurance company by midnight on 13 December 2006.

3.7 *Tax reliefs on contributions and assets*

For a contribution to be a personal term assurance contribution, two conditions must be met. These are:

- the scheme uses a non-group life policy to insure the provision of the individual's death benefits under the scheme; and
- the policy is not a protected policy, because it was started after certain dates.

HMRC's Helpsheet 347 contains a flowchart. In brief, the Q & A's to the individual are:

Does your pension scheme use non-group life insurance policies?

– if no, your contribution is not a personal term assurance contribution and may get tax relief

– if yes, is your non-group life policy a protected policy?

– if yes, your contribution is not a personal term assurance contribution and may get tax relief

– if no, part or all of your contribution is a personal term assurance contribution.

However, life assurance premiums paid by an employer for the benefit of his employees may continue if they are to a group policy and the other members covered by the policy are not connected with the individual paying the premiums (ie spouse, relative or civil partner).

METHODS OF GIVING TAX RELIEF ON CONTRIBUTIONS

3.7 Relief on contributions is normally given through the PAYE system. RACs and pension annuity contracts were brought within PAYE on 6 April 2007. There are some differing methods of claiming tax reliefs, which are available only in specified circumstances and depend on the method chosen by the scheme. The different methods are described under their relevant headings below.

Focus

- Personal pension schemes must use the 'relief at source' method to obtain tax-relief

---

Relief at source

3.8 Personal pension schemes must use the 'relief at source' (RAS) method for tax relief on member contributions – see HMRC's Pensions Newsletter 55 as at *http://www.hmrc.gov.uk/pensionschemes/newsletter55.pdf* for an update. RAS is granted under *FA 2004, s 192*, and the *Registered Pension Schemes*

(Relief at Source) Regulations 2005 (SI 2005/3448). Occupational pension schemes may use either the RAS method or the net pay method (see **3.10** below) In practice, almost all occupational schemes use the net pay method. One notable exception is NEST, which is a statutorily established scheme that employers may use as one of the vehicles to satisfy their automatic enrolment duties from October 2012 onwards.

The terms RAS and 'net pay' are often incorrectly taken as being the other way round. Contributions to a personal pension, under the RAS method, are taken from net salary, ie salary that has already been reduced for income tax. (They are therefore frequently confused with the 'net pay' method.) On receipt of the contribution, the personal pension provider grosses it up by an amount equal to the basic rate of income tax and reclaims that amount from HMRC. Thus, an £80 contribution is grossed up by the provider, when it comes into the provider's hands, to become £100. A £100 contribution taken from net salary is grossed up to become £125. It is particularly important to bear this in mind in connection with GPPs. GPPs are, as the name suggests, individual policies arranged on a group basis, but where the grouping is for employees of a particular employer.

Employees therefore need to know how their contributions are to be expressed – as a percentage of gross salary or net salary, ie before or after tax relief. This is even more important now that the AA has been reduced to £40,000; when making a large contribution or when calculating scope available under the allowance, it needs to be borne in mind that the insurer will add on 20% tax relief, thereby increasing the contribution.

It is common to express contributions as a percentage of gross basic salary, but to deduct the net amount from pay. Thus, an employee earning £25,000 pa and paying a 10% contribution might actually have £25,000 × 10% × 80% = £2,000 deducted from his net pay over the year instead of £2,500. The additional £500 would be added by the provider and reclaimed from HMRC.

This method is fine for people whose highest rate of tax is at the 20% basic rate, as they are getting all their tax relief immediately. The position is different for higher rate taxpayers as they need to claim additional tax relief – it is not granted automatically. It has been estimated that up to 250,000 higher rate taxpayers omit to claim this additional relief. There are two ways in which a higher rate taxpayer can claim this tax relief:

- via the self-assessment process at the end of the relevant tax year; or
- by writing to HMRC and requesting that their tax code is changed to reflect the contributions they are paying.

Employees can find the address of their local tax office by calling HMRC on 0845 900 0444 and quoting their NI number.

If employee contributions are moved onto a salary sacrifice basis, there is no longer any need to reclaim higher rate relief separately as, under salary sacrifice, the gross salary can be reduced by the gross amount of the contribution; also, since it is now an employer contribution instead of an employee contribution, it will not be grossed up by the provider upon receipt.

3.9 *Tax reliefs on contributions and assets*

However, if member contributions are moved onto a sacrifice basis and some members have already had their tax codes adjusted for higher rate relief, they will need to revise these tax codes to avoid excessive in-year relief and a subsequent tax bill after the end of the tax year.

The personal pension provider/ scheme administrator must obtain the following information about the member before they can claim back basic rate tax relief on a member's contributions:

- the member's full name and address;
- their date of birth; and
- their NI number, or a statement that they don't have one (the information isn't needed if the member is under 16, or a non-UK citizen who isn't living in the UK).

Additionally, the member's employment status must be determined. The member will need to make declarations, including one to tell their pension scheme if they make a contribution that doesn't qualify for tax relief. Pension schemes normally collect all the required information and member declarations as part of the application form to join the scheme.

HMRC's Pensions Newsletter 56 dated January 2013 (see *http://www.hmrc.gov.uk/pensionschemes/newsletter56.pdf*) describes the process for obtaining higher rate relief for personal pensions.

HMRC's Pensions Newsletter 63 dated July 2014 (see *http://www.hmrc.gov.uk/pensionschemes/newsletter63.pdf*) stated as follows:

> 'Following the changes to the process for registering a pension scheme with HMRC, applications for relief at source will not be accepted until the scheme is registered. Any applications for relief at source made before a scheme is fully registered will not be processed until a decision on registration status has been made. Therefore you should not complete APSS103 and APSS103A until you have received a valid registration certificate.
>
> The RPSCOM100(Z) for the tax year 2013–14 is due to be submitted to HMRC by 6 October 2014. This is a reminder that failure to submit by the deadline will hold up any subsequent repayments pending receipt of the completed RPSCOM100(Z). You can find more information on relief at source repayments and the member information we may ask for relating to relief at source, in HMRC's RPSM.
>
> You should already have received a notice to provide this information. If you have not received a notice please email pensions.businessdelivery@hmrc.gsi.gov.uk'

Net pay arrangement

3.9 The net pay arrangement has been in place for many years (*FA 2004, s 193*), and the present method is unchanged. This is the procedure whereby an employer deducts the contribution from an individual's employment taxable income before operating PAYE. This contribution is now termed a 'relievable pension contribution'. The employer pays the gross contribution into the pension scheme.

Tax relief is enjoyed by the individual at his marginal rate of income tax without needing to make an additional claim unless, exceptionally, full relief cannot be given through the operation of net pay. Therefore, if a member makes a relievable pension contribution of £100, the employer will deduct £100 from the individual's employment income and pay £100 into the pension scheme.

A person who contributes under a net pay arrangement can claim tax relief under self-assessment, PAYE coding or a repayment claim.

Relief on making a claim

3.10 This approach means that no relief is given to the member when the contribution is paid. The individual makes gross contributions to the scheme and claims tax relief on his relievable pension contributions. Therefore, where an individual makes a relievable pension contribution of £100, £100 will be paid to the scheme. The individual then claims the tax relief from HMRC. Relief is given by way of a deduction from the individual's total income.

Gross contributions are only available to ongoing RACs where the RAC does not operate the relief at source system.

PUBLIC SERVICE PENSION SCHEMES

3.11 Some members of public service pension schemes, such as general practitioners and dentists, are taxed on some of their relevant UK earnings under *ITEPA 2003, Pt 2*, through being self-employed.

If they choose to pension these earnings in a registered pension scheme set up in accordance with the *National Health Service Acts*, they will be unable to use the net pay arrangement to obtain tax relief on their contributions. The member should make a claim for tax relief to HMRC, through their self-assessment tax return if possible.

COMPENSATION PAYMENTS

3.12 Compensation may be awarded at the instruction of a court or ombudsman for a range of failings by the scheme administrator or other parties. This could include compensation for poor advice, mis-selling, poor administration or poor performance.

Where the monetary compensation is paid to a registered pension scheme, this could constitute a relievable contribution. There are therefore issues where contributions, including the compensation amount, exceed the AA.

There is also a problem where the member has enhanced or fixed protections. Compensation paid to a DC scheme, which is treated as a relievable

3.13 *Tax reliefs on contributions and assets*

contribution, will generally result in the loss of enhanced or fixed protections. The obvious answer to such a problem is to make sure that compensation is paid directly to the member where possible.

> **Focus**
> - The annual allowance continues to be cut back

REDUCED ANNUAL ALLOWANCE

3.13 The AA was introduced on A-Day as one of the two cornerstones of the new pension tax regime, the other being the LTA. The AA restricted the tax-relievable amount of contributions and benefit accrual that could occur each year. It effectively replaced the pre A-Day limits on contributions and funding, while the LTA imposed an overall cap on the maximum benefit that a person could accumulate from tax-relieved funds over their lifetime, thus replacing the pre A-Day benefit limits. If accrual over a year exceeds the AA, or total benefits exceed the LTA, the excess is subject to a charge, the point of which is to claw back the tax relief which had been granted on the contributions and fund accumulation.

Up to 2011/12, the AA was not a concern of most pension scheme members. Its level was established at £215,000 in 2006/07, a level high enough only to concern very high earners looking to make large pension contributions. It increased gradually to £255,000 in accordance with the table below until 2011/12, when its level was drastically cut to £50,000. It was cut again, to £40,000, from 2014/15:

Tax year	Annual allowance
2006/07	£215,000
2007/08	£225,000
2008/09	£235,000
2009/10	£245,000
2010/11	£255,000
2011/12	£50,000
2014/15	£40,000

The reduced AA of £50,000 from tax year 2011/12 was brought in by *FA 2011, Sch 17*, and described in HMRC's Pensions Newsletter 56 dated January 2013 (see *http://www.hmrc.gov.uk/pensionschemes/newsletter57.pdf*).

The current AA level of £40,000 as from 2014/15 was brought in by *FA 2013, s 49*, and described in HMRC's Pensions Newsletter 57 dated May 2013 (see *http://www.hmrc.gov.uk/pensionschemes/newsletter56.pdf*).

Although there is no limit on the contributions that may be paid to a registered pension scheme there are limits on the amount of tax relief available (see **3.2**

Tax reliefs on contributions and assets **3.13**

above). The AA is tested for DC schemes against the contributions made, and for DB schemes on the accrual of a pension. The AA applies to each tax year. An AA charge arises on any excess input (*FA 2004, s 227*). *FA 2011, Sch 17*, replaced the excess charge rate of 40% with the 'appropriate rate'. The appropriate rate is the marginal rate which applies to the taxpayer concerned for the current year.

Before the reduced AA was introduced, there was an exemption that excluded input from the AA in the year when all benefits under that arrangement came into payment. That previous exemption has been removed, which means that contributions made in a year of retirement must now be valued against the AA. The charge applies in the year pension benefits are drawn. The opening value of rights under defined benefit schemes is subject to a revaluation rate.

Schemes must report the AA charges on the quarterly AFT return. So, for example, AA charges that arose in the 2011/12 tax year needed to be reported by the quarter ending 31 March 2014, with the AFT return filed and the tax charge paid by 15 May 2014.

Inflation-linked increases in expected pensions for deferred members of schemes do not count when determining the excess AA charge.

The AA charge is not treated as income for any of the purposes of the *Taxes Acts*, and it applies whether or not the administrator or member are resident, ordinarily resident or domiciled in the UK.

Excess monies may remain in the scheme and any excessive tax withheld by the scheme may be refunded to the member. If tax relief has been given on an excess, it will be clawed back from the fund. The allowance cannot be set off against the AA from one year to another if the value of a DB falls during the year.

To see if the AA is exceeded in any tax year, it is necessary to aggregate the total pension input amounts during the pension input period of each pension arrangement of the individual ending in the tax year concerned.

In a DC arrangement, the pension input amount is the sum of any member and employer contributions paid during the input period. In a DB arrangement, pension input amounts are calculated as the difference between the accrued pension at the end of the input period and the accrued pension at the end of the previous input period. The previous figure is adjusted for inflation and the difference multiplied by a factor of 16. (Prior to 2011/12, the factor was 10, and there was no inflation adjustment.)

The pension input period is the period over which the pension input amount is measured. Pension input periods are usually 12 months long, but an input period may be ended earlier or later by the member or administrator nominating a new end date.

Full tax relief is still available on member contributions, and employer contributions remain deductible for the employer and exempt from a benefit-in-kind charge on the employee. Another change brought in with the reduced AA is the carry forward of unused allowance from up to three previous tax

3.13 *Tax reliefs on contributions and assets*

years – see **3.20** below. However, it is necessary to have been a member of a registered pension scheme at some point in the tax year from which an unused allowance is to be brought forward. When carrying forward from any of the tax years 2008/09 to 2010/11, the AA is treated as if it were £50,000 instead of the actual allowance that applied in those tax years. Similar adjustment is made from 2014/15 for the reduced AA of £40,000.

Pension input periods, pension input amounts and the carry-forward provisions are described in further detail in **3.16** to **3.22** below.

The ongoing reductions in the level of the AA mean that significantly more people are now brought within the scope of the AA provisions. DC members will find it easier to cope with than DB members, due to the more flexible nature of DC pension provision. The rules of DB schemes can be rigid in nature, and DB members may find they have inadvertently exceeded the AA following a pay rise or simply through the accrual of additional service. Where the allowance is exceeded due to an exceptional pay rise, the carry-forward provisions might be relied on to cover the excess. However, if the ongoing accrual of benefits, or the payment of contributions, would mean that the AA is constantly exceeded year on year, it may be appropriate to revisit the design of an employer's pension scheme. Some options that might be considered are:

- Agreeing a contribution cap, or a cap on benefit accrual, at the AA of £40,000 to prevent it being exceeded. It needs to be borne in mind that, at some point in the future, the AA may once again start to increase each year (although this is seeming increasingly unlikely), and this will need to be taken into account when devising new arrangements.

- Offering contributions or benefit accrual of up to £40,000 with any excess provided as cash remuneration. While this works well with DC arrangements, it is more difficult to achieve with DB arrangements, and it will need careful consideration by the scheme actuary.

- Maintaining current contribution levels and helping those who exceed the AA to establish the likely tax charge or calculate the allowance that can be carried forward. If a member proves to be consistently above the AA, however, a longer-term solution may be needed.

- Providing contributions or benefit accrual of up to £40,000 plus additional accrual in an unfunded EFRBS (see **Chapter 11** below). While EFRBS are generally unattractive post *FA 2011*, an unfunded arrangement may still continue largely as before (again, see **Chapter 11** below). This may be a useful option if the employer does not object to carrying a pension liability on its balance sheet. However, anyone considering the use of an unfunded EFRBS as a top-up to a registered pension scheme needs to make sure that any inter-operation between the two schemes does not jeopardise tax relief for the registered pension scheme. *FA 2004, s 196A* curtails tax relief if the benefits to be provided under a registered pension scheme or an EFRBS are dependent on the benefits that will be provided under the other scheme. In other words, if it is found that there is some scope under the registered pension scheme, the EFRBS benefit cannot be reduced to augment the registered pension scheme benefit by a corresponding amount without jeopardising tax relief.

HMRC's Pensions Newsletter 57 dated May 2013 (see *http://www.hmrc.gov.uk/pensionschemes/newsletter57.pdf*) describes the latest reduction to the AA.

Exemptions

3.14 There are a few situations where the AA does not apply. The AA does not apply in cases of death, nor does it apply in cases of serious ill-health where any of the following conditions are met:

- benefits have been fully commuted on grounds of serious ill-health (ie the payment meets the conditions for a serious ill-health lump sum);
- the member is unlikely to work again; or
- injury compensation has been paid to ex-military personnel.

In addition, the following exemptions do not count towards the allowance:

Where a member:

- dies;
- retires due to severe ill-health; or
- is a deferred member whose benefits do not increase beyond certain levels.

Deferred pensions in a DB scheme are excluded from the AA provided that their revaluation in deferment is no greater than the increase in the CPI or the rate provided under the rules of the scheme as they stood at 14 October 2010. As a result, discretionary pension increases would be caught by the AA. There are no concessions for enhancements in redundancy situations, or early retirement situations where an employer may want to enhance benefits to reward past service.

There is no exemption for deferred pensions that maintain a salary link. Such pensions may need to be tested against the AA each year. While the increase itself is unlikely to exceed the allowance, it would need to be taken into account if any other contributions have been paid or any other benefit accrued.

Provision of information

3.15 Under the changes made to the AA from 6 April 2011, and from 6 April 2014, scheme trustees, pension providers and employers are obliged to comply with new information requirements. Where contributions or accrual in respect of any active member under the scheme exceed the AA, the scheme administrator (ie trustees or provider) must automatically provide those members with a 'pensions savings statement' (see below). Where a member has two or more arrangements in the scheme, the input amounts (see **3.19** below) must be aggregated to see if the AA has been exceeded.

3.15 *Tax reliefs on contributions and assets*

Scheme administrators must provide the pensions savings statement no later than 6 October following the end of the tax year in which the excess contributions or accrual occurred. However, in the case of a DB arrangement where the employer has not provided the trustees with the information they need to produce a pensions savings statement, the timescale for trustees is extended to three months from when the employer finally does provide them with the information they need.

A pensions savings statement must contain the following information:

- the pension input amount over the input periods for arrangements of the member under the scheme;
- the AA for the tax year in which the input periods end;
- the pension input amounts for input periods ending in each of the three preceding tax years;
- the AA for each of those three preceding tax years (the figure of £50,000 should be provided where any of the preceding tax years is 2008/09, 2009/10 or 2010/11, adjusted to 40% for later years); and
- where the input amount occurred over an input period that began before 14 October 2010 but ended in the 2011/12 tax year, the pension input amount attributable to contributions or accrual from 14 October 2010 to the end of the input period.

The latest carry-forward provisions for the AA are described in **3.20** below.

A pensions savings statement must be provided automatically where the AA has been exceeded, but must also be provided upon the request of a member (or former member) even where the AA has not been exceeded. This allows members of more than one scheme to obtain the necessary information to establish whether contributions/accrual in all schemes have in aggregate exceeded the allowance. The member's request must be in writing and the information must be supplied within three months or, if later, by 6 October following the end of the tax year.

Employers with DB schemes must provide the scheme trustees with the information they need to calculate active members' pension input amounts over input periods ending in the tax year in question. The information must be supplied by no later than 6 July following the end of the tax year. Trustees may ask the employer for information to allow them to calculate input amounts for members' input periods, for example ending in the 2008/09, 2009/10 or 2010/11 tax years. Their request must be in writing, and employers must supply the information within three months of the request. If trustees or the employer fail to provide the required information by the deadline, they will be liable to a fine of up to £300 plus a fine of up to £60 for each day the information remains outstanding. Deadlines for 2011/12 were extended by 12 months, although trustees and employers could choose to implement their processes in advance to help those members potentially caught.

Tax reliefs on contributions and assets **3.16**

> **Focus**
> - The complex rules for calculating the pension input period for contributions are explained

PENSION INPUT PERIODS

3.16 With the reduction of the AA from £255,000 to £50,000, and subsequently to £40,000, many more pension savers have been affected by the pension tax regime. This may mean having to get to grips with one of the more complicated aspects of the regime – pension input periods – if they are to assess correctly their own tax and complete their self-assessment returns.

Pension input amounts, to be tested against the AA, are calculated over the pension input period ending in the tax year in question. The pension input period is usually any 12-month period over which DC contributions are paid or DB benefits accrue. The input period is specific to the pension arrangement at the individual member level; if a member has more than one arrangement (for example, a DB arrangement with a DC AVC arrangement), a different input period could apply to each.

The first pension input period under an arrangement starts on the first date after 5 April 2006 when a contribution is first paid to a DC arrangement or when benefits start to accrue under a DB arrangement.

When a pension input period ends depends on whether the arrangement was in existence before 6 April 2011. *FA 2011* simplified input period end dates, but only in respect of new arrangements from 6 April 2011 onwards. New arrangements started from 6 April 2011 onwards would have a default input period end date of 5 April in the tax year in which the arrangement commenced. Subsequent input periods in the same arrangement would end on each subsequent 5 April.

The position was more complicated for arrangements in existence at 6 April 2011. In such cases, the first input period ended on the anniversary of the start date – this would be 12 months and one day later, rather than exactly 12 months. However, the second and subsequent input periods ended exactly 12 months later, without the extra day.

Example of a pre-2011 DC arrangement:

- the first contribution was made on 7 July 2009;
- the first input period therefore started on 7 July 2009 and ended on 7 July 2010;
- as it ended in the 2010/11 tax year, it would have been tested against the AA of £255,000; and
- the second input period started on 8 July 2010 and ended on 7 July 2011.

3.17 *Tax reliefs on contributions and assets*

Example of a pre-2011 DB arrangement (pre-2006 joiner):

- a member started to accrue benefits on 7 August 2005 (ie before 6 April 2006);
- the first input period therefore started on 6 April 2006 and ended on 6 April 2007;
- as it ended in the 2007/08 tax year, it would have been tested against the AA of £225,000; and
- the second input period started on 7 April 2007 and ended on 6 April 2008.

Example of a pre-2011 DB arrangement (post-2006 joiner):

- a member started to accrue benefits on 7 June 2007;
- the first input period therefore started on 7 June 2007 and ended on 7 June 2008;
- as it ended in the 2008/09 tax year, it would have been tested against the AA of £235,000; and
- the second input period started on 8 June 2008 and ended on 7 June 2009.

CHANGING INPUT PERIOD END DATES

3.17 The situation described above is the default position imposed by tax legislation. However, it is not necessary to adhere to the default input period end date if another date would be more convenient for either the member or the scheme administrator. The input period end date for one or more tax years can be changed by a simple written nomination.

Before *FA 2011*, the tax rules allowed an input period end date nomination to be made for a date that had already passed. However, *FA 2011* removed this option with effect from 19 July 2011. From that date is has no longer been possible to nominate an end date before the actual date on which the nomination is made.

In the case of a DC arrangement, the nomination may be made by either the member or the scheme administrator (the trustees or the personal pension provider). If the member nominates the pension input period, the member must notify the scheme administrator of this, unless the scheme administrator has already notified the member that it has nominated an alternative end date for that tax year (in such a case, the member's nomination is ineffective).

In the case of a DB arrangement, the nomination may be made only by the scheme administrator (ie the trustees). The trustees must notify the member of the pension input period they have selected.

Scheme administrators may notify members of their nominated input period end dates in several ways: they may write to each member; they may set out the nominated date in the scheme rules or scheme booklet; or they may place

Tax reliefs on contributions and assets **3.17**

a notice on the employer's website or the pension scheme's website, so that it is available to all members.

In nominating input periods, it is important to remember that each arrangement must have only one input period end date in each tax year. Subject to that proviso, an input period may be shortened to less than 12 months. An input period may also be lengthened beyond 12 months if it started on or after 6 April 2011. The input period may be lengthened beyond 12 months as long as the end falls somewhere in the following tax year. Note, however, that the £50,000 allowance (later, the £40,000 allowance) would apply to all accrual over the lengthened input period. The convenience of changing an input period in this fashion, therefore, needs to take into account any potential tax consequences. HMRC's guidance on the launch of the carry-forward position in 2011 is still a useful source of reference. HMRC has stated that, for the purpose of carrying forward unused AA to the 2014/15 tax year, the AA for each of the previous three tax years (2013–14, 2012–13 and 2011–12) remains at £50,000 (see **3.20** below). The 2011 guidance is as follows:

> 'A scheme can only have one pension input period in each income tax year and each pension input period must not exceed 12 months. Therefore, following the introduction of the annual allowance charge on 6 April 2006, any scheme that did not nominate to change their pension input period to an alternative date in their first year will have a first pension input period ending on 6 April 2007 and will have pension input periods ending on 6 April going forward.
>
> It would seem that some scheme administrators did not realise that this was the case and thought that if they had not nominated for an alternative end date for their first pension input period, the default was to the tax year, so that their pension input period runs to the 5 April each year. Having realised that this is not so, they are now looking to change their pension input period so that it does align with the income tax year. The nomination rules mean that a scheme can bring forward the end date of pension input period to a date earlier in the tax year.
>
> Under the current legislation a scheme can, where no previous nomination has been made, make a retrospective nomination to unwind their pension input period back to the first pension input period. By retrospectively nominating for their first pension period to end on 5 April 2007, the scheme can align their pension input period to the income tax year for all subsequent periods. Once you have made a nomination to change the PIP then you can't make a second nomination for the same tax year.
>
> Changing the scheme's pension input period in this way may have an impact on a member's tax liability, as it may result in a member's contributions or benefit accrual falling within a different tax year for the purposes of the annual allowance charge. If the scheme has always worked on the basis that their pension input period ended on the 5 April this is likely to have little if any effect and is only likely to

3.18 *Tax reliefs on contributions and assets*

affect members who have made large contributions close to the end or beginning of the income tax year. However, it is worth noting that members will be liable to any annual allowance charge that arises as a result of the change in the pension input period and will be able to claim any repayment of any overpayment that may arise as a result of the change. A repayment claim can be made up to four years after the end of the tax year in which the overpayment arises.

The scheme must advise their members if they nominate for their first pension input period to end other than on the scheme anniversary. If a scheme does not do so, that member's pension input period automatically defaults to the anniversary of the date they joined the scheme or 6 April if the member joined the scheme before 6 April 2006.

If a scheme wishes to retrospectively nominate for their first pension input period to end on 5 April 2007, they need to do so before the draft legislation receives Royal Assent. Under the draft legislation, from 6 April 2011 it will not be possible for a nominated date to be a date before the date on which the nomination is made.'

TRANSITIONAL INPUT PERIODS

3.18 The reduced AA of £50,000 applies for input periods ending in the 2011/12 tax year. The reduced AA of £40,000 applies for input periods ending in the 2014/15 tax year (see **3.20** below). When the first reduction came into effect, some adjustment was needed to ensure a smooth transition to the changed regime, as input amounts of more than £50,000 could have been made before 14 October 2010, the date on which the reduced allowance was announced, for an input period ending in 2011/12. Pension input periods that started in the 2010/11 tax year (for which an AA of £255,000 applied) and ended in the 2011/12 tax year (for which the £50,000 reduced AA applied) were therefore affected.

Any pension input periods which started after 14 October 2010 and ended in the 2011/12 tax year were fully subject to the reduced AA of £50,000.

Any pension input periods which commenced before 14 October 2010 and ended on or before 5 April 2011 were subject to the full AA of £255,000.

Any pension input periods which had already commenced before 14 October 2010 and which ended in the 2011/12 tax year were subject to the transitional provisions. The transitional provisions allowed input of up to £50,000 from 14 October 2010 to the end of the input period, but total input over the input period must not have exceeded £255,000. This is illustrated by the following example.

Example

Jessica had a pension input period running from 7 April 2010 until 6 April 2011. As this is a straddling period, the transitional provisions applied.

The contributions made to her personal pension between 7 April 2010 and 13 October 2010 were £200,000. Between 14 October 2010 and 6 April 2011, her contributions were £65,000. This is a total of £265,000 over the input period.

To determine if there could be an AA charge for the post-announcement period (14 October 2010 to 6 April 2011 inclusive), the allowance of £50,000 was deducted from the contributions paid (£65,000). The result of £15,000 was potentially subject to the AA charge.

The second stage was to test contributions in the pre-announcement period (7 April 2010 to 13 October 2010 inclusive). This was done by taking the AA of £255,000 and deducting the lower of £50,000 and the contributions paid after 13 October 2010 (£65,000). This left £205,000 which was the allowance available to cover her contributions in the pre-announcement period. In this case, her £200,000 contributions were covered by the available allowance.

PENSION INPUT AMOUNTS

3.19 Most arrangements in UK pension schemes will be either DC or DB. How the pension input amounts are calculated is quite different depending on whether the arrangement is DC or DB.

HMRC recognises two types of DB arrangement: cash balance; and 'other'. There are only a few cash balance schemes in the UK, although their popularity as occupational schemes may increase if employers get a greater appetite for risk-sharing arrangements. The normal structure of a cash balance scheme is that the employer promises that a certain pot of money will be available at retirement, which the employee must convert into an income, usually by purchasing an annuity from an insurance company. The employer bears the investment risk, while the employee bears the longevity risk.

'Other' DC arrangements are by far the most common. All group personal pension schemes fall within that category. HMRC uses the term 'money purchase' in its RPSM Glossary as follows:

> 'An arrangement is an other money purchase arrangement where the member will be provided with money purchase benefits, and the amount that will be available to provide those benefits is calculated purely by reference to payments made under the arrangement by or on behalf of the member. This means that in an other money purchase arrangement the capital amount available to provide benefits (the member's "pot") will derive wholly from actual contributions (or credits or transfers) made year on year.
>
> The scheme administrator or trustees may use the payments made under the arrangement to make investments of any kind on behalf of the member (for example, cash on deposit, shares, other investment assets, a life assurance policy on the member's death). As long as the pot ultimately used to provide benefits is wholly derived from

3.19 *Tax reliefs on contributions and assets*

the original payments, the arrangement is an other money purchase arrangement. The subsequent investment income and any capital gains are derived from payments made under the arrangement, and they themselves become part of the member's pot.

It is a feature of other money purchase arrangements that the member bears all the investment and mortality risk. The scheme simply pays out whatever benefits the amount in the pot, including the proceeds of all the investments that have been made using the payments into the scheme, will support.'

Determining the pension input amount for such an arrangement is relatively straightforward. It is the sum of the contributions made by the member and the employer during the pension input period that counts towards the AA. However, the following are not counted as pension input:

- Contracting-out minimum contributions or flat-rate rebates plus age-related rebates paid by the Government to a contracted-out money purchase occupational scheme or an appropriate personal pension. (Contracting-out on this basis was discontinued with effect from 6 April 2012, although rebates were received in the 2012/13 tax year in respect of the 2011/12 tax year.)

- Member contributions in excess of 100% of earnings (or £3,600 if greater).

- Investment growth within DC arrangements.

- Transfers from one registered pension scheme to another.

- The payment of AVCs to buy added years (that would be a DB arrangement).

- Contributions to non-registered schemes.

- Input in cases of death or serious ill-health. There are three strands to the ill-health exemption: if benefits have been fully commuted; if the member is unlikely to work again; or if injury compensation has been paid to ex-military personnel.

The previous exemption where all benefits are taken at retirement has been removed, which means that contributions made in a year of retirement must now be valued against the AA.

The timing of contribution payments can be quite important, as it may determine whether a contribution is to be treated as falling one side or the other of a tax year or an input period end date. For the purpose of including a contribution in an input period, it is the date when it is treated as received by the scheme administrator that counts.

Legislation does not provide the level of detail needed to resolve such a question. It can generally be inferred that the relevant date is the day on which the scheme administrator receives the money, but it seems to be open to interpretation in certain circumstances. HMRC has adopted a practical approach. In particular, it makes a distinction between a one-off payment or irregular payment, such as a cheque or bank transfer, and a payment which is part of a series of regular contributions.

Where an employer deducts regular contributions from an employee's pay on the same day each month but does not pay them to the scheme administrator until sometime in the following month, HMRC would be prepared to accept the date of deduction as the relevant date. A similar argument applies for contributions made by direct debit. Where a debit is to be made on a certain day each month but is not made until a day or two after that regular date because it is a weekend or bank holiday, HMRC would be prepared to accept the regularly specified date on the debit as the relevant date, as long as the scheme administrator holds a fully completed direct debit mandate.

Where a contribution is expressed as due for, say, March, but the direct debit specifies it is to be taken on, say, 10 April in respect of March, the relevant date would be 10 April. If a direct debit fails (eg due to lack of funds in the transferring account) and is reprocessed, HMRC would not be prepared to accept the original due date as the relevant date.

Evidently, where timing is outside the control of the payer, HMRC accepts that contributions could be treated as made on the date intended and expected by the payer.

However, HMRC takes a stricter line on one-off payments. Because there is no reliance on a series of previously established regular contributions being processed at a particular time each month, the parties have obviously taken a conscious action to make a separate payment and therefore necessarily must have had regard to the timescales involved in the transaction. A payment by cheque would be treated as received on the day the cheque is actually received by the scheme administrator (whether delivered by hand or by post). A one-off bank transfer would be treated in the same way as a cheque; it should be treated as received on the day the funds are in the scheme administrator's hands, ie when credited to the administrator's account.

HMRC considers that, where the timing of payments results in a tax charge and the bank is in error due to late actioned instructions, that would be a matter to be resolved between the bank and the person who has suffered the tax charge as a consequence.

Input amounts in DB arrangements are harder to value. HMRC defines a DB arrangement as follows:

> 'An arrangement other than a money purchase arrangement that provides only defined benefits. "Defined benefits" are calculated by reference to the earnings or the service of the member, or by any other means except by reference to an available amount for the provision of benefits to or in respect of the member, (thus making the definitions of money purchase and defined benefit arrangements mutually exclusive). A defined benefit arrangement is, typically, a "final salary" scheme, that is, one where the level of benefits paid is calculated by reference to the member's final salary and length

3.19 *Tax reliefs on contributions and assets*

of service with the employer. Contributions are often made to such an arrangement, and so there may be a pension fund or pot, but the benefits that may be paid are not calculated by reference to that fund or pot.'

To calculate the input amount, a valuation factor of 16 is applied to the increase in accrued pension over the input period regardless of age, sex or normal retirement age. The accrued pension at the end of the previous input period is uprated by the CPI before subtracting it from the accrued pension at the end of the current input period. If the result is negative, it is taken as nil. The following example illustrates this method of calculating the input amount and how it differs from the method that applied before the 2011/12 tax year (when the valuation factor was 10).

Example

At 6 April 2010, a member's completed pensionable service was ten years, the scheme's accrual rate was 60ths, and final pensionable salary was £45,000. By 6 April 2011, the member had 11 years' service and final pensionable salary had increased to £50,000. The measure of inflation to be used is the CPI, which in this example was 3.1% for the year.

Element	Old method	New method
Accrued pension at end of last input period	£7,500 (10/60 × £45,000)	£7,500 (10/60 × £45,000)
Opening value	£75,000 (£7,500 × 10)	£123,720 (£7,500 × 16 × 1.031)
Accrued pension at end of current input period	£9,167 (11/60 × £50,000)	£9,167 (11/60 × £50,000)
Closing value	£91,670 (£9,167 × 10)	£146,672 (£9,167 × 16)
Increase in capital value	£16,670 (£91,670 – £75,000)	£22,952 (£146,672 – £123,720)

In the example above, the change in the calculation method resulted in the pension input amount being £22,952 instead of only £16,670. This was still within the £50,000 AA which applied at the time; but, as service and salary increase, more DB members will fall foul of the AA, as illustrated in the following table. The table indicates the input amount attributable to a DB pension accrued over a year if an active member's pensionable salary has increased by 3%, 6%, 9% or 12% at the end of the year. It assumes that the scheme provides 60ths accrual and that the CPI rise is 2.5%. It can be adapted for post 6 April 2014 calculations to reflect the further reduction in the level of the AA to £40,000 (see **3.20** below).

Member with ten years' service at start of year

Pensionable salary	Increase in pensionable salary			
	3%	6%	9%	12%
£250,000	£72,000	£94,000	£116,000	£138,000
£225,000	£64,800	£84,600	£104,400	£124,200
£200,000	£57,600	£75,200	£92,800	£110,400
£175,000	£50,400	£65,800	£81,200	£96,600
£150,000	£43,200	£56,400	£69,600	£82,800
£125,000	£36,000	£47,000	£58,000	£69,000
£100,000	£28,800	£37,600	£46,400	£55,200
£75,000	£21,600	£28,200	£34,800	£41,400
£50,000	£14,400	£18,800	£23,200	£27,600
£25,000	£7,200	£9,400	£11,600	£13,800

In the actual calculation to be performed for the AA test, it is the scheme's definition of final pensionable salary that should be used to calculate the accrued pension figures.

If a DB pension is actuarially reduced for early payment, the unreduced amount must be added back into the closing value for the input calculation. Opening and closing values must also be adjusted for the effect of any sharing orders and normal transfers into and out of the scheme.

There is a problem when it comes to valuing the increase in an active member's DB pension if part of that pension does not accrue, as such, but the member receives an actuarial uplift for late payment. This could be the case for a member aged between 60 and 65, where one tranche of pension has an age 65 normal payment age and another tranche has an age 60 normal payment age. If the two tranches can be treated as separate arrangements, it should be possible to apply the deferred pension exemption to the age 60 tranche that receives the actuarial uplift; this would then not count towards the annual allowance. If both tranches are treated as one arrangement, the total increase would count towards the annual allowance. Whether the pension is treated as comprised of one or two arrangements would be for the scheme trustees to decide, as they are the scheme administrator and responsible for performing the input calculations. However, it should not be difficult for them to designate the two tranches as separate arrangements, which should mean that a lower input amount arises, although trustees may well wish to take advice on the method of doing this and any other implications.

CARRY-FORWARD PROVISIONS

3.20 The ability to carry forward unused AA from three previous tax years was introduced when the AA was reduced from £255,000 to £50,000 with effect from 6 April 2011.

3.21 *Tax reliefs on contributions and assets*

HMRC's Pensions Newsletter 56 dated January 2013 (see *http://www.hmrc.gov.uk/pensionschemes/newsletter56.pdf*) was published on 29 January 2013 and covered the current changes to the carry forward rules. It stated:

> 'Following the Autumn Statement we have had a number of enquiries about carry forward in connection with the reduction to the annual allowance from tax year 2014–15.
>
> No changes to the carry forward rules have been announced.
>
> If your total pension savings for the tax year are more than the annual allowance you can still carry forward any unused allowance from the previous three years to the current tax year. You only have to pay tax on any amount of pension savings in excess of the total of the annual allowance for the tax year plus any unused annual allowance you carry forward from the previous three years.
>
> This means that the amount of any unused allowances arising from the tax years 2011–12 to 2013–14 and available for carry forward to 2014–15 and subsequent years will still be based on the £50,000 limit.
>
> Therefore for 2014–15 you will be able to carry forward up to £50,000 unused annual allowances from each of the tax years 2011–12 to 2013–14.
>
> For 2015–16 you will be able to carry forward up to £50,000 unused annual allowances from 2012–13 and 2013–14, and £40,000 from 2014–15.'

Carry forward provisions may have been introduced in order to accommodate 'spikes' in DB accrual, but it can also be used by members of DC schemes to pay additional contributions in excess of their normal allowance.

Carry forward can therefore be an extremely valuable feature for DC members. Those who have both the means to pay and the necessary earnings to support additional tax-relievable contributions may wish to calculate how much scope they have left at the end of a year.

Similarly, anyone who has exceeded their AA may need to calculate their scope from previous years to determine whether or not they need to pay an AA charge.

HMRC's Pensions Newsletter 59 dated October 2013 (see *http://www.hmrc.gov.uk/pensionschemes/newsletter59.pdf*) covered the position where an individual has exceeded the AA in the carry forward rules. It states that further information on carry forward can be found at http://www.hmrc.gov.uk/pensionschemes/calc-aa.htm

Conditions

3.21 To be eligible for carry forward, the person concerned must have been a member of a registered pension scheme at some point in the tax year from which they want to carry forward unused allowance. This point is sometimes overlooked when carrying out scope assessments. If they were not a member of a scheme throughout the entire tax year, that year cannot be used for carry forward.

That said, the definition of 'member' for carry-forward purposes is drawn very widely. A member is any active member, pensioner member, deferred member or pension credit member of any registered pension scheme.

A person is an active member 'if there are presently arrangements made under the pension scheme for the accrual of benefits to or in respect of the person'.

A pensioner member is someone who 'is entitled to the present payment of benefits under the pension scheme and is not an active member'.

A deferred member is someone who 'has accrued rights under the pension scheme and is neither an active member nor a pensioner member'.

A pension credit member is someone who 'has rights under the pension scheme which are attributable (directly or indirectly) to pension credits and if a person dies having become entitled to pension credits but without having rights attributable to them, the person is to be treated as having acquired, immediately before death, the rights by virtue of which the liability in respect of the pension credit is subsequently discharged'.

It is not necessary to have been a contributing member of the pension scheme for the tax year in question. Simply having a deferred pension in an occupational scheme or a paid-up personal pension policy will be enough to qualify for carry forward. It is also possible simply to have been a member of an employer's group life assurance scheme – if the life assurance scheme was registered with HMRC as a pension scheme, even though no pension accrued, this too would count as being a member and would qualify the person for carry forward.

There are, therefore, some situations where the entire AA could be carried forward from a previous tax year.

Timing

3.22 There is a strict order in which the AA must be used up: the full AA in the current tax year must be used first; then any unused allowance from the three previous years is used up, using the earliest tax year first.

It is important to remember that the AA operates on the basis of pension input periods. These may not necessarily tie in with the tax year or with each other if there are two or more arrangements. Contributions (or accrual of benefits) are always assessed over the input period that ends in the relevant tax year when testing against the AA. Therefore, when assessing how much scope remains, it is important for members to know when the input periods of each of their arrangements start and finish. With the recent changes brought about by the introduction of a reduced AA, many scheme administrators (trustees or pension providers) have amended the start and end dates of members' input periods to tie in with the tax year or some other convenient date, such as scheme year end, pay review date, accounting year or flexible benefits

3.22 *Tax reliefs on contributions and assets*

year end. Details of members' input periods can be obtained from the scheme administrator.

Examples

Unused allowance of £15,000 could be carried forward to 2014/15 (once pension contributions of at least £50,000 are made in 2014/15):

	2011/12	**2012/13**	**2013/14**
AA	£50,000	£50,000	£50,000
Contributions	£35,000	£60,000	£40,000
Unused allowance	£15,000	£Nil	£10,000
Cumulative	£15,000	£5,000	£15,000

Note that, in 2012/13, the £10,000 excess over the allowance eats into the £15,000 to be carried forward from 2011/12, resulting in only £5,000 being allowed for carry forward.

However, the legislation is slightly different when carrying forward from the pre-FA 2011 years, ie 2008/09, 2009/10 and 2010/11. The AA for carry-forward purposes is £50,000, and an excess will *not* eat into a previous year's carry-forward, as in the following example:

	2008/09	**2009/10**	**2010/11**
AA	£50,000	£50,000	£50,000
Contributions	£35,000	£60,000	£40,000
Unused allowance	£15,000	£Nil	£10,000
Cumulative	£15,000	£15,000	£25,000

This may not have been the original intention behind the measure, but HMRC have accepted this and re-issued guidance to the above effect on 25 November 2011. For the years from 2014/15 the position is unchanged but for the reduced level of the AA (see **3.17** above). For further details are provided at RPSM06108010 onwards, and in the *Examples* below:

Example 1

It should be noted that, in *Example 1* of **3.2** above, John has unused tax relief available of £40,000 (£50,000 AA less £10,000 tax relief given) for 2013/14, in *Example 2* of **3.2** above Jim has unused tax relief available of £15,000 (£50,000 AA less £35,000 tax relief given) for 2013/14, and in *Example 3* of **3.2** above Joyce has no unused tax relief available as she has used up all her AA for 2013/14.

Example 2

Alan had UK earnings in 2013/14 of £100,000. He paid total contributions of £20,000 to his registered pension scheme in 2013/14. He qualifies for tax relief on the total contributions of £20,000 (100% of UK earnings) and has £30,000 (£50,000 AA less £20,000) unused tax relief. However, he has £25,000 unused tax relief available from 2010/11, nil unused tax relief available from 2011/12 and £10,000 unused tax relief available from 2012/13. His total unused tax relief for these three years is £35,000 of which £30,000 can be set against the sum of £30,000 unused tax relief in 2013/14. This leaves a balance of £5,000 of unused tax relief from 2012/13 which can be carried forward to 2014/15 or 2015/16 if necessary.

EMPLOYER CONTRIBUTIONS

General principles

3.23 As is the case with member contributions, there are no statutory limits on the amount of employer contributions that can be paid, only on the amount of the tax reliefs that are available. Tax relief is given on contributions that are paid on behalf of a member by any employer, corporate body or legal entity; but, if the contribution is made by anyone other than the employer itself, it will be deemed to have been made by the scheme member (who should receive any tax relief which is due). BIM46000 onwards address the matter of tax reliefs, including those for multi-employer schemes (see below).

Where a company is a member of a group registered pension scheme, relief will be given in respect of its contribution amount to the scheme:

- although the levels of contribution may not reflect the individual circumstances of a particular employer, this does not prevent a deduction being allowed if payments are apportioned between the employing companies on a reasonable basis; and

- where, say, the parent company pays the contributions and each employing subsidiary is recharged an appropriate amount relating to its employees, the intra-group recharge may be accepted as being a contribution paid by the employer in the period of account in which the parent company paid the contribution.

In the case of non-group schemes:

- the payment of a pension contribution is part of the normal costs of employing staff, and so it will usually be allowable expenditure; and

- the above also applies where the contribution is to a multi-employer scheme for companies that are not in the same group (eg an industry-wide scheme), even though employees elsewhere in the industry may benefit from the payment.

Tax-relievable contributions

3.24 Tax relief is given on employer contributions to a registered pension scheme against the employer's trading receipts. The contributions may include the cost of any management expenses which the employer pays to the scheme.

3.24 *Tax reliefs on contributions and assets*

HMRC give the following guidance (at RPSM05102010):

> 'Tax relief on employer contributions to a registered pension scheme is given by allowing contributions to be deducted as an expense in computing the profits of a trade, profession or investment business, and so reducing the amount of an employer's taxable profit.
>
> In the case of a trade or profession, employer contributions will be deductible as an expense provided that they are incurred wholly and exclusively for the purposes of the employer's trade or profession ICTA\S74(1)(a) – corporation tax and ITTOIA\S34 – income tax. Where the employer is a company with investment business the employer contributions will be deductible as an expense of management ICTA\S75.
>
> The pension tax legislation amends the normal rules as to what is an allowable deduction and as to the timing of a deduction. The details of these amendments can be found on RPSM05102020. But briefly the 2 main points are
>
> - pension contributions are not treated as capital payments if they otherwise would be, and
> - a deduction can only be given for the period in which the contribution is paid.
>
> The HMRC officer dealing with the Income Tax/Corporation Tax return of the employer will consider questions as to whether the contribution is an allowable expense. More specific guidance about whether contributions to registered pension schemes are an allowable expense is in the Business Income Manual at BIM46001.
>
> As a contribution needs to meet the "wholly and exclusively" rule if tax relief is to be given in computing the profits of a trade or profession for tax purposes, special consideration needs to be given in making any risk assessment to
>
> - schemes with multiple employers – see RPSM05102160, and
> - contributions paid in respect of members who are controlling directors or are connected to a controlling director – see RPSM05102170.
>
> In order to prevent avoidance of the spreading rules, see RPSM05102060, certain payments by an employer are treated for spreading purposes as if they are contributions to a registered pension scheme. For more details see page RPSM05102025.
>
> Tax relief can only be given on contributions that have actually been paid. The amount shown in the profit and loss account in respect of obligations in respect of defined benefit schemes may be substantially different from the amount of contributions paid to the scheme. But it is only the amount actually paid that can be considered for tax relief.

Tax reliefs on contributions and assets **3.27**

There are transitional provisions for some employers who received tax relief before 6 April 2006 for a contribution actually paid after 5 April 2006 – see RPSM05102150.

Tax relief on large contributions may be spread forward into future tax years – see RPSM05102060 to RPSM05102130.

Detailed guidance on the deduction in computing trading profits for employer's contributions to a registered pension scheme can be found in the Business Income Manual at BIM46000 onwards.

Detailed guidance on the deduction in computing profits for employer's contributions to a registered pension scheme by an Investment Company is in the Company Taxation Manual at CTM08340 onwards.'

Deductible expenses

3.25 RPSM05102020 states that employer contributions will not be treated as capital payments if they otherwise would be for the purposes of *Case I* or *II* of *Schedule D* or in computing trading profits for the purposes of the *ITTOIA 2005*. The contributions can only be deducted for the period of account in which they are paid. It is not possible to carry contributions back or forward to other periods.

Employers with investment business

3.26 Tax relief on employer contributions is given as an expense of management of the employer's investment business under *CTA 2009, Pt 16, Ch 2. Ch 2*, is modified so that:

- relief is available where, ordinarily, a contribution would not be allowed under *Ch 2* because the contribution represents an expense of a capital nature; and
- the contribution can only be referred to the accounting period in which it is paid.

Employers who are life assurance companies

3.27 Tax relief on employer contributions is given as an expense under *ICTA 1988, s 76*.

This section was modified so that:

- the contributions are brought into account in step 1 of *s 76(7)* if they would not otherwise be (and so are not regarded as capital expenses); and
- the contributions can only be referred to the accounting period in which they are paid.

LAM at Chapter 12A contains further details about *s 76*.

3.28 *Tax reliefs on contributions and assets*

> **Focus**
> - Spreading rules apply for large employer contributions

THE SPREADING RULES

3.28 *FA 2004* retained the main spreading rules which were in place as at A-Day. The relevant statutory references are *FA 2004, ss 197* and *198*. Pre A-Day periods of spread continued to apply until the spread had run its course or the employer ceased business, whichever first occurred.

Links to numerous examples of how to calculate periods of spread are provided at RPSM05102000. In brief, a large contribution may be spread, for tax deduction purposes, over two or more accounting periods. The main criterion is that contributions exceeding 210% of an amount paid in a preceding accounting year must be considered for spreading. The spread is applied to the amount by which the contribution paid in the current accounting period exceeds 110% of the amount of the contribution paid in the previous accounting period.

Major exceptions are:

- spreading will not apply to any payment which has not exceeded £500,000;
- on a cessation of business, where a period of spread is already in place, the relief may be allowed in an earlier accounting period of the employer choice; and
- contributions which are paid to fund cost of living increases for pensioners, or to meet future service liabilities for new entrants, are excluded from spreading.

FA 2008, s 90, prevented the avoidance of spreading by means of interposing a new company and financing it to pay the contribution, with effect from 10 October 2007.

Employer contributions must be physically alienated from the employer, in the relevant accounting period. If they are paid in a later period, the tax relief is only granted for that period.

Tax relief will only be given on cash contributions made, not on the amount shown in the company accounts. The spread will be for up to four years, which is the maximum period applicable where the excess contributions are £2 million or more. *FA 2004, Sch 36, Pt 4, para 42* contained transitional protection for existing arrangements as at A-Day.

The accounting period

3.29 Spreading means that the relief which is due to an employer on the contribution is not given entirely in the chargeable period in which the payment is made. Instead, part of the relief due is spread forward into future periods. The 'chargeable period' means a period of account (where a contribution relates to a trade or profession) or an accounting period (where it relates to an investment business or to the basic life assurance and general annuity business of a life insurance company).

DEFICIENCY PAYMENTS

3.30 Statutory payments by employers, to cover deficiencies in the assets of a registered pension scheme under *PA 1995, s 75*, are deemed to be relievable contributions. Further details on granting relief are provided in RPSM05102040.

LEVY PAYMENTS

3.31 Levy payments under *PA 2004, Pt 2*, by employers are not strictly contributions. However, the *Pension Protection Fund (Tax) Regulations 2006 (SI 2006/575)* deem them to be so, meaning that tax relief is available on any levy payments and the relief will not be spread.

IN SPECIE CONTRIBUTIONS

3.32 As is the case for member contributions (see **3.4** above, and **14.7** below), contributions into registered pension schemes by employers may be made other than in cash form. From a tax efficiency viewpoint, an investor who wishes to make contributions into a registered pension scheme could find it more beneficial to transfer assets than to realise those assets into cash for the purpose of making a payment. However, again, the payments must be expressed as cash sums. For example:

- ABC Property Developers Limited ('ABCPDL') agrees with the trustees of the ABCPDL pension scheme to pay a monetary amount into the pension scheme;
- ABCPDL offers to meet its obligation by effecting a transfer of assets into the pension scheme, of market value equal to the debt;
- the trustees of the scheme agree to accept the transfer of assets in settlement of the debt; and
- the transfer of assets is made and treated as a contribution into the scheme.

The 'payment' must be made within the employer's relevant accounting period, in order for the tax relief to be given. Records should therefore be kept of the arrangement by the parties for the future.

It should be noted that certain transactions may attract CGT and stamp duty at the time of transfer.

3.33 *Tax reliefs on contributions and assets*

RESTRICTIONS ON TAX RELIEF

3.33 Examples of circumstances in which tax relief may be restricted on employer contributions are given in RPSM05102140. The relevant regulations are the *Registered Pension Schemes (Restriction of Employers' Relief) Regulations 2005 (SI 2005/3458)*.

In summary, HMRC may restrict tax relief where:

1. any of the member's benefits are dependent on the non-payment of a benefit that they were expecting to receive from an EFRBS; or
2. payment of benefits to the member from an EFRBS would reduce the transfer value of any rights in a registered pension scheme.

The Manual states that the process for 1 and 2 is to calculate the pension input amount for each of the member's arrangements under the scheme in relation to the employer's period of account in which the contributions are paid. The amount of the restriction on the relief is an amount equal to the aggregate of the pension input amounts for the period of account in question in respect of each arrangement under the scheme relating to the member. Where the pension input period is being calculated in the case of cash balance arrangements and DB arrangements, the amount of any relievable pension contributions paid by or on behalf of the member during the period of account in question is deducted from the closing value of the pension input amount. In the case of other DC arrangements, the pension input amount is established by taking into account only the employer's contributions paid in respect of the member during the period of account in question.

Additionally, RPSM05102170 addresses the matter of contributions for directors or individuals connected to a controlling director. It states that, broadly, it is accepted that a contribution will be treated as wholly and exclusively for the purposes of the trade, and so will be tax relievable, if it is paid in respect of a controlling director or a connected employee in line with a contribution that would have been made for an unconnected employee in a similar situation. Further detail, including the possibility of an Inspector challenging the allowability of a contribution, is given in BIM46000 onwards.

> **Focus**
> - The ongoing reductions to the lifetime allowance are explained

REDUCED LIFETIME ALLOWANCE

3.34 Tax exemptions apply to contributions to a registered pension scheme and the growth on investments within the scheme. To prevent excessive relief being given away, the tax rules impose two restrictive allowances: the AA; and the LTA. The AA controls tax relief on the way in; the LTA is a mechanism of clawing back excessive tax relief on the way out.

Benefits from a registered pension scheme must be tested against the LTA on the occurrence of various BCEs. See **Appendix 1** for the list of BCEs and the

Tax reliefs on contributions and assets **3.34**

amounts crystallised by such events. If the aggregate of a person's benefits crystallised to date exceed the LTA, a tax charge is imposed on the excess at the crystallisation point.

The LTA was introduced on 6 April 2006 and was broadly designed to take the place of the earnings cap that had applied until then. It has changed as follows:

Tax year	LTA	Change
2006/07	£1.5m	
2007/08	£1.6m	+ £100,000
2008/09	£1.65m	+ £50,000
2009/10	£1.75m	+ £100,000
2010/11	£1.8m	+ £50,000
2011/12	£1.8m	No change
2012/13	£1.5m	– £300,000
2013/14	£1.5m	No change
2014/15	£1.25m	– £250,000

Note the sharp reductions to £1.25m for the 2014/15 tax year. The reasons for the reductions are complex. They are based on the continuing austerity measures imposed by government on registered pension schemes and their members. The creation of a 50% income tax rate in 2010/11 for those earning more than £150,000 pa. had triggered the first move, which had been to cut back on 50% tax relief being given to high earners' pension contributions. The HIERC was to be introduced on the pension accrual of those earning over £150,000 pa. In the meantime, another complicated set of rules, known as 'anti-forestalling', was to be introduced to prevent high earners taking advantage of higher rate tax relief in the period up to the introduction of the HIERC.

The change of Government in May 2010 meant that the charge was scrapped before its commencement date. The incoming Government sought to raise the same amount of tax revenue from pensions in general, so affecting a far greater number of people. It was decided that this would be done through a combination of a very severely reduced AA and a reduced LTA. The AA was consequently reduced by *FA 2011, Sch 17* (see **3.13** above) from £255,000 to £50,000, and the LTA was reduced by *FA 2011, Sch 18*, from £1.8m to £1.5m. It was further cut back to £1.25 million from 6 April 2014 (*FA 2013 s 48* and *Pt 1 Sch 22*).

There are several types of protection available to those who have benefits in excess of the LTA. Primary and enhanced protection (PP and EP respectively) were available when the LTA was introduced on A-Day; fixed protections were available when the LTA was reduced on 6 April 2012 (FP 2012) and again on April 2014 (FP 2014) and individual protection also applies from 6 April 2014 (IP 2014). These protections are described in **Chapter 9** below. It

3.35 *Tax reliefs on contributions and assets*

is generally inefficient to have large pension savings in a registered pension scheme that ultimately exceed the LTA. Any excess over the LTA may be drawn as a lump sum under the tax rules, but there would also need to be a power in the scheme's rules to allow this. Most schemes are written so as to allow the scheme administrator to make lump sum payments that fall within the definition of authorised lump sums. Where the excess is drawn as pension, a one-off tax charge of 25% of the crystallised amount applies and income tax is payable on the pension. Where the excess is drawn as a lump sum, a one-off tax charge of 55% applies against the lump sum. It would therefore be prudent to structure remuneration packages and pension saving targets so that the LTA is not exceeded.

HMRC's Pensions Newsletter 57 dated May 2013 (see *http://www.hmrc.gov. uk/pensionschemes/newsletter57.pdf*) describes the latest reduction to the LTA.

Testing against the lifetime allowance

3.35 The aggregate pensions saving in tax-advantaged schemes over a member's lifetime must be taken into consideration for the purpose of testing against the LTA. However, this does not include any dependants' pensions; these are not subject to the LTA.

The method of testing against the LTA is not as complex as that for the AA. Nevertheless, it does still depend on the nature of schemes and arrangements under which the member's pension entitlements have accrued.

The amount crystallised by each BCE is shown in **Appendix 1**. Broadly speaking, however, the amounts to be tested against the LTA can be summarised as follows:

- *DB schemes*: Pensions must be valued on a factor of 20:1. If the pension increases under the relevant scheme exceed the retail prices index, or a fixed 5% per annum, or aggregate survivors' benefits exceed the member's pensions, a special factor can be agreed with HMRC. Where separate lump sums are payable under a scheme (that is, cash sums which do not derive from a pension commutation), these amounts are added on after the calculation has been made.

- *Pensions in payment on A-Day*: Where a pension has already come into payment as at A-Day, a factor of 25:1 is applied to the pension in order to determine its capital value. Where an unsecured pension is in payment from a money purchase scheme at A-Day, the maximum drawdown level as at 5 April 2006 is used, even if the actual drawdown amount being taken is less than the maximum. The valuation of pre-A-Day rights only needs to be taken into account if a benefit crystallisation event occurs in relation to the member after A-Day.

- *DC schemes in general*: These are measured as the market value of the sums and assets held under the arrangement in respect of the member.

In addition to the exemption for dependants' pensions, the following exemptions apply:
- partnership retirement annuities, but excluding other RACs;
- transfers to other registered pension schemes; and
- discretionary augmentations given across the board to pensions in payment (these do not have to be tested against the LTA if there are at least 50 pensioners under the scheme and the increase applies to a class of at least 20 pensioner members).

SCHEME ADMINISTRATOR RESPONSIBILITIES

3.36 The scheme administrator has three responsibilities before, at and after the time when a BCE occurs in a member's lifetime:

(a) establishing whether a chargeable amount arises at the BCE;

(b) accounting to HMRC for the LTA charge due on any chargeable amount that arises at the BCE (on a quarterly basis); and

(c) providing the member after the BCE with a statement confirming the total level of the member's LTA that has been used up under the scheme; and, if a chargeable amount arose at the BCE, a notice confirming:
 - the level of chargeable amount that arose at the BCE;
 - the LTA charge due; and
 - whether or not they have accounted for the due charge, or intend to do so in due course.

There is no regulatory method laid down for establishing the available allowance at a BCE; schemes can adopt the method which best suits their design and operation.

The following text is an extract from RPSM11100030:

> 'When calculating the percentage of the standard lifetime allowance being used up at any BCE the scheme administrator need only be concerned with the benefits currently being tested under their particular scheme. They do not require specific details of any other benefits the member may have (which in turn avoids the need to obtain details of other rights when the individual joins the scheme). However, in order to calculate whether the member has enough available lifetime allowance to cover the amount crystallising at that BCE (and whether or not a lifetime allowance charge is due) the scheme administrator may well require details from the member of the previous percentages of the "standard lifetime allowance" they have used up under other registered pension schemes at earlier BCEs.'

Lifetime allowance examples

3.37 The following examples show methods of testing against the LTA on successive events. They are taken from RPSM and are still extant on that site.

3.37 *Tax reliefs on contributions and assets*

At RPSM11100030:

> 'How the lifetime allowance is measured
>
> When a member becomes entitled to draw benefits from a registered pension scheme, they use up a proportion or percentage of their lifetime allowance. That is how the lifetime allowance test works, by reference to percentages of the individual's lifetime allowance used up in particular circumstances.
>
> There is no measure for lifetime allowance purposes of any benefits held by the individual until entitlement to those benefits arises. The exceptions to this rule are
>
> - where the member reaches age 75 without having taken benefits,
> - where the member transfers to a certain sort of overseas scheme, or
> - where certain payments prescribed in regulations are made, for example, after the member's death because entitlement to those benefits for the purpose of the tax rules could not be established before the death.
>
> In these cases any undrawn entitlement is tested for lifetime allowance purposes at that time.
>
> In addition, where the member reaches age 75 having previously designated funds after 5 April 2006 in a money purchase arrangement as available for the payment of drawdown pension (known as unsecured pension before 6 April 2011), the amount by which the value of their drawdown pension fund at that time exceeds the value of the funds previously designated is tested for lifetime allowance purposes.
>
> The circumstances where a lifetime allowance test occurs are referred to in the legislation as benefit crystallisation events (BCEs). At each BCE a capital value is attributed to the benefits that crystallise. This capital value (the amount crystallising) is converted into a percentage of the standard lifetime allowance for the tax year the BCE occurred in. That percentage is then measured against the member's available lifetime allowance at the point of testing.
>
> The percentage of the member's lifetime allowance being used up as a consequence of a BCE is added to any percentage used up previously by the member, whether under the same scheme or a different registered pension scheme. Where the total of these percentages exceeds the individual's lifetime allowance, the excess (or the chargeable amount) is subject to a specific tax charge (the lifetime allowance charge).

Example

> Mike crystallises benefits with a capital value of £150,000. The standard lifetime allowance at that point is £1.5 million, so the

percentage used up is 10%. If Mike had not crystallised any other benefits previously, he will have 90% of his lifetime allowance still available for the next BCE.

The same process occurs when Mike crystallises benefits at a future date.

This time Mike crystallises a further £450,000 when the standard lifetime allowance is £1.8 million. So Mike has used up a further 25% of the standard lifetime allowance. In total Mike has used up 35% (10% + 25%) of his lifetime allowance.

The percentage of the standard lifetime allowance used up at a particular BCE in a particular tax year remains constant year by year even though the standard lifetime allowance is changed in subsequent tax years. So the 10% of the standard lifetime allowance used up in the example above when the standard lifetime allowance is £1.5 million remains constant at 10% in the later year when the allowance has risen to £1.8 million. This process ensures that the original crystallisation amount of £150,000 maintains a fixed percentage, despite subsequent changes to the lifetime allowance.

RPSM11100040 explains the logic behind this process in more detail, and the example in RPSM11100090 illustrates this principle.

When calculating the percentage of the standard lifetime allowance being used up at any BCE the scheme administrator need only be concerned with the benefits currently being tested under their particular scheme. They do not require specific details of any other benefits the member may have (which in turn avoids the need to obtain details of other rights when the individual joins the scheme). However, in order to calculate whether the member has enough available lifetime allowance to cover the amount crystallising at that BCE (and whether or not a lifetime allowance charge is due) the scheme administrator may well require details from the member of the previous percentages of the "standard lifetime allowance" they have used up under other registered pension schemes at earlier BCEs.

RPSM11103000 onwards explains in more detail the lifetime allowance testing process and the responsibilities imposed under the tax rules on each party.'

Similarly, at RPSM11100090:

'Lifetime allowance: basic principles: worked example

On 9 October 2006, Judy decides to draw some of her benefits from a registered pension scheme. She wants to take the maximum lump sum and use the residual funds to purchase a lifetime annuity. The scheme administrator calculates the capital crystallised value of the level of benefits she wants to draw as being £750,000.

3.38 *Tax reliefs on contributions and assets*

The scheme administrator writes to Judy telling her how much will crystallise for lifetime allowance purposes and the percentage of the current standard lifetime allowance this will represent (50% of the standard lifetime allowance for the 2006/07 tax year). They ask Judy to provide a statement within 1 month confirming the level of lifetime allowance she anticipates being available on the anticipated BCE date, and to say whether or not she anticipates any other BCE occurring either on or before that date under another scheme. They also ask her whether she is entitled to an enhanced lifetime allowance and, if so, to provide evidence of the certificate confirming the exact level of enhancement, as provided by HMRC.

Judy has not drawn any pension benefits from any other source previously and is subject to the standard lifetime allowance. She provides the requested statement confirming she has not used up any lifetime allowance previously and does not anticipate another BCE occurring either by or on the proposed date of the BCE.

The scheme administrator is satisfied that there is no chargeable amount and pays the benefits in full. They send Judy a statement verifying that she has used up 50% of the standard lifetime allowance at the BCE. Judy keeps this for future reference.

In the 2010/11 tax year Judy decides to draw the rest of her benefits under the scheme. The scheme administrator calculates the capital crystallised value of these remaining benefits as £180,000. The standard lifetime allowance is now £1.8 million so this second tranche of pension benefits represents 10% of the standard lifetime allowance at that time.

The scheme administrator writes to Judy outlining the above and asking her again about her anticipated available lifetime allowance at the time she wants to draw benefits. Judy still has 50% of her lifetime allowance available.

The new tranche of benefits will take Judy up to 60% of her lifetime allowance (50% plus 10%), so again there is no chargeable amount on this BCE. Judy declares to the scheme administrator that she has 50% of the standard lifetime allowance available at that time.

Benefits are paid out by the scheme administrator.

The scheme administrator sends a statement to Judy telling her she has now in aggregate used up 60% of her lifetime allowance (the standard lifetime allowance) through the scheme. Again, this certificate helps Judy keep track of the lifetime allowance she has used up, and evidence this fact where necessary.'

FUND ASSETS AND YIELD

3.38 Chapter 5 below describes the current investment rules. The funds of registered pension schemes receive considerable tax reliefs similar to the tax reliefs which applied to exempt approved schemes prior to A-Day. The investment yield of such schemes is free of income tax and CGT, and lump sum benefits are free of tax subject to the limits described in **Chapter 4** below.

Special tax consequences arise in respect of certain schemes IRPS, typically SIPPs and SSASs, investing in taxable property which includes residential property and personal chattels. These are detailed in **Chapter 12** below.

The main tax reliefs and exemptions for registered pension schemes are:

- any income received by a registered pension scheme in respect of its investments, deposits or other activities are free of tax *(FA 2004, s 186)*;
- any profits or gains arising in respect of transactions in certificates of deposit are free of tax *(ICTA 1988, s 56)*;
- any underwriting commissions which are applied for the purpose of a registered scheme are free of any charge *(FA 2004, s 186(1)(b))*;
- any profits from sale and repurchase agreements (Repos) and manufactured payments are free of tax *(Manufactured Payments and Transfer of Securities (Tax Relief) Regulations 1995 (SI 1995/3036))*; and
- there is no CGT on gains on the disposal of investments *(TCGA 1992, s 271)*, including income from futures and options *(FA 2004, s 186(3))*.

Income from futures contracts and options contracts are deemed to be all from investments, as is any income derived from transactions relating to futures contracts or options contracts *(FA 2004, s 186(3))*.

Focus

- The annual and lifetime allowance excess tax charges are explained

---

ANNUAL ALLOWANCE CHARGE

3.39 The AA charge is a freestanding charge imposed on pension input amounts that exceed the AA. All pension input amounts accruing during all pension input periods that end in the same tax year must, in aggregate, be tested against the AA for that tax year. As the charge relates solely to the input to registered UK pension schemes, it will be incurred whatever the residence or domicile of the administrator or member.

As the AA charge is freestanding, it is not permitted to offset the charge against general tax repayments or against other tax allowances or any losses. DWP legislation preventing the surrender of pension rights has been amended, so that it is now possible to meet the AA charge from pension benefits. It should be noted that the excessive amount is not treated as pension income (or any other income) for the purposes of UK bilateral double taxation conventions.

Liability to the charge does not prevent tax relief on contributions being given in the first place. Rather, the purpose of the charge is to claw back the tax

3.39 *Tax reliefs on contributions and assets*

relief that has been given (member and employer contributions are deductible in assessing income tax or CT, and employer contributions are exempt from a benefit-in-kind charge on employees).

The AA charge was 40% up to the 2010/11 tax year. From 2011/12 onwards, the charge depends on the taxpayer's marginal rate of income tax. The amount of tax due is determined by adding the excess input over the AA to other taxable income. This means that, once the AA is exceeded, there will effectively be no tax relief available.

Previously, the AA charge had to be declared and submitted by taxpayers through the self-assessment process. In recognition of the fact that many more people would be caught by the reduced AA, and they may not have the necessary free resources to pay the charge when due, the Government introduced the facility whereby taxpayers could have the charge paid by their pension scheme in return for a deduction in pension rights.

Members have the right to opt for AA charges to be met from their pension benefits if the charge is £2,000 or more. This will be done on their self-assessment forms/submissions. However, it is only mandatory for schemes to pay the member's tax charge and reduce benefits where the tax charge relates solely to pension savings in that pension scheme.

If the tax charge arises as a result of membership of numerous pension schemes, a particular pension scheme could pay all of the tax, if requested to by the member, but it is not required to do so.

Pension schemes do not have to pay the charge if:

- the scheme is in a PPF assessment period, or enters one after the member has elected for the scheme to pay his tax and before this is implemented, or
- there are exceptional circumstances, such as where scheme administrators are able to demonstrate that it would detrimentally affect the overall health of the scheme.

Schemes have a wide degree of flexibility to decide how benefits should be reduced in exchange for paying a member's tax charge. The only proviso is that the reduction is broadly fair and accurate so that the individual and other members of the scheme will not be advantaged or disadvantaged as a result.

The deduction is reasonably straightforward in a DC scheme. The member's account would be reduced by the amount of AA charge paid to the scheme administrator.

It is not so straightforward in a DB pension scheme. Some possible methods are:

- Adopt a debit approach similar to pension sharing on divorce. This builds up a negative deferred pension to be applied against the normally accrued DB pension when it comes into payment.
- Pay the tax from any DC benefits held in the DB scheme, eg AVCs.
- Treat it as a negative money purchase pot; ie treat the amount of tax paid as a loan which rolls up with an interest assumption until benefits

are payable at retirement, transfer or death. If the 'loan' is to be realised against a pension when it comes into payment, the pension will need to be actuarially reduced.

Scheme trustees will need to take advice from their actuary on the best method for their scheme and the terms which should apply.

As from 6 April 2011, scheme trustees, pension providers and employers are obliged to comply with new information requirements to aid the effective operation of the new regime (see **3.15** onwards and **Chapter 7** below). Therefore, by 6 October each year, members should be aware if an AA charge has arisen either from the statement they have received from schemes in which they have exceeded the AA, or as a result of an individual request for information to their pension schemes. Members may then decide to pay the tax from their net income, or from their pension benefits. If they decide the latter, they must report this on their self-assessment return and make an irrevocable election to their pension scheme by 31 July after the deadline for self-assessment. The pension scheme would then pay the tax and reduce the scheme benefits. The scheme must pay the tax by December of the same year via the AFT return.

In the year of retirement, any election to deduct the tax charge from benefits must be made before benefits are taken. Tax-free lump sums will be 25% of the value of pension rights after any AA charge has been deducted.

If an AA charge has already been paid and it is discovered that this has been overpaid, it would be possible for schemes to reinstate part of the scheme benefit and reclaim the overpaid tax by amending the AFT return that has already been submitted.

SPECIAL ANNUAL ALLOWANCE CHARGE

3.40 The £20,000 SAAC applied for the 2009/10 and 2010/11 tax years for those with relevant income of £150,000 or more. Anyone with gross income of £180,000 or more would have tax relief cut to the basic rate (20%). Those with gross income of £150,000 and above but under £180,000 would have relief cut back on a sliding scale from 50% (the top rate of income tax at April 2010) to 20%. The £20,000 allowance was increased to as much as £30,000 if infrequent (ie less frequent than quarterly) DC contributions had been paid. Input for the purpose of the SAAC was measured in the same way as for the normal AA, with the exception that it was measured over a tax year instead of a pension input period.

Protected pension input amounts ate into the SAAC but did not attract a tax charge if they exceeded it. Details were provided in the previous version of this book.

LIFETIME ALLOWANCE CHARGE

3.41 Where the LTA has been exceeded on a BCE, the LTA charge becomes payable on the chargeable amount. The rate of the charge on the

3.41 *Tax reliefs on contributions and assets*

excess over the LTA is 25% if a pension is taken. If a lump sum is taken, the rate is 55%. The charge is intended to negate the tax reliefs which the relevant funds will have attracted over time, both on the contributions and the fund growth. The scheme administrator may deduct the charge, and the member should normally declare the payment in his tax return and offset the tax deducted.

The liability for the charge falls jointly and severally on the member and the administrator, or on the recipient in the case of a lump sum death benefit. The charge is payable regardless of the residency or domicile of the administrator or member. Any withholding tax accounted for by the scheme may be offset against the member's liability. The administrator may reclaim any excessive tax which has been paid and repay it to the member.

The scheme administrator may apply to HMRC to be absolved of liability to pay the charge where the administrator acted in good faith and concluded that no charge was due. If the charge arises on the payment of certain lump sum death benefits following the death of the individual, the recipient is liable for the charge (not the member's personal representatives or the scheme administrator making the payment). However, the member's personal representatives are responsible for establishing whether a chargeable amount arises following the payment of such a lump sum death benefit, and both the member's personal representatives and the scheme administrator have a duty to report to HMRC.

If the member does not pay the LTA charge, or suffer a reduction in rights to pay for it, but the scheme administrator instead pays the charge (a 'scheme-funded tax payment'), the charge must be grossed up as if it were part of the member's rights. RPSM11105220 explains this further:

> 'The amount that actually crystallises through a BCE over and above the member's available lifetime allowance is referred to as the basic amount of the chargeable amount.
>
> This basic amount will be made up of either a lump-sum amount or retained amount (or a combination of the two) depending on the events taking place. From this breakdown the level of lifetime allowance charge due can be identified (see RPSM11105210).
>
> For BCEs other than those dealing with the entitlement to a scheme pension the actual lifetime allowance charge paid by the scheme administrator is referred to in the legislation as a "scheme-funded tax payment", and is added on to the basic amount to form part of the chargeable amount. This is because, for these BCEs, the amount crystallised is the net amount after tax (so the net lump sum paid by the scheme, the net amount being designated to provide a drawdown pension fund, before 6 April 2011 an unsecured pension fund, etc.). Adding the tax paid by the scheme administrator ensures that the taxable amount is the gross amount before tax.
>
> Where a scheme-funded tax payment needs to be added to the basic amount to form the chargeable amount, the scheme administrator

Tax reliefs on contributions and assets **3.41**

will want to ensure that the tax they pay, which forms the scheme-funded tax payment, is the same amount that will be due on the gross chargeable amount.

For example, if a member, aged between 55 and 75, with no available lifetime allowance has uncrystallised funds of £100,000 in a money purchase arrangement and wishes to use it to provide a lifetime annuity, the scheme administrator is likely to use £75,000 to purchase the annuity and pay £25,000 to HMRC to cover the lifetime allowance charge due. This will mean that the basic amount is the £75,000 crystallising through BCE 4, the scheme-funded tax payment is £25,000 and the chargeable amount is £100,000. The tax due on the chargeable amount is £25,000, the same amount that the scheme administrator has paid.

If the scheme administrator allowed the full £100,000 to be used to purchase a lifetime annuity, and to fund the tax out of the scheme's own resources, then the amount crystallising through BCE 4 would be £100,000. The scheme administrator would need to pay £33,333 of lifetime allowance charge to HMRC as a scheme-funded tax payment – so the chargeable amount would be £133,333 and the charge due (and already paid) would be £33,333.

RPSM11105250 provides an example illustrating the above.'

RPSM11105250 reads:

'Matthew has already used up 100% of his lifetime allowance. He still holds £300,000 uncrystallised funds in a money purchase arrangement. Matthew decides to draw these benefits on 3 October 2011 when he is 72 years old.

Matthew tells the scheme administrator that he has no available lifetime allowance, so the scheme administrator knows that any amount crystallising will be a chargeable amount.

The scheme rules give Matthew the option of drawing some or all the chargeable amount as a lifetime allowance excess lump sum or as an authorised pension benefit. Matthew chooses to draw two thirds of the chargeable amount as a lump sum, and use the remaining amount to generate a drawdown pension. A pension commencement lump sum may not be paid as his lifetime allowance has already been fully used.

Before making the payments the scheme administrator calculates the lifetime allowance charge due on the chargeable amount.

Two BCEs occur: the payment of the lifetime allowance excess lump sum (BCE 6) and the designation of funds to provide drawdown pension (BCE 1).

The amount potentially crystallising on the payment of a lifetime allowance excess lump sum (through BCE 6) is £200,000. But the

3.42 *Tax reliefs on contributions and assets*

lump sum will be reduced by the scheme administrator to reflect the lifetime allowance charge due on this sum. The lump sum attracts a lifetime allowance charge at the rate of 55% so the lifetime allowance charge due on this part of the chargeable amount is £110,000. The net lifetime allowance excess lump sum paid to Matthew by the scheme is £90,000 (£200,000 – £110,000).

The amount crystallising through BCE 6, plus the lifetime allowance charge paid by the scheme administrator in relation to this payment (a scheme-funded tax payment), represent the lump sum amount of the chargeable amount. The lump sum amount is the £90,000 crystallising through BCE 6 on the payment of the (net) lifetime allowance lump sum, plus the £110,000 scheme-funded tax payment paid by the scheme in respect of the lump sum amount. The £90,000 crystallising through BCE 6 forms part of the basic amount, but the scheme-funded tax payment of £110,000 does not.

The amount crystallising on the designation of funds to provide drawdown pension (through BCE 1), plus the scheme-funded tax payment paid by the scheme administrator in relation to this designation represents the retained amount of the chargeable amount. This sum attracts a lifetime allowance charge at the rate of 25%.

The scheme administrator will fund the lifetime allowance charge due on the designation of uncrystallised funds to provide a drawdown pension direct from those funds. The lifetime allowance charge due on this part of the chargeable amount will be £25,000 (25% of £100,000). So only £75,000 of the £100,000 uncrystallised funds being crystallised is designated to provide a drawdown pension (with the other £25,000 being used to fund the charge due).

The retained amount is the £75,000 crystallising through BCE 1 on the designation of funds to provide a drawdown pension, plus the £25,000 scheme-funded tax payment paid by the scheme in respect of the retained amount. The £75,000 crystallising through BCE 1 forms part of the basic amount, but the scheme-funded tax payment of £25,000 does not.

The total lifetime allowance charge paid is therefore £135,000 (£110,000 + £25,000).

The drawdown pension paid from the drawdown pension fund is still taxable as pension income on Matthew through PAYE.'

There could be a second LTA test in circumstances where a member is in drawdown (see **4.14** below).

Salary sacrifices

3.42 Salary sacrifices were traditionally a means for members to increase their pension provision beyond the 15% limit on employee contributions which applied before A-Day. Also, they could be seen to be tax-efficient, by saving the employer and the employee from paying NICs and potentially taxation on the forgone salary. The relevant statutory reference at *ITEPA 2003 s 62*.

In the past, salary sacrifices were mainly used to give up of rights to future cash remuneration in return for the employer's contributions to a registered pension scheme. Now they can apply to any situation where an employee gives up a right to future cash remuneration in return for a benefit-in-kind.

Salary sacrifices of taxable income for high earners must be in accordance with HMRC earnings guidelines (EIM42750), which includes the following example of a sacrifice:

> 'An employee's current contract provides for cash remuneration of £40,000 a year with no benefits. The employee agrees with the employer that for the future the employee will be paid cash remuneration of £34,800 a year and 52 childcare vouchers a year, each with a face value of £100. This would be referred to as a salary sacrifice.'

The introduction of the new tax regime from A-Day reduced the need for many salary sacrifice arrangements. However, the relatively generous AA level has since been severely restricted on two occasions since its introduction, as described above. This means that salary sacrifices are undergoing a new period of popularity. Salary sacrifices fall within employment law and not tax law, and it is therefore somewhat outside the remit of HMRC to rule on their effectiveness. Nevertheless, the HMRC website contains full details of what constitutes an effective salary sacrifice. The employee has to give up his future entitlement to the benefit and suffer a reduction in income in place of a non-cash benefit. EIM42753 says:

> 'In a salary sacrifice arrangement the contract is changed or varied. The employee may agree to a smaller cash salary in return for a non-cash benefit.
>
> The change in the entitlement should be reflected in the contract. If the contract is not effectively varied, the employee remains entitled to the elements of the remuneration package previously specified.

Varying the contract can be achieved in a number of ways:

- Rewriting the document in part or whole

- Setting out agreed changes in a separate document that is attached to the main contract. This may be a letter or a pro-forma.

- Employees may be informed of proposals to make changes by the employer. The employer may specify that if an employee has not indicated his/her wish not to participate in the changes by a certain date, the absence of an "opt out" will be regarded as an "opt in". This approach is often used when wholesale changes to all employees' terms and conditions are proposed.

3.42 *Tax reliefs on contributions and assets*

> For example, changes to the employer's occupational pension scheme.
>
> The first two points on the bulleted list are easily recognised as effective changes as the employee will usually signify his/her agreement by signing the document. The third arrangement is also effective if the employees:
>
> - have been fully informed of the proposals
> - are given a specified date by which time the "opt out" must be made
> - continue working after the opt out date
> - continue working after the first pay-day when the changes have been implemented without protest
>
> When these conditions have been satisfied, the employees have indicated their agreement to the variation by their conduct and the revised agreement is legally binding on both parties.'

In practice, a salary sacrifice letter should be signed by the employee and the employer must state the date on which the level of the employee's salary will be reduced, and the amount or percentage of pay or monetary amount by which it shall be reduced. It is common for the employer to state that it will pay a sum of money directly into the company's pension scheme for the employee's benefit in a separate document. This has long been the practice as the employee could not have an indefeasible right to revert to their full salary or income tax and NICs would be chargeable on the full amount under the doctrine of 'money's worth'. The relevant principle was established in *Heaton v Bell (46TC211)*.

However, although the reduced salary will be a permanent variation to the employee's contract of employment, the employer may offer an annual option to cancel the waiver for future years. Sacrifices must not reduce the rate of pay to be less than the minimum wage figure. Any agreement to reduce pay below the minimum wage is void, and so employers might find themselves on the hook, both for the higher wage legally and the additional benefit contractually.

HMRC does also now acknowledge that, in exceptional circumstances, an employee may be given the right to revert to the original salary level. Exceptional circumstances may include hardship or unexpected lifestyle event changes.

The timing of an effective salary sacrifice is important, as it hinges on the date when the contractual right to cash remuneration has been reduced. There are two conditions that have to be met:

- the employment contract must be effectively varied before the changes are implemented. Any right to receive cash wages/salary must be given up before the employee is entitled to receive the remuneration.
- the true construction of the revised contractual arrangement between employer and employee must be that the employee is entitled to lower cash remuneration and a benefit.

Bonus waivers are similar to salary sacrifices and can appeal in particular to high earners (see **11.20** below). The advent of disguised remuneration under *FA 2011, Sch 2*, (see **Chapter 11** below) brought into doubt the effectiveness of salary sacrifices for some schemes, such as EFRBS. However, following a long consultative process, HMRC confirmed that bona fide sacrifices are not caught by the legislation.

Statutory clearance from HMRC of the effectiveness of existing waivers can be obtained in certain circumstances by writing to: HMRC Clearances Team, Alexander House, 21 Victoria Avenue, Southend-on-Sea, Essex, SS99 1BD; email *hmrc.southendteam@hmrc.gsi.gov.uk*.

THE PENSIONS REGULATOR

3.43 The Regulator published two updated COPS, with supporting guidance, on reporting late contributions as from 20 September 2013. They are:

- Code of Practice 05 – *Reporting Late Payment of Contributions to Occupational Money Purchase Schemes*.
- Code of Practice 06 – *Reporting Late Payment of Contributions to Personal Pension Schemes*.

The Codes apply, regardless of the number of scheme members. Reports must be made to members within 30 days of reporting to the Regulator (see the *Pensions Act 2004 (Codes of Practice) Appointed Day Order 2013 – SI 2013/2316*).

VAT

3.44 VAT implications can often be overlooked, as pension schemes are generally not liable for direct tax. Nevertheless, VAT can be an important consideration for some funded schemes, in particular in respect of rental income or charges for financial services. It can be possible to offset VAT incurred by a scheme on its administration costs against the VAT received on rent from property it leases or to take advantage of the VAT exemption on financial services or to adopt the VAT flat-rate scheme.

The main source of guidance was Customs HMRC VAT Notice 700/17 (November 2011). It was superseded by HMRC Reference: Notice 700/17 (January 2013). A general VAT Guide Notice 700 was issued in August 2013.

The January 2013 Notice focussed on pensions, and covered them in detail. The main extracts are reproduced below. However, as VAT is constantly under the spotlight (as are VAT tax avoidance schemes, which fall within the DOTAS legislation), it is advisable to check the latest standing guidance on a regular basis. The main subjects covered by the guidance are reproduced in the extract below:

'1.5 What happens if I make exempt supplies?

Where you make exempt supplies the amount of input tax you can deduct may be restricted. You are entitled to deduct the input tax incurred on costs that you

3.44 *Tax reliefs on contributions and assets*

use or intend to use in making taxable supplies. You cannot normally deduct input tax incurred on costs that relate to your exempt supplies. If your input tax relates to both taxable and exempt supplies, you can normally deduct only the amount of input tax that relates to your taxable supplies. You can find more information in Notice 706 Partial exemption.

2. Guidance for employers about claiming input tax

2.1 What pension scheme activity forms part of my business activities?

The management of your own employee pension scheme is a part of your normal business activities. If you are a VAT registered employer, and set up a pension fund for your employees under a trust deed, the VAT incurred in both setting up the fund and on its day-to-day **management** is your input tax. This applies even where responsibility for the general management of the scheme rests (under the trust deed) with the trustee, or the trustees pay for the services supplied. A clear distinction is, however, made between "management" and "investment" costs – see paragraph 2.2.

2.2 What pension scheme activity does not form part of my business activities?

When the trustees make investments, acquire property and collect rents from property holdings, these activities (all termed "investment" activities for the purposes of this Notice) are quite separate from your business. It follows that tax incurred in carrying on **investment** activities is not your input tax even if you pay such expenses on behalf of the trust.

2.3 On what kinds of "management" services can I claim input tax?

You can claim for:

1. making arrangements for setting up a pension fund;
2. management of the scheme, that is collection of contributions and payment of pensions;
3. advice on reviewing the scheme and implementing changes to it;
4. accountancy and auditing relating to management of the scheme, such as preparation of the annual accounts;
5. actuarial valuation of the assets of a fund;
6. general actuarial advice connected with administration of the fund;
7. providing general statistics in connection with the performance of a fund's investments or properties; and
8. legal instructions and general legal advice, including drafting trust deeds, insofar as it relates to the management of the scheme.

2.4 On what kind of "investment" services can't I claim input tax?

You can't claim for:

- advice connected with making investments;
- brokerage charges;

- rent and service charge collection for property holdings;
- producing records and accounts in connection with property purchases, lettings and disposals or investments;
- trustee services, that is services of a professional trustee in managing the assets of the fund;
- legal services paid on behalf of representative beneficiaries in connection with changes in pension fund arrangements; and
- custodian charges.

2.5 What evidence will I need to claim input tax?

You should hold tax invoices made out in your name. If the trustees pay for the supplies on your behalf you should arrange for the invoices to be made out in your name by the suppliers.

2.6 What if I am reimbursed by the trustees or charge them for costs I incur in managing the pension scheme?

If the management services are of the kind described in paragraph 2.3 then you should not charge output tax. This is because these costs are treated as your own business costs. Where, however, similar arrangements are adopted for services that consist of investment advice, or other services connected with the pension funds own business activities, you must account for output tax.

2.7 What if a third party manages the scheme?

A fund manager, property manager or professional trustee may be appointed to manage the scheme. Usually their charges will cover both management as well as investment services proper to the trust. You only receive the management services for the purposes of your business. Therefore, you can only treat the tax connected with the management of the scheme as your input tax.

If the supplier issues a single tax inclusive invoice for both kinds of services you will have to split the costs between management and investment services. You may, by way of a simplification agreed with the sector, treat 30% of the costs as for management services when a third party:

- provides both the pension fund's management and investment services; and
- issues one single tax invoice.

If you do not consider that 30% is a fair proportion of the costs attributed to management services you will have to provide evidence to HMRC in support of this view.

The supplier may themselves apportion their supply between investment and management services and issue separate invoices. When this happens you should treat the whole of the tax incurred on management services as input tax.

If you claim input tax:

- on a separate invoice for management services; and
- on a single invoice for both management and investment services.

3.44 *Tax reliefs on contributions and assets*

it may be that to apply 30% of the costs to management services will not give a fair and reasonable result. When the result of the apportionment is not fair you must use an alternative method. The alternative method should reflect the proportion of the supply attributable to management services. You should provide evidence to HMRC to support the alternative method.

Further information on attributing services between 'management' and 'investment' is given in section 5.

2.8 What is the position when pensions are provided for the employees of more than one employer?

This paragraph does not apply where employers are members of the same VAT group registration – see section 4.

Some pension funds provide pensions for the employees of several employers who may have a commercial link or be entirely separate from each other. In such cases each employer can only treat as input tax that proportion of the management services proper to their own employees.

Where a person supplying management services to the fund issues a single invoice one of the employers, or in the case of entirely separate employers, the trustee, may act as paymaster and treat all the VAT on management services as input tax provided they recharge each of the other employers with their share of the costs plus VAT. A person acting as paymaster must issue a VAT invoice to each of the respective employers who, in turn, can treat the tax as their input tax.

2.9 What is the position if I cease to be in business?

If you cease trading, and therefore cease to be an employer, you no longer have any entitlement to input tax on management of the pension scheme. Where, however, the trustees are themselves VAT registered on account of business activities carried out by the pension scheme they may treat the tax incurred on services connected with the continuing management of the scheme as their input tax, subject to the normal rules. This means that where the trustees are required to restrict recovery of input tax because they make exempt supplies not all the tax on the management services may be recovered – see paragraph 1.5.

Where a professional trustee is appointed to run a pension scheme e.g. where the sponsoring employer ceases to exist. VAT incurred on the management of the pension fund can only be recovered by the trustee insofar as it is a clear cost component of an onward supply of that management of the pension fund.

3. Guidance for trustees about claiming input tax

3.1 Do I need to be VAT registered?

A pension fund has no legal status in itself being represented by its trustees. If you are the trustee(s) of a fund and it makes taxable supplies, for example following an election to waive exemption in relation to supplies of property, you must consider whether you need to be VAT registered (see notice 700/1 Should I be registered for VAT?)

3.2 On what kinds of services can I claim input tax?

If you are VAT registered you can treat as input tax VAT incurred on goods and services used, or to be used, for the purposes of your business. VAT on supplies connected with the management of a pension scheme is normally not your input tax (but see paragraph 2.9 where an employer has ceased business) as these supplies are primarily regarded as being the responsibility of the employer. Where you make exempt supplies your recovery of input tax may be restricted – see paragraph 1.5.

3.3 What if a third party manages the scheme?

If a third party:

- provides both management and investment services; and
- issues only one inclusive invoice

as explained in paragraph 2.7 we will, by way of a simplification agreed with the sector, accept that 70% of these services are investment services supplied for the purposes of the trustee's activities. Any claim that this is not an accurate apportionment will need to be supported by suitable evidence.

4. Group registrations and pension schemes

4.1 Can the sole trustee of a fund be included in a VAT group registration?

Yes, provided it is a corporate body, it may be possible for that trustee to form part of a group registration with the employer (see notice 700/2 Group treatment).

4.2 What is the result of a corporate trustee being included in a group registration?

This has implications for both your outputs and inputs.

4.2.1 Outputs

When a corporate trustee is included in a VAT group registration any business supplies made by the trustee, including dealing in the assets of the fund, are treated as being made by the representative member.

4.2.2 Inputs

Tax incurred on supplies to the trustee can be treated as received by the representative member.

If the fund provides pensions for employees of companies outside the VAT group any VAT incurred on management of the scheme for those companies is not seen as being for the purposes of the representative member's business. Tax incurred should be apportioned so that only so much as relates to group members is treated as received by the representative member. Alternatively the representative member may elect to use the paymaster arrangement – see paragraph 2.8.

VAT incurred by group members is recoverable by the representative member to the extent that it is attributable to supplies made to persons outside the

3.44 *Tax reliefs on contributions and assets*

group which carry the right to deduct input tax. Any non-business and exempt supplies made by the employer or trustee must be taken into account when considering VAT recovery.

4.3 Has a corporate trustee liability for meeting VAT debts of the representative member?

Normally all group members are jointly and severally liable for tax due from the representative member. In the case of a corporate trustee, however, we are advised that this liability does not extend to the assets of any trust, for example a pension fund of which the corporate trustee is the trustee, except to the extent the group VAT debt is attributable in whole or in part to the administration of the trust.

5. Attribution of services incurred in connection with funded pension schemes

This list sets out our view of how services incurred in connection with funded pension schemes are to be attributed for VAT purposes.

Services	Attribution	
	Management	**Investment**
Regular meetings with clients	Yes	Yes
Regular meetings with consulting actuaries	Yes	
Cash management	Yes	Yes
Investment management – asset allocation and stock selection		Yes
Investment research, including relevant travel – UK and overseas		Yes
Economic research, including relevant travel – UK and overseas		Yes
Dealing in securities in UK and overseas markets on behalf of clients		Yes
Keeping detailed accounts of all investments, receipts, disbursements other transactions		Yes
Review and control of investment portfolios		Yes
Preparation of contract notes		Yes
Preparation of performance statistics	Yes	Yes
Preparation of schedules of transactions		Yes
Preparation of specialist market commentaries		Yes
Preparation of valuations	Yes	Yes

Tax reliefs on contributions and assets 3.44

Services	Attribution	
	Management	Investment
Submission of data to independent performances monitoring service	Yes	
Safekeeping of property and securities in own name or name of nominee or in bearer form		Yes
Appointment of and responsibility for sub-custodians domestic or foreign		Yes
Provision of nominee service		Yes
Maintenance of securities accounts, stock registration and transfer		Yes
Collection of dividends and interest and obtaining new coupon sheets		Yes
Recovery of tax		Yes
Administration in respect of • capital repayments; and • capitalization issues		Yes
Administration in respect of company meetings and, in particular, executive of forms of proxy as appropriate • conversions; • exchanges; • liquidation • distributions; • redemptions; • right issues; and • payment of calls		Yes
Programming and provision of relevant computer support for • investment management; and • investment administration and control		Yes
Programming and provision of relevant computer support for • valuations and performance statistics.	Yes	

Your rights and obligations

Your Charter explains what you can expect from us and what we expect from you. For more information go to Your Charter.

3.45 *Tax reliefs on contributions and assets*

Do you have any comments or suggestions?

If you have any comments or suggestions to make about this notice, please write to:

HM Revenue & Customs
VAT Deductions & Financial Services
Room 3C/12
100 Parliament Street
London
SW1A 2BQ

Please note this address is not for general enquiries.

For your general enquiries please phone our Helpline 0300 200 3700.

Putting things right

If you are unhappy with our service, please contact the person or office you have been dealing with. They will try to put things right. If you are still unhappy, they will tell you how to complain.

If you want to know more about making a complaint go to hmrc.gov.uk and under quick links, select Complaints and appeals.'

REFUNDS TO THE EMPLOYER

3.45 Any refunds made to an employer remain chargeable at 35% (*FA 2001, s 74*).

CHECKLIST

- Despite the major policy changes by recent governments which have attacked tax-efficient pension provision for savers, the accumulated fund of a registered pension scheme in respect of income and gains remains almost entirely tax-free

- HMRC's RPSM at RPSM02103010 provides an 'at a glance' list of the main tax reliefs and exemptions

- There are no formal limits on the amount of member contributions that may be paid by a member or other person in respect of a member, only on the amount on which the member may enjoy tax relief

- In order to qualify for tax relief on relievable pension contributions, the individual must be an active member of a registered pension scheme, and a relevant UK individual in the tax year in which the contribution is paid

- While contributions must be expressed as cash, it is possible for members to agree to pay a monetary contribution and transfer an asset in settlement of that debt (i.e. in specie)

- Restrictions apply to life assurance premiums and pension term assurance

Tax reliefs on contributions and assets **3.45**

- Relief at source is described
- Net pay arrangements are described
- The taxation of certain members of public service pension schemes, such as general practitioners and dentists, is described
- Compensation payments, and their implications for the AA are discussed
- The reductions to the AA are explained
- Pension input periods are explained
- Pension input amounts are explained
- The carry forward of unused AA is described
- There are no statutory limits on the amount of employer contributions that can be paid, only on the amount of the tax reliefs that are available
- The main spreading rules for employer contributions are described
- Statutory payments by employers, to cover deficiencies in the assets, are tax-relievable
- Levy payments under *PA 2004, Pt 2*, are not strictly contributions, but *Regulations* deem them to be so
- The reductions to the LTA are explained
- The scheme administrator has three responsibilities when a BCE occurs
- The AA charge is a freestanding charge
- The LTA charge becomes payable on the chargeable amount. The rate of the charge on the excess over the LTA is 25% if a pension is taken. If a lump sum is taken, the rate is 55%
- Salary sacrifices are becoming popular again
- The Pensions Regulator has published two updated COPS on reporting late contributions
- Guidance is given on VAT, which can be an important consideration for some funded schemes
- Refunds to Employers are taxed at 35%

Chapter 4

> **SIGNPOSTS**
>
> - There is no overall limit on the amount of pension which can be paid.
> - Pensions will normally be taxed as earnings under *ITEPA 2003*
> - Significant changes and relaxations have been made to the drawdown rules
> - Pension commencement lump sum must only be paid in connection with a pension coming into payment.
> - Protected lump sums are described
> - Major changes have been made to the trivial pensions and small pension pots rules
> - BCE's are referred to, and are listed in **Appendix 1**

Benefit rules

INTRODUCTION

4.1 The concept of imposing limits on the benefits payable by tax-advantaged pension schemes had largely disappeared from A-Day, with the introduction of a new pension tax regime under *FA 2004*. The exception to this was where transitional provisions contained in the *Pension Schemes (Modification of Rules of Existing Schemes) Regulations 2006 (SI 2006/364)* applied to a scheme and had not been disapplied by the trustees or managers of the scheme. These regulations operated so as to continue some of the pre A-Day limits, most notably the earnings cap, and were primarily designed to protect against a potential leap in scheme liabilities as a result of the removal of the old limits. The regulations expired on 6 April 2011 (see **2.14** above).

FA 2004 divided payments from registered pension schemes into authorised payments and unauthorised payments (see **Chapter 15** below). If a payment is unauthorised, it does not mean it cannot be paid; it means that the payment is subject to a range of unauthorised payment charges which can, in some cases, be quite severe. Authorised payments have a far more favourable tax treatment, so it is important that member and survivor benefits paid from registered pension schemes should comply with the rules for authorised member payments contained in *FA 2004, ss 164–171*. The tax treatment of authorised member payments varies. Depending on the payment, they can be tax-free, subject to income tax, or subject to the LTA charge (see **3.41** above).

Unfortunately, although the removal of most pre A-Day benefit limits and the earnings cap simplified administrative costs, the recent savage attacks on tax-relievable contributions and fund levels (see **Chapter 3** above) has imposed a far stricter and less attractive regime for ordinary pension savers as well as the higher earners. Furthermore, new complex rules have been introduced and the 'one-tax' regime for all no longer exists as a real concept.

The payment of a benefit from a registered pension scheme may be subject to the LTA of the person receiving the benefit, or to the LTA of the person in respect of whom it is paid (in the case of a death benefit). The payment of such a benefit, or the first payment of such a benefit if it is a pension, is known a BCE (see **Appendix 1** to this book).

This **Chapter** looks at the rules for authorised member payments, the types of benefits which can be paid, the drawdown facility, at present primarily available only to DC schemes (but this restriction is a matter of ongoing consultation), the minimum age for payment, death benefits, pension sharing and the general application of BCEs.

Focus
- Pensions must be paid in forms which are acceptable under *FA 2004*
- No limit applies to the level of pension which may be paid

PENSION RULES

4.2 There is no overall limit on the amount of pension which can be paid. The pre A-Day requirement that a member must have left employment for a benefit to be paid was removed (with the exception of ill-health retirements and protected low pension ages in **4.30** below).

Pension can only be paid in one of the following forms:

- Scheme pension (this is normally paid under a DB arrangement, but can be paid by a DC scheme under a guarantee – see **4.3** below).
- Lifetime annuity.
- Drawdown pension (see below).

Pensions will normally be taxed as earnings under *ITEPA 2003*.

Scheme pension

4.3 Scheme pension must be paid under a DB arrangement and may be paid under a DC arrangement. It must meet the following conditions:

- It must be payable by the scheme administrator or by an insurance company selected by the scheme administrator.
- It must be payable in at least annual instalments until the member's death or until the later of the member's death and a guaranteed period of up to ten years.

4.4 *Benefit rules*

- The level of scheme pension must not decrease from one year to the next, except in permitted circumstances.
- If it is paid under a DC arrangement, the member must first have had the choice to select a lifetime annuity.

The permitted circumstances in which a scheme pension may decrease are:

- Reduction of an ill-health pension upon full or partial recovery.
- A reduction applying to all pensions in payment.
- Reduction to take account of integration with the state pension (bridging pension).
- Pension sharing order or provision.
- Forfeiture of pension under provisions allowed by *PA 1995*.
- Court order.
- Abatement under a public service pension scheme.
- Certain other circumstances relating to the PPF, contracted-out rights affected by GRA 2004, and admission to the Royal Hospital at Chelsea.

Effect of reduction of pension

4.4 If the level of a pension decreases other than in permitted circumstances, future instalments will be subject to unauthorised payment charges.

Furthermore, if the level of a pension in payment is reduced to below 80% of its original level, any tax-free lump sum paid in connection with the pension will become an unauthorised payment. Care must therefore be taken in any matter which involves the reduction or cessation of a pension in payment.

Lifetime annuity

4.5 A lifetime annuity may be paid under a DC arrangement. It may be purchased either from uncrystallised funds or drawdown funds and must meet the following conditions:

- It must be payable by an insurance company.
- The member must have had an opportunity to select the insurance company (open market option).
- It must be payable until the member's death or until the later of the member's death and a guaranteed period of up to ten years.
- It must not decrease in payment, except where the variation relies on investment performance, tracks an investment index or tracks inflation. A lifetime annuity may also be reduced in consequence of a pension sharing order.

- No payment, either directly or indirectly, of a capital sum may be given on the member's death, with the exception of an annuity protection lump sum death benefit.

Where a guaranteed annuity is provided, it may be assigned during the guarantee period either by the terms of the member's will, or by the personal representatives, to allow:

- a testamentary disposition or the rights of those entitled on an intestacy; or
- an appropriation of the annuity to a legacy or a share or interest in an estate.

There is no firm definition of the meaning of the term 'annuity' in the legislation. Ultimately, the decision must be one of legal opinion if there is any uncertainty in the minds of the trustees or administrator as to the appropriate risk of a product.

HMRC's Newsletter No 62 dated May 2014 as at *http://www.hmrc.gov.uk/ pensionschemes/newsletter62.pdf* contains a significant pointer to HMRC's views on, and treatment of, the payment of arrears of annuities. It says:

> 'HMRC has been made aware that some lifetime annuity contracts have been set up under which the annuity provider agrees to backdate the periodic payments to the member to the date from which that member would have had the right to be paid a pension under the scheme rules; the annual rate of the lifetime annuity reflects that it is effectively being paid for longer. Until we became aware of this, it had been our understanding that the annuity provider would only consider itself to be contractually bound to pay the annuity for the future period starting from the date the contract was made.
>
> So, on the basis that it is possible to backdate the regular annuity payments, the question then arises as to whether a payment of arrears is authorised for the purposes of the pension tax rules. To qualify for tax treatment as a lifetime annuity, an annuity must satisfy the conditions in paragraph 3 of Schedule 28 Finance Act [*sic* 2004].
>
> ....
>
> One of these conditions is that 'the amount of the annuity must not decrease' (paragraph 3(1)(d)).
>
> We consider that contractual annuity income in respect of a period before the annuity was set up could be paid without breaching this requirement. In our view, the 'amount of the annuity' is the amount regularly paid as annuity income. Depending on the circumstances, annuity income can be paid at different intervals, for example, monthly or annually. Where an amount of arrears in respect of a period before the contract was set up is paid at the time the annuity starts, we would not consider that the 'amount of the annuity' had decreased, if the amount paid in respect of the earlier period was paid at the same rate pro rata as the payments made going forward.

4.6 *Benefit rules*

For the avoidance of doubt, our guidance set out in the Registered Pension Schemes Manual (RPSM) on page RPSM11102050 (meaning of 'entitlement' for the purposes of the tax rules) is not affected by this clarification. The 'entitlement' to the lifetime annuity still arises when all the necessary steps have been taken. The entitlement to the pension commencement lump sum therefore still arises immediately before that time, and it can be paid up to six months before that date (or 12 months afterwards).

Arrears of lifetime annuity can be considered to be authorised pension payments under section 165 Finance Act 2004 where the amount of the periodic payment is not decreased, as set out above. We are considering whether any changes need to be made to our guidance in RPSM in order to clarify our interpretation. If any changes are needed, we will include these in the next RPSM update (likely to be in autumn 2014).'

Compulsory insurance

4.6 It was originally stated in *FA 2004, Sch 28, para 2(1)*, that pensions had to be secured with an insurance company for any schemes which had fewer than 50 members. After consultation, it was decided to drop this requirement, and it was removed by *FA 2005, Sch 10*.

Focus

- The drawdown facilities have been greatly modified, and further changes are pending

---

EASING OF FUND ACCESS RULES, DRAWDOWN

Background

4.7 Drawdown is available to DC schemes. There has been a great deal of tinkering about with the drawdown rules in recent years, with limits going up and down like a yo-yo, and sometimes disappearing altogether. Indeed, another very significant change is about to be introduced.

It is helpful to understand when the first major changes to the post A-Day rules were envisaged, and subsequently brought into effect, in order to follow the latest developments accurately. The first indications of a major change were described in the previous edition of this book and contained in statute under *F(No 2)A 2010, s 6, Sch 3*. That *Act* introduced some preliminary changes pending the abolition of ASP. The changes are summarised briefly in **4.10** and **4.11** below.

The rules concerning pension and pension death benefit rules for unsecured pensions, secured pensions, lump sums, ASPs and pension and lump sum death benefit rules were changed so that any reference (in the then current legislation) to an age of 75 was a reference to the age of 77. They applied to an annuity that was purchased on or after 22 June 2010.

Unsecured pension rules – pre 6 April 2011

4.8 Unsecured pension was determined by returns on widely invested funds which deliver growth rather than security up to age 75, or age 77 as appropriate, as described in **4.7** above. Under *FA 2004, Sch 28, para 1*, a maximum annual income withdrawal of 120% was permitted of the basis amount of the flat-rate single life annuity that could be bought out of the member's credit with five-yearly reviews. The basis amount was the annuity which could have been bought, applying theoretical annuity rates from the GAD.

ASP Rules – pre 6 April 2011

4.9 Under ASP rules, the minimum and maximum ASP levels were a percentage of the notional annuity that could be provided based on the GAD's tables. The notional annuity was a single life, level annuity applicable for someone aged 75 or 77 as appropriate, as described in **4.7** above. The minimum ASP level was 55% of the notional annuity, the maximum was 90%. If the member drew less than the minimum amount, the scheme administrator was liable for a 40% tax charge on the difference between the minimum and the amount actually drawn. Moneys held in ASP by a member aged 75 or 77 as appropriate, as described in **4.7** above, or over were subject to IHT at 40% when the investor died in respect of assets over the nil rate band.

There are provisional protections for existing unsecured pensions and ASP within the current lifespan of such arrangements.

Capped drawdown from 6 April 2011

4.10 *FA 2011* made considerable easements with effect from 6 April 2011. The *FA 2004, s 165*, compulsory annuity purchase requirement at age 75 or 77 as appropriate, as described in **4.7** above (unless an ASP was provided), was repealed together with ASP. New drawdown facilities replaced unsecured pension and existing drawdown rules, subject to transitional provisions for continuing arrangements.

The new forms of drawdown were brought in with effect from 6 April 2011 by *FA 2011, Sch 16*.

Members of DC schemes (who have not yet taken a pension) could defer their decision to take benefits indefinitely from that date. The compulsory annuity purchase provisions were repealed from the same date.).

The main form of drawdown is commonly referred to as 'capped drawdown'. There is also a 'flexible drawdown' (uncapped) facility for high earners, and this is described in **11.23–26** below.

Certain conditions apply to 2011 capped drawdown:

4.10 *Benefit rules*

- The maximum amount must be determined at least every three years, until the end of the year in which the member reaches the age of 75.
- Thereafter, annual reviews must be carried out.
- Any withdrawals which are made whilst a member is resident overseas (for a period of less than five full tax years) will be taxed for the tax year in which the member becomes UK resident again.
- Any tax-free cash sum must be taken when income drawdown commences.
- the age 75 limit for taking cash was removed.
- an individual may take no income at all in a year.
- the drawdown rules only apply where an individual has ceased to be an active member of any registered pension schemes, and any future pension savings by that individual anywhere will attract the excess AA charge.

Someone taking drawdown will have had their crystallised benefits tested against the LTA whenever they first started drawdown. Unfortunately, this is not the end of the matter as far as the LTA is concerned, as the tax rules are designed to ensure that members draw income from their tax-advantaged pension savings.

A drawdown fund will be tested again against the LTA when the member reaches the age of 75, or upon purchase of an annuity with the drawdown fund if earlier. Upon a member reaching age 75 while still in receipt of income drawdown, the amount tested against the LTA is the remaining fund less the original amount crystallised by going into drawdown. If the member has not drawn enough income in the meantime, this could result in some funds being exposed to a LTA charge. It may therefore be advisable to draw income rather than face additional tax.

The same applies for a lifetime annuity purchased out of drawdown funds. The amount crystallised is the annuity purchase price, but this is reduced by the amount (or an appropriate proportion of the amount) previously crystallised on going into drawdown.

An alternative may be to transfer the drawdown fund to a drawdown arrangement under a QROPS (see **Chapter 13** below). There will be a LTA test on the funds at the point of transfer, but no other LTA test will be applied in the receiving overseas scheme, ie there will be no second LTA test at age 75. The tax benefit of transferring to a QROPS to ensure this second test, and potential charge, do not arise should be weighed against the costs of selecting a suitable overseas jurisdiction, establishing membership of a scheme, transferring the funds and the ongoing charges in the overseas scheme. Any currency conversion issues would also need to be addressed.

If any uncrystallised DC funds remain by age 75, they will be subject to a LTA test at 75. There are no further LTA tests after age 75 (with the exception of a BCE3, large increase in scheme pension; see **Appendix 1**).

Any amount over the LTA threshold will be subject to a tax charge. Where excess monies are paid out in lump sum form, a charge of 55% arises on the amount paid out ('the chargeable amount'). The administrator shall withhold the charge, and remit it to HMRC. Any remaining part of the chargeable amount is referred to as the 'retained amount'. This is the amount that will be retained by the scheme (or an overseas pension scheme) or an insurance company to fund pension benefits etc. The retained amount is subject to a lower charge than the lump-sum amount to reflect the fact that those funds will be taxed at a later point when paid from the scheme, ie when paid as a pension. The LTA charge on the retained amount is therefore 25%.

Accordingly practitioners may wish to compare the value of a tax-relievable contribution combined with investment yield in a registered scheme (and an ultimate 55% charge on any excess over the allowance) with a cash payment by the employer.

The table below summarises the drawdown changes at 6 April 2011.

Feature	Before 6 April 2011		After 6 April 2011
Name	Unsecured pension (USP)	Alternatively secured pension (ASP)	Drawdown pension
Age range	55 to 75	75+	55+
Minimum pension	0%	55%	0%
Maximum pension	120% of GAD	90% of GAD	100% of GAD
Death benefit charge	35%	82% (70%+IHT)	55%

Access

4.11 This is what a scheme member could access from the scheme fund under 2011 capped drawdown:

(a) Up to 100% of the equivalent annuity which could be purchased out of the fund whilst such member retains the fund.

(b) No minimum annual withdrawal amount.

The following is an example of phased drawdown:

Example

Bill was 58 in 2007/08. He had pension rights in his DC pension scheme of £640,000. He decided to take a tax-free cash lump sum of £65,000 and continue working. He had to draw an unsecured pension from £195,000 of his

4.12 *Benefit rules*

fund (£260,000 less 25%, £65,000 = £195,000), leaving £380,000 (£640,000 less £260,000) in his fund not subject to payment of the unsecured pension. by 2011/12 his fund had grown to £450,000 and he decided to take a further tax-free cash lump sum of £48,000 and continue working part-time. He had to take a drawdown pension from £144,000 of his fund (£192,000 less 25%, £48,000 = £144,000) leaving £258,000 (£450,000 less £192,000) in his fund not subject to his two drawdown pensions, the original unsecured pension having become a drawdown pension on 6 April 2011. In 2015/16 Bill finally retires and decides to take the remainder of his benefits from his fund now worth £280,000. He decides to take a further tax-free cash lump sum of £70,000 (£280,000 @ 25%) and with the balance of £210,000 plus the funds supporting his drawdown pensions, purchase a lifetime annuity.

NB – It is most important that at each stage where a cash lump sum is taken that Bill ensures he avoids any problems with the provisions of recycling lump sums (see **10.7** below).

Inheritance tax

4.12 IHT is not chargeable on drawdown funds which remain in the scheme, whatever age the beneficiary is when they die. Additionally, IHT is not chargeable on drawdown funds under QROPS or QNUPS (although the Government is considering bringing in new rules for the latter). However, IHT charges will apply in circumstances where the scheme trustees have no discretion over the payment of lump sum death benefits and to lump sums from non-registered pension schemes or RNUKS.

Capped drawdown from 27 March 2013

4.13 The following changes to capped drawdown applied under *FA 2013, s 50*, from 27 March 2013:

- The maximum drawdown level was increased to 120%.

- The 120% maximum income level also applies to dependants' drawdown pension.

The EU Gender Directive, from 21 December 2012, means that the scheme administrator should use the GAD table for men to obtain the relevant annuity rate for women if the individual:

- is aged over 23 with a reference period starting on or after 21 December 2012 (including when the nominated period is before that date);

- is aged 75 or over with a drawdown pension year starting on or after that date (including when the nominated period is before that date); and

- is aged over 23 and her basis amount needs recalculating following one of the events described at RPSM09103570 occurring on or after 21 December 2012.

Capped drawdown from 27 March 2014, and further proposals for change

4.14 The following changes to capped drawdown applied from 27 March 2014:

- The maximum drawdown level was increased to 150%.

- The 150% maximum income level also applies to dependants' drawdown pension.

The above change was announced in the Chancellor's Autumn Statement on 5 December 2013. A consultation document was published entitled *'Freedom and Choice in Pensions'*.

The change is introduced by *FA 2014*, s 41. HMRC published a Draft Guidance Note on 17 July 2014 entitled *'Pension Flexibility: Transitional issues associated with the pension changes that came into force on 27 March 2014'*.

However, in his Budget speech on 19 March 2014, the Chancellor announced that it is intended that major changes for DC schemes will have effect from 2015/16. They are:

- complete freedom for individuals to draw down as much or as little of their pension pot as they want, anytime they want, from age 55 (to rise to 57 in 2028);

- a removal of all caps and drawdown limits;

- no one will have to buy an annuity;

- there will be a new right to advice on decision-making.

The proposal to allow complete freedom to permit individuals to withdraw their total DC fund has met with a very mixed reception. There was also concern that new, and discriminatory, rules accompanied the announcement. The matter clearly needed to be looked at in depth, and this is subject to an ongoing process. The debate is becoming of considerable length. It is hoped that the following resume will help the reader to focus on the potential advantages and pitfalls that it identifies.

It is well known that the UK level of state retirement provision compared with its European neighbours is very low. The UK has always encouraged individuals, through tax incentives, to secure additional pensions through private means. The Government has abandoned most of this concept for DC savers as evidenced by the Pensions Minister's following assertion after the Budget announcement:

> 'If people do get a Lamborghini, and end up on the state pension, the state is much less concerned about that, and that is their choice'.

The opportunity to completely collapse their retirement savings will be attractive to some, particularly if they are in financial distress. However, this does not bode well for their living standards in retirement. It can be argued,

4.14 *Benefit rules*

and it has been by Government, that the move gives people the right to self-determination, but the announcement was clearly one-sided. It did not apply drawdown to DB members, and HM Treasury stated that it would ban or restrict transfers from DB to DC schemes for public sector workers, and would consider imposing the same restriction on private sector members 'if the risks and issues around doing so can be shown to be manageable'.

Following the initial Budget announcement, the pensions industry's representative bodies actively entered the debate. Among the most significant responses were those summarised below:

- At the NAPF conference on 20 May 2014 the chair of the parliamentary committee charged with scrutinising pensions policy said she was sceptical whether the government had fully considered all its options before selecting its chosen route. However, the NAPF now seems to have largely approved of the change.

- The ABI has stated that members of DB schemes currently have the right to transfer their benefits to a DC, and this right must be retained (whilst recommending that conditions should be placed on the right to transfer, including a requirement for those wishing to transfer to take regulated financial advice).

- The ACA backed the government's plans to give DC savers more flexibility, but urged it not to ban transfers from DB schemes.

Another industry concern was that the UK may find itself in the situation whereby millions of pensioners will be living in comparative poverty if they collapse their pension pots without investing the proceeds.

There has since been some movement by Government on its clearly selective proposal for change. On 21 July 2014 it announced a relaxation in its approach to transfers between DB and DC funds. Most members will have freedom to effect such transfers but not members currently drawing down their DB pensions or still, apparently, those who wish to make transfers from unfunded public sector pensions. Additionally, HM Treasury stated, in its response to consultation, that the relaxation is subject to the members of DB schemes seeking (potentially expensive) regulated financial advice. The cost of the advice will fall on the member, unless the transfer is from a DB to a DC arrangement within the same scheme, or as a result of an employer led incentive exercise, in which case it will fall on the employer. This is despite the fact that the Government has promised that it will:

> 'guarantee that individuals approaching retirement will receive free and impartial face-to-face guidance to help them make the choices that best suit their needs. We will introduce a new duty on pension providers and schemes to deliver this "guidance guarantee" by April 2015. We have asked the Financial Conduct Authority to make sure this guidance meets robust standards, working closely with consumer groups. And we will make available a £20 million development fund to get the initiative up and running'.

Benefit rules **4.14**

The Pensions Minister had subsequently said to the Select Committee on Work and Pensions on 29 April 2014 that it was

> '15 minutes' worth of guidance, to which £20 million was being committed over the next two years. It is only 15 minutes' worth'.

The parliamentary debates on the Finance Bill 2014 during its progress to *FA 2014* revealed concern by some Select Committee members on the degree of accuracy of this statement as there was industry perception, borne of long experience, that the guidance would need to last at least two hours.

HM Treasury also stated on 21 July 2014 that members who take advantage of the new freedom to withdraw tax-free cash from their accumulated pension pot will suffer big cuts to their AA on future pension contributions if they subsequently reinvest that cash into a new pension and receive tax relief again. There will be a £10,000 annual cap on future pension savings for those who access their pensions from April 2014. Individuals who are already in capped drawdown will be able to retain the £40,000 limit. In addition, HMRC's guide 'Pension flexibility 2015' states that individuals

> 'who have accessed their pension savings flexibly from a flexi-access drawdown fund will retain an annual allowance for defined benefits pension savings of up to £40,000, depending on the value of new money purchase pension savings' and 'All existing funds used for pre-6 April 2015 flexible drawdown will automatically become flexi-access drawdown funds'.

HMRC issued its first response to consultation on 21 July 2014. The main points for DC schemes were reiterated, with some proposed relaxations DB schemes:

- There will be unrestricted access to pension pots for DC, and it will be possible to plan withdrawals so that only marginal tax is paid on what is taken out.

- The promised guidance remains 'free', but does not have to be face-to-face (e.g. it may be by means of telephone calls or online). It will be funded by a levy on insurers that will be paid for through higher charges on pension schemes.

- It is intended to extend the facility to all pension savers, including DB and career average schemes.

- The Pensions Advisory Service and Money Advice Service will lead the way in providing the guidance guarantee, supported by Age UK and Citizen's Advice. It be closely monitored by the FCA.

- There will be rules to stop 'pension recycling' and reduction in death taxes, and to prevent those over age 55 from diverting parts of their salary into pension recycling

- Lump sums may be taken over and above the 25% tax-free limit and tax-relievable contributions may still be paid subject to a limit of £10,000 p.a.

4.14 *Benefit rules*

- The 55% charge on death on pensions in a drawdown account will be reduced by an amount to be decided in the Autumn Statement.
- It will be permitted to provide annuities that can decrease and increase in value, as the annuitant chooses. Additionally, lump sums may be taken from annuities.
- The intended ban on transferring out of DB into DC will not be imposed, but transferees must pay for financial advice which could significantly diminish their pension pots.

Members of unfunded public sector schemes will still be banned from transferring.

There is to be consultation on taking withdrawals directly from DB schemes.

HMRC Newsletter 64 dated August 2014 contains links to the draft Taxation of Pension Bill at *https://www.gov.uk/government/publications/draft-legislation-the-taxation-of-pensions-bill* and HMRC's Tax Information and Impact Note (TIIN) at *https://www.gov.uk/government/publications/pension-flexibility-2015.*

The changes in the draft clauses will:

- remove the higher tax charges where people take pensions under DC savings as they wish;
- increase the flexibility of the income drawdown rules by removing the maximum 'cap' on withdrawal and minimum income requirements for all new drawdown funds from 6 April 2015;
- enable those with 'capped' drawdown to convert to a new drawdown fund once arranged with their scheme;
- enable pension schemes to make payments directly from pension savings with 25% taken tax-free (instead of a tax-free lump sum);
- introduce a limited right for scheme trustees and managers to override their scheme's rules to pay flexible pensions from money purchase pension savings;
- remove restrictions on lifetime annuity payments;
- ensure that individuals do not exploit the new system to gain unintended tax advantages by introducing a reduced annual allowance for money purchase savings where the individual has flexibly accessed their savings; and,
- increase the maximum value and scope of trivial commutation lump sum death benefits.

It is clear that Government is expecting a windfall tax receipt by making the impending drawdown change, as any member's DC fund which is withdrawn will be subject to the member's marginal rate of tax. Clearly some tax-planning on the timing of withdrawals by individuals would be prudent. Whether the melt-down windfall will occur is by no means certain, but the move against

DB to DC transfers indicated that HM Treasury was immediately alerted to the potentially large drain on the Treasury fund if public sector workers in (often unfunded or largely unfunded) occupational pension schemes were to transfer-out.

There has already been a marked impact on the insurance market and providers of annuity products, as demand for annuities has fallen noticeably since the Budget announcement. The ongoing developments will be interesting, as new products and bonds are being designed. In addition to the Government's first response to consultation described above, the concept of a 'one-year annuity' as an interim measure had already been mooted, and there is some concern over potential loss to the investor if annuity rates are even smaller than they are now by the time that people retire.

There will need to be far-reaching changes made to existing legislation in order to accommodate the latest change for DC schemes. *FA 2014* removes the revaluation factor for determining how much of the commutation limit is used up by crystallisation of previous pension rights, and the 55% tax charge on lump sums taken in excess of 25% is reduced to the individual's normal marginal tax rates.

Job shifting

4.15 *FA 2004* brought in significant easements to pension provision for individuals who change their jobs. Such persons may be members of any type of registered pension scheme concurrently (including occupational and personal pension schemes). They may also remain in a registered pension scheme even if they are temporarily unemployed or away from work.

Registered pension schemes may be open to all, whatever the employment or residence status of the individual concerned. Individuals may join non-associated multi-employer schemes and industry-wide schemes enjoying the benefit from the economies of scale this can bring. They can also join cross-border schemes and transfer their funds to QROPS (see **Chapter 13** below) of which they are a member. Such persons (and their employers) may also benefit from tax reliefs made to overseas pension schemes in specific circumstances.

The good news for retirement planning is that individuals who are internationally mobile will be able to remain in one scheme wherever they work in the EU if they wish to do so and they are eligible persons. Their employer will be able to contribute to the overseas pension scheme.

All the above scenarios are covered in detail in this book. In the main, they are a rare example of simplification which has survived the significant erosion of that principle, both before and since its introduction. However, the rules which apply to transfers to QROPS and the reporting requirements following the acceptance of a transfer from a registered pension scheme by a QROPS have become increasingly stringent (see **Chapter 13** below).

There are some general pitfalls to be wary of when changing jobs. These mostly concern the potential loss of EP or FP 2012 or FP 2014 (see **Chapter 9**

4.15 *Benefit rules*

below). Apart from some limited circumstances, protections are lost upon the holder becoming a member under a new arrangement in a registered pension scheme. Under automatic enrolment rules (see **2.2** above), employers must put the majority of their workforce into a pension scheme. The scheme must be registered with HMRC if it is a UK scheme. This would occasion the loss of EP or FP 2012 or FP 2014. However, if the member opts out within the statutory period (one month of being enrolled), they are treated as never having become a member, and their EP or FP 2012 or FP 2014 remains in place. The problem does not go away; every three years the employer must re-enrol opt-outs, so those with EP or FP 2012 or FP 2014 may find themselves having to opt out again.

The provision of group life assurance is a common employee benefit, but it is usually set up as a registered pension scheme, even though only a lump sum death benefit is provided. Membership of a life assurance only scheme can be compulsory, so those with EP or FP 2012 or FP 2014 may need to take steps to ensure they are not put into the scheme upon joining a new employer; protection would be lost if they are covered for life assurance under a registered pension scheme. The problem can be avoided by using an excepted group life policy, which is not a registered pension scheme and will therefore not jeopardise protection.

It is possible to be a member of more than one registered pension scheme at the same time and to contribute to those schemes. However, care must be taken with the reduction of the annual allowance from £255,000 to £40,000 (see **3.13** above). The £40,000 allowance covers contributions to all schemes in a tax year; it operates on an aggregate not an individual scheme basis.

Perhaps unsurprisingly, the back-lashes to the intended crash out drawdown changes are still-escalating. The Fabian Society said on 22 September 2014 that the

> '"revolutionary" policy unleashed by Chancellor George Osborne in March would leave retirements "permanently diminished"'.

A left think tank has said that Labour should reverse the pension freedoms announced in the Budget 2014 if it wins the general election in May 2014.

Additionally, an Australian consultancy has warned the UK to take a firm stance against political tampering with pensions. It has expressed deep concern with the political game of 'ping-pong' in the UK over pension provision.

Wherever pensions end up in this melee, it is certain than that scheme members and their advisers should be made fully aware of what is happening and how they should ensure that they reach the best solution for themselves.

Focus
- The entitlement to receive a lump sum is linked to pension entitlement

LUMP SUM RULES

Pension commencement lump sum

4.16 A pension commencement lump sum must only be paid in connection with a pension coming into payment. *FA 2004, Sch 29, para 1(1)(c),* states that, where a member becomes entitled to a cash lump sum benefit, the cash lump sum must be paid within an 18-month period starting six months before, and ending 12 months after, the date when the member becomes entitled to the related pension. A change under *FA 2014, Sch 5,* has widened the six month window to 18 months in order to give DC members who have already taken their pension commencement lump sum flexibility to delay drawing their pension until after April 2015. As from that date, such members will have the option of taking their benefits in cash rather than by means of annuity purchase (see **4.14** above).

The additional rules which apply generally to pension commencement lump sums are as follows:

- for pension benefits not taken until after 75, a pension commencement lump sum may now also be paid to a member aged 75 or over;

- a pension commencement lump sum must be tested against the LTA as a BCE 6. If the entitlement to pension and the pension commencement lump sum arises shortly before the member reaches age 75, it is possible that they may not be paid their pension commencement lump sum until after they have reached that age.

- In the scenario above, where the lump sum is payable under a DC arrangement, the funds which will be used to pay the lump sum will have been treated as remaining unused funds when the member reached age 75 and tested against the LTA as a BCE 5B at that time. Therefore, to prevent double testing, there is no BCE 6. The only BCE that occurs is a BCE 5B. So, contrary to the usual position, the amount of the lump sum will be tested against the member's LTA after rather than before the pension in connection with which it is paid is tested. This will affect the amount of the member's available LTA at the time their pension commencement lump sum is tested.

In a DC arrangement, the lump sum is expressed as one third of the annuity purchase price, where a lifetime annuity is provided, or one third of the sums designated for income withdrawal. This equates to 25% of funds being vested, but expressing it in such a manner ensures the lump sum calculation is tied to the amount of funds actually crystallised at the time.

Under a DB arrangement, calculation of the pension commencement lump sum is more complicated. The lump sum is calculated according to the formula ¼ (LS + AC) where:

- LS is the amount of lump sum actually taken; and

- AC is the amount crystallised by the scheme pension coming into payment (normally 20 times the initial rate of scheme pension in a DB arrangement).

4.17 *Benefit rules*

In a DB arrangement where a lump sum is provided by the commutation of pension, the maximum amount of lump sum depends on the commutation rate used within the scheme. The lump sum formula may more usefully be expressed as:

(20 × full pension × commutation factor) / (20 + 3 × commutation factor)

Therefore a £10,000 pa pension in a DB scheme with a commutation rate of, say, £14 per £1 pa may be partially commuted for a lump sum of up to:

(20 × 10,000 14) / (20 + 3 × 14) = £45,161

The residual pension will be 10,000 − 45,161 / 14 = £6,774.21 pa.

Note that the lump sum will always be $6^{2}/_{3}$ times the residual pension in a DB arrangement, unless transitional protection applies (but see **4.19** below). If a person has taken a lump sum prior to A-Day, this will be taken into consideration for the purpose of calculating the maximum lump sum that may be taken from the same arrangement after A-Day. Additionally, any person who has taken a lump sum prior to A-Day, but deferred his or her pension until after A-Day, will not be permitted to take a further tax-free lump sum in relation to that employment.

Lump sums from AVCs

4.17 Any rights derived from AVCs that were not commutable before A-Day because they were started after 8 April 1987 may be commuted subject to scheme rules permitting.

Where DC AVCs have been paid under a DB scheme, the entire AVC fund may be used first to provide a pension commencement lump sum before it is necessary to commute DB pension, subject again to scheme rules permitting.

Two or more schemes relating to the same employment

4.18 Payment of pension commencement lump sum is linked to the pension being brought into payment, not the member's service with an employer. It is therefore not possible to draw lump sum from a separate scheme of the same employment in the way it was before A-Day. This is, however, still possible if a member has both DB and DC rights *in the same scheme*, for example by having benefits in two sections under the same scheme.

Overall lump sum limit

4.19 Unless transitional protection applies (see **Chapter 9** below), the maximum pension commencement lump sum that may be taken tax-free is limited to 25% of the available LTA. This is calculated according to the following formula:

¼ × (CSLA − AAC × CSLA / PSLA)

where:

- CSLA is the standard LTA at date of vesting
- AAC is the aggregate of the amounts crystallised by previous benefit vestings
- PSLA is the standard LTA at each respective previous BCE
- The following examples from the RPSM illustrate this.

RPSM09104550: Pension commencement lump sum: Maximum amount: Available portion (extract):

'Example 1 – calculating the available portion of the member's lump sum allowance

John has £450,000 of uncrystallised funds in a money purchase arrangement. He does not have an enhanced lifetime allowance. In the 2010/11 tax year he decides to use all the funds held in the arrangement to provide an unsecured pension and the maximum pension commencement lump sum permitted.

Before paying out benefits the scheme administrator writes to John telling him that he will crystallise £450,000 for lifetime allowance purposes, which represents 25% of the standard lifetime allowance for that tax year (25% of £1.8 million). The scheme administrator also asks John to

1. provide a statement confirming his anticipated available lifetime allowance at the time he wishes to draw benefits, expressed as a percentage of the standard lifetime allowance for that current tax year, based on statements he will have been provided by other scheme administrators, where benefits have been crystallised previously under other registered pension schemes, and
2. confirm whether or not he is entitled to an enhanced lifetime allowance.

John has used up 85% of his lifetime allowance previously. John confirms that he will have 15% of the standard lifetime allowance of £1.8 million available when he draws benefits. He also confirms he is not entitled to an enhanced lifetime allowance.

The scheme administrator applies the percentage available (15%) to the standard lifetime allowance for that year (£1.8 million), and divides this by four to obtain the available portion of the lump sum allowance.

So 15% × £1.8 million = £270,000.

This figure divided by four gives £67,500.

The permitted maximum is therefore capped at £67,500.

4.19 *Benefit rules*

The scheme administrator will also have identified a chargeable amount of £180,000 (£450,000 − £270,000). This can be paid as a lifetime allowance excess lump sum (minus the lifetime allowance charge due).'

RPSM09104560: Pension commencement lump sum: Maximum amount: Available portion (extract):

'Example 2 – calculating the available portion of the member's lump sum allowance

Chris has £450,000 of uncrystallised funds in a money purchase arrangement. He is also entitled to an enhanced lifetime allowance of 150% of the standard lifetime allowance. (So he has a lifetime allowance enhancement factor of 0.5). Chris has not protected any lump sum rights in existence on 5 April 2006.

In the 2010/11 tax year Chris decides to use all the funds to provide an unsecured pension and the maximum pension commencement lump sum. In this tax year his lifetime allowance is £2.7 million (£1.8 million + {£1.8 million × 0.5}).

Chris has already used up 90% of the standard lifetime allowance. So at the point he will draw benefits, he will have an available lifetime allowance of 60% of the standard lifetime allowance (150% − 90%). This means Chris can crystallise £1.08 million (60% of £1.8 million) before exceeding his available lifetime allowance.

Before Chris draws benefits the scheme administrator writes to him asking him for details of previous crystallisations under other schemes and whether or not he is entitled to an enhanced lifetime allowance.

Chris provides the scheme administrator with the number on the HMRC certificate confirming his entitlement to an enhanced lifetime allowance as evidence of his entitlement. He also tells the administrator that he has already used 90% of the standard lifetime allowance.

The scheme administrator uses this information to work out whether or not Chris has enough available lifetime allowance to cover the amount crystallising under their scheme at that time. The scheme administrator can also use this information to identify what Chris's available portion of the lump sum allowance actually is.

The scheme administrator now knows that Chris has used up 90% of the current £1.8 million standard lifetime allowance at the point benefits are crystallising for lifetime allowance purposes. This means that previous crystallisations, adjusted by reference to the changes in standard lifetime allowance level, or "AAC", represent £1.62 million (90% of £1.8 million).

So the scheme administrator knows that the available portion of the lump sum allowance is a quarter of £180,000 (£1.8 million − £1.62 million). This is £45,000.

Benefit rules **4.20**

The permitted maximum for Chris is therefore £45,000 (not the applicable amount of £112,500).

But no chargeable amount arises, as the amount crystallising is covered by his available lifetime allowance.'

When entitlement to a pension commencement lump sum arises on or after 6 April 2011, the normal rules apply, but with a number of amendments (see **Appendix 1** for detail of BCEs).

Amendments effective from 6 April 2011

4.20   RPSM09104195 provides:

'1. In relation to pension benefits not taken until after he has reached age 75, a pension commencement lump sum can be paid to a member aged 75 or over so any reference to entitlement to the lump sum having to arise before age 75, eg at page RPSM09104140, can be ignored.

2. When a member's entitlement to a pension commencement lump sum arises (this is immediately before the entitlement to the pension in connection with which the lump sum is being paid arises) the amount of the pension commencement lump sum is tested against the member's lifetime allowance as a BCE 6. However, where the member's entitlement to the pension and the pension commencement lump sum arises shortly before the member reaches age 75, it is possible that he may not be paid his pension commencement lump sum until after he has reached that age. If the pension commencement lump sum is being taken in respect of a money purchase arrangement then the funds which will be used to pay the lump sum will have been treated as remaining unused funds when the member reached age 75 and tested against the lifetime allowance as a BCE 5B at that time. To prevent double testing against the lifetime allowance, in these particular circumstances, the legislation provides that there is no BCE 6 see RPSM11104730 for more detail, so the only BCE that occurs is a BCE 5B. This means that contrary to the usual position, the amount of the pension commencement lump sum will be tested against the member's lifetime allowance after rather than before the pension in connection with which it is paid is tested. This will affect the amount of the member's available lifetime allowance at the time their pension commencement lump sum is tested.

3. When calculating the applicable amount (see pages RPSM09104300 onwards), the amount crystallised in relation to the connected pension (AC in the statutory formula) is, where the member became entitled to the pension before reaching age 75, the amount crystallised by reason of the member becoming entitled to the pension or, where the member becomes entitled

4.20 *Benefit rules*

to the pension after reaching age 75, the amount that would have crystallised had there been a BCE in relation to the pension.

4. One of the conditions for paying a pension commencement lump sum is that the member has available lifetime allowance. The maximum pension commencement lump sum that can be paid is usually dependent on the amount of the member's available standard lifetime allowance. See for example the guidance at RPSM09103500. However, where the lump sum is being paid after age 75 from uncrystallised funds or rights, those funds or rights will have already been tested against the member's lifetime allowance under BCE 5B or BCE 5 respectively when the member reached age 75. This BCE will have used up some or all of the member's available lifetime allowance at that time.

So, solely for the purposes of deciding whether the member satisfies the condition that they have available lifetime allowance, when they take a pension commencement lump sum after age 75:

- the fact that a BCE 5 or 5B has occurred is disregarded. This means that any LTA used up by that BCE does not count in calculating whether the member has available lifetime allowance, and

- if the member has already taken benefits from the same or another arrangement under a registered pension scheme after reaching age 75 or some other event has occurred that would have been a BCE but for the fact that the event occurred on or after the member reaching age 75, then, again solely for the purposes of calculating whether the member has available lifetime allowance, those events are treated as though they were BCEs and so are treated as having used up lifetime allowance.

Example

George has taken benefits worth 60 per cent of the standard lifetime allowance before reaching age 75. George has no form of protection. George still has £900,000 pension saving that he has not yet taken (uncrystallised funds) when he reaches age 75 on 15 July 2011. These pension savings are held under a money purchase arrangement and so, although no benefits are taken at the time, are tested against the lifetime allowance as a BCE 5B when George reaches age 75. The standard lifetime allowance is £1.8 million, so these benefits use up 50 per cent of the standard lifetime allowance.

When this is added to the 60% lifetime allowance George has already [used] this up this means he has used up 110% of the standard lifetime allowance. He has exceeded his lifetime allowance by 10% so £180,000 (10% of £1.8 million) is liable to a lifetime allowance charge. As George has not yet taken (crystallised) these pension savings the rate of the lifetime allowance charge is 25 per cent. The

Benefit rules **4.20**

scheme administrator deducts the £45,000 tax due from George's fund and pays the tax to HM Revenue & Customs. So George's fund is now £855,000. George makes no further contributions to his fund.

On 28 February 2012, George takes some more benefits amounting to £630,000 into payment. George wants to take part of this amount as a pension commencement lump sum and the rest as pension. In deciding if he can have a PCLS, and how much lifetime allowance is available

- the BCE 5B is ignored, and
- as George has not crystallised any other benefits since his 75th birthday there is nothing to add back at this stage.

This means that for the purposes of the pension commencement lump sum George has 40 per cent available lifetime allowance. The standard lifetime allowance for 2011–12 is £1.8 million so George has £720,000 available lifetime allowance. He can take a pension commencement lump sum of £157,500. This is 25 per cent of George's crystallising funds (£630,000) and less than 25 per cent of his available lifetime allowance of £180,000 (25% of £720,000).

This tranche of benefits would have used up 35 per cent (£630,000/£1.8m × 100) of the standard lifetime allowance if it had occurred before George was 75.

On 31 March 2012 George takes benefits in respect of the rest of his uncrystallised funds. As a result of investment growth, these funds are now worth £250,000. George wants to take part of this amount as a pension commencement lump sum. In deciding if he can have a pension commencement lump sum and how much available lifetime allowance George has:

- the BCE 5B is ignored, and
- as George has taken benefits since his 75th birthday which would have used up 35 per cent of his lifetime allowance had he taken them before age 75, these must be taken into account.

This means that for the purposes of the pension commencement lump sum, George now has 5 per cent available lifetime allowance (40% available at age 75 less 35% worth of benefits taken since age 75)). He can therefore take a pension commencement lump sum of £22,500 as this is 25 per cent of his £90,000 available lifetime allowance (5% of £1.8m). The remainder of the funds is used to provide pension income.

As George was over age 75 at the time there are no BCEs and so no possibility of a lifetime allowance charge in relation to the benefits he takes on 28 February 2012 and 31 March 2012.

These adjustments to the PCLS rules mean that effectively the amount of PCLS George can take in relation to pension rights is the same regardless of his age.'

4.21 *Benefit rules*

A further protection was provided, for lump sum rights exceeding £375,000 with primary protection. Individuals can choose, subject to scheme rules, how much lump sum they wish to take from each scheme. So an individual may take all the benefits from a particular scheme as a stand-alone lump sum. This can happen where:

- the member is aged less than 75 (this condition does not apply after 5 April 2011);
- the member has reached the normal minimum pension age (or any earlier protected pension age they may have under the scheme) or is taking benefits earlier due to ill-health; and
- all the member's uncrystallised rights under the scheme come into payment as a single BCE.

Payment of a stand-alone lump sum is a BCE 6, and so it is liable to the LA charge if there is insufficient LA to cover the payment. The amount of the stand-alone lump sum is limited by the formula:

VULSR – APCLS

Where:

- VULSR is the value of the member's uncrystallised lump sum rights as at 5 April 2006 increased in line with the increase of the standard LA or, from 6 April 2012, by 20% until such time as the prevailing standard LA taken is more than £1.8 million when the previous method of determining the increase re-applies; and
- APCLS is the value of any PCLS and/or stand-alone lump sum that has previously been paid to the member (increased in line with the increase of the standard LA). From 6 April 2012, the lump sum paid previously is increased by multiplying the amount of that lump sum by £1.8 million (or the standard LA at the time the further lump sum is paid if this is greater), then dividing by the standard LA at the time of payment. For example, if the further lump sum had been paid in tax year 2012/13 when the standard LA was £1.5 million, and the previous lump sum (£300,000) was paid in tax year 2007–08 when the standard LA was £1.6 million, the previous lump sum was increased as follows – £300,000 × £1.8 million/£1.6 million giving an increased amount of £337,500.

Focus
- Lump sums which are protected from A-Day are a valuable asset and care should be taken not to inadvertently lose that protection

Protected lump sums

4.21 The available protections for lump sums as at A-Day are described in **Chapter 9** below. In summary, many members of DB schemes enjoy a higher level of tax-free lump sum as their rules provided the necessary flexibility.

Benefit rules **4.23**

Members of most PPS effectively enjoy a continuation of their existing entitlements, namely 25% of their fund values. Members of occupational money purchase schemes are less likely to benefit from the 25% limit, as their existing 3/80ths or uplifted 80ths final salary formula may have been higher due to lower levels of contributions. However, FA 2004, Sch 36, paras 31–34, offered protection for accrued lump sums greater than 25% in cases where all the following conditions are met:

(a) the relevant member must have become entitled to all pensions payable to him under the scheme on the same date;

(b) the pension scheme must have been an approved occupational pension scheme (meaning approved under *ICTA 1988, Ch 1, Pt XIV*, a relevant statutory scheme, a parliamentary fund, a section *32* policy or a former superannuation fund under *ICTA 1970, s 208*);

(c) the value of the member's uncrystallised lump sum rights on 5 April 2006 must have exceeded 25% of the value of his uncrystallised rights on 5 April 2006;

(d) where the lump sum entitlement at A-Day exceeded £375,000, notice of intention to rely on either PP or EP must *not* have been given; and

(e) the member must not have requested and received a transfer of his benefits out of the scheme on or after A-Day.

If all pension rights of a member are transferred out of his scheme, post A-Day protection will be lost unless the transfer is part of a block transfer (see **4.24**) or rights are transferred to a buy-out policy upon scheme wind-up. If a partial transfer occurs, the protected lump sum in the ceding scheme must be reduced by one quarter of the transfer value.

Valuing lump sum rights at 5 April 2006

4.22 To assess whether lump sum protection applies to a member's rights within an arrangement, it is necessary to value the member's uncrystallised lump sum and pension rights in the arrangement as at 5 April 2006. This can prove to be a complicated matter due to the need to have regard to pre A-Day HMRC limits.

The method of calculation was described in the previous edition of this book.

Valuing lump sums – more than one scheme relating to the same employment

4.23 The amount of lump sum rights that may be protected must not exceed HMRC limits as at 5 April 2006. Similarly, in working out the amount of a member's pension rights for the 25% test, HMRC limits must not be exceeded. The situation is particularly complicated if a member has rights under more than one arrangement relating to the same employment. In this case, where the aggregate lump sums or pension rights exceed HMRC limits, each benefit must be reduced in proportion to the excess of aggregate rights.

4.24 *Benefit rules*

This may mean that some lump sums which were thought to benefit from protection actually do not, and vice versa. Examples of the rules which applied are contained in the previous edition of this book.

Block transfers

4.24 Block transfers provide an easement to the loss of lump sum protection (and low normal pension age protection) for an individual's rights on making a transfer, the main purpose being to avoid unnecessary restrictions on genuine corporate reconstructions. If a member with a protected lump sum becomes a member of another pension arrangement as a result of a block transfer, he will not lose his lump sum protection. Successive block transfers can be made without affecting protection. It is therefore important to understand the conditions applicable to a block transfer. HMRC describe a block transfer as follows (at RPSM03106070 for low pension age protection and RPSM03105521 for lump sum protection):

> 'A transfer is a block transfer if it involves the transfer in a single transaction of all the sums and assets representing accrued rights under the scheme from which the transfer is made which relate to the member and at least one other member of that pension scheme. To be a single transaction
>
> - all of the sums and assets must be transferred from the transferring scheme to only one receiving scheme. Two or more partial transfers to two or more different schemes cannot be a transfer in a single transaction; and
>
> - the transaction must be made under a single agreement for a single transfer between the two schemes.
>
> It is not necessary that all of the sums and assets are all physically passed from the transferring scheme to the receiving scheme on the same day – there may be legal or administration reasons why this is not possible. However they should all be transferred in relation to the agreement to transfer and within a reasonable timescale.
>
> There is no restriction on the type of registered pension scheme receiving the transfer. So a personal pension scheme can receive a block transfer as long as the other block transfer conditions are met.'

Note that, for protection to continue to apply, the member whose rights are transferring under the block transfer must not have been a member of the receiving scheme for more than 12 months before the date of transfer. This is a point that is sometimes overlooked and will be very important if employees' deferred pension rights in one scheme are being transferred to a successor scheme in the same employment.

Payment of protected lump sum

4.25 Once it comes to be paid, the amount of a protected lump sum is calculated according to the following complicated formula:

VULSR × ULA / FSLA + ALSA, and

ALSA = ¼ × (LS + AC − VUR × CSLA / FSLA)

where:

- VULSR is the value of uncrystallised lump sum rights on 5 April 2006
- ULA is the underpinned LTA, ie the greater of the prevailing LTA and the relevant limit shown in Chapter 9 below
- CSLA is the current standard LTA (ie at the time of paying the lump sum)
- FSLA is the LTA
- LS is the amount of lump sum actually taken
- AC is the amount crystallised by bringing the annual pension into payment, and
- VUR is the value of uncrystallised rights under the scheme on 5 April 2006.

If ALSA (additional lump sum amount) is a negative number, it is taken to be nil.

The formula set out above reflects an amendment made by *FA 2008*. Prior to the amendment, ALSA was only taken into account in the formula if relevant benefit accrual had occurred post A-Day. Relevant benefit accrual is, in the case of a DC arrangement, the payment of a contribution and, in the case of a DB arrangement, the payment of pension above a certain level that is not easily ascertained and which consequently led to the amendment of the formula.

The formula was also amended by *FA 2011* to take account of the reduction in the standard LTA. £1.8 million can still be used to uprate the A-Day protected amount in the first part of the formula but is not used in the second part of the formula, which is designed to take account of post A-Day accrual and must reflect the current level of the LTA.

If use of the protected lump sum formula leads to a figure that is less than the normal formula for calculating a pension commencement lump sum, the normal calculation can be used instead.

Note that, post A-Day, scheme administrators are not obliged to pay the maximum protected lump sum. If scheme rules permit, they may pay a lump sum of up to the protected amount.

Stand-alone lump sum

4.26 The *Taxation of Pension Schemes (Transitional Provisions) (Amendment No 2) Order 2006, SI 2006/2004* provides rules for the calculation of stand-alone lump sums. A stand-alone lump sum is a tax-free lump sum which constitutes the whole of a person's rights under a pension scheme on 5 April 2006. It includes not just the scenario of a cash-only scheme but also

4.27 *Benefit rules*

the situation where the maximum HMRC approvable lump sum is greater than the value of the commutable pension rights on 5 April 2006. As long as there is no relevant benefit accrual post A-Day (which would be the case if there were no further pensionable service under a DB arrangement and no further contributions paid under a DC arrangement), the lump sum may be paid tax-free whatever its value has grown to by investment growth or revaluation.

Protected lump sums – interaction with overall lump sum limit

4.27 The maximum amount of pension commencement lump sum that can be paid is normally limited to 25% of the available LTA (see **4.19** above). Protected lump sums which are greater than 25% override the above restriction, meaning that a member who does not register for PP or EP may continue to have a lump sum entitlement greater than £375,000 if that entitlement was greater than 25% of the value of his rights at A-Day. The protection conditions in *FA 2004, Sch 36, paras 31–34*, must be met.

Short service refund lump sum

4.28 Where a member of an occupational pension scheme has less than two years' qualifying service, refunds of contributions made by the member will be permitted. If the refund was made in any of the tax years 2006/07 to 2009/10, the first £10,800 is taxed at the rate of 20% and the balance is taxed at the rate of 40%.

If the refund is made in the 2010/11 tax year or later, the first £20,000 is taxed at the rate of 20% and the balance is taxed at the appropriate higher rate.

The scheme administrator may deduct the tax they are liable to from the actual payment made to the individual, where the rules of the scheme making the payment allow this. This will not change the level of charge due; the tax charge applies to the gross amount of the lump sum before the deduction of the tax.

It is the scheme administrator who is liable to the tax charge and not the person who receives the lump sum payment. So if the recipient is a non-taxpayer they cannot make any repayment claim in respect of the tax paid. There is no further tax due for the person who receives the lump sum payment, even if they are a higher rate tax payer. Also, the person receiving the payment cannot off-set the tax paid against any other taxable income.

A refund of excess contributions lump sum is not subject to any income tax charge. It is paid tax-free. This reflects the fact that no tax relief has been granted on the contributions being refunded in the first place.

See **4.29** if interest is paid on a refund of contributions.

Scheme administration member payment

4.29 A short service refund lump sum may only be paid up to the amount of member contributions actually made. If a refund of member contributions

Benefit rules **4.29**

is paid from a money purchase scheme, it may incorporate investment gains or losses. If the sum paid to the member is higher than the amount of his contributions due to investment gains, or if interest is otherwise added to the refund payment, the investment gain or interest would not fall within the parameters of a short service refund lump sum. However, the investment gain or interest could still be an authorised payment if it falls within the parameters of a scheme administration member payment. See the following extract from the Registered Pension Schemes Manual (at RPSM09104740):

'Interest paid on the short service refund lump sum

The definition of a short service refund lump sum includes an upper limit equal to the amount of actual contributions made by the member to the scheme. But the scheme rules may provide for the refund to consist of other monies on top of the actual contributions being refunded. The scheme administrator must determine the nature of the payment according to the scheme rules. The interest may be paid as a separately calculated amount or may form part of the lump sum payment.

Interest as a separately calculated amount

A registered pension scheme's rules may provide for interest to be paid in addition to the contributions being refunded. The interest may arise simply because of a delay in making a payment or may be a payment over and above the computed lump sum for some other reason. If it qualifies to be treated as a scheme administration member payment (see below) for tax purposes, a payment of interest on top of the refunded contributions is an authorised payment.

A scheme administration member payment is a payment for the administration or management of the scheme. Such payments should be made on an arm's length, commercial basis. So any interest paid by a scheme on a refund of contributions should be no more than a reasonable commercial rate if it is to be a scheme administration member payment. Any excess will be an unauthorised member payment and taxed accordingly – see RPSM04104020 and RPSM04104040.

Interest payments associated with a short service refund lump sum that meet the definition of scheme administration member payment are taxable under section 369 Income Tax (Trading and Other Income) Act 2005 (formerly Case III Schedule D). The scheme administrator should make the payment without deducting income tax, and the recipient should include the interest in a self-assessment tax return or notify their HMRC income tax office of liability if they do not receive a notice to make a return.

Interest as part of the lump sum

If the contributions to be refunded are less than the statutory maximum then schemes may be able to provide for interest to be paid as part of the lump sum. For example, the lump sum may be computed with

4.30 *Benefit rules*

reference to an interest rate. If the interest is part of the lump sum, and the lump sum paid is within the statutory maximum, the tax treatment set out in section 205 Finance Act 2004 applies.'

Serious ill-health lump sum

4.30 Serious ill-health commutation is permitted for registered pension schemes (*FA 2004, Sch 29, para 4*) out of uncrystallised benefits. The administrator must obtain written medical evidence that the member's life expectancy is less than one year and must notify HMRC.

There is no charge to income tax on payment of a serious ill-health lump sum paid to a member who has not reached the age of 75, either on the individual or the scheme administrator, unless the LTA would be exceeded.

A serious ill-health lump sum paid on or after 6 April 2011 to a member who has reached the age of 75 is liable to a charge to income tax at the rate of 55%. The scheme administrator is the person liable for paying this charge, so they will normally deduct the tax from the lump sum before payment.

Focus

- The rules which apply to trivial pensions and small pension pots have been relaxed.

Trivial commutation, and small pension pots

4.31 In recent years there have been long drawn-out discussions on how to free up small pension funds. This has always been a thorn in the side for for the annuity providers, who often cannot provide annuities on a commercial basis. There has also been a desire from pensioners to realise their capital from funds which provide miniscule pension payments.

Traditionally, HMRC regularly reviewed the maximum level of trivial pensions that it would permit to be paid in cash form in order to assist with a solution. However, at last there has been some positive move to overcome this problem by legislative change, although, perhaps unsurprisingly in the light of recent developments, a most complex set of conditions have been introduced, which run through two threads of access to funds.

The new, complex, rules, are contained in *FA 2014, s 42* and are summarised below:

Trivial pensions: The trivial commutation lump sum amount had previously been set at £18,000 – which had replaced the earlier maximum of 1% of the LTA. The latest rules are that, from 27 March 2014, individuals aged over 60 who have not touched their pension pot, and whose total pension savings are no more than £30,000, can withdraw all of their savings. The first 25% will be tax-free, and the remainder will be taxed as the top slice of their income in the tax year of withdrawal. The affected payments are payments that would be trivial commutation lump sums but for the continuing payment of an annuity,

Benefit rules **4.31**

and which satisfy the other conditions set out in *reg 10* of the *Registered Pension Schemes (Authorised Payments) Regulations 2009 (SI 2009/1171)*.

In order to qualify for this facility, there must be no other trivial commutation paid. All benefits under the pension arrangement must be extinguished. *FA 2013, Sch 22, para 8(4)*, revised the calculation of the maximum amount that can be paid where the individual has previously taken some pension benefits. From 6 April 2014 the calculation is by reference to any change in the trivial commutation limit.

An individual's pension rights must be valued at no more than the commutation limit on what is called the 'nominated date'. The member has an opportunity to nominate the date when their pension rights are valued for triviality purposes, but it cannnot be earlier than three months before the first trivial commutation lump sum paid to the member by any registered pension scheme.

If the lump sum is being paid after age 75 from uncrystallised rights or funds, those rights or funds will have been tested against the member's LTA under BCE 5 or BCE 5B respectively when the member reached age 75. This BCE will have used up some or all of the member's available LTA at that time. This means that, for the purposes of deciding whether the member satisfies the condition that they have available LTA, the fact that a BCE 5 or 5B has occurred is disregarded. In other words, any LTA used up by that BCE does not count in calculating whether the member has available LTA. However, if the member has already taken benefits from the same or another arrangement under a registered pension scheme after reaching age 75 or some other event has occurred that would have been a BCE but for the fact that the event occurred on or after the member reaching age 75, then, solely for the purposes of calculating whether the member has available LTA, those events are treated as though they were BCEs.

With regard to the required procedures to benefit, HMRC's Pensions Newsletter 57 dated 14 May 2013 describes trivial commutation payments through RTI. It also announced improvements to the P53 form and process and reporting trivial commutation payments through RTI. The P53 is a trivial pension/annuity in-year repayment claim form and will include a version that can be completed online. Pension schemes must report to HMRC through RTI any payments they make where tax is deducted under PAYE.

Small pots: The size of the lump sum small pot that can be taken from occupational pension schemes was increased to £10,000 from 27 March 2014. This represents the total pension savings that can be taken from age 60 as a taxed lump sum, and the aggregate total from other small pots is now £30,000, meaning that there has been an increase in the number of pots that can be taken to three. All benefits under the pension arrangement must be extinguished. The small pot limit had previously been set at £2,000. Small pots can be taken without taking into account other pension benefits (*FA 2004, s 164(1) (f)*). There must not have been a transfer-out of the scheme in the 3 years preceding the date of payment and the first 25% of the payment is tax-free (unless the pension is in payment, when the whole amount is liable to IT) with the remaining 75% taxable under PAYE.

4.31 *Benefit rules*

If a member has small benefits in a non-occupational pension, such as a personal pension, *section 32* (buyout policy), stakeholder plan or RAC, it may be possible to cash them in even if the main rules above have not been met. The payment must extinguish all their pension rights under the arrangement, and they must not have previously received more than two payments under one of these types of scheme. This excludes any separate lump sum under the special rule for occupational schemes only. The first 25% of the payment is tax-free, with the remaining 75% taxable under PAYE. If the pension is in payment, the whole amount is liable to income tax.

The rules which apply differ depending on whether the individual is a member of a company or public pension scheme, or a personal pension scheme, as shown in the following examples:

Example 1 – company or public sector pension scheme

If the individual's pension pot is worth £10,000 they may take their pension pot as a lump sum subject to the conditions:

Condition 1:

They must take all their pension pots with the same pension scheme as a lump sum.

Condition 2:

They must not have transferred any funds out of the pension scheme in the last three years.

Condition 3:

They are not a controlling director – or someone connected with a controlling director (i.e. a director of a limited company who owns or controls 20% or more of the ordinary share capital of the company inclusive of that person's immediate family – whether or not the director owns or controls at least 20% of the company) of an employer that participates in the pension scheme.

Condition 4:

They belong to more than one company or public sector scheme for the same job and their total pension pots are worth £10,000 or less.

If they meet the first 3 conditions but not condition 4 they may still be able to take their whole pension pot as a lump sum but they will need to check with their scheme administrator.

Example 2 – Personal pension scheme

If the individual's pension scheme isn't a company or public sector scheme they may still be able to take all their pension pot as a lump sum if their pension pot is worth no more than £10,000. They must take all the money in that pension pot as a lump sum.

They may only take a lump sum 3 times (previously 2) under this rule.

Only 75% of the lump sum is taxable. The scheme administrator will deduct any tax due at the basic rate of 20% using PAYE and the member a P45 showing how much tax has been paid. If the individual normally doesn't pay tax, they can claim back the overpaid tax from HMRC. If they are a higher or additional rate taxpayer they may need to pay more tax through self-assessment.

Excessive lump sums

4.32   HMRC gives the following explanation of the treatment of the payment of excessive lump sums (at RPSM09104030):

> **'What happens when the limits on authorised lump sums are exceeded?** (extract):
>
> If a registered pension scheme makes a lump sum payment that does not fit into any of the seven authorised member lump sum payment definitions it is an unauthorised member payment, and will be taxed as such (see RPSM04104020 and RPSM04104040).
>
> Where a scheme makes a payment that meets the definition of an authorised lump sum payment, but the amount paid simply exceeds the limit specified in the legislation, this does not mean that the whole payment becomes unauthorised in all cases.
>
> For the following lump sum payments
>
> - a pension commencement lump sum,
> - a stand-alone lump sum – see RPSM03105155 and RPSM03105202,
> - a short service refund lump sum,
> - a refund of excess contributions lump sum, and
> - a winding-up lump sum
>
> the part of the payment that is within limits will still represent an authorised lump sum payment, as appropriate. Any excess will not be treated as being part of that lump sum payment, and will become either
>
> - another form of authorised lump sum payment or scheme administration member payment (where it falls within the relevant definition), or
> - an unauthorised member payment, and be taxed as such.
>
> With the other forms of authorised member lump sum payments, either

4.33 *Benefit rules*

- the limit is an integral part of the definition (so if the limit is breached the whole payment falls out of the definition, as with payment of a trivial commutation lump sum), or
- there are no limits as such, although the amounts paid are tested for lifetime allowance purposes (as with payment of a serious ill-health lump sum or lifetime allowance excess lump sum).'

PENSION AGES

Normal minimum pension age

4.33 Pensions payable to members of registered pension schemes must not come into payment before the member has reached normal minimum pension age. This is currently age 55 but had been age 50 before 6 April 2010. The exception to this is where a pension is brought into payment on grounds of ill-health. An ill-health pension is subject to the following rules:

- the member must have left the employment to which the pension relates; and
- the administrator must obtain proper medical evidence that the member is incapable of continuing in his current occupation.

An ill-health pension may cease, where scheme rules permit or require, if the member recovers sufficiently to return to his original job.

The normal ill-health qualification is where a member satisfies the scheme's ill-health condition, and so is and will continue to be, medically incapable (either physically or mentally) for work as a result of:

- Injury;
- sickness;
- disease; or
- disability.

Focus
- Transitional protection rules apply for low retirement ages for certain individuals
---

Protected low retirement age

4.34 If benefits are taken before normal minimum pension age under protective measures, an abatement of 2.5% per annum must be applied to the LTA. Transitional provisions existed to protect individuals who had unqualified rights on 5 April 2006 to take a pension before the normal minimum pension age. Where certain conditions are met, these individuals may take benefits at an age earlier than the normal minimum pension age

Benefit rules **4.34**

without incurring a tax charge. This is known as the member's protected pension age (see RPSM03106010).

The later developments for personal pension schemes and occupational pension schemes or deferred annuity contracts, are explained in **4.35** and **4.36** below respectively.

The individuals who are most likely to have protected low retirement ages are sportsmen or those in hazardous occupations (the *Registered Pension Schemes (Prescribed Schemes and Occupations) Regulations 2005 (SI 2005/3451)*).

(See *the Registered Pension Schemes (Prescribed Schemes and Occupations) Regulations 2005 (SI 2005/3451, reg 3)*.

RPSM03106035 provides the following list:-

- Athletes,
- Badminton players,
- Boxers,
- Cricketers,
- Cyclists,
- Dancers,
- Divers (saturation, deep sea and free swimming),
- Footballers,
- Golfers,
- Ice hockey players,
- Jockeys – flat racing,
- Jockeys – national hunt,
- Members of the Reserve Forces,
- Models,
- Motor cycle riders (Motocross or road racing),
- Motor racing drivers,
- Rugby League players,
- Rugby Union players,
- Skiers (downhill),
- Snooker or billiards players,
- Speedway riders,
- Squash players,
- Table tennis players,
- Tennis players (including real tennis),

4.35 *Benefit rules*

- Trapeze artists, and
- Wrestlers.

Personal pension schemes

4.35 Some members of retirement annuity contracts or personal pension schemes will be able to protect their right to take pension and lump sum benefits at their request before the normal minimum pension age (see RPSM03106030). The age at which the member has the right to take a pension on 5 April 2006 will become their protected pension age.

Where pension benefits are taken before age 50, the member's LTA may be reduced (see RPSM03106080).

In order to exercise the above right, the member must on 5 April 2006

- be or have been in a prescribed occupation described in **4.34** above, and
- have had an unqualified right to take a pension before the age of 50 (an unqualified right is when no other party need consent to the individual's request before it becomes binding upon the scheme or contract holder).
- become entitled to all uncrystallised pension and/or lump sum rights under the scheme on the same day; and
- cease any relevant employment on drawing benefits.

Benefits may only become payable on cessation of any related employment. The right will be lost upon a transfer of benefit, but not if it is part of a block transfer.

Occupational pension schemes

4.36 Members of occupational pension schemes or deferred annuity contracts with a low normal retirement age will be able to retain that right (see RPSM03106020) if:

- the member had the right on to take a pension and/or lump sum before the age of 50 (or 55 by 6 April 2010);
- the right is unqualified (in that no other party need consent to the individual's request before it becomes binding upon the scheme or contract holder);
- the provision to take benefits before age of 50 (or 55 by 6 April 2010) was set out in the governing documentation of the retirement benefit scheme or deferred annuity contract on 10 December 2003;
- the member becomes entitled to all of his uncrystallised pension and/or lump sum rights under the scheme on the same day;
- the member has left the employment to which the scheme relates;

- the member either:
  - had the right under the scheme or contract on 10 December 2003, or
  - acquired the right in accordance with the scheme provisions as they were on 10 December 2003 upon joining the scheme after that date.

On transferring out of the pension scheme, a member will normally lose his right to a protected low retirement age. However, where the transfer is part of a block transfer, members with a right to a low normal retirement age may continue to hold that right under the new arrangement.

The LTA abatement (see **4.34** above) will not apply if an individual is taking his benefits from one of the following schemes:

- Armed Forces Pension Scheme,
- British Transport Police Force Superannuation Fund,
- Firefighters' Pension Scheme,
- Firemen's Pension Scheme (Northern Ireland),
- Gurkha Pension Scheme,
- Police Pension Scheme,
- Police Service of Northern Ireland Pension Scheme,
- Police Service of Northern Ireland Full Time Reserve Pension Scheme, or
- a scheme established solely for the receipt of additional voluntary pension contributions from members of the schemes above.

PENSION DEATH BENEFIT RULES

General rules

4.37 There is generally no limit on the amount of dependant's pension that can be paid from a registered pension scheme. The payment of a dependant's pension does not count as a BCE and is therefore not subject to the LTA. Dependants' pensions are, however, subject to income tax under PAYE.

It is no longer a necessity that a dependant's pension payable to a surviving spouse is payable for the life of the spouse (or until earlier remarriage).

Dependants' pensions from DB arrangements are generally unrestricted. The exception to this is a dependant's pension payable on death in retirement, where death occurs after age 75 and the member's pension commenced after 5 April 2006. In this case, the dependant's pension must not exceed the level of the member's pension at date of death plus 5% of any retirement lump sum taken.

4.38 *Benefit rules*

On the death of a member of a DC arrangement before retirement, a dependant may choose to purchase an annuity or to take income withdrawals. On the death of the member after retirement, a dependant may continue to take income withdrawals if the member had been taking income withdrawals, or purchase an annuity. If the member was in receipt of an annuity at date of death, the terms of the annuity could provide for payment of a dependant's annuity. In summary, the only benefits a DC arrangement is authorised to provide on the death of a (pensioner) member in receipt of a scheme pension entitlement are a dependants' scheme pension, dependants' annuity, or dependants' drawdown pension. These may be payable to any dependant of the member,

A ten-year guarantee may be provided on members' pensions from DB schemes and on lifetime annuities.

Where a scheme provides for a dependant's pension, it may be possible, depending on scheme rules, to convert it into a lump sum death benefit before the dependant becomes entitled to it.

In order to receive a dependant's pension, the recipient must meet the definition of dependant set out in *FA 2004*.

Meaning of dependant

4.38 A person who was married to, or who was a civil partner of, the member at the date of death is a dependant. A dependant may also be someone who was married to, or who was a civil partner of, the member at the time when the member's pension commenced, as long as the rules of the scheme provide for this.

A child of the member is a dependant if he has not reached the age of 23 or, if he has reached that age, he was, in the opinion of the scheme administrator, dependent on the member because of physical or mental impairment.

A person who is not a child of the member, not married to the member and not a civil partner of the member may still be a dependant if, in the opinion of the scheme administrator, at the date of the member's death:

- he was financially dependent on the member,
- his financial relationship with the member was one of mutual dependence, or
- he was dependent on the member because of physical or mental impairment.

Transitional protection – children's pensions

4.39 Although children's pensions must normally cease by age 23, transitional provisions ensure that a right to a child's pension continues after A-Day and the pension would be payable until the later of the child reaching age 23 and ceasing full-time education or vocational training. For this to apply, one of the following three conditions must be met:

Condition 1

- The pension was in payment to a child of the member on 5 April 2006 or the member had died on or before 5 April 2006 and a pension was due to come into payment to the child; and
- The rules of the pension scheme allowed a pension to be paid to a child of the member following the death of that member until the child ceased full-time education or vocational training.

Condition 2

- The pension was in payment to a member on 5 April 2006;
- The rules of the pension scheme allowed a pension to be paid to a child of the member following the death of that member until the child ceased full-time education or vocational training; and
- The child was born on or before 5 April 2007.

Condition 3

- The rules of the pension scheme on 10 December 2003 allowed an irrevocable election to be made designating part of the sums or assets representing the member's rights as available for the payment of a pension to a child of the member following the death of that member until the child ceased full-time education or vocational training; and
- Such an election had been made by the member and accepted by the scheme administrator on or before 5 April 2006.

Focus

- Lump sum death benefits are subject to complex rules, dependent on the nature of the arrangement and the date of payment

---

LUMP SUM DEATH BENEFIT RULES

General rules

4.40 As with dependants' pensions, there is no limit to the amount of lump sum death benefit that may be paid from a registered pension scheme. However, the lump sum will either be subject to the LTA or subject to a special tax charge if it is paid after age 75 or in respect of crystallised rights.

Where a trivial commutation lump sum death benefit is concerned, the payment must be made to dependants (see **4.43** below). If lump sum death benefits are not paid directly to the legal personal representative, that person must be notified of the payment. It is also a requirement that the amount of the LTA used up is declared, and a charge of 55% on any excess over the LTA will fall on the beneficiary.

The type of lump sum death benefit payable will depend on whether the arrangement from which it is paid is defined benefit or money purchase.

4.41 *Benefit rules*

Where an individual died before 6 April 2014, and lump sum benefits were not paid until on or after that date, the lump sum is tested against the standard LTA at the time of the individual's death.

Defined benefit arrangements

4.41 If the member died on or after 6 April 2011, a DB lump sum death benefit can be paid, whatever age the member was when he died.

If the member died before his 75th birthday, the DB lump sum death benefit must be paid within two years of the earlier of:

- the date the pension scheme administrator first knew of the member's death, and
- the date the scheme administrator could reasonably have been expected to know of the member's death.

If the member was 75 or over when he died, the two-year time limit for paying the lump sum does not apply.

On death before age 75, the lump sum must be tested against the member's LTA. If the total benefits taken in respect of the member are more than his LTA, the excess is liable to the LTA charge at 55%. Otherwise, it is tax-free.

There is no LTA test on death after age 75. However, the lump sum will be taxed at 55%. So, if a £100,000 lump sum is payable, the amount of tax due is £55,000. The scheme administrator is responsible for paying this tax, not the person who received the lump sum death benefit. The scheme administrator can deduct the tax due before paying the lump sum. The scheme administrator should pay the tax due using the AFT return procedure.

IHT will not normally apply. All the IHT charges that arose before 6 April 2011, on pension funds left over on death, no longer apply. Similarly, the IHT charges that were due when a person chose not to take any benefits from his scheme no longer apply.

DB schemes may also pay what HMRC refer to as 'pension protection lump sum death benefits' in respect of pensions in payment. When a member starts to be paid a scheme pension, he may be able to choose to guarantee that a set amount of pension will be provided. If the member dies before the guaranteed amount of pension has been paid, the balance can be paid as a lump sum. This lump sum is called the pension protection lump sum death benefit.

If the member died on or after 6 April 2011, a pension protection lump sum death benefit can be paid, whatever age the member was when he died. There is no time limit for the payment of this lump sum.

The maximum pension protection lump sum that can be paid is the crystallised amount for LTA purposes when the scheme pension started, less any amount of scheme pension paid. The legislation limits the level of pension protection lump sum death benefit that may be paid on the member's death using the following formula:

$$AC - AP - TPLS$$

AC is:

- where the member became entitled to his pension after 5 April 2006 and before his 75th birthday, the amount crystallising through BCE 2;

- Where the member became entitled to his scheme pension after 5 April 2006 aged 75 or over, the amount that would have crystallised as a BCE 2 if that BCE could occur; and

- where the member became entitled to his pension before 6 April 2006, 25 times the annual rate of the pre 6 April 2006 pension.

AP is the amount of scheme pension paid up to the point the member died. If the scheme pension started before 6 April 2006, only payments made on or after 6 April 2006 are included.

TPLS is the amount of pension protection lump sum death benefit previously paid under the scheme (or by any insurance company that entitlement is secured with) in relation to the member's scheme pension entitlement.

Pension protection lump sum death benefits are not tested against the LTA, but a special tax charge is due. The scheme administrator is responsible for paying this tax charge; but, where the lump sum death benefit is paid by an insurance company, the company becomes liable for the charge due. The person who received the lump sum is not liable to this tax charge. The scheme administrator (or insurance company making the payment) can deduct the tax due before paying the lump sum. Where the member died before 6 April 2011, the rate of the tax charge is 35%. Where the member died on or after 6 April 2011, the rate of the tax charge is 55%. IHT, which would have arisen before 6 April 2011, no longer applies.

Money purchase arrangements

4.42 DC arrangements may pay lump sum death benefits from both uncrystallised rights and rights that have come into payment.

An uncrystallised funds lump sum death benefit can be paid from funds that have not yet been put into payment. If the member died on or after 6 April 2011, an uncrystallised funds lump sum death benefit can be paid, whatever the age of the member when he died. If the member died before the age of 75, the uncrystallised funds lump sum death benefit must be paid within two years of the earlier of the following dates:

- the date the pension scheme administrator first knew of the member's death, and

- the date the scheme administrator could reasonably have been expected to know of the member's death.

If the member died age 75 or over, there is no two-year time limit on making the payment of an uncrystallised funds lump sum death benefit.

The amount of uncrystallised funds lump sum death benefit paid must be no more than the value of the uncrystallised funds, as were held in the

4.42 *Benefit rules*

arrangement when the member died, at the point of the lump sum payment. So any growth of those uncrystallised funds up to the point of payment may be covered in the payment.

If the member was aged under 75 when he died, the lump sum must be tested against the LTA. If the total benefits taken in respect of the member are more than his LTA, the excess is liable to the LTA charge at 55%. Otherwise, it is tax-free.

If the member was aged 75 or over when he died, the uncrystallised funds lump sum death benefit is not tested against the LTA, but it is subject to a special tax charge of 55%. The scheme administrator, not the recipient, is responsible for paying this special tax charge, and the tax may be deducted from the payment due. IHT will not apply (a change brought in by the *FA 2011*).

An annuity protection lump sum death benefit can be paid where the deceased member was in receipt of a lifetime annuity. When the annuity was purchased, the member would have been able to choose to guarantee that a set amount of pension would be provided. If the member dies before the guaranteed amount of pension has been paid, the balance can be paid as a lump sum.

If the member died on or after 6 April 2011, an annuity protection lump sum death benefit can be paid, whatever age the member was when he died. There is no time limit for the payment of this lump sum. The maximum amount that can be paid as a lump sum death benefit is the amount that had been crystallised for LTA purposes when the annuity was purchased, less any amount of pension paid. It is limited by the following formula:

AC – AP – TPLS

AC is:

- where the member became entitled to his pension after 5 April 2006 and before his 75th birthday, the amount crystallising through BCE 2 or BCE 4 when the member became entitled to his lifetime annuity;

- where the member became entitled to his pension after 5 April 2006 aged 75 or over, the amount that would have crystallised as a BCE 2 or BCE 4 if that BCE could occur for someone aged 75 or over; and

- where the member became entitled to his pension before A-Day, 25 times the annual rate of the pre-A-Day pension.

AP is the amount of scheme pension paid up to the point the member died. If the pension started before 6 April 2006, only payments made on or after 6 April 2006 are included.

TPLS is the amount of annuity protection lump sum death benefit previously paid under the scheme in relation to the member's lifetime annuity.

An annuity protection lump sum death benefit is not tested against the LTA, but it is subject to a special tax charge. This is 35% if the member died before 6 April 2011, and 55% if the member died on or after 6 April 2011. There is no longer an IHT charge.

If a member is in receipt of income drawdown (that is not classed as a short-term annuity), the remainder of the fund may be paid out on death as a lump sum (a drawdown pension fund lump sum death benefit). If the member died on or after 6 April 2011, the lump sum can be paid, whatever the age of the member when he died. There is no time limit for the payment of this lump sum. A drawdown pension fund lump sum death benefit cannot be more than the value of the drawdown pension fund held in the arrangement when the member died, at the point of the lump sum payment. Any growth of that drawdown pension fund up to the point of payment may be covered in the payment. (Any sum used to purchase a short-term annuity cannot go towards the lump sum death benefit, which must simply be a return of existing funds.) The lump sum death benefit is not subject to the LTA, but it is subject to a special tax charge of 35% (death before 6 April 2011) or 55% (death on or after 6 April 2011). The IHT charge that would have arisen before 6 April 2011 no longer applies.

Trivial commutation lump sum death benefit

4.43 The payment of trivial pension in lump sum form to a dependant is a useful facility, and there have been some recent relaxations in the rules which apply. These are described below.

Where the member died before 6 April 2011 and was under age 75:

A dependant of that member could become entitled to authorised pension death benefits within the triviality limit that applied at the time (see **4.31** above), and the scheme could provide for those pension entitlements to be commuted and paid as a lump sum (along with any lump sum death benefit entitlement). Generally, such a dependant's pension entitlement could be trivially commuted immediately as it arose or at any time thereafter.

However, a trivial commutation lump sum death benefit could only be paid where both

- the member giving rise to the entitlement died before reaching age 75, and
- the payment was actually made before the date the member would have reached their 75th birthday.

The payment must extinguish the dependant's entitlement to any form of authorised death benefit under the registered pension scheme in respect of the deceased member. A trivial commutation lump sum death benefit is taxable as pension income of the dependant receiving the payment

Where the member died on or after 6 April 2011:

On death on or after 6 April 2011, similar rules apply, subject to the following changes:

4.44 *Benefit rules*

- The previous age 75 restrictions no longer apply.
- From 6 April 2012, if the lump sum paid exceeds £18,000, only the amount up to the £18,000 limit can be treated as a trivial commutation lump sum death benefit. This is a maximum amount per scheme, not the maximum across all schemes.
- The benefit can be paid whatever age the member was when they died, and there is no time limit for making the payment.
- The dependant can commute a dependant's pension that is just about to start or one that is already being paid.

The whole lump sum is taxable as pension income of the dependant. The pension scheme administrator should apply PAYE to the lump sum payment (*ITEPA 2003 ss 579A, 579D, 683* and *Income Tax (PAYE) Regulations 2003, reg 11 (SI 2003/2682)*).

IHT will not apply if the lump sum is paid at the discretion of the pension scheme trustees (or provider). The IHT charges that arose before 6 April 2011 on ASP left over on death no longer apply.

Funeral grant

4.44 The rules of some occupational pension schemes allow a one-off tax-free payment to be made on the death of a member in order to fund funeral expenses. Where the member was over the age of 75 at the date of death, such a payment would not be an authorised lump sum. The *Taxation of Pension Schemes (Transitional Provisions) Order 2006 (SI 2006/572)* created a new authorised payment, called a life cover lump sum, to provide protection in these circumstances. The conditions that have to be met are:

- the registered pension scheme was, immediately before A-Day, a retirement benefit scheme approved for the purposes of *ICTA 1988, Pt XIV*;
- the member had a right under the pension scheme to a life cover lump sum on 5 April 2006;
- the rules of the pension scheme on 10 December 2003 included provision conferring such a right on some or all of the persons who were then members of the pension scheme, and such a right was either then conferred on the member or would have been had the member been a member of the scheme on that date;
- the rules of the scheme in relation to life cover lump sums have not been changed since 10 December 2003; and
- the member was in receipt of benefits from the scheme on or before 5 April 2006 or entitled to one or more life cover lump sums amounting to £2,500 or less.

The payment is tax-free by virtue of *ITEPA 2003, s 636A*. It is not listed as being included in the lifetime allowance, as it is not defined as a relevant lump sum death benefit for the purpose of BCE's (*FA 2004, s 216* and *Sch 32*).

A 'dependant' may include an ex-wife or civil partner who had been married or a civil partner to the member when the pension commenced.

Charity lump sum death benefit

4.45 A charity lump sum death benefit is a lump sum paid to a charity if the member (or dependant) is in receipt of a drawdown pension and dies when there are no other dependants of the member.

If the member (or dependant) died on or after 6 April 2011, there is no requirement for the member (or dependant) to be age 75 or over when he died. The lump sum can be paid, whatever the age of the member (or dependant).

A charity lump sum death benefit can also be paid if the member dies on or after 6 April 2011 and all the following apply:

- the member was 75 or older when he died,
- the member had uncrystallised rights under any type of arrangement when he died, and
- there are no dependants of the member.

If the lump sum is being paid because of the death of a member on or after 6 April 2011, the lump sum must be paid to a charity selected by the member.

If the lump sum is being paid because of the death of a dependant who died on or after 6 April 2011, the lump sum must be paid to either:

- a charity selected by the member, or
- if the member had not chosen a charity, a charity selected by the dependant.

Where the lump sum is being paid in respect of someone who died on or after 6 April 2011, the scheme administrator cannot choose the charity receiving the payment.

A charity lump sum death benefit is not tested against the LTA. There is no special tax charge, and there is no tax charge on the charity receiving the payment, as long as it is used for charitable purposes.

Focus
- Specific rules apply to the effect of pension debit and credit on a member's benefits

---

PENSION SHARING

Pre A-Day pension debit and credit

4.46 Pension sharing on divorce operates so as to reduce a member's pension rights by a pension debit, and to award the ex-spouse with a pension credit. Before A-Day, a pension debit counted against the HMRC maximum benefit that a member was allowed to accrue under the pre-A-Day tax regime.

4.47 *Benefit rules*

The pension credit was ignored in assessing the HMRC maximum benefit of the ex-spouse.

Post A-Day pension credit

4.47 The position changed on 6 April 2006. If a person acquires a pension credit post A-Day, it will count towards that person's lifetime allowance. However, in a case where the pension being shared is one that has been brought into payment on or after 6 April 2006, the person receiving the pension credit can apply for an uplift to their LTA. Since the pension being shared will already have been tested against the LTA once before, when it was brought into payment, it would be unfair to test it against a LTA a second time. The uplift is calculated according to the formula

APC/SLA

where:

- APC is the appropriate amount of the pension credit rights at the date they were acquired (ie that part of the original member's cash equivalent transfer value which was split in favour of the ex-spouse), and
- SLA is the standard LTA at the time when the pension credit rights were acquired.

For example, if £1 million worth of pension rights were shared in the 2007/08 tax year in the proportion 50:50, the pension credit recipient is entitled to an uplift of £500,000 / £1,600,000 = 0.3125, which is rounded up to two decimal places, 0.32. If the person with pension credit draws benefits in the 2010/11 tax year when the LTA was £1.8m, their LTA would have increased to £1.8m × 1.32 = £2,376,000.

To receive this uplift, the recipient of pension credit has to notify HMRC on form APSS201 by 31 January five years after the 31 January following the tax year in which the pension sharing order took effect.

A similar uplift is available for anyone who acquired pension credit before 6 April 2006, given that pre A-Day pension credit did not count against HMRC limits. The uplift is available whether or not the pension credit relates to rights which were already in payment. The uplift is calculated according to the formula

IAPC/SLA

where:

- IAPC is the appropriate amount of the pension credit rights at the date they were acquired (i.e. that part of the original member's cash equivalent transfer value which was split in favour of the ex-spouse), and
- SLA is the standard LTA for the 2006/07 tax year (ie £1,500,000).

To determine the amount of IAPC, it is increased in line with increases in the RPI from the month in which the pension credit was acquired up to April 2006.

Anyone seeking an uplift for pre A-Day pension credit had to notify HMRC on form APSS201 on or before 5 April 2009. Note, however, that this uplift is not available for pre A-Day pension credit if the person with pension credit is also relying on PP.

Post A-Day pension debit

4.48 For those subject to a pension debit before A-Day, the good news is that this does not count towards the post A-Day LTA, despite the fact that it counted towards pre A-Day HMRC limits. This means that someone with a pension debit acquires scope to fund their benefits up to their original level. However, if any transitional protection is being relied on that requires the calculation of HMRC maximum benefits on 5 April 2006, the pension debit may have to be taken into account for those purposes.

For the seriously wealthy, this means divorce may not necessarily be all bad news post A-Day. If 100% of pension rights are given away post A-Day as part of a divorce settlement, the person giving the rights away will be able to fund up to the LTA once again, essentially benefiting from contribution tax relief twice.

Focus
- Benefit crystallisation events can trigger a test against the lifetime allowance
- The number of different benefit crystallisation events has increased in recent years

---

BENEFIT CRYSTALLISATION EVENTS

4.49 BCEs are events where a test is triggered against the LTA limit. However, crystallisation is not just the initial payment of a benefit from a scheme; it includes a number of other events. The list of BCEs and their application has grown considerably in recent years. A comprehensive list is provided, together with some explanatory notes from HMRC's RPSM, in **Appendix 1**.

The scheme administrator has duties to perform both at and after a BCE in a member's lifetime. They are:

(a) establishing whether a chargeable amount arises;

(b) accounting to HMRC for any LTA charge due (on a quarterly basis); and

(c) providing the member with a statement confirming the total level of the member's LTA that has been used up under the scheme. Additionally, if a chargeable amount arose, a notice confirming:
- the level of chargeable amount that arose;
- the LTA charge; and
- whether or not the scheme administrator has accounted for the due charge, or intends to do so in due course.

4.50 *Benefit rules*

> **Focus**
> - The government is preparing to introduce collective defined contribution schemes, based largely on a 'Dutch-style' form of DC provision

COLLECTIVE DEFINED CONTRIBUTION SCHEMES

4.50   CDC's were unveiled in the Queen's Speech on 4 June 2014. They have been referred to in a recent DWP consultation and are to be based largely on a 'Dutch-style' form of DC provision. The Netherlands has experienced some significant losses in CDC fund values recently, and the Pensions Industry had previously voiced some concerns over this proposed move, including consultant Ros Altmann who warned against 'over-optimistic claims' about performance.

The theory is that CDCs will benefit employers more than expensive and heavily regulated DB schemes in which the employer bears the risk, and that members will benefit more from CDCs than DC schemes. The Government intends to introduced them in 2016.

However, Ros Altmann said:

> 'In practice, they still suffer from market and actuarial risks and new pension freedoms may mean they are less attractive for members. Lower earners may subsidise higher earners – younger members may subsidise older members.'

Accordingly, there is currently a lack of certainty about whether CDCs will succeed in the market-place, particularly with the pending introduction of freedom to collapse DC schemes in their entirety. Nevertheless, there are some positive perceptions. Ros Altmann outlined the potential pros and cons of the new proposed CDC schemes as follows:

Possible advantages

- Employers pay fixed contributions (typically being 10–12% of salary)
- No balance sheet risk for employers
- Members are offered a 'target' level of pension, related to average salary
- Members are offered inflation protection for their pensions
- Less risk for employers and members than pure DC
- Pooling investments allows lower management costs
- Pooling investments in large funds offers chance for better spread of assets to deliver higher returns – CDC could include assets such as infrastructure, forestry etc.
- Government estimates CDC pensions could be up to 30% higher than pure DC.

Benefit rules **4.50**

Possible disadvantages

- Pensions in payment could fall
- Pensions are at the mercy of market forecasts – and actuarial accuracy
- If pensions are too generous due to forecast errors, they will have to be cut
- Younger members may end up with lower pensions than older members
- On average, lower earners live less long than high earners, so low earners may subsidise the pensions of the high earners
- Relies on trust between generations and requires ongoing pool of new members coming in and contributing
- Sounds rather like with-profits which did not always work out well due to unexpected market movements.

In June 2014 new legislation was put to parliament, and the government re-branded such schemes as DABs. Employers and advisers will wish to track the development of this product in the future, and obtain guidance on whether it is appropriate to their needs.

CHECKLIST

- There is no overall limit on the amount of pension which can be paid. The pre A-Day requirement that a member must have left employment for a benefit to be paid was largely removed
- Pensions must normally take the form of scheme pensions, drawdown or lifetime annuities. They will normally be taxed as earnings under *ITEPA 2003*
- There have been major changes to the drawdown rules following the abolition of ASP and the age 75 rule. Further changes are envisaged. These matters are described in detail
- Schemes may be open to all, whatever the employment or residence status of the individual concerned. Individuals may join non-associated multi-employer schemes and industry-wide schemes enjoying benefits from the economies of scale, and they can also join cross-border schemes and transfer their funds to QROPS
- Pension commencement lump sum must only be paid in connection with a pension coming into payment. Under *FA 2004* the cash lump sum must be paid within an 18-month period starting six months before, and ending 12 months after, the date when the member becomes entitled to the related pension. However, a change under the *FA 2014* has widened the six month window to 18 months in order to give DC members who have already taken their pension commencement lump sum flexibility to delay drawing their pension until after April 2015

4.50 *Benefit rules*

- Rights derived from AVCs that were not commutable before A-Day because they were started after 8 April 1987 may be commuted subject to scheme rules permitting

- Examples are provided for the purpose of calculating the pension commencement lump sum limit

- Protected lump sums are described

- A member of an occupational pension scheme with less than two years' qualifying service may take a refund of contributions

- Serious ill-health commutation is permitted

- Trivial pensions and small pension pots may be commuted, under new and complex rules. Working examples are provided

- The treatment of the payment of excessive lump sums is described. Working examples are provided

- Normal minimum pension age is currently age 55. The exception to this is where a pension is brought into payment on grounds of ill-health

- Transitional provisions exist to protect low normal retirement ages that members of registered pension schemes may have been entitled to on 5 April 2006

- The rules which apply to pension death benefits for DB and DC schemes are described

- The rules which apply to lump sum death benefits for DB and DC schemes are described

- The meaning of a 'dependant' is given

- Transitional provisions ensure that a right to a child's pension continues after A-Day

- Pre A-Day arrangements for a one-off tax-free payment to be made on the death of a member in order to fund funeral expenses may still be paid

- A charity lump sum death benefit may be paid if the member (or dependant) is in receipt of a drawdown pension and dies when there are no other dependants of the member

- The effect of pension-sharing on divorce on the LTA is described

- BCE's are referred to, and are listed in **Appendix 1**

- Collective defined contribution schemes are envisaged by Government

Chapter 5

> **SIGNPOSTS**
>
> - Pension schemes may contain wide powers of investment
> - Investment in residential property and certain other 'taxable property' is not permitted for investment-regulated pension schemes
> - Occupational pension schemes no longer have to be subject to trust law to become registered pension schemes

Investment rules

INTRODUCTION

5.1 The investment rules that were introduced on A-Day, following *FA 2004* and subsequent Acts, largely reflected the pre A-Day rules. However, some important relaxations had been announced in *FA 2004*. Despite this very welcome and bold move by the simplification team of HMRC and HM Treasury, unexpected and major restrictions were to follow for certain schemes by virtue of *FA 2006*.

The first investment restriction which was removed by revision of *FA 2004* was on residential property. However, by the time that A-Day had been reached, the opening up of UK registered pension schemes to investment in residential property on commercial terms had been withdrawn for schemes which were classified as IRPS (see **Chapter 12** below). A concept of taxable property was introduced, with attaching severe tax charges and penalties.

Until this first attack on simplification, the long-standing reliance that had been placed on the prudence of, and compliance with, the statutory duties of trustees or administrators as the determining factor on investment activity and management had not been prejudiced. The rules had been the underlying principles of England and Wales law since 1925 (the Scottish statute was effective from 1921). However, in England and Wales trust law, and under Scottish trust law and EU law, they remain in place.

This U-turn by UK government was the first indication of an erosion of the principle of simplification. *FA 2004* and simplification are now distant memories. The *Act* has changed dramatically, and the regulatory floodgates have been opened. Complex changes and tax charges and penalties followed on targeted pensions vehicles and individuals. These disturbing developments have largely destroyed the true concept of even-handedness and affordable pension provision in the UK, which is constantly being diminished.

Admittedly, the UK (like its EU neighbours) is experiencing increased longevity of its citizens. However, the reduction in tax rates for high earners,

5.2 *Investment rules*

and the attacks on the disadvantaged, are peculiar features of the UK's attitude to recovery and the provision of care. Of course it is important to keep industrialists and high earners within the UK, but with state pension provision and care provision in the UK at an alarmingly low level compared with its EU neighbours, there seems to be real reason for concern.

Whatever UK governments may do in the future to erode private pension provision, trust law still protects the beneficiaries of the trust, and requires trustees to accumulate and enhance capital in their interests. Additionally, investments must be held securely and under a 'prudent person' principal. Satisfactory arrangements must be in place for holding the scheme's assets, which must be separate from the employer's account. Trustees/scheme administrators have a statutory duty to consult with the employer about the scheme's statement of investment principles.

As the UK removed the need for its tax-relievable pension schemes to be subject to trust law from A-Day perhaps, in the light of the UK developments in recent years, the UK may abandon the above, or some of the above, basic principles of law and prudence. Nevertheless, this cannot happen if the UK remains an EU member state.

The current rules for schemes, other than taxable property under IRPS, are shown under the following headings.

Focus
- Schemes may contain wide powers of investment

THE MAIN RULES WHICH APPLY TO ALL REGISTERED PENSION SCHEMES

5.2 The main permitted transactions are:

(a) loans, other than member loans;

(b) borrowing;

(c) transactions between an employer's or member's business and the scheme;

(d) investment in land and buildings;

(e) loans to the employer or other party that is unconnected to the member;

(f) investment in property, including (in some circumstances) residential property;

(g) disposals of assets on a commercial basis other than in order to avoid tax charges which should lawfully be incurred;

(h) purchases of assets by scheme members or connected persons from the scheme on a commercial basis;

(i) sale of assets by a member to a registered scheme on an arm's-length basis;

(j) investment in quoted or unquoted shares; and

(k) trading activities by the trustees or scheme manager.

The *Occupational Pension Schemes (Investment) Regulations 2005 (SI 2005/3378)* contain the following provisions:

(a) Assets must be invested in the best interests of members and beneficiaries; and, in the case of a potential conflict of interest, in the sole interest of members and beneficiaries.

(b) The powers of investment, or the discretion, must be exercised in a manner calculated to ensure the security, quality, liquidity and profitability of the portfolio as a whole.

(c) Assets must consist predominantly of investments admitted to trading on regulated markets, and other investments must be kept to a prudent level. There must also be diversification of assets, and special rules apply to derivatives and collective investment schemes.

(d) The requirements of the *IORPS Directive* are adopted in a proportionate and flexible manner, where appropriate using the 'small scheme exemption' which is contained in *Article 5*. Schemes with fewer than 100 active and deferred members are exempted from many of the requirements of the regulations, but are still required to have regard to the 'need for diversification on investment' rule.

(e) A triennial review of the statement of investment principles is required. The previous requirements on the statement's contents are largely restated.

(f) Trustees must consider 'proper advice' on the suitability of a proposed investment, and there are specific requirements in relation to borrowing and a restriction on investment in the 'sponsors' undertaking' to no more than 5% of the portfolio (where a group is concerned, the percentage is no greater than 20%).

The Pensions Regulator set out its expectations of trustees, employers and advisers involved in making pension scheme investment decisions on 10 November 2010. It provided a pdf guidance note as at *http://www.thepensionsregulator.gov.uk/press/pn10-21.aspx.*

Member loans

5.3 Loans to members are not permitted. One effect of this is that personal pension schemes and retirement annuities that have no sponsoring employer are unable to make loans to their members' businesses or partnerships where a partner is the scheme member.

Loans to third parties

5.4 Loans to third parties are permitted, but they must be on fully commercial terms.

5.5 Investment rules

Employer loans

5.5 Employer loans are permitted for all schemes.

Loans to the employer fall to be treated as 'employer-related investments' under the *Occupational Pension Schemes (Investment of Scheme's Resources) Regulations 1992 (SI 1992/246)* and the *Occupational Pension Schemes (Investment) Regulations 1996 (SI 1996/3127)*. These regulations require that:

- not more than 5% of the current market value of the resources of a scheme may at any time be invested in employer-related investments; and
- none of the resources of a scheme may at any time be invested in any employer-related loan.

There are exemptions for small schemes, as described below.

Loans may be for up to five years' duration and 50% of fund value. The other conditions are:

(a) the permitted loan interest rate is an average of the base rates of a specified group of banks;

(b) the chargeable rate for the purposes of *FA 2004, s 179*, is 1% more than the reference rate found on the reference date preceding the start of the period (see the *Pension Schemes (Prescribed Interest Rates for Authorised Employer Loans) Regulations 2005 (SI 2005/3449)*);

(c) the reference date is the twelfth working day preceding the operative date in the following month; the operative date means the sixth working day of each month;

(d) if it is not possible for an employer to repay a loan within the agreed period, the loan may be rolled over once for a maximum period of five years; and

(e) loans must be secured against assets of at least equal value.

Where a scheme is not an occupational pension scheme, there can be no sponsoring employer. Any loans made by the scheme to an employer who is connected to the member will attract a tax charge on the member.

Employer shares

5.6 The *Occupational Pension Schemes (Investment) Regulations 2005 (SI 2005/3378)* revoked the *Occupational Pension Schemes (Investment) Regulations 1996 (SI 1996/3127)*, and supplemented changes made to *PA 1995* by *PA 2004*. They included provisions to implement certain requirements of the *IORPS Directive*, in particular of *Articles 12* and *18*. The *2005 Regulations* cover the following matters:

- They impose requirements on trustees of occupational pension schemes in relation to the statement of investment principles required under *PA 1995, s 35*, and in relation to the choosing of investments.

Investment rules **5.7**

- They impose restrictions on borrowing and the giving of guarantees by trustees and in respect of employer-related investments.
- They set out requirements in respect of the statement of investment principles required under *PA 1995, s 35*.
- They set out modified requirements in respect of such statements for schemes in relation to which there is more than one employer.
- They set out requirements in respect of choosing investments.
- They set out restrictions in respect of borrowing and guarantees.
- They disapply *PA 1995, s 35*, and disapply or modify certain requirements of *regs 2* to *5*, in respect of certain schemes.
- They define the expressions 'connected persons' and 'associated persons' as they apply in the *Regulations*.
- They prescribe certain investments as employer-related investments in addition to those specified in *PA 1995, s 40(2)*, and set out the restrictions on employer-related investments. They also prescribe investments to which the restrictions do not apply. Special provision is made as regards the application of the restrictions to schemes in relation to which there is more than one employer.
- They make special provision in the case of a scheme undertaking cross-border activities.

There is a limit on the level of permitted shareholdings in the sponsoring company and associated/connected companies. The limit is 5% of the fund value under the *Occupational Pension Schemes (Investment of Scheme's Resources) Regulations 2002 (SI 1992/246)*. The *Occupational Pension Schemes (Investment) (Amendment) Regulations 2010 (SI 2010/2161)* were made to comply with the IORPS Directive which imposes a 5% limit on the amount of resources an occupational pension scheme can invest in the sponsoring employer. The *Regulations* apply to investments by an operator of collective investment schemes and to investments subject to certain transitional protection. Certain investments by operators of such a scheme fall within the meaning of employer-related investments. *Regulation 2(3)* removed transitional protection from schemes to which *regulation 5(2)(d)* of the *Occupational Pension Schemes (Investment of Scheme's Resources) Regulations 1992 (SI 1992/246)* applied immediately before 6 April 1997.

RPSM07105020 explains that a scheme may acquire shares of more than one sponsoring employer of the scheme provided that, at the time the payment is made, the market value of the shares is less than 20% of the total of the sums and the market value of the assets held for the purpose of the pension scheme.

The *IORPS Directive* gives exemption for schemes with fewer than 100 members.

Borrowing

5.7 Borrowing must not exceed 50% in total of the net fund value of the scheme at the date of borrowing (*FA 2004, ss 182(2), 184(2)*).

5.8 *Investment rules*

If there are multiple members' arrangements in the scheme, borrowing can be at arrangement level (*FA 2004, s 163(4)*). In the case of a money purchase scheme, the value of any funds which are providing pensions in payment must be deducted from the fund value for the purpose of the 50% test (*FA 2004, s 182(3)*).

Excessive borrowing will be deemed to be a scheme chargeable payment (*FA 2004, ss 183(2), 185(2)*) and subject to a scheme sanction charge of 40% (*FA 2004, s 240*).

Debts

5.8 Any debts between the scheme, the employer and the member must be on commercial terms. Unpaid debts will be taxed as unauthorised payments.

Third party investments

5.9 All investments, including loans to third parties described above, must be on commercial terms. They must not remove value from the fund.

Annuities

5.10 Annuities must not normally provide for a return of the balance of insurance funds on death (breaches will be taxed as unauthorised payments).

Trading income

5.11 Trading income is taxable under the self-assessment procedure. RPSM07101050 states:

> 'There are no restrictions to prevent a registered pension scheme from entering into trading activities. But as income derived from trading is not investment income or income from deposits, the tax exemptions (including those relating to capital gains on assets used by a scheme for trading purposes) do not apply. So a registered pension scheme is liable to pay tax on any income derived from a trading activity.'

BIM56930 states as follows:

> 'Pension funds
>
> There is a strong presumption that a pension fund is an investment, not a trading vehicle. This is not to say that pension funds cannot undertake activities which amount to a trade. If such an activity is clearly trading, the status of the pension fund cannot change that. But if the position is unclear, it will be necessary to investigate the purpose of the transaction to see if this was a trading one or part of the investment activities.
>
> The latter point was considered in the case of *Clarke v Trustees of British Telecom Pension scheme & others* [2000] STC 222. The point

at issue was whether commissions from sub-underwriting activities carried on by the trustees came from a separate trade. In that case it was held that they did not, because there was no intention to trade and the sub-underwriting was carried out in relation to the shareholding policy pursued by the trustees in the course of the investing activities. Thus, even though the sub-underwriting was not essential to the holding of shares, and involved different parties, it was still integrated with, and took colour from, the investing transactions.

Other types of fund

It is a question of fact whether such funds are trading or investing. As with companies and individuals, you look at all the relevant circumstances before coming to a decision. The badges of trade have limited value (see BIM56840), and the use of derivative instruments (see BIM56890) or the adoption of particular strategies (see BIM56920), are not, by themselves, decisive either, although of course they are likely to be relevant circumstances to be considered.

General guidance on funds based in the UK is in the Company Taxation Manual (CTM) and those based overseas in the Offshore Funds Manual (OFM) (available via the Collective Investment Schemes Centre page on the HMRC internet).

For offshore funds which are trading, the Investment Manager Exemption may be relevant – see INTM269000+.'

Non-commercial use of assets by a member or associate

5.12 Any non-commercial use of assets by a member or associate will attract a benefit-in-kind charge on the member.

Underwriting commissions etc

5.13 Underwriting commissions which are applied for the purposes of a scheme are not liable to income tax. Other forms of income, such as stock-lending fees, and income derived from futures and options contracts are also exempt from tax.

Property investment limited liability partnership

5.14 Income derived from investments or deposits held as a member of a property investment limited liability partnership is liable to tax.

Stock-lending fees, and income derived from futures and options

5.15 Stock-lending fees, and income derived from futures and options contracts, are exempt from tax.

5.16 *Investment rules*

Residential property

5.16 Where residential property is let, the rent could be invested in the member's scheme on a tax-free basis. It is possible that profit achieved by capital growth could also be invested in the fund without incurring capital gains tax. The property becomes an asset of the pension fund, and there is a requirement to put all rental income into the pension fund so it is locked away and cannot be accessed until authorised benefits are paid.

If the property is made available to a member of the scheme or members of their family, it will give rise to a benefit-in-kind tax charge if a market rent is not paid (even if they choose not to use it).

Borrowing to fund a property purchase cannot exceed 50% of the value of the pension arrangement. Putting any previously owned property into the pension scheme will trigger any unrealised chargeable gain on the property, and transaction costs such as stamp duty.

Disposals of assets whilst retaining the ability to use

5.17 Any disposals of assets whilst retaining the ability to use them will normally attract income tax on the retained benefit.

Liquidity

5.18 RPSM07101030 states that:

> 'when deciding the scheme's investment policy, the administrators/ trustees will need to bear carefully in mind the need to have sufficient liquid funds to pay pension benefits.'

It further says:

> 'For example, investment in land and buildings may be a good long-term investment when the members are many years from retirement but becomes less appropriate as their retirement approaches, particularly where the scheme has only one or two members. Even if the purchase of the member's, widow's/widower's or dependant's annuity is deferred, it is appropriate to ensure that the scheme is in a position to buy an annuity or provide benefits in the form of Alternatively Secured Pension without becoming involved in a forced sale of property. This is particularly so if the property purchased is an important part of the employer's own commercial premises or even the member's own residential property and thus potentially difficult to realise.'

Focus
- Certain activities are not permitted, and can incur unauthorised payment charges

Category A, B and C transactions

5.19 RPSM07102130 concerns non arm's-length transactions and connected parties. It identifies three classes of transaction, which are described below:

Category A Transactions

Any transactions between the scheme and the member or sponsoring employer.

Category B Transactions

Any transactions between the scheme and people connected with members and or connected employers. 'Connected' for this purpose means anyone who falls within the definition of *ICTA 1988, s 839* (RPSM07103180), now *CTA 2010, s 1122*.

Category C Transactions

Any transactions between the scheme and a third party, which is directly or indirectly for the benefit of a member or sponsoring employer.

Where there is a transaction between the scheme and anyone within category A, B or C, it must be made as an arm's-length bargain. If it is not an arm's-length bargain, and as a consequence value passes to the member, the difference will be taxed as an unauthorised payment (see RPSM07108010). Scheme trustees should ensure that, when a connected party transaction is being made, they take a sensible, commercial and prudent course and obtain relevant valuations from suitably qualified valuers.

Example

For example: a scheme sells an asset worth £1m to a member at a price of £500,000. There is value passed to the member of £500,000 and this amount will be taxed as an unauthorised payment.

Market value

5.20 Scheme transactions must be made at market value. It means the market value of an asset under *TCGA 1992, s 272*, and the price which those assets would reasonably be expected to fetch on a sale in the open market.

All employer transactions must be made on an arm's-length basis if they are not to be treated as unauthorised payments.

All member transactions must be conducted on a commercial basis, and member loans are prohibited. A member's business may purchase or sell assets to the member's pension scheme, provided this is done on an arm's-length basis. CGT may be payable when the asset is sold, and it is the responsibility of the member to declare the sale on his self-assessment tax return.

Value shifting

5.21 Value shifting will attract tax charges. Types of transaction which have the effect of shifting value from the scheme to a person who is, or has

5.22 Investment rules

been, a scheme member or a connected person, or to a person who is, or has been, a sponsoring employer, will be caught. Value may be shifted by either increasing the value of an asset or decreasing a liability of a scheme member or sponsoring employer without actually creating a payment.

Where value is passed from the scheme to either a member (or a person who has been a scheme member) or a sponsoring employer (or a person who has been a sponsoring employer), the amount of the value shifted out of the scheme is treated as an unauthorised payment if the amount passed is other than what can be expected on arm's-length terms. A scheme sanction charge will also be made on the scheme.

Member use of assets

5.22 *FA 2004* does not prevent a member or his family or household from using scheme assets. The disadvantage in doing this is that, if the beneficiary has use of the assets, he will be taxed on the value of the benefit in the same way as an unauthorised payment charge. This charge will be offset by any amount the member has contributed towards the asset use, such as payment of rent.

Property rental, whether in respect of properties owned by the sponsoring employer and/or the member, is permitted at commercial rates. If commercial rates are not paid, an unauthorised payment charge will be incurred.

The term 'member of family' includes:

- a member's spouse;
- a member's children and their spouses;
- a member's parents; and
- a member's dependants.

The term 'members of a household' includes:

- a member's domestic staff; and
- a member's guests.

There is a formal requirement to report member use of assets. Reports must be sent in by 17 July following the tax year in which the circumstance arose, and the benefit-in-kind will be calculated on a cash equivalent basis.

Non-income producing assets

5.23 Subject to the taxable property and tangible moveable asset provisions (see **Chapter 12**), non-income producing assets, such as works of art, may be held by a registered pension scheme if acquired on a proper commercial basis. Transactions may take place without restriction, so schemes may purchase such assets from, and sell them to, scheme members. Members may also be able to enjoy the use of the asset itself on a commercial footing. However, if an asset is deemed to be a wasting asset, an unauthorised payment charge of 40% and an additional scheme sanction charge of 15% will arise on the member.

Waivers of debt

5.24 Whenever a member debt is waived by a registered scheme, it is deemed to be a loan to the member. As such, it will be taxed as an unauthorised payment.

Wasting assets

5.25 Any scheme which invests in wasting assets will incur a scheme sanction charge on the scheme administrator. A tax charge will also be made on the member of a scheme if he receives the benefit. Wasting assets are described in *TCGA 1992, s 44*, as assets that have an anticipated life of less than 50 years. Examples of such assets are properties with less than 50-year leases, cars, racehorses, and plant and machinery.

Financial service regulation

5.26 The regulation of financial services was the responsibility of the FSA. It impacted on the investment by schemes in regulated property. The FSA was replaced in 2013 with a subsidiary prudential regulator under the Bank of England. The new regulator is comprised of two bodies, the FCA and PRA.

The Pension Regulator's defined contribution code

5.27 The Pension Regulator's DC Code of Practice 13 entitled 'Governance and administration of occupational defined contribution trust-based schemes' came into effect on 21 November 2013. It contains guidance in areas such as lifestyling and the investment of contributions, reviewing performance, changing funds and monitoring and reviewing the scheme's default strategy. A default strategy of investment should be selected automatically for a member joining the scheme, unless the member chooses to set their own strategy and chooses funds themselves from those made available by the trustees.

CHECKLIST

- The first investment restriction which was removed by revision of *FA 2004* was on residential property. By A-Day the opening up of UK registered pension schemes to investment in residential property on commercial terms had been withdrawn for schemes which were classified as IRPS
- Trust law prevails in England and Wales, and Scotland, and the EU relies on the 'prudent man' principle
- The UK removed the need for its tax-relievable pension schemes to be subject to trust law from A-Day
- The main permitted investment activities of registered pension schemes are explained

5.27 *Investment rules*

- The FSA was replaced in 2013 with a subsidiary prudential regulator under the Bank of England. The new regulator is comprised of two bodies, the FCA and the PRA
- The Pension Regulator's DC Code contains guidance in areas such as lifestyling and the investment of contributions, reviewing performance, changing funds and monitoring and reviewing the scheme's default strategy

Chapter 6

> **SIGNPOSTS**
> - Transfers may be made freely between registered pension schemes and QROPS
> - A registered pension scheme may receive a transfer from another scheme that is not a registered pension scheme (eg an EFRBS)
> - Specialist, changing, rules apply to transfers from DB schemes to DC schemes under the proposed new freedom to allow full access to DC pots
> - Transitional protection for low retirement ages or tax-free lump sums greater than 25% may be lost on a transfer-out
> - The scheme administrator must include in the HMRC Event Report any transfer to a QROPS and any transfer that is an unauthorised payment

Transfers

INTRODUCTION

6.1 The relaxation in the transfer rules under the post-6 April 2006 tax regime attracted a great deal of attention. There was a considerable widening in the rules which apply to transfers, much of which had been brought about by the impact of the *IORPS Directive* and a draft *Portability Directive*. Subsequently, the *Portability Directive* was adopted by the EC in June 2013. It requires member states to implement minimum requirements for the acquisition and preservation of pension rights for people who go to work in another EU country. The Directive is one step closer to reality after representatives from the EP and EU member states reached an agreement on some of the details of the legislation recently.

Although the EU is concerned with easing transferability of members' pension and employment rights between member states, it has been necessary to free up some of the UK transfer restrictions internally and internationally in order to achieve a level playing field. **Chapter 13** below describes the specific application of the new transfer rules where overseas schemes are concerned. In this **Chapter**, attention is given to transfers to and from UK registered pension schemes.

PERMITTED TRANSFERS

6.2 The introduction of the LTA in 2006 applied the same overall cap on tax-advantaged pension savings to both occupational pension schemes and

6.3 *Transfers*

personal pension schemes. As a result, there were no longer restrictions on the transfer of rights from one type of scheme to the other, there was no need to certify transfer amounts and lump sums, and there was no requirement to seek HMRC approval for certain transfers mainly associated with high earners. Transfers may now be made freely between the various forms of occupational and personal schemes that exist in the UK without the same restrictions that applied before A-Day, subject only to scheme rules permitting. Any certificates given before A-Day are redundant, although they would have to have been taken into account for the purpose of valuing benefits at 5 April 2006 for anyone registering for PP or EP.

However, if a transfer is made from a registered pension scheme that does not meet the definition of a 'recognised transfer' in *FA 2004, s 169*, it will be an unauthorised payment and subject to the range of unauthorised payment charges (see **Chapter 15** below). A recognised transfer is defined in *FA 2004, s 169* as:

> 'a transfer of sums or assets held for the purposes of, or representing accrued rights under, a registered pension scheme so as to become held for the purposes of, or to represent rights under another registered pension scheme or a qualifying recognised overseas pension scheme, in connection with a member of that pension scheme.'

The unauthorised payment charges may be disapplied if the scheme administrator made the transfer in good faith and based on false or incorrect information from the member.

There is no prohibition on a registered pension scheme receiving a transfer from a non-registered scheme.

TRANSFERS BETWEEN REGISTERED PENSION SCHEMES

6.3 A transfer from one registered pension scheme to another registered pension scheme is a recognised transfer. No tax charges or sanctions apply to recognised transfers. However, transfers must be made directly between the schemes concerned; funds should not be routed through intermediaries. Where the receiving scheme is an insured scheme but the transfer value is not paid directly to the scheme administrator or insurance company, the transferring scheme administrator will be liable to a penalty of up to £3,000.

A recognised transfer from one registered pension scheme to another is not a BCE and therefore not subject to the LTA. A recognised transfer from a registered pension scheme to a QROPS, however, *is* a BCE, and the transfer value must be tested against the member's LTA. If the transfer value exceeds the available LTA, it is subject to a tax charge of 25%.

A recognised transfer is not a contribution, and no tax relief is due in respect of the transfer.

The making of transfer payments has implications when assessing the value of a member's rights against his AA. If benefits are transferred from a DB arrangement, the amount of annual pension transferred is added back in the member's closing value at the end of the input period. If a transfer is received by a DB arrangement, the annual pension transferred in is excluded from the member's closing value at the end of the input period. In a DC arrangement, only the contributions paid are tested against the AA, and a transfer should therefore have no effect with regard to the AA.

Transfers may be made in cash, *in specie* or as a combination, subject only to the rules of the schemes concerned. Sums and assets transferred should represent the full value of the member rights being transferred.

A recognised transfer can be made from a registered pension scheme to a deferred annuity contract, as the deferred annuity contract is automatically treated as a registered pension scheme. The assignment of an annuity policy which does not provide for immediate payment of benefits is also a recognised transfer.

Partial transfers were not normally permitted under the pre A-Day tax rules. This is no longer a problem, and partial transfers may now be made in respect of members' uncrystallised rights. This is subject to scheme rules permitting. Pension practices and arrangements, especially DC arrangements, may therefore now be designed with this flexibility in mind. It is possible to transfer only part of a pension fund to another arrangement for the purpose of providing an income, while the original fund continues to remain invested and receive contributions.

Specialist rules apply to transfers from DB schemes to DC schemes under the proposed new freedom to allow full access to DC pots. The latest developments are described in **4.14** above.

Where a pension scheme contains rights that relate to contracting out of the additional state pension, DWP legislation imposes some further conditions on the transfer. However, contracting out on a DC basis (to produce funds known as 'protected rights') was discontinued on 6 April 2012, and all protected rights funds now treated as ordinary DC rights. The tax regime's ease of transferability has therefore been extended to those pension funds that were formerly protected rights.

Focus
- Transfers to non-registered pension schemes, other than QROPS, are not recognised and will be treated as unauthorised payments

TRANSFERS FROM REGISTERED PENSION SCHEMES TO NON-REGISTERED SCHEMES

6.4 A transfer from a registered pension scheme to a UK scheme that is not a registered pension scheme is not a recognised transfer. An unauthorised payment charge of 40% of the payment will be levied on the member. A 15% unauthorised payment surcharge will also be levied on the member if

6.5 *Transfers*

the transfer payment (together with any other unauthorised payments in the previous 12 months) exceeds 25% of the member's rights.

The scheme administrator will be liable for a scheme sanction charge of 40% of the payment, although this is reduced to 25% where the member has paid the unauthorised payment charge. If amounts transferred are 25% or more of the funds held in the scheme, HMRC may deregister the scheme, and a 40% deregistration charge would become payable.

Note that the amount transferred is not included in the member's closing value at the end of an input period for the purpose of the AA.

The transfer is not a BCE and therefore will not be taken into account against the member's LTA.

TRANSFERS FROM NON-REGISTERED SCHEMES TO REGISTERED PENSION SCHEMES

6.5 There is no prohibition on a registered pension scheme receiving a transfer payment from another UK scheme that is not a registered pension scheme (eg an EFRBS).

The transfer payment would not count against the AA, and it would benefit from the tax-advantaged investment environment of a registered pension scheme. However, it would be subject to the LTA once it was brought into payment from the registered pension scheme.

Such a transfer payment will not be treated as a contribution, and no tax relief will be available on the payment. It should therefore be questioned whether such a transfer is the best course of action, or whether the benefits from the non-registered scheme should be drawn first and then paid to a registered pension scheme as a contribution (assuming the member has enough earned income to obtain full tax relief on the contribution).

A registered pension scheme may receive a transfer from an OPS. Where this is from a ROPS the member may receive an uplift to his LTA to reflect the value of any rights transferred in that have not benefited from UK tax relief.

LOSS OF PROTECTION

6.6 Members of registered pension schemes who benefit from transitional protection for low retirement ages or tax-free lump sums greater than 25% or £375,000 can lose these protections if they transfer their rights in certain circumstances:

Low retirement ages. RPSM03106070 states that protection will be retained where a member with a protected pension age becomes a member of another registered pension scheme or a QROPS as a result of a block transfer. This applies to both uncrystallised and crystallised rights. If a transfer is not a block transfer there will be no protected pension age under the receiving scheme. The meaning of 'block transfer' is explained in *RPSM03106070*.

Tax-free lump sums greater than 25% or £375,000. Lump sum protections can be lost in similar circumstances on transfer. RPSM03105521 and RPSM03201040 respectively provide relevant guidance.

TRANSFER OF RIGHTS IN PAYMENT

6.7 A transfer of pension rights, once they had come into payment, was not generally possible under the pre A-Day tax rules. Under the post A-Day rules, a transfer of crystallised rights is possible.

A scheme pension, once it has started to be paid, may be transferred to another arrangement and will be a recognised transfer as long as it takes the same form and is paid at the same level in the receiving arrangement (although reasonable administrative costs relating to the transfer may be deducted). The scheme pension under the receiving arrangement will be treated as if it were still payable under the transferring arrangement. It will not therefore be treated as a BCE, and any guarantee will run from the original start date.

A lifetime annuity, once it has come into payment, may be transferred from one insurance company to another. The transferred annuity would be treated as a continuation of the original annuity and would not be a BCE. Any annuity protection lump sum death benefit must be by reference to the original annuity.

The *Registered Pension Schemes (Transfer of Sums and Assets) (Amendment) Regulations (SI 2014/1449)* came into force on 1 July 2014. They clarify that where a pension already in payment at A-Day is transferred to a new scheme pension on or after 6 April 2014, but prior to the scheme member's first LTA charge valuation or BCE, the new scheme pension is to be treated as if it were the original pre-A-Day pension.

Where a member or dependant is in receipt of drawdown, he may transfer his drawdown fund to another arrangement set up for the purpose of the transfer. A partial transfer is not possible. All the sums and assets relating to his drawdown fund must be transferred to the new arrangement, and the receiving scheme must not mix the transferred rights with other rights of the member existing at that time. The administrator of the receiving scheme must be provided with the necessary information relating to review periods etc to enable him to administer the drawdown fund as if it were still administered in the ceding arrangement.

MUST A SCHEME RECEIVE A TRANSFER?

6.8 It is not compulsory for the trustees or managers of a scheme to receive an incoming transfer unless its rules so provide. The one exception to this was stakeholder pension schemes, which had to accept transfers-in at the request of a member.

REPORTING TO HMRC

6.9 The scheme administrator of a registered pension scheme must include in the HMRC Event Report any transfer to a QROPS and any transfer

6.10 *Transfers*

that is an unauthorised payment. Event Reports must be received by HMRC by 31 January following the end of the tax year in which the transfer took place. New rules for reporting QROPS transfers are described in **Chapter 13** below.

If a scheme administrator is requested to complete a pension scheme return by HMRC, they would have to report amounts transferred to other pension schemes in the tax year and transfer amounts received from other pension schemes. The scheme return must be received by HMRC by 31 January following the tax year to which it relates.

HMRC RESPONSE TIME TO A REQUEST FOR CONFIRMATION OF STATUS OF RECEIVING SCHEME

6.10 HMRC states at *http://www.hmrc.gov.uk/news/pensionliberation.htm?WT.ac=PENSIONSCHEMES_TACKLIB* as follows:

> 'To help scheme administrators decide whether to make a transfer, HMRC has revised the process for responding to requests for confirmation of the registration status of the receiving scheme. Under this new process HMRC will respond to requests for confirmation of the registration status without seeking consent from the receiving scheme. However HMRC will only provide confirmation where the receiving scheme is registered and the information held by HMRC does not indicate a significant risk that the scheme was set up, or is being used, to facilitate pension liberation. Otherwise, a response will be issued setting out the conditions in which HMRC will confirm registration status and explain that one or both of the conditions are not satisfied.'

CHECKLIST

- There was a considerable widening in the rules which apply to transfers, much of which had been brought about by the impact of the *IORPS Directive* and a draft *Portability Directive*
- The *Portability Directive* was adopted by the EC in June 2013
- Transfers may be made freely between the various forms of occupational and personal schemes that exist in the UK, and QROPS
- A transfer from a registered pension scheme to a UK scheme that is not a registered pension scheme is not a recognised transfer and penal charges can be incurred
- There is no prohibition on a registered pension scheme receiving a transfer payment from another UK scheme that is not a registered pension scheme (eg an EFRBS)
- Specialist rules apply to transfers from DB schemes to DC schemes under the proposed new freedom to allow full access to DC pots

Transfers **6.10**

- Members of registered pension schemes who benefit from transitional protection for low retirement ages or tax-free lump sums greater than 25% lose these protections if they transfer their rights to another pension scheme A scheme pension, once it has started to be paid, may be transferred to another arrangement and will be a recognised transfer as long as it takes the same form and is paid at the same level in the receiving arrangement

- A lifetime annuity, once it has come into payment, may be transferred from one insurance company to another. It would be treated as a continuation of the original annuity

- It is not compulsory for the trustees or managers of a scheme to receive an incoming transfer unless its rules so provide

- The scheme administrator must include in the HMRC Event Report any transfer to a QROPS and any transfer that is an unauthorised payment

- HMRC's may be sent a request to confirm the status of a pension scheme

Chapter 7

> **SIGNPOSTS**
> - The reporting rules have been greatly extended, and are largely broadened to encompass QROPS
> - Event Reports and accounting for tax returns must be submitted to HMRC
> - Most information must be submitted online
> - The self-assessment tax return (SA970) normally is no longer required
> - EFRBS must submit reports from time to time
> - Appeals may be made against any tax charges or penalties incurred

Reporting rules

INTRODUCTION

7.1 The pre A-Day reporting requirements underwent significant change as from A-Day. The *Registered Pension Schemes (Provision of Information) Regulations 2006 (SI 2006/567)* introduced the reporting service on HMRC's Pension Schemes Online (see the *Registered Pension Schemes and Overseas Pension Schemes (Electronic Communication of Returns and Information) Regulations 2006 (SI 2006/570)*, as amended). HMRC's Pensions Newsletter 63 dated July 2014 (at *http://www.hmrc.gov.uk/pensionschemes/newsletter63.pdf*) provides an update on the conversion of HMRC forms to i-forms. The main information requirements under *FA 2004* are contained in *s 251* under the heading 'General requirements'. This section also empowers HMRC to make regulations requiring persons of a prescribed description to provide information to HMRC. The regulation-making power extends to requirements to give information to other parties. These powers have since been greatly extended, as described under the remaining headings in this **Chapter.**

Section 252 states that HMRC may issue notices requiring persons to produce information to HMRC, to be available for inspections in respect of any documentation required by HMRC, and to provide such other information as they deem appropriate.

Any notices issued under *s 252* will specify the compliance period. The period may not end earlier than 30 days beginning with the day on which the notice is given. Both *ss 251* and *252* extend to EFRBS (see **Chapter 11** and **Chapter 15** below for more information). The main penalties remain in place if the information requirements are not met. The normal range of penalties begins at £300, with an additional £60 per day for any continuing failure to comply. However, where fraud or negligence relates to tax returns, transfer payments, statements, declarations and information provision, fines of up to £3,000 per event may be levied. The penalty provisions are described in greater detail in **Chapter 15** below.

A right to appeal against notices is contained in *s 253* of the *Act* (see **7.20** below for the latest procedures that apply).

The main governing legislation

7.2 The rules under *SI 2006/567* have been subject to many extensions and amendments since their inception. Under *FA 2008, Sch 36*, HMRC was given extensive powers to request information and documents. The information can be requested from a taxpayer or third party for the purpose of checking a taxpayer's tax position. HMRC can also require information from a third party for the purpose of checking another person's tax position where that person's identity is not known.

The later changes to legislation and practice are described below:

- The *Registered Pension Schemes (Provision of Information)(Amendment) Regulations 2011 (SI 2011/301)* amended *SI 2006/567* and changed the information which the scheme administrator of a registered pension scheme is required to report to HMRC in respect of certain events.

- The *Registered Pension Schemes (Provision of Information) (Amendment) Regulations 2013 (SI 2013/1742)* further amended *SI 2006/567* and reflected the changes made by *FA 2013* (see **1.4** above).

- The following is a summary of the main extended information requirements under the foregoing *Regulations*:

    - As from 6 April 2011, only the member's NI number is required for most reports (previously, the date of birth, address and NI number had to be provided)

    - In respect of unauthorised payments, if the person is neither an individual nor a company, the scheme administrator must obtain a number from HMRC and provide it in the Event Report.

    - Sponsoring employers must supply the scheme administrator with the information required to calculate the pension input amount relating to an employee or director for a tax year by 6 July following the end of that tax year.

- The scheme administrator must provide HMRC with additional information, including the reference number issued by HMRC under the *Registered Pension Schemes and Relieved Non-UK Pension Schemes (Lifetime Allowance Transitional Protection) (Notification) Regulations 2013 (S.I. 2013/1741)*).

- Scheme administrators must provide HMRC with additional information where there is a recognised transfer to a QROPS.

7.2 Reporting rules

- The member of a registered pension scheme must give additional information to the scheme administrator when they make a request for a recognised transfer.

The *Registered Pension Schemes and Overseas Pension Schemes (Miscellaneous Amendments) Regulations 2013 (SI 2013/2259)* have further amended the above information requirements. There is transitional provision for the scheme administrator and member to provide information in relation to transfers from registered pension schemes to QROPS which were in existence immediately before 6 April 2012 if they would have ceased to meet the necessary conditions for QROPS status as at 6 April 2012 (see the *Registered Pensions Schemes and Overseas Pension Schemes (Miscellaneous Amendments) Regulations 2012 (SI 2012/884)* and **Chapter 13** below.

Where the transfer request made by the member to the scheme administrator in respect of the transfer or the transfer itself took place on or after 6 April 2102 but before 14 October 2013, the time limits for the delivery of information from the scheme administrator to HMRC and from the member to the scheme administrator were extended.

FA 2014, Sch 7, greatly increased HMRC's powers in the following areas:

- applications for registration;
- power to inspect documents in relation to applications for registration;
- penalties for failure to comply with information notices etc;
- penalties for inaccurate information in applications;
- penalties for inaccurate information or documents provided under information notice;
- penalties for false declarations;
- de-registration process;
- HMRC power to require information or documents for purpose of considering if scheme administrator is fit and proper;
- HMRC power to inspect documents for purpose of considering if scheme administrator is fit and proper;
- penalties for failure to comply with information notices etc;
- penalties for inaccurate information or documents provided under information notice.

The following sub-headings set out the reporting duties of each party involved with a registered pension scheme and the person to whom information must be given.

Focus
- The scheme administrator is largely responsible for making reports to HMRC and other persons

---

EVENT REPORTS

Scheme administrator to HMRC

7.3 The scheme administrator must report as follows:

- Where scheme rules are changed to:
    - (a) entitle any person to require the making of unauthorised payments; or
    - (b) permit investment other than in policies of insurance.
- A change in scheme rules where the scheme was treated immediately before 6 April 2006 as two or more separate schemes within *ICTA 1988, s 611*.
- Where the legal structure of the scheme changes from one of the following categories to another:
    - (a) a single trust under which all of the assets are held for the benefit of all members of the scheme;
    - (b) an overall trust within which there are individual trusts applying for the benefit of each member;
    - (c) an overall trust within which specific assets are held as, or within, sub-funds for each member;
    - (d) an annuity contract;
    - (e) a body corporate.
- Membership movements – where the number of scheme members falls in a different band at the end of a tax year from that in which it fell at the end of the previous tax year. The bands are:
    - 0
    - 1–10
    - 11–50
    - 51–10,000
    - 10,000 plus.
- This applies to total membership of a scheme.
- A BCE in relation to a member where:
    - (a) the amount crystallised exceeds the standard LTA, or exceeds the standard LTA when taken with other crystallised amounts; and
    - (b) the member relies on enhanced protection, FP 2012 or FP 2014.
- Payment of a lump sum death benefit payment which, either alone or together with other lump sum death benefits from the scheme, is more than 50% of the standard LTA.

7.3 Reporting rules

- Payment of benefits to a member who is under normal minimum pension age (55 from 6 April 2010) where the member was at that time or within the previous six years:

    (a) a director or a person connected with a director in relation to the sponsoring employer or an associated company;

    (b) the sponsoring employer, whether alone or with others; or

    (c) a person connected with the sponsoring employer.

- A change in the country or territory in which the scheme is established.
- Payment of a lump sum death benefit in respect of a member aged 75 or over (see the changed rules in **Chapter 4** above).
- Payment of pension commencement lump sum which, when added to the crystallised amount, exceeds 25% of the total, and which is more than 7.5%, but less than 25%, of the current standard LTA.
- Payment of a pension commencement lump sum where the member has primary or enhanced protection, FP 2012, FP 2014 or IP 2014 and the lump sum exceeds 25% of the standard LTA.
- Payment of a serious ill-health lump sum to a member who is (or was in the previous six years):

    (a) a director or a person connected with a director of the sponsoring employer or an associated company;

    (b) the sponsoring employer, whether alone or with others; or

    (c) a person connected with the sponsoring employer.

- Suspension of an ill-health pension.
- Transfers to QROPS, including wwhere the transfer was requested before 6 April 2012.
- Unauthorised member or employer payments.
- On acquiring or losing IRPS status.
- On making a scheme chargeable payment (income or gains from taxable property).
- Payment of a stand-alone lump sum greater than 7.5% of the standard LTA or where the member has PP or EP, FP 2012, FP 2014 or IP 2014 and lump sum rights exceeded £375,000 on 5 April 2006.
- Scheme becomes or ceases to be an occupational pension scheme.
- Termination of scheme administrator appointment.
- Scheme wind-up (three-month notification period).
- Making changes to the rules of pre A-Day 'split scheme' rules;
- A transfer of a lump sum death benefit;

- Attaining or losing the status of an occupational pension scheme.
- Either a member or dependant moving into flexible drawdown – 2012–13 onwards.

Scheme administrator to member

7.4 The scheme administrator must report the following information to scheme members:

- On a BCE, the level of LTA used up.
- To each member:
    (a) to whom a pension is being paid, at least once in each tax year; or
    (b) in respect of whom a BCE has occurred, within three months of that event,
- a statement of the cumulative total percentage of the LTA crystallised, at the date of statement, by the events in respect of the scheme and any other scheme from which that scheme has received a transfer payment.
- Where a scheme has made an unauthorised payment to a member, before 7 July following the tax year in which the event took place, the following information:
    (a) the nature of the benefit provided;
    (b) the amount of the unauthorised payment which is being treated as being made by the provision of the benefit; and
    (c) the date on which the benefit was provided.
- Where the scheme administrator makes a payment on account of his liability to pay for the LTA charge, within three months of the BCE, details of:
    (a) the chargeable amount on which the charge arises;
    (b) how the chargeable amount is calculated;
    (c) the amount of the tax charge; and
    (d) whether he has accounted for the tax or intends to do so.
- Where a member's pension input amount in the scheme has exceeded the AA, the Scheme administrator must supply the member with a pension savings statement (see **3.15**).

Member to Scheme administrator

7.5 If EP, PP, FP 2012, FP 2014 or IP 2014 is to apply, the member must report to the scheme administrator the protection certificate reference number given by HMRC.

Scheme administrator to scheme administrator

7.6 If part or all of a member's pension rights are transferred from one scheme to another (scheme A to scheme B), the scheme administrator of scheme A must provide to the scheme administrator of scheme B, within three months of the transfer, a cumulative total percentage of the standard LTA crystallised by the event in respect of scheme A and any scheme from which that scheme has received (directly or indirectly) a transfer payment.

Scheme administrator to personal representatives

7.7 On the death of a member, the scheme administrator must report to the personal representatives:

- The percentage of the standard LTA crystallised by, and the amount and date of payment of, a defined benefit or uncrystallised funds lump sum death benefit paid by the scheme in relation to the member (no later than the last day of the period of three months beginning with the day on which the final such payment was made).

- The cumulative total percentage crystallised by BCE's in respect of the deceased member under the scheme or any schemes from which assets have been transferred (whether directly or indirectly), in respect of the deceased member's pension rights, but excluding any amount in respect of lump sum death benefit in respect of the deceased member. The information must be provided no later than the last day of the period of two months beginning with the day on which a request is received from the member's personal representatives.

Scheme administrator of annuities in payment – provided to and by scheme administrator, insurance company and annuitant

7.8 If, on the crystallisation of a member's pension rights, an insurance company receives funds to provide (whether from a secured or unsecured pension) a scheme pension or lifetime annuity, the scheme administrator must, within three months of annuity purchase, provide the insurance company with details of the percentage of the standard LTA crystallised both before and after such a purchase.

At least annually, the insurance company must provide the annuitant with a statement of the percentage of the standard LTA crystallised at the date of the statement in respect of the annuity.

Employer company

7.9 If an unauthorised employer payment is made to a company, that company must provide the following information to HMRC:

(a) details of the scheme that made the payment;

(b) the nature of the payment;

(c) the amount of the payment; and

(d) the date on which the payment was made.

The information must be provided to HMRC no later than 31 January following the tax year in which the payment was made.

Insurance company etc to personal representatives on death

7.10 Where an insurance company or similar provider has paid an annuity from the assets of the scheme and the person concerned has died, the provider must, on request, provide the following information to the personal representatives within two months of the request:

(a) the date the annuity was purchased; and

(b) the amount crystallised as a percentage of the standard LTA.

Personal representatives to HMRC

7.11 Where a DB or uncrystallised funds lump sum death benefit is paid which, either alone or when aggregated with other similar payments, results in a LTA charge, the following information must be provided within 13 months of the death of the member, or 30 days from the date the personal representatives became aware of the event giving rise to the charge:

(a) the name of the scheme and the name and address of the administrator;

(b) the name of the deceased member;

(c) the amount and date of the payment; and

(d) the chargeable amount on which the charge arises.

If a requirement to report arises after expiration of the above period, the information must be provided within 30 months of the death of the member. On the discovery of further information after the expiry of such a period, a report must be made within three months of discovery.

RECORD KEEPING

7.12 The general rule is that all records which are held by administrators, trustees, advisers, employers or directors must be kept for a period of at least six years.

Accounting for tax reports

7.13 The accounting for tax return APSS302 (AFT), which replaced Forms 1(SF) and 2(SF) in their entirety, must be submitted to HMRC covering:

7.14 *Reporting rules*

(a) LTA charges,
(b) tax due on lump sums repaid,
(c) taxable death benefits,
(d) taxable refunds of surpluses, and
(e) de-registration charges.

The return must be made on a quarterly basis and must be provided within 45 days of the relevant quarter end. The due dates are:

- for tax charged in the period ending with 31 March, no later than 15 May;
- for tax charged in the period ending with 30 June, no later than 14 August;
- for tax charged in the period ending with 30 September, no later than 14 November; and
- for tax charged in the period ending with 31 December, no later than 14 February.

Registered pension scheme return

7.14 Under *FA 2004, s 250*, HMRC may give notice to the scheme administrator of a registered pension scheme that it requires a registered pension scheme return to be completed. The information required by the return is as follows:

- contributions made under the scheme;
- transfers of monies or assets representing accrued rights;
- income and gains from investments or deposits held by the scheme;
- other receipts of the scheme;
- sums and other assets held for the purposes of the scheme;
- the scheme's liabilities:
- provision of benefits by the scheme;
- other expenditure of the scheme;
- membership of the scheme; and
- any other matter relating to administration of the scheme.

The normal timescale for submission applies, being 31 January following the relevant tax year (or three months after any notice which is given after 31 October in the relevant tax year, or three months from the completion of the winding up of a scheme which wound up before that date).

There are two different versions of the return, one for occupational schemes and the other for non-occupational schemes.

Focus
- The online reporting forms are listed

Online registration and reporting

7.15 Not all reports of information come under the mandatory HMRC e-filing protocol (see **2.5** above, which also Includes a list of the online registration and notification forms).

The following table sets out the further information which must be submitted online.

Form number	Description
AAG1	Disclosure of avoidance scheme
AAG2	Notification by scheme user where offshore promoter does not notify HMRC
AAG3	Notification by scheme user where there is no promoter, or the scheme is promoted by lawyer unable to make full notification
AAG4	Disclosure of avoidance scheme. (Notification of scheme reference number by scheme user)
AAG5	Continuation form
AAG6	A form for providing scheme reference numbers to users of notifiable Stamp Duty Land Tax arrangements
APSS 146	Registered Pension Scheme Registration for Income Tax Repayments
APSS 146A	Registered Pension Scheme Repayments Third Party Authority
APSS 146B	Registered Pension Scheme Repayments Specimen Signatures
APSS 150	Authorising and de-authorising a practitioner
APSS 151	Add Scheme Administrator for second and subsequent notifications of pre A day Scheme Administrators or for any post A day Scheme Administrators
APSS 151	Add Scheme Administrator for first notifications of Pre A day Scheme Administrators – to be completed online
APSS 152	Amend Scheme Details
APSS 153	Change of Scheme Administrator/Practitioner user details
APSS 154	Associate Scheme Administrator to Scheme
APSS 155	Election to vary a Contracting out or Appropriate Scheme Certificate
APSS 155A	Election to vary a Contracting out or Appropriate Scheme Certificate
APSS 155B	Election to surrender/Request to cancel a contracting-out or appropriate scheme certificate

7.15 Reporting rules

Form number	Description
APSS 160	Cessation of Scheme Administrator
APSS 161	Pre-register as a Scheme Administrator/Practitioner
PS 199	Scheme Wind-Up pre A day
APSS 200	Protection of Existing Rights
APSS 201	Enhanced Lifetime Allowance (Pension Credit Rights)
APSS 202	Enhanced Lifetime Allowance (International)
APSS 203	To authorise HMRC to allow scheme administrators to view lifetime allowance certificates
APSS 209	Request by Scheme Administrator for Lifetime Allowance Certificate Details
APSS 227	Fixed protection
APSS 250	QOPS notification
APSS 251	QROPS/ROPS notification
APSS 251A	QROPS – Change of details
APSS 251B	QROPS – Change in status and notification of fund value
APSS 252	Report of BCE's
APSS 252 (Insert)	Supplementary page for relevant migrant members
APSS 253	Payments in respect of Relevant Members
APSS 253 (Insert)	Supplementary page for APSS 253
APSS 254	Election for deemed BCE on event
APSS 254 Notes	Election for a deemed BCE Completion notes
APSS 262	Transferring UK tax-relieved assets to a QROPS (amended due to *SI 2013/1742* – the new regulations for recognised transfers apply to transfer requests made by the member from 12 August 2013)
APSS 263	Member information
APSS 300	Event Report (and supplementary pages)
APSS 300A	Amendment to registered pension scheme event report for 2006/07 or 2007/08
APSS 300B	Amendment to registered pension scheme event report for 2008/09 onwards
APSS 301	Registered Pension Scheme Return for Occupational Pension Schemes
APSS 301 Notes	Amendment to information declared on the original occupational pension scheme return – Guidance notes

Form number	Description
APSS 302	Accounting for Tax by Scheme Administrator
APSS 313	Amendment to a Registered Pension Scheme Return for Non-Occupational Pension Schemes
APSS 315	Form to complete to report the value of payments to an individual in tax year ending 5 April 2012 from a flexible drawdown pension. For later tax years, payments must be reported on the online Event Report
APSS 413	Notice of Appeal and Application to Postpone Payment
PS 199	Scheme Wind-Up pre-A Day
R63N	Tax Claim for Exempt Approved Retirement Benefit Schemes
SA970	Tax Return for Trustees of Registered Pension Schemes
SA 975	Guide to completing the tax return for trustees of an approved self-administered pension scheme.

Accounting and auditing requirements

7.16 The following regulations govern the required accounting and auditing actions for registered pension schemes:

- the *Registered Pension Scheme (Accounting and Assessment) Regulations 2005 (SI 2005/3454)*; and

- the *Registered Pension Scheme (Audited Accounts) (Specified Persons) Regulations 2005 (SI 2005/3456)*.

SELF-ASSESSMENT

Pension schemes

7.17 Since 6 April 2007, pension schemes have only been issued with a self-assessment tax return (form SA970) if they have previously been liable to tax or if a repayment of tax has been claimed. For most registered pension schemes, a self-assessment tax return is therefore no longer necessary. The SA970 can be filed in paper form. Form SA975 provides a guide to completing the tax return for trustees of an approved self-administered pension scheme.

The SA970 self-assessment return is not to be confused with the pension scheme return, which may be requested by HMRC in addition.

Members

7.18 Members of registered pension schemes may need to complete self-assessment tax returns if they receive interest on short service refund lump

7.19 *Reporting rules*

sums. If they do not receive a notice to make a return, they should inform HMRC of chargeability.

Self-assessment tax returns cover any member liability to the AA charge. Self-assessment returns should also be used for any unauthorised member payments.

REPORTING EMPLOYER-FINANCED RETIREMENT BENEFIT SCHEMES

7.19 The *Employer-Financed Retirement Benefits Schemes (Provision of Information) Regulations 2005 (SI 2005/3453)* state that the term 'responsible person' has the same meaning as in *ITEPA 2003, s 399A*.

The information requirements run on a year of assessment basis, being a year beginning 6 April in any year and ending the following 5 April. The *Regulations* state that the responsible person is the prescribed person for the purpose of their requirements. The main requirement is that the responsible person must notify HMRC before 31 January following the year of assessment after the coming into existence of the EFRBS.

The responsible person is also responsible for providing details of the relevant benefits which have been paid during the year of assessment (with certain exceptions which are otherwise chargeable to tax). The information required is:

(a) the name, address and NI number of the recipient of the relevant benefit;

(b) the nature of the relevant benefit provided; and

(c) the amount of the relevant benefit calculated in accordance with *ITEPA 2003, s 398(2)*.

The information must be provided no later than 7 July following the end of the year of assessment in which the benefit was provided.

Appealing against a decision

7.20 Appeals may be made against any tax charges or penalties incurred for a failure to meet the reporting standards above, or for any of the charges described in **Chapter 15** below. However, the General Commissioners and the Special Commissioners were both abolished with effect from 31 March 2009. They were replaced with effect from 1 April 2009 by a single Tribunal (see *EA 2007* and the *Transfer of Tribunal Functions and Revenue and Customs Appeals Order 2009 (SI 2009/56)*).

Tax appeals in the First-tier Tribunal are allocated to one of four procedural tracks according to their ascending order of complexity and value. The Upper Tribunal principally replaced the Chancery Division of the High Court for tax appeals. The Upper Tribunal can hear complex cases of sufficient value transferred from the First-tier Tribunal. Appeals against a First-tier or Upper Tribunal decision go on to the Court of Appeal. So, on the pensions front, all appeals made against HMRC's tax charges, adverse decisions etc go to the Tribunal. Appeals pending before 31 March 2009 also go to the Tribunal.

Appeals are normally to be made within 30 days of the relevant event. The events include appeals:

- against a failure to register a scheme;
- against an action to de-register a scheme;
- against a decision to exclude a recognised overseas pension scheme;
- against notices requiring documents or particulars; and
- in respect of the discharge of the LTA charge.

There is also is a statutory option, to be exercised within 30 days from the date the decision was issued, to call for an appealable decision to be reviewed by HMRC. The following process will then apply:

- to settle the matter by agreement with the officer who made the decision; or
- to opt for a HMRC review of the decision (either by accepting an offer of review from HMRC, or by requesting it directly); or
- to notify the appeal to the tribunal in writing.

If the person chooses the second option above, they will still be able to take their case to the Tribunal once the review has been completed. If they receive a review offer, it is important that they either accept the review offer or notify the Tribunal of the appeal within the 30 day time limit or their appeal will be treated as settled (subject to the Tribunal accepting a late appeal or HMRC accepting a late review acceptance).

Exoneration/discharge from liability

7.21 There may be cases where scheme administrators have been provided with false information by scheme members, for example in connection with the LTA. Scheme administrators can ask HMRC for a discharge under *FA 2004, s 267*, from the LTA charge if they think that it is fair and reasonable to do so. This may also apply where the unauthorised payment or scheme sanction charges have been incurred.

Payments made in error

7.22 It is necessary to report any payments made in error to HMRC. However, *Regulation 13* of the *Registered Pension Schemes (Authorised Payments) Regulations 2009 (SI 2009/1171)* provides some protection from charge in justifiable cases of genuine error. The *Regulations* apply to a payment which is had been intended to represent a payment permitted by the pension rules or the pension death benefit rules to or in respect of a member, where the scheme administrator or insurance company making the payment (in either case), believed that:

7.22 *Reporting rules*

(a) the recipient was entitled to the payment; and

(b) the recipient was entitled to it in that amount.

Further information can be found in RPSM09108010. Details of this potentially important facility are given below:

- The *Regulations* can apply to payments of both a member's pension as well as to payments of a dependant's pension.
- They enable payments that are made in circumstances involving both error and good faith to stand undisturbed by the unauthorised payment charges that would otherwise apply.
- The relevant payments will normally take the form of over-payments of benefits, although the regulations can have wider effect.
- Reports of overpayment of pension will need to satisfy the following conditions:
  - the payment was genuinely intended to represent the payment of a pension permitted by the pension rules or the pension death benefit rules, as appropriate, and
  - the payer believed that the recipient was entitled to the payment, and
  - the payer believed that the recipient was entitled to the amount of the payment that was paid in error:

  but if however the error related to the recipient having died, (e.g. overpayment due to not having been aware of the death), the above does not apply by virtue of RPSM09108020.
- Where an error is discovered before a payment was made, the payment may still qualify as an authorised payment, subject to the following two possibilities:
  - The first is where the payment in error is actually a further pension payment made after payment(s) made under *Regulation 13*. Those earlier payment(s) must have been of a similar nature to this one, been paid to the same recipient and been provided in similar circumstances (apart from the fact the error has now been discovered);
  - The second applies where there was no earlier payment error under *Regulation 13*. It only applies to cases where the payment(s) would have been covered by *Regulation 13* if the error had not yet been discovered.
- If a payment comes within one of the above two possibilities, then it must meet one or more of the following conditions to be an authorised payment. The conditions are that:
  - the payer took reasonable steps to prevent the error-payment being made, or being made in that amount; or
  - the payment is made while the scheme administrator is taking a reasonable amount of time to consider whether to change the rules of the scheme, so that such extra payments would in future be normal authorised payments under the tax rules, or

- the payment is made while the scheme administrator is taking a reasonable amount of time to change the rules of the scheme, so that such extra payments will in future be normal authorised payments under the tax rules.

It may be necessary for the scheme administrator to issue a revised statement to the member showing the amount of LTA used up by reference to the amount of pension to which the member was actually entitled where a statement had been issued by reference to the over-paid pension.

The above *Regulations* were amended by the *Registered Pension Schemes (Authorised Payments) (Amendment) Regulations 2013 (SI 2013/1818)* to accommodate the abolition of contracting out in relation to DC pension schemes from 6 April 2012.

Focus
- There are new, consolidated, disclosure rules

Replacement disclosure regulations

7.23 The disclosure requirements which applied to occupational pension schemes and personal pension schemes have also been of great complexity. They have been somewhat simplified by the DWP's revised rules which encompass both forms of pension provision. The *Regulations* are the *Occupational and Personal Pension Schemes (Disclosure of Information) Regulations 2013 (SI 2013/2734)*, which had effect from 6 April 2014. It is important that scheme administrators and advisers comply with the new rules which are, in brief, described below:

- There must be automatic provision of basic information:
- Basic information includes (where appropriate):
  - lifestyling;
  - statutory money purchase illustrations;
  - retirement and death benefits;
  - changes to benefits in payment;
  - changes to scheme information;
  - scheme modifications made by the Pensions Regulator;
  - a summary of the funding statement;
  - automatic enrolment information; and
  - winding-up rules.
- Other information must be made available on request, including:
  - scheme documentation;
  - employer details;
  - annual reports and accounts;

7.24 Reporting rules

- defined benefit funding principles;
- winding-up procedures;
- transfer information; and
- a statement of non-money purchase benefits.

TAX AVOIDANCE

7.24 Tax avoidance is described in **Chapter 15** below. Tax avoidance by a registered pension scheme must be reported. The relevant forms are listed in **7.15** above. Where the disclosure is made by the promoter, the scheme administrator must include the reference number allocated by HMRC in the tax return for the pension scheme for the year in which the tax advantage arises.

CHECKLIST

- The *Registered Pension Schemes (Provision of Information) Regulations 2006 (SI 2006/567)*, as amended, introduced the reporting service
- The *Registered Pension Schemes and Overseas Pension Schemes (Electronic Communication of Returns and Information) Regulations 2006 (SI 2006/570)*, as amended, apply to online submissions.
- There are numerous Event Reports which must be complied with and submitted to HMRC
- Records must be kept for a period of six years
- Accounting for tax return APSS302 must be submitted to HMRC
- HMRC may give notice to the scheme administrator it requires a registered pension scheme return to be completed
- A table sets out the information which must be submitted online
- Regulations govern the required accounting and auditing actions for registered schemes
- For most registered pension schemes, a self-assessment tax return (SA970) is no longer necessary
- The *Employer-Financed Retirement Benefits Schemes (Provision of Information) Regulations 2005 (SI 2005/3453)* require EFRBS to submit reports from time to time
- Appeals may be made against any tax charges or penalties incurred
- There are provisions for exoneration from charge and genuine errors
- There are simplified disclosure regulations
- Tax avoidance is described in **Chapter 15**

Part Two

General taxation and tax planning considerations for individuals and employers

Chapter 8

> **SIGNPOSTS**
> - Employer contributions are not a taxable benefit, and contributions by employers and members, or for the benefit of members, are tax-relievable subject to certain limitsr
> - Lump sums are tax-free, within permitted limits
> - There are few tax charges on scheme investments
> - There are exemptions for schemes from IHT in most circumstances

Tax considerations

INTRODUCTION

8.1 **Part Two** of this book describes the tax exemptions and charges for registered pension schemes. It also contains the protections from the standard LTA and general comment on tax-planning for individuals.

Contributions, income tax and NIC

8.2 Employer contributions are not a taxable benefit. Additionally, within the permitted limits, contributions by employers and members, or for the benefit of members, are tax-relievable. The AA charge is payable on any amounts in excess of the AA in the circumstances described in **Chapter 3** above.

In addition, for DB schemes, the PPF levy has to be paid. The PPF is to use a bespoke risk scoring system to calculate scheme levies from 2015/16.

In June 2014, the Conservative party resurrected the idea of merging NI into income tax. This move is proposed for a future Parliament.

Pensions

8.3 Pension income is taxable on the amount that accrues in a tax year. This includes both members and dependants scheme pensions; lifetime annuities; short-term annuities, and drawdown.

Unauthorised pensions paid will also be chargeable to income tax as pension income unless the unauthorised pension has been assessed to income tax as an unauthorised payment.

PAYE is to be deducted from such pensions. The payer of the pension must operate PAYE in accordance with the PAYE rules before paying the pension.

8.4 *Tax considerations*

> **Focus**
> - Lump sums described below are tax-free within permitted limits

Lump sums

8.4 Lump sums are generally tax-free, within the permitted limits described in **Chapter 4** above. Otherwise, the following lump sums are taxable:

- a short service refund lump sum;
- a pension protection lump sum death benefit;
- an annuity protection lump sum death benefit;
- a drawdown pension fund lump sum death benefit;
- a LTA excess lump sum;
- a trivial commutation lump sum;
- a winding up lump sum;
- a payment of commuted equivalent pension benefits;
- a trivial commutation lump sum death benefit;
- a winding up lump sum death benefit;
- a defined benefits lump sum death benefit paid in respect of a member who was aged 75 or over when they died;
- an uncrystallised funds lump sum death benefit paid in respect of a member who was aged 75 or over when they died; and
- a serious ill-health lump sum paid to a member aged 75 or over. Details are provided in **Chapter 3** above.

> **Focus**
> - Most investments are tax-free

Investments

8.5 There are few tax charges on scheme investments. In general, the investments may accrue on a tax-free basis on:

- income derived from investments or deposits held for the purposes of the scheme;
- underwriting commissions applied for the purposes if they would otherwise be chargeable to tax under *Case VI* of *Schedule D*. Most references to Schedule D, Case VI occur in *ICTA 1988* (see also BIM14030);
- income from futures contracts and options contracts;
- profits or gains arising from transactions in certificates of deposit;
- profits from sale and repurchase agreements (repos) and 'manufactured payments';

Tax considerations **8.7**

- a gain arising from the disposal of investments.

However, a registered pension scheme is restricted in the amount that can be invested in the shares of a sponsoring employer company.

Details are provided in **Chapter 5** above.

The exemptions above do not apply to income derived from investments or deposits held as a member of a property investment LLP.

Taxable property held in an IRPS is subject to certain tax charges. Details are provided in **Chapter 12** below.

Focus

- There is generally exemption from inheritance tax

Inheritance tax

8.6 There is no general exemption from IHT for registered pension schemes. However, *IHTA 1984* includes specific provisions, primarily for trust-based schemes, which take them outside the usual IHT charges on these settlements, viz:

- contributions by individuals or close company employers are not regarded as chargeable transfers;
- scheme funds are not subject to the IHT charges (which would otherwise arise every 10 years on the current market value;
- IHT charges do not apply to distributions of capital from a scheme, for example, those to provide a lump sum on a member's retirement or a death benefit to a member's widow or widower;
- on the death of a scheme pensioner or annuitant, their estate for IHT purposes is regarded as not including any part of the scheme funds relating to that pension or annuity.

These exemptions extend to the schemes themselves, those who contribute to them and those who benefit from them.

Details can be found in RPSM04100060.

Transitional protections

8.7 The valuable transitional protections from tax charges are described in described in **Chapter 9** below. This is particularly pertinent following the serious abatements in the AA and the LTA in recent years (as described in **Chapter 3** above).

As the rules are very complex, detailed explanations of how they operate are contained in the **Chapter**.

8.8 *Tax considerations*

Tax-planning

8.8 **Chapter 10** below contains comments on tax-planning in general.

OTHER SPECIALIST MATTERS

8.9 The remaining **Parts** of this book concern specialist matters, including: the different types of scheme which can benefit certain individuals; overseas matters and the tax charges which can be avoided. A brief summary of the subject matter of each **Chapter** is given below.

High earners

8.10 **Chapter 11** below considers the options which can benefit high earners, including bonus sacrifices, flexible drawdown EFRBS, IRPS, and bonus sacrifices.

Overseas considerations

8.11 **Part Four** provides a step-by-step guide through the attractive but complex world of overseas pension schemes and how to avoid incurring tax charges and penalties.

Other forms of retirement savings

8.12 **Part Five** considers alternative means of savings which may be attractive in appropriate circumstances, in addition to registered pension scheme pension provision.

Tax charges and DOTAS

8.13 **Part Six** considers the potential pitfalls which must be avoided if penal tax charges are to be avoided by UK schemes and UK citizens.

CHECKLIST

- Employer contributions are not a taxable benefit
- Within the permitted limits, contributions by employers and members, or for the benefit of members, are tax-relievable
- Pension income is taxable on the amount that accrues in a tax year
- Lump sums are generally tax-free, within the permitted limits
- There are few tax charges on scheme investments
- There are exemptions for schemes from IHT in most circumstances

Chapter 9

> **SIGNPOSTS**
>
> - Primary protection and enhanced protection were available from A-Day
> - Lump sum protection was available from A-Day
> - The meaning of 'relevant benefit accrual' is given
> - Fixed protection 2012, fixed protection 2014 and individual protection 2014 are described, together with lump sum protections and death benefits

Transitional protection

INTRODUCTION

9.1 The pension tax regime which was introduced by *FA 2004* on A-Day differed from the introduction of previous tax regimes in one very important aspect: it was retrospective. The introduction of previous pension tax regimes permitted those already accruing benefits in their particular occupational scheme to continue to do so on the same tax terms in the future, while new employees had to be pensioned under the new tax terms. Not only did this 'grandfathering' lead to inequalities in the employment context, but it also gave rise to a complicated system of tax controls with each new layer of legislation or HMRC discretionary practice.

FA 2004 ensured that no future benefits would accrue on historical tax terms. This applied also when the AA and LTA were reduced in April 2011 and April 2012 (see **3.13** and **3.34** above, respectively).

However, without a system of protection for pre-2006 accrued rights, many would have been faced with controversial tax bills whenever they came to retire. As one of the main goals of *FA 2004* had been simplification, the method of protecting members' pre-2006 accrued rights also had to be simple. Two methods were devised to try and achieve this: EP (enhanced protection); and PP (primary protection).

Similar thinking was applied when the LTA reduced from £1.8m to £1.5m on 6 April 2012, and again to £1.25m on 6 April 2014, but the concept of simplicity had long disappeared. A complex system of protections has developed – FP 2012 (fixed protection 2012); FP 2014 (fixed protection 2014) and IP 2014 (individual protection 2014). These protections are described later in this **Chapter**. The path towards greater confusion and complexity in the future sadly seems to be set.

9.2 *Transitional protection*

Unfortunately, the rules for each type of post A-Day protection are not exactly the same. It is therefore imperative that these rules are fully understood, and that HMRC certificates of protection are kept in a safe and accessible place, if these valuable protections are not to be lost at a later date. Some of these protections can be lost by further relevant benefit accrual or certain transfer activity. Administrators and advisers will wish to hold copies of the certificates as they will need to consult them at some time. However, such persons are likely to change during an individual's lifetime, and so it important that the member retains a copy of their personal protection certificate.

Member protection

9.2 The effect of EP is to ensure that scheme members are able to protect their pre A-Day accrued rights and avoid the LTA charge completely. EP also provides an exemption from the AA charge. Certain conditions had to be met in order to achieve and retain EP. The most important of these is that no further 'relevant benefit accrual' has occurred in respect of the individual concerned. For the meaning of 'relevant benefit accrual', see **9.29** below.

PP, on the other hand, allows further benefit to accrue after A-Day. It provides a simple protection on accrued rights by offering an uplift to an individual's LTA in the form of a LTA factor based on the amount of pension rights already accrued at A-Day. However, further benefit accrual is likely to attract a LTA charge as it is, almost by definition, above the protected amount.

Scheme members had until 5 April 2009 to notify HMRC that they would be relying on EP and/or PP, although the nature of EP would have effectively meant that they needed to take a decision before A-Day.

The rules and timescales which apply to FP 2012; FP 2014 and IP 2014 are described later. To make matters more confusing, relevant benefit accrual for the fixed protections differs from the definition of relevant benefit accrual for EP purposes; it is therefore important for the reader to make sure that they are referencing the correct section, EP; FP 2012 or FP 2014, when considering what constitutes relevant benefit accrual.

Scheme protection concerning pre A-Day limits

9.3 It was also recognised by *FA 2004* that references to pre A-Day HMRC limits had been incorporated into the rules of tax-approved pension schemes. Removing the effect of HMRC limits overnight could have increased the rights of a number of members unintentionally, thereby exposing pension schemes and their sponsors to additional costs. A set of transitional regulations therefore imposed some of the pre A-Day limits on schemes that had been tax-approved on 5 April 2006. These limits could have been disapplied by a statutory resolution made by the trustees of the scheme. This was usually done at the same time as the trustees used their amendment power to make other changes related to the post A-Day tax regime. This scheme protection fell away on 6 April 2011 (see **2.14** above), and so pension trustees had to ensure that any necessary changes were made before then.

Furthermore, if members had a right to benefits that did not meet the form of the new authorised payments, the payment of such benefits would bring unauthorised payment charges to both the member and the scheme. In this case, the regulations override trustees' obligations to pay the benefits and instead grant them the discretion to make the payment.

This **Chapter** looks at all the current forms of member protection – PP, EP, FP 2012, FP 2014 and IP 2014.

RPSM examples

9.4 A number of useful examples have been taken from HMRC's RPSM. The examples referred to in the text below can be found in Chapter 3 of the RPSM (RPSM03100000 onwards), but those that concern the changes from A-Day until the post-2011 changes are also reproduced at the end of this **Chapter** for ease of reference.

Focus

- Protections from the standard lifetime allowance and post A-Day lump sum limits are valuable protections and should not be inadvertently lost

---

VALUING PRE A-DAY RIGHTS FOR PRIMARY OR ENHANCED PROTECTION

9.5 Whether PP or EP was chosen, or both, it was necessary to value the rights that had accrued at 5 April 2006. In the case of PP, this was necessary because an amount no greater than the maximum pension under the applicable pre A-Day regime could be protected. In the case of EP, the amount of benefit above the appropriate pre A-Day limit (if any) had to be surrendered. Rights were valued in the same manner for both these purposes, but there were some extra easements when calculating pre A-Day limits. Also, the value of benefits was not based on one of the traditional actuarial methods, eg transfer value, but on the standard HMRC valuation factor.

Rights not yet in payment

9.6 The valuation of rights which had not yet come into payment at A-Day depended on the type of arrangement from which they derived (DC, DB, cash balance or hybrid).

Money purchase/DC arrangements

9.7 For DC arrangements, which include both personal pensions and occupational DC schemes, the value of a member's uncrystallised rights was the sum of any cash held under the scheme and the market value of the other assets held to provide the member's benefits on 5 April 2006.

9.8 *Transitional protection*

Note that, where PP applies, it was possible to recalculate the value of rights as at 5 April 2006 in a case where compensation for poor performance of an investment owned by the scheme was paid between 6 April 2006 and 5 April 2009. *Regulations 9, 10* and *11* of the *Taxation of Pension Schemes (Transitional Provisions) Order 2006 (SI 2006/572)* apply.

Cash balance arrangements

9.8 For a cash balance scheme, the value of a member's uncrystallised rights was the amount that would be available for the provision of immediate benefit if the member had been entitled to receive it on 5 April 2006. For this purpose, it was assumed that the member was in good physical and mental health and had reached either age 60 or, if a different age was specified in the rules at 10 December 2003 as the minimum age at which benefits could be paid without reduction, that age.

Defined benefit/DB arrangements

9.9 For a DB arrangement, the value of a member's uncrystallised rights was calculated by the formula:

(RVF × ARP) + LS

where:

- RVF is the relevant valuation factor (ie 20)
- ARP is the annual rate of pension to which the member would be entitled if he acquired an actual rather than a prospective right to receive it on 5 April 2006
- LS is the amount of lump sum the member would have received otherwise than by commutation (ie only applicable for schemes that provide separate pension and lump sum).

As for cash balance arrangements, it was assumed that the member was in good physical and mental health and had reached either age 60 or, if a different age was specified in the rules at 10 December 2003 as the minimum age at which benefits could be paid without reduction, that age.

Hybrid arrangements

9.10 In a hybrid arrangement, the value of uncrystallised rights was simply calculated on whichever of the bases produced the highest result.

HMRC pre A-Day limits

9.11 The value of uncrystallised rights had to be restricted to comply with pre A-Day HMRC limits where those rights derived from one of the following occupational pension schemes:

(a) a retirement benefit scheme approved for the purpose of *ICTA 1988, Ch I, Pt XIV*;

(b) a scheme formerly approved under *ICTA 1970, s 208*;

(c) a relevant statutory scheme as defined in *ICTA 1988, s 611A*, or a pension scheme treated by HMRC as such; or

(d) a deferred annuity contract securing benefits under any of the three types of scheme above.

The restriction is expressed by the formula:

20 × MPP

where:

- MPP is the maximum permitted pension that could be paid to the individual on 5 April 2006 under the arrangement without giving HMRC grounds for withdrawing tax approval. See **Appendix 3** for the main features of the pre A-Day tax approval regime.

In arriving at MPP, it was assumed that the member was in good physical and mental health and had reached either age 60 or, if a different age was specified in the rules at 10 December 2003 as the minimum age at which benefits could be paid without reduction, that age. For a member still in service on 5 April 2006, it was assumed that he left employment on that date.

As an example, if a member of a DB scheme was subject to the pre-1987 regime, was still in service on 5 April 2006, had 30 years' potential service to his normal retirement date, and had 20 years' service accrued to 5 April 2006, his HMRC maximum permitted pension at 5 April 2006 would be calculated as the higher of:

(a) 20/60 × final remuneration, and

(b) 20/30 × (40/60 × final remuneration − retained benefits).

In this case, the member has more than 10 years' service to his normal retirement date and, as the pre-1987 regime applies, he can therefore count on the uplifted 60ths scale, which gives him a maximum pension ('P') of 40/60. Retained benefits must then be deducted, if necessary, and the result multiplied by N/NS, where N is service accrued, in this case, to 5 April 2006, and NS is potential service to normal retirement date (20 years and 30 years respectively in this example) (see HMRC Practice Notes IR12 (2001), para 7.47).

Retained benefits did not have to be taken into account if the member's P60 earnings from pensionable employment did not exceed £50,000 in the 2004/05 tax year, even for controlling directors. If pensionable service did not continue for the whole of the 2004/05 tax year, a *pro rata* calculation applied. If pensionable service ceased before 6 April 2004, retained benefits did not have to be taken into account if P60 earnings in the last complete tax year before date of leaving did not exceed £25,000. These easements were introduced by Update 159 (now incorporated into Practice Notes, para 7.6a) and were

9.12 *Transitional protection*

applicable on and from 5 April 2006. See also paragraph 16.55a of the Practice Notes on the valuation of DC benefits. Retained benefits could also be ignored under the other administrative easements described in paragraphs 7.5 to 7.7 of the Practice Notes.

Note that HMRC limits were subject to the requirements of the preservation legislation. This meant that it was not always possible to restrict MPP to the N/60 or N/NS × (P − RB) formulae above. This is an especially important consideration for members of occupational DC pension schemes. For example, the maximum permitted pension for a member of such a scheme approved after 1991 would be the pension he could have received if he had retired on ill-health grounds at the date of leaving, ie using potential service up to his normal retirement date.

In an occupational DC pension scheme, the calculation of MPP should be carried out on the appropriate preservation basis depending on when the scheme was approved. The appropriate preservation basis will be the version of HMRC's limits calculation that was set out in the Practice Notes at the time of approval. Under PP, where the value of uncrystallised rights was greater than 20 × MPP, note that the excess over 20 × MPP was not lost, nor did it have to be surrendered (as it would for EP). 20 × MPP was simply the maximum value that could be taken into account when calculating the LTA enhancement factor. The excess rights remain in the scheme, but are obviously more likely to be subject to a LTA charge.

Rights in payment

9.12 Where rights had come into payment, they were valued as 25 times the annual rate of pension that was being paid. Note that any lump sum already paid was not taken into account; this was already catered for by multiplying the pension in payment by 25 instead of 20. There was no need to test pensions in payment against HMRC pre A-Day limits, as this had already been done when the benefits were brought into payment.

Where the rights in payment were in the form of income drawdown, they were valued as 25 times the maximum annual rate of drawdown that could have been received on 5 April 2006. For this purpose, it was not necessary to obtain a new drawdown valuation as at 5 April 2006; the maximum rate established at the last review would have been sufficient.

Lump sum rights

9.13 The method of valuing lump sum rights on 5 April 2006 was described in the previous edition of this book.

The Practice Notes IR12 (2001) are stored online in the national web archive, but they can be accessed, together with earlier links, on the HMRC website at:*www.hmrc.gov.uk/pensionschemes/former-regime.htm*.

PRIMARY PROTECTION

Method of protection

9.14 PP was achieved by working out an uplift to be applied in individual cases to the standard LTA, called a LTA enhancement factor, and registering the details with HMRC. The enhancement factor is the percentage by which the value of rights on 5 April 2006 exceeds £1,500,000 and is expressed in the following formula:

(RR − SLA)/SLA

where:

- RR is the value of pension rights on 5 April 2006
- SLA is the standard LTA for the 2006/07 tax year (£1,500,000)

For example, if the value of an individual's total pension rights on 5 April 2006 was £1,830,000, his LTA enhancement factor would be 0.22, calculated as:

(1,830,000 − 1,500,000)/1,500,000 = 0.22

This means that he would be entitled to a personal LTA 22% greater than the underpinned LTA at the time he takes benefits (the underpinned LTA is the standard LTA up to 5 April 2012, and the greater of the prevailing standard LTA and £1.8m from 6 April 2012 onwards).

When calculating a LTA enhancement factor, the factor should be rounded up to two decimal places. When advising a member of the percentage of LTA used by any BCE, this should be rounded down to two decimal places. Further information is provided in RPSM11100040.

Note that *Articles 9, 10* and *11* of the *Taxation of Pension Schemes (Transitional Provisions) Order 2006 (SI 2006/572)* provided transitional protection for individuals who qualify for PP but whose pre-commencement rights had been undervalued on 5 April 2006 due to the poor performance of investments held by the scheme. If the scheme received compensation in respect of the poor performance on or after A-Day, this compensation became potentially chargeable to the LTA charge. *Article 9* sets out the conditions which the individual needed to satisfy to qualify for the transitional protection. *Article 10* modifies the valuation of uncrystallised rights. The compensation payment had to be made between 6 April 2006 and 5 April 2009.

PP was only available if the amount of an individual's relevant pension rights exceeded £1.5M on 5 April 2006 and he had notified HMRC of his intention to rely on primary protection before 6 April 2009.

For pension rights to be relevant, they must derive from one or more of the following arrangements:

(a) a retirement benefit scheme approved under *ICTA 1988, Ch I, Pt XIV*;

(b) a scheme formerly approved under *ICTA 1970, s 208*;

9.15 *Transitional protection*

(c) a relevant statutory scheme;

(d) a *section 32* buy-out policy (named after *FA 1981, s 32*, now repealed);

(e) a parliamentary pension fund;

(f) a RAC (also known as a *section 226* annuity, named after *ICTA 1970, s 226* now repealed); or

(g) a personal pension scheme approved under *ICTA 1988, Ch IV, Pt XIV*.

Rights built up in a FURBS or UURBS (see **Chapter 11** below) did not count as relevant pension rights, nor did any entitlement to a pension which would arise on the death of another.

The value of uncrystallised relevant pension rights must not have exceeded the maximum approvable limit by reference to the appropriate tax regime applicable to each of an individual's occupational pension scheme rights on 5 April 2006. If the valuation of uncrystallised relevant pension rights *did* exceed the value of the maximum permitted pension, the excess was not lost, nor did it have to be surrendered, but it could not be taken into account in working out the LTA enhancement factor.

If PP applies and an individual's pension rights are decreased by a pension debit as a result of pension sharing on divorce, the LTA enhancement factor needs to be recalculated by reference to the value of rights that remain after the pension debit is deducted. If this reduces the value of rights below £1.5M, PP is lost and the individual will be subject to the standard £1.5m LTA.

Registration for protection

9.15 The *Registered Pension Schemes (Enhanced Lifetime Allowance) Regulations 2006 (SI 2006/131)* set down the procedural and administrative requirements for notification, certification and compliance for those wishing to rely on PP and/or EP.

Notification of a member's intention to rely on PP had to be made by him, on the appropriate form, to reach HMRC by 5 April 2009. The notification had to be signed and dated by the individual. Only in exceptional circumstances could someone other than the individual sign the notification form. Where someone was incapable by reason of mental disorder or physical disability, a person having responsibility for managing the individual's affairs, or having power of attorney, could sign on the individual's behalf. Where an individual had died, his personal representatives had the power to complete the notification form and otherwise do whatever the individual could have done with regard to notification.

Notification of intention to rely on EP could be made on the same form, and there was also a section for notifying HMRC of lump sum entitlements greater than £375,000 on 5 April 2006.

The individual to whom a protection certificate is issued must preserve it until no further BCE can occur. Each certificate has a unique reference number.

Where HMRC issued a protection certificate, they had the power to instigate a review of any information given in connection with the certificate within a period of 12 months from the date on which the notification was given to them. Even where the 12-month period has passed, HMRC may still instigate a review at any time if they have reason to believe that any information in connection with the notification was, or has become, incorrect. Individuals must keep records relating to the protection notification for at least six years.

Pension benefits

9.16 The amount of a benefit crystallised at a BCE event is usually tested against the standard LTA at the time of crystallisation. Under PP, the crystallised amount is tested against an individual's personal LTA, ie the underpinned LTA as increased by his LTA enhancement factor. The underpinned LTA is, up to 5 April 2012, the prevailing standard LTA; and, from 6 April 2012 onwards, it is the greater of the prevailing LTA and £1.8m.

If the standard LTA is (say) £1.5m, an individual has an enhancement factor of 0.22, and he crystallises benefits valued at £2,100,000 in the 2012/13 tax year, he would still have escaped the LTA charge as illustrated by the following:

- personal LTA = underpinned LTA of £1,800,000 × 1.22 = £2,196,000, which is greater than the crystallised amount of £2,100,000.

If an individual vests benefits at different times, the application of the personal LTA is operated in the same way as the standard LTA. See the example in RPSM03102030 at the end of this **Chapter**.

Lump sum benefits greater than £375,000

9.17 Where an individual has applied for PP and has registered lump sum rights at 5 April 2006 which are greater than £375,000, the normal rules for calculating pension commencement lump sums (see **4.16** above) at a BCE event do not apply. Instead, the pension commencement lump sum is calculated as the amount registered at A-Day increased by the factor:

ULA/FSLA

where:

- ULA is the underpinned LTA (the prevailing standard LTA up to 5 April 2012 and, from 6 April 2012 onwards, the greater of the prevailing standard LTA and £1.8m)
- FSLA is the standard LTA for 2006/07 (£1.5m).

For example, if lump sum rights of £400,000 were registered at A-Day, and in the year of vesting, eg 2010/11, the standard LTA had increased to £1.8m, the maximum lump sum that could be paid would be:

£400,000 × 1,800,000/1,500,000 = £480,000

9.18 *Transitional protection*

If the tax year of vesting were 2012/13, when the standard LTA was £1.5m, the maximum lump sum that could be paid would still be £480,000 due to the operation of the underpinned LTA in the formula.

Note that the sum registered at A-Day relates to the aggregate of all lump sum rights that an individual may have under several pension arrangements. If lump sums are taken from two different schemes at two different times, the protected lump sum amount will have to be adjusted to take account of the first lump sum paid. This is done by increasing the first lump sum by the factor ULA/PSLA and then deducting it from the increased protected lump sum amount at the second payment date. ULA is the underpinned LTA as above, and PSLA is the standard LTA at the time the member became entitled to the first lump sum.

In the example above, if a £200,000 lump sum had been paid in the 2007/08 tax year when the standard LTA was £1.6m, then the maximum lump sum that could be paid on vesting in 2010/11 would have been:

(£400,000 × 1,800,000/1,500,000) − (£200,000 × 1,800,000/1,600,000) = £255,000

With lump sum protection under PP, it may be possible to transfer protected lump sum allowance from one scheme to another, and even commute the benefits entirely from one scheme if this would still be within the protected lump sum allowance. This, of course, would be subject to scheme rules permitting such commutation. See the example given in RPSM03105160 at the end of this **Chapter**.

The amount of lump sum payable tax-free must not exceed the amount of LTA available. It is therefore very important to take great care over the timing of different lump sum payments to ensure that valuable tax-free lump sum rights are still within the LTA available. If an individual uses up too much of his personal LTA by vesting benefits in pension form first of all, he may find that there is insufficient LTA left to cover all of a protected lump sum being vested later on. The examples in RPSM03105170 and RPSM03105180 reproduced at the end of this **Chapter** illustrate the danger of this.

Death benefits

Normal protection

9.18 Payment of a DB lump sum death benefit and an uncrystallised funds lump sum death benefit (see **4.41** above). are tested against an individual's LTA. If the total benefits taken in respect of the member are more than his LTA, the excess is liable to the LTA charge at 55%. Otherwise, it is tax-free if paid before age 75. If it is paid after age 75 the lump sum will be taxed at 55%. Excess amounts over the available LTA will not be subject to a LTA charge if they are paid in the form of dependants' pensions, although the pension will be subject to income tax at the recipient's marginal rate.

Under PP, a lump sum death benefit is tested against the deceased's personal LTA (ie as increased by the application of the LTA enhancement factor) instead of the standard LTA.

The 55% tax charge described above also applies to DC schemes, subject to the rules described in **4.41** above.

Protected life cover

9.19 An increased form of protection is available if lump sum death benefits, payable in respect of death on 5 April 2006, were greater than the sum of an individual's crystallised and uncrystallised pension rights. In such a case, a higher LTA enhancement factor can be claimed by the deceased's beneficiaries in the event of death post A-Day. The higher LTA enhancement factor is based on the value of lump sum death benefit rights instead of pension rights. For protected life cover to apply, all the following conditions must be met:

(a) P applied immediately before the member's death.

(b) Either a DB lump sum death benefit (**4.41**) or a DC lump sum death benefit (is paid, as described above.

(c) The recipients inform HMRC of their intention to rely on protected life cover.

(d) The value of lump sum death benefits under all approved pension arrangements relating to the member on 5 April 2006 is greater than the value of his crystallised and uncrystallised pension rights on the same date.

(e) If the lump sum death benefits had been paid on 5 April 2006, they would not have exceeded HMRC limits. If they exceeded HMRC limits on 5 April 2006, only the amount up to HMRC limits can be used for protected life cover.

(f) The member had been employed by the same or a connected employer continuously from 5 April 2006 to the date of his death.

(g) The member's employer participated in the scheme on 5 April 2006.

(h) The member had not started to receive payment of benefits under the pension scheme before his death.

There are further conditions where the death benefits are insured and the scheme is not an occupational scheme with at least 20 members on 5 April 2006. In this case, protected life cover is only available if:

(a) a sum is paid under the insurance policy when the member actually died, and

(b) the terms of the policy have not been varied significantly between 5 April 2006 and the date of death.

Care must therefore be taken when re-broking life assurance policies held by small schemes, as re-broking would be a significant variation.

9.20 *Transitional protection*

ENHANCED PROTECTION

Method of protection

9.20 As long as an individual retains EP, he will have no liability for the LTA charge at any BCE. It will also not be possible for him to receive payment of a LTA excess lump sum.

Two conditions must exist for EP to apply. The first is that an individual must have given notice to HMRC of his intention to rely on it. The second is that the valuation of his uncrystallised rights derived from all occupational pension schemes on 5 April 2006 did not exceed an amount calculated as 20 × MPP, where MPP is the maximum permitted pension that would be allowed by reference to the appropriate tax regime in force before A-Day.

ER will be lost if relevant benefit accrual occurs (see RPSM03104520).

For an explanation of MPP and information on the valuation of uncrystallised rights on 5 April 2006, see **9.5** above.

Surrender of relevant excess

9.21 If an individual's uncrystallised occupational pension scheme rights on 5 April 2006 exceeded 20 × MPP, the excess had to be surrendered if EP was to be relied on. This was addressed by the *Registered Pension Schemes (Surrender of Relevant Excess) Regulations 2006 (SI 2006/211)*.

These regulations modified the rules of a pension scheme so as to allow members to be able to surrender those rights in excess of 20 × MPP. At the same time, the provisions of the *Occupational Pension Schemes (Assignment, Forfeiture, Bankruptcy etc) Regulations 1997 (SI 1997/785)* were amended so that such a surrendered EP did not fall foul of the inalienability requirements of the *PA 1995*.

FA 2005, Sch 10, para 38 inserted a new *s 172A* into *FA 2004*, which provides that, where a member surrenders any benefit to which he had a prospective entitlement, it is to be treated as an unauthorised payment. The *Registered Pension Schemes (Surrender of Relevant Excess) Regulations 2006 (SI 2006/211)* exempts the surrender of relevant excess from *FA 2004, s 172A*, as long as the following conditions are met:

(a) the value of rights surrendered is determined in accordance with *FA 2004, s 212* (ie the usual method of valuing uncrystallised rights), and

(b) the surrendered rights do not include:
- a surrender in respect of a pension sharing order,
- a surrender in exchange for additional dependant's benefit,
- a surrender for the purpose of transferring rights to another arrangement under the pension scheme relating to the member or a dependant,

- a surrender which constitutes an assignment of benefits, or
- rights to prospective entitlement which an individual has as a dependant of another individual.

Any surrender of rights greater than the relevant excess will be an unauthorised payment in accordance with *FA 2004, s 172A*.

Note that it was not necessary to surrender rights in the pension scheme in which the excess arose. Rights could have been surrendered from any one or more other schemes in order to come within the EP requirements.

There was no requirement to make a payment to a member in return for any rights surrendered; the value of rights surrendered could have been distributed elsewhere within the pension scheme. However, where a payment was made to a member in respect of the surrender, such a payment would most likely have been an unauthorised member payment and subject to the unauthorised payments charges. If the payment included a return of surplus AVCs, some of the unauthorised payments charges might be mitigated, depending on particular circumstances.

The value of rights surrendered could alternatively be paid to a sponsoring employer if it met the requirements of the *Registered Pension Schemes (Authorised Surplus Payments) Regulations 2006 (SI 2006/574)*.

Registration for protection

9.22 Notification of a member's intention to rely on EP had to be made by him, on the appropriate form, to reach HMRC by 5 April 2009. However, because an application for EP involved making certain decisions about the accrual of benefit beyond A-Day, most people were not able to wait until 2009 and had to consider their position before A-Day. The *Registered Pension Schemes (Enhanced Lifetime Allowance) Regulations 2006 (SI 2006/131)* apply.

A notification of intention to rely on PP could be made at the same time as a notification for EP, provided an individual's rights were valued at more than £1.5m on 5 April 2006. In fact, an individual with A-Day rights greater than £1.5m who registered for EP would have been advised to register for PP as well. If EP were ever lost, then at least PP would provide a fallback position.

This proved to be a bit of a stumbling block when the fixed protection concept was introduced, firstly with effect from 6 April 2012. To make use of FP 2012 or FP 2014, a person had to have neither EP nor PP. For example, someone with EP, who had rights valued between £1.5m and £1.8m, might have found it advantageous to make use of FP 2012, which guaranteed a £1.8m LTA. However, while EP could be given up, PP could not. Therefore, those who had EP and who also took the precaution of getting PP were prevented from making use of fixed protection.

The notification process for EP included a section on the form for notifying HMRC of lump sum entitlements greater than £375,000 on 5 April 2006.

9.23 *Transitional protection*

Records relating to the protection notification must be kept for at least six years.

If the notification form was completed by someone else on the individual's behalf, the individual still had to sign the form unless he was physically or mentally incapable of doing so. An individual's personal representative could also sign the form if the individual had died. Anyone notifying HMRC of EP should have received a certificate from them showing the details of their protection.

Pension benefits

9.23 Since there is no liability for a LTA charge, the payment of a member's pension benefits may proceed, subject only to income tax and the scheme administrator receiving appropriate notice of the member's EP status.

Payment of lump sum benefits greater than £375,000

9.24 Where an individual has applied for EP and has registered lump sum rights at 5 April 2006 which are greater than £375,000, the normal rules for calculating pension commencement lump sums (see **4.16** above) do not apply. Instead, the pension commencement lump sum is calculated as the same percentage of rights being crystallised at the vesting date as the percentage arrived at by dividing uncrystallised lump sum rights at A-Day by the value of uncrystallised rights at A-Day and multiplying by 100. This is best demonstrated by an example:

At A-Day

If the value of uncrystallised lump sum rights on 5 April 2006 = £400,000

and the value of uncrystallised rights on 5 April 2006 = £2,000,000

the lump sum percentage on 5 April 2006 = (£400,000/£2,000,000) × 100 = 20%.

At retirement

If the value of rights crystallised at retirement = £2,400,000

the maximum lump sum at retirement = 20% × £2,400,000 = £480,000.

If an individual had more than one pension arrangement, the maximum lump sum that could be taken from each arrangement would be limited by the percentage derived from the total uncrystallised lump sum rights at A-Day divided by the total uncrystallised rights and multiplied by 100. This means that, if one arrangement paid a lump sum less than this percentage, the excess could not be taken from another arrangement. See the example in RPSM03105210 reproduced at the end of this **Chapter.**

Death benefits

Normal protection

9.25 The application of EP to lump sum death benefits depends on whether the arrangement is a DC arrangement or a DB arrangement.

In the case of a DC arrangement, an uncrystallised funds lump sum death benefit may be paid equal to the accumulated value of the assets in a member's pension fund at the date of death, and EP would not be lost. The situation becomes complicated, however, if an insured lump sum is payable.

If the proceeds of a life assurance policy would form part of the member's overall fund and the scheme rules simply provide for a death benefit calculated as a return of fund, as opposed to a defined benefit (eg four times salary), the total fund including the life policy proceeds could be paid as a lump sum without jeopardising EP.

However, the payment of tax-relievable life assurance premiums in respect of a DC arrangement would normally constitute relevant benefit accrual (see **9.29** below). EP would therefore be lost unless the conditions for protected life cover (see **9.26** below) are satisfied. Note also that HMRC stated in Simplification Newsletter No 8 (published on 23 December 2005) that, if such premiums were paid out of the existing assets of a member's scheme, this would not jeopardise EP.

In the case of a DB arrangement, a lump sum may be paid to the extent of the usual appropriate limit (see **9.29** below) without jeopardising EP. If a lump sum is paid that is greater than the usual appropriate limit, this is relevant benefit accrual and would normally cause the loss of EP at the point of payment. The exception to this is if protected life cover applies (see **9.27** below) in which case a higher appropriate limit may be relied on.

If any benefit is paid in the form of dependants' pensions, EP would not be lost as this does not constitute a BCE.

Protected life cover – money purchase/DC arrangements

9.26 Premiums paid to a life assurance policy under a DC arrangement do not count as relevant benefit accrual (see **9.29** below) where the following conditions are met:

(a) The contribution is only used for the payment of premiums under an insurance policy on the life of the member.

(b) The policy is issued, or issued in respect of insurances made, before 6 April 2006.

(c) There is no right to surrender any rights under the policy.

(d) The terms of the policy must not be varied significantly in the period between 6 April 2006 and the member's death so as to increase the benefit or extend the cover term.

9.27 *Transitional protection*

(e) No benefits may be paid under the policy except by reason of the member's death.

Re-broking a life assurance policy would therefore seem to cause the loss of EP, as premiums to the new policy would not be able to benefit from this protection. There are exemptions, however, where a new scheme is set up to comply with age discrimination legislation or to comply with the *PA 2004* prohibition on life assurance-only categories in occupational pension schemes.

Protected life cover – defined benefit arrangements

9.27 A higher appropriate limit may be claimed by beneficiaries on the death of a member with EP. For a higher appropriate limit to apply, the following conditions must be met:

(a) Either a DB lump sum death benefit (**4.41** above) or a DC lump sum death benefit (**4.42** above) is paid.

(b) The recipients inform HMRC of their intention to rely on protected life cover.

(c) If the lump sum death benefits had been paid on 5 April 2006, they would not have exceeded HMRC limits. If they exceeded HMRC limits on 5 April 2006, only the amount up to HMRC limits can be used for the appropriate limit.

(d) The member had been employed by the same or a connected employer continuously from 5 April 2006 to the date of his death.

(e) The member's employer participated in the scheme on 5 April 2006.

(f) The member had not started to receive payment of benefits under the pension scheme before his death.

There are further conditions where the death benefits are insured and the scheme is not an occupational scheme with at least 20 members on 5 April 2006. In this case, a higher appropriate limit is only available if:

(a) a sum is paid under the insurance policy when the member actually died, and

(b) the terms of the policy have not been varied significantly between 5 April 2006 and the date of death.

Care must therefore be taken when re-broking life assurance policies held by small schemes, as re-broking would be a significant variation.

The new appropriate limit is calculated as the aggregate of the maximum amounts that could have been paid, if the member had died on 5 April 2006, as lump sum death benefits from the DB arrangement in question, together with lump sum death benefits from any other DB arrangement relating to the same employment. Note the requirement to take into account only so much of these benefits as would not have prejudiced HMRC approval at 5 April 2006. If this is higher than the appropriate limit that would otherwise have applied, it may be relied on instead. The revised appropriate limit may be increased in the same ways applicable to the appropriate limit normally (see **9.29** below), including salary growth.

HMRC would consider a group life assurance scheme to be a DB scheme only where the rules of the scheme determine the lump sum death benefit to be paid. If the rules of the scheme do not specify a certain benefit, but simply provide for the lump sum death benefit payable to be the proceeds of an insurance policy (even if the policy provides a DB), HMRC have stated they would consider this to be a DC scheme. Given that contributions to a DC arrangement may constitute relevant benefit accrual, it may be necessary to determine whether a group life scheme is DC or DB in nature. If the scheme is not a DB scheme (contributions to a DB arrangement do not constitute relevant benefit accrual), it will be important to ensure that the conditions in **9.26** above continue to be met.

Because of the somewhat confusing conditions relating to protected life cover, its limitations and the fact that putting a new recruit with EP into a registered group life scheme will cause the loss of that protection, employers have been keen to take out excepted group life policies. Excepted group life policies sit outside the registered pension scheme regime and can be used to provide life assurance for those with EP without jeopardising that protection. See **10.17** for further information.

Loss of enhanced protection

9.28 Loss of EP may be occasioned by any of the following:

1. Relevant benefit accrual (see **9.29** below).
2. Impermissible transfer (see **9.30** below).
3. Transfer that is not a permitted transfer (see **9.31** below).
4. Creating a new arrangement under a registered pension scheme other than:
    (a) to receive a permitted transfer,
    (b) as part of an exercise to comply with age discrimination legislation, or
    (c) as part of an exercise to comply with the *PA 2004* prohibition on life assurance-only categories.
5. Voluntarily surrendering EP by writing to HMRC.

Focus
- Relevant benefit accrual can cause loss of valuable protections
---

RELEVANT BENEFIT ACCRUAL

9.29 For EP to remain valid, there must be no relevant benefit accrual on or after A-Day. If relevant benefit accrual occurs, EP will be lost at the time relevant benefit accrual occurs.

9.29 *Transitional protection*

Relevant benefit accrual occurs under a DC arrangement (but not a cash balance arrangement) if a contribution is paid which is:

(a) a tax-relievable contribution paid by or on behalf of the individual;

(b) a contribution in respect of the individual by his employer;

(c) any other contribution which becomes held for the benefit of the individual.

See **9.26** above for an exemption for premiums in respect of protected life cover.

Relevant benefit accrual occurs under a cash balance or DB arrangement if, at the time a benefit is paid, or on a permitted transfer to a DC arrangement, the crystallised value of the benefit exceeds the appropriate limit. The appropriate limit is the higher of (1) and (2) below:

(1) the value of an individual's rights on 5 April 2006 increased to the date of payment by the highest of:

– 5% pa compound;

– the increase in the relevant index; and

– an increase specified in statutory order (relating to contracting-out and preservation legislation);

(2) the benefit derived by using pensionable service to 5 April 2006, the scheme's accrual rate, and the amount of pensionable earnings at the actual date of payment, which may be some time after A-Day.

See **9.27** above for calculation of the appropriate limit in the case of protected life cover.

There are some restrictions on the earnings that can be used under option (2). The elements included in earnings must be the same elements that were pensionable prior to A-Day.

If the member was subject to the post-1989 regime on 5 April 2006, his earnings were limited to the highest earnings in any consecutive 12-month period in the three years before retirement, leaving service or death, or to 7.5% of the underpinned LTA if that is lower. If the member leaves service without retiring, the earnings figure may be indexed in line with the relevant index, 5% pa compound or order made by HMRC. The underpinned LTA is, up to 5 April 2012, the prevailing standard LTA; and, from 6 April 2012 onwards, it is the greater of the prevailing standard LTA and £1.8m.

If the member was not subject to the post-1989 regime on 5 April 2006, his earnings are similarly calculated as the highest earnings in any consecutive 12-month period in the three years before retirement, leaving service or death; but if they exceed 7.5% of the underpinned LTA they must be restricted to a three-year average, or to 7.5% of the underpinned LTA, whichever is greater. If the member leaves service without retiring, the three-year average of earnings to the date of leaving may be indexed in line with the relevant index, 5% pa compound or order made by HMRC.

This means that it is feasible for DB to continue to accrue post A-Day under EP, as long as the eventual amount crystallised on retirement does not exceed the appropriate limit for the arrangement as set out above. This allows for modest pay rises to the date of retirement; but, more importantly, it allows for normal accrual to continue and for early retirement to be taken where the early retirement reduction factor takes the value of the actual benefit paid under the appropriate limit. See the examples in RPSM03104590, RPSM03104600 and RPSM03104610 reproduced at the end of this **Chapter**, which illustrate when benefit accrual in a DB arrangement would and would not occasion the loss of EP.

Impermissible transfers

9.30 An impermissible transfer covers the following actions:

- Conversion of a DB arrangement into a DC arrangement.
- Transfer of sums into a DC arrangement from somewhere other than another pension arrangement of the member.

A transfer of pension rights pursuant to a pension sharing order in connection with divorce proceedings is exempt.

Permitted transfers

9.31 A permitted transfer would take place where some or all of the benefits under a DB or a DC arrangement are transferred to a DC arrangement. The value of the sums and assets received by the DC arrangement must be actuarially equivalent to the rights being transferred.

Partial transfers may be effected without losing EP. Under the original wording of the FA 2004, partial transfers would have caused the loss of EP. *FA 2007* introduced an amendment to remove the bar on partial transfers. The amendment is deemed to have effect from 6 April 2006.

A transfer from one DB arrangement to another is permitted in certain circumstances. These are where:

- A scheme is winding up and a transfer is made to another DB scheme relating to the same employment.
- A business or undertaking is being transferred from one person to another, it involves the transfer of at least 20 employees, and the transferor and transferee are not treated as members of the same group of companies.

Otherwise, a transfer to a DB scheme is not a permitted transfer, and EP would be lost.

Note that, on a transfer from a DB arrangement to a DC arrangement, the transfer value must be tested against the appropriate limit (see **9.29** above). Although the transfer may be a permitted transfer, if the transfer value exceeds the appropriate limit, it will cause the loss of EP.

9.32 *Transitional protection*

Any transfer of rights which is made to a scheme for an ex-spouse following a pension sharing order is a permitted transfer.

FIXED AND INDIVIDUAL PROTECTIONS

Background

9.32 The HIERC was due to be implemented on 6 April 2011. This would have levied a tax on the pension contributions or pension accrual, on a tapering scale, of those earning more than £150,000 in a tax year. The tax charge was designed to claw back some of the, then current, 50% tax relief so that only 20% basic relief would have been given.

On coming to power in May 2010, the Coalition Government replaced HIERC with reductions in the AA from 6 April 2011; and the LTA from 6 April 2012. Some form of protection was needed against the drop in the LTA, to cater for those who had already accrued rights between £1.5m and £1.8m and would be immediately and unfairly caught by the change. Additionally, anyone with rights already over £1.8m would be facing a much higher tax bill as a result of the change.

The solution was the introduction of FP 2012. As long as no further benefit accrued from 6 April 2012 onwards, someone with FP 2012 would be treated as having a LTA of £1.8m instead of £1.5m. If the standard LTA rises above £1.8m in future, those with FP 2012 can rely on the higher allowance from that time.

The legislation governing FP 2012 can be found in *FA 2011, s 67* and *Sch 18*.

The later introductions of FP 2014 and IP 2014, and the rules which apply to both, are described in **9.44** below.

Conditions for fixed protection 2012

9.33 Under FP 2012 the standard LTA was replaced by a figure of £1.8 million when calculating the enhancement factor where the individual is relying on protection under *FA 2004, ss 220, 222, 223* or *224*, (which apply a lifetime enhancement factor in respect of pension credits, relevant overseas individuals and transfers from QROPS). The substitution related only to events taking place before 6 April 2012.

A person could obtain FP 2012 if the following conditions were met:

- They had one or more arrangements under a registered pension scheme on 6 April 2012.
- They did not have PP.
- They did not have EP.
- Notice of intention to rely on FP 2012 had been given to HMRC before 6 April 2012.

To notify HMRC of intention to rely on FP 2012, form APSS227 had to be completed and received by HMRC before 6 April 2012.

It was not necessary to have rights in excess of £1.5m in order to apply, and it was not necessary to provide any valuation of pension rights with the notification. Once the application had been processed, HMRC issued a FP 2012 certificate.

Where a scheme member wishes to rely on FP 2012 when crystallising benefits, they must tell the scheme administrator of this fact and provide their FP 2012 certificate number. The scheme administrator may then proceed on the basis that the member's LTA is £1.8m instead of any lower standard LTA.

If a scheme member does rely on FP 2012 when crystallising benefits, the scheme administrator must notify HMRC as part of the scheme's Event Report. Any liability to a LTA charge must be reported on the scheme's AFT return and paid at the same time. Scheme administrators must give members a statement showing how much of the standard LTA has been used up by a BCE. In the case of someone with FP 2012, the percentage shown in the statement should be calculated as a percentage of the FP 2012 LTA of £1.8m (or the standard LTA if that is higher).

EP could be given up through notification on form APSS227 at the same time as applying for FP 2012, but not PP. Anyone with PP, therefore, could not have made use of FP 2012. This would also have affected anyone who took EP but decided to take out PP as well as a safeguard against potentially losing their EP.

Effect of fixed protection 2012

9.34 The effect of FP 2012 is essentially to apply the post A-Day tax regime, contained in *FA 2004, Pt 4*, as if the standard LTA were the higher of the prevailing standard LTA and £1.8m. Thus, in calculating any LTA charge, BCEs are tested against £1.8m instead of £1.5m from 6 April 2012 onwards.

The same applies to the calculation of lump sum retirement benefits. Pension commencement lump sums are normally limited to 25% of the prevailing standard LTA. However, £1.8m may be used in calculating this limit for someone with FP 2012. Assuming there is no scheme-specific lump sum protection, the maximum pension commencement lump sum will therefore be the lower of:

- 25% of the available LTA set by FP 2012, which will be £1.8m, and
- 25% of the amount crystallising under the scheme at that time.

This means that, if the member has not previously taken any benefits and is crystallising £1.8m or more, their maximum tax-free lump sum would be £450,000.

Loss of fixed protection 2012

9.35 FP 2012 will cease to apply if, at any time from 6 April 2012 onwards, any of the following events occur:

9.36 *Transitional protection*

- There is benefit accrual in relation to the individual under an arrangement in a registered pension scheme.
- There is an 'impermissible transfer' into any arrangement under a registered pension scheme relating to the individual.
- A transfer of sums or assets under an arrangement is made that is not a 'permitted transfer'.
- An arrangement relating to the individual is made under a registered pension scheme otherwise than in permitted circumstances.

These four circumstances are elaborated on in **9.36** to **9.41** below.

Note that FP 2012 can be lost if benefit accrual occurs at any time from 6 April 2012 onwards. This is an ongoing test. The test is straightforward in a DC arrangement, as it will be when a relevant contribution is paid. The test is more complicated in a DB arrangement (see **9.38** below for details).

If FP 2012 is lost under any of the four circumstances above, the member must notify HMRC of this fact within 90 days of the event that gave rise to the loss. The address to write to is:

HM Revenue & Customs
Pension Schemes Services
FitzRoy House
Castle Meadow Road
Nottingham
NG2 1BD

Failure to notify the loss of protection can result in a penalty of up to £300, with daily penalties of up to £60 thereafter.

Once FP 2012 has been lost, the standard LTA will apply to all BCEs taking place after the date on which protection was lost.

Benefit accrual

9.36 Having any 'benefit accrual' from 6 April 2012 onwards is one of the four ways in which FP 2012 can be lost. Note that benefit accrual for the purpose of FP 2012 is not the same as relevant benefit accrual for the purpose of EP. The following three sections describe what is meant by benefit accrual in DC arrangements, DB and cash balance arrangements, and hybrid arrangements.

Other money purchase arrangements

9.37 If a 'relevant contribution' is paid on or after 6 April 2012 to an 'other money purchase (viz: DC) arrangement' (ie one that is not a cash balance arrangement), this will cause the loss of FP 2012 at the time the contribution is paid. 'Relevant contributions' can be any of the following three types:

1. A 'relievable contribution', ie a contribution paid by the member or by someone else (but not the employer) on behalf of the member. However, the following are excluded from the definition of relievable contribution:

    (a) DC contracting-out rebates.

    (b) Contributions paid by the member or someone else on the member's behalf (other than the employer) after the member has reached age 75.

    (c) Contributions to a registered pension scheme to purchase personal term assurance (life assurance premiums paid for non-group death benefits that are not tax-relievable).

2. A contribution paid by the member's employer in respect of the member.

3. A contribution that is not paid by the member, by anyone else on behalf of the member or by the member's employer, but where that contribution is subsequently allocated to the member's arrangement.

Compensation payments may be awarded for poor advice, misselling, poor administration or poor performance. Where the compensation is paid into another DC arrangement instead of directly to the member, it will generally result in the loss of FP 2012.

Defined benefit and cash balance arrangements

9.38 FP 2012 will be lost if there is an increase in the value of the member's rights under a DB or cash balance arrangement at any time on or after 6 April 2012. However, increases can be ignored if they do not exceed the 'relevant percentage' in a tax year.

Increases in value are based on the valuation assumptions in *FA 2004, s 277*. Whenever the benefit accrual test is carried out, the member's rights are valued as the amount he would be entitled to, assuming that the member:

- is of an age at which no reduction would apply to the payment of an immediate benefit, and

- is in good physical and mental health at the time of the test.

The 'relevant percentage' is an annual rate of increase specified in a scheme's rules as at 9 December 2010 or, if there is no such rate specified, the percentage increase in the consumer prices index (CPI) to September in the previous tax year. The rate specified in scheme rules can include the rules of a predecessor arrangement from which a transfer has been received.

In the case of a cash balance arrangement, an increase occurs if there is an increase in the amount that would, on the valuation assumptions, be available for the provision of benefits to or in respect of the member. If it exceeds the relevant percentage, FP 2012 will be lost.

9.38 *Transitional protection*

In the case of a DB, an increase occurs if there is an increase in the formula

(P × RVF) + LS

where:

- P is the annual rate of pension which would, on the valuation assumptions, be payable to the member under the arrangement;
- RVF is the relevant valuation factor (20, unless another has been agreed with HMRC); and
- LS is the annual rate of lump sum to which the member would, on the valuation assumptions, be entitled (otherwise than by way of commutation of pension).

If it exceeds the relevant percentage, FP 2012 will be lost.

Where the relevant percentage is determined under scheme rules as at 9 December 2010, this may only apply to certain categories of membership. It is common for rules to apply percentage increases to deferred pensions. Late retirement factors may also be applied where the drawing of benefits is deferred beyond the scheme's normal pension age. However, the accrual of DBs for active members is usually expressed as the product of pensionable salary, service and an accrual rate.

If someone with FP 2012 remains an active member after 5 April 2012, it is quite possible that they will have benefit accrual that exceeds the increase in CPI, thereby causing the loss of FP 2012. However, once an active member becomes a deferred member, the deferred pension revaluation rate specified in scheme rules can be relied on instead of the CPI increase, assuming the rule was in place on 9 December 2010. If scheme rules are subsequently changed to apply a higher increase rate, FP 2012 will be lost when the first increase occurs after 5 April 2012. This is particularly important to remember because of changes in the statutory method used to revalue deferred pensions. For example, where a scheme uses CPI for revaluation but a rule change is executed to provide revaluation by reference to the often higher RPI, this would cause the loss of FP 2012 upon the first increase that is higher than the CPI rate.

The following example, taken from HMRC guidance RPSM11106090, illustrates the loss of FP 2012 protection where someone continues in active membership:

> 'Roger is a member of a defined benefits scheme. His scheme gives him a pension of 1/60th of pensionable salary for each year of service. To get a lump sum Roger has to give up (commute) part of his pension. If Roger dies before he starts drawing his pension a lump sum of four times salary will be paid.
>
> Roger applies for fixed protection but continues to build up benefits under his scheme after 5 April 2012. From 2012–13 onwards Roger needs to check each tax year to see if he has lost fixed protection. He does this by testing whether or not the value of his pension rights

have gone up by more than the "relevant percentage" in the tax year. The relevant percentage, is either

- an annual rate specified in the rules of the pension scheme on 9 December 2010, or where there is no rate specified
- the annual percentage increase in the consumer prices index (CPI) for the month of September in the previous tax year.

The rules of Roger's pension scheme do not set a percentage by which member's benefits are increased each year. So Roger needs to check that his pension rights have not gone up by more than the annual CPI increase.

On 5 April 2012 Roger has 35 years of service and a pensionable salary of £132,000. He has built up a pension of

35/60 × £132,000 = £77,000pa.

The value of Roger's pension rights on 5 April 2012 is therefore

£77,000 × 20 = £1,540,000.

On 5 April 2013 Roger's pensionable salary has gone up by only £500 to £132,500. Roger has now built up an annual pension of

36/60 × £132,500 = £79,500.

This means the value of his pension rights is now

£79,500 × 20 = £1,590,000.

The annual increase in the consumer prices index (CPI) to September 2011 is, say, 3%. This means that as long as Roger's pension rights over the tax year have not increased by more than 3% he will keep fixed protection.

The value of Roger's pension rights as at 5 April 2012 increased by CPI is

£1,540,000 × 103/100 = £1,586,200.

This is less than the value of Roger's pension rights at the end of 2012–13. Roger has lost fixed protection.'

Whether a late retirement factor is within the definition of 'relevant percentage' may hinge on how it is worded in scheme rules. Although the *FA 2011* requires there to be 'an annual rate of increase specified in a scheme's rules', HMRC accept that, just because a specific rate (eg 12%) is not mentioned, it does not necessarily mean that the late retirement factor will not qualify as a relevant percentage. If a rate is not explicitly mentioned, a late retirement factor will still be a relevant percentage if:

- the annual rate, once calculated, can be expressed in percentage terms; and
- the scheme trustees have no discretion over whether to pay the late retirement factor.

9.38 *Transitional protection*

The late retirement factor may therefore vary from year to year and from member to member without it necessarily failing to be a relevant percentage. It is also not necessary for the trustees to take actuarial advice in setting the late retirement factors, but the rate should do no more than compensate the member for the delayed payment of his pension.

Where part of a member's pension is put into payment, this does not in HMRC's view provide further scope to increase benefits above the relevant percentage without benefit accrual occurring. Upon part-crystallisation of benefits, the rights immediately before part-crystallisation should be valued to see if benefit accrual has occurred. If FP 2012 has not been lost, the ongoing benefit accrual test still applies but by reference to the residual benefits. Further accrual can only occur up to the relevant percentage increase, taking account of any increase that accrued before part-crystallisation. The following example from HMRC guidance at Pensions Newsletter *'Fixed Protection Special Edition November 2011'* illustrates the issue:

> 'At 6/4/2012, Fiona has uncrystallised defined benefits pension rights of £80,000 (pension before commutation); the value of her uncrystallised rights is £1.6m.
>
> Fiona has applied for fixed protection.
>
> Fiona remains in active membership of the scheme and the "relevant percentage" for tax year 2012–13 is the annual increase in the CPI for September 2011 which is 5.2%.
>
> Fiona is therefore aware that if her rights increase by more than 5.2% she will lose her fixed protection. £1.6m increased by 5.2% is £1,683,200.
>
> On 30 October 2012, Fiona takes a pension of £50,000 from her arrangement. By that time her total accrued rights were to a pension of £82,000.
>
> The value of her prospective rights immediately before crystallisation is therefore £1.64m (£82,000 × 20). This is an increase of 2.5%.
>
> There has been no increase in Fiona's rights above the relevant percentage so she has not lost fixed protection.
>
> However, the £32,000 remaining uncrystallised pension rights have already received a 2.5% increase (in effect the uncrystallised rights were worth £31,220 at the start of the year and have increased by 2.5% to £32,000).
>
> The uncrystallised rights may still give rise to benefit accrual if they are increased beyond the relevant percentage during the tax year.
>
> In measuring this it is necessary to take account of all increases during the tax year including those increases previously occurring before part crystallisation.
>
> Any further increase in the value of those remaining uncrystallised rights in 2012–13, in excess of 2.7% of £31,220, will lead to loss of fixed protection.

Similarly, if Fiona's rights had been increased by 5.2% by the time the pension of £50,000 was taken, she loses her fixed protection if the remaining uncrystallised rights are increased at all during the remainder of the tax year.'

Hybrid arrangements

9.39 Benefit accrual under a hybrid scheme is a combination of the DC and DB/cash balance tests. If benefits under the hybrid arrangement include DC benefits, FP 2012 will be lost if a relevant contribution is paid. FP 2012 will also be lost if there is an increase of more than the relevant percentage in the value of the member's rights under the arrangement.

Transfers

9.40 FP 2012 is lost on the occurrence of an 'impermissible transfer'. This is the same definition of 'impermissible transfer' as applies for EP. It covers the conversion of a DB arrangement into a DC arrangement, and the transfer of money into a DC arrangement from somewhere other than another pension arrangement of the member. However, a transfer of pension rights under a pension sharing order following divorce may be made without jeopardising FP 2012.

Transfers of pension rights that are not 'permitted transfers' will also cause the loss of FP 2012. The following are permitted transfers:

1. The transfer of some or all of the benefits under a DB or a DC arrangement to another DC arrangement (the value of the sums and assets received by the DC arrangement must be actuarially equivalent to the rights being transferred).

2. A transfer from one DB arrangement to another only in the following situations:
   - The scheme is being wound up and a transfer is made to another DB scheme relating to the same employment.
   - A business or undertaking is being transferred from one person to another, it involves the transfer of at least 20 employees, and the transferor and transferee are not treated as members of the same group of companies.
   - The transfer is part of a 'retirement benefit activities compliance exercise'. This is where life assurance-only members need to be removed from an occupational pension scheme to avoid falling foul of *PA 2004, s 255* (which limits scheme activities to the provision of pension benefits and ancillary benefits for pension members).

3. A transfer of rights to a scheme for an ex-spouse following a pension sharing order.

9.41 *Transitional protection*

New arrangements

9.41 FP 2012 will cease to apply if an arrangement relating to an individual is made under a registered pension scheme otherwise than in permitted circumstances. The permitted circumstances are:

- The new arrangement is set up to receive a permitted transfer (see **9.40** above).

- The new arrangement is set up as part of a 'retirement benefit activities exercise' (see **9.40** above).

- The new arrangement is set up as part of an 'age equality compliance exercise'. This is where one arrangement is cancelled and a new arrangement is set up in order to comply with age discrimination legislation under *EA 2010*.

Therefore, if new recruits with FP 2012 are put into a group life assurance scheme set up as a registered pension scheme, they would lose FP 2012. Where employees are automatically enrolled into a registered pension scheme under new employer duties from October 2012 onwards, this constitutes a new arrangement and would cause the loss of FP 2012. Employees with FP 2012 who have been automatically enrolled under these provisions would need to exercise their statutory right to opt out within the one-month deadline if they are to maintain their protection.

Where someone takes out a new personal pension policy but subsequently cancels the policy under FCA rules, this would be viewed by HMRC as creating a new arrangement and would cause the loss of FP 2012.

PAYMENT OF PROTECTED LUMP SUM

9.42 Once it comes to be paid, the amount of a protected lump sum is calculated according to the following complicated formula:

$$\text{VULSR} \times \text{ULA} / \text{FSLA} + \text{ALSA}, \text{ and}$$

$$\text{ALSA} = \tfrac{1}{4} \times (\text{LS} + \text{AC} - \text{VUR} \times \text{CSLA} / \text{FSLA})$$

where:

- VULSR is the value of uncrystallised lump sum rights on 5 April 2006

- ULA is the underpinned LTA, ie the greater of the prevailing LTA and £1.8 million

- CSLA is the current standard LTA (ie at the time of paying the lump sum)

- FSLA is the LTA for 2006/07 (£1.5 million)

- LS is the amount of lump sum actually taken

- AC is the amount crystallised by bringing the annual pension into payment, and

- VUR is the value of uncrystallised rights under the scheme on 5 April 2006

If ALSA (additional lump sum amount) is a negative number, it is taken to be nil.

The formula set out above reflects an amendment made by *FA 2008*. Prior to the amendment, ALSA was only taken into account in the formula if relevant benefit accrual had occurred post A-Day. Relevant benefit accrual is, in the case of a DC arrangement, the payment of a contribution and, in the case of a DB arrangement, the payment of pension above a certain level that is not easily ascertained and which consequently led to the amendment of the formula.

The formula was also amended by *FA 2011* to take account of the reduction in the standard LTA from £1.8 million to £1.5 million. £1.8 million can still be used to uprate the A-Day protected amount in the first part of the formula but is not used in the second part of the formula, which is designed to take account of post A-Day accrual.

If use of the protected lump sum formula leads to a figure that is actually less than the normal formula for calculating a pension commencement lump sum, the normal calculation can be used instead.

Life cover

9.43 The provision of group life assurance for employees with FP 2012 may lead to the loss of that protection in certain circumstances.

In a DB arrangement, 'benefit accrual' for the purpose of FP 2012 (see **9.38** above) is expressed in terms of the benefit to which the member is entitled, not the benefits to which the member's dependants are potentially entitled. Therefore, where death benefits are provided on a DB basis before 6 April 2012, and they continue to be provided on the same basis after 5 April 2012, this would not cause the loss of FP 2012.

However, HMRC would consider a group life assurance scheme to be a DB scheme only where the rules of the scheme determine the lump sum death benefit to be paid. If the rules of the scheme do not specify a certain benefit, but simply provide for the lump sum death benefit payable to be the proceeds of an insurance policy (even if the policy provides a DB), HMRC have stated that they would consider this to be a DC scheme. Relievable contributions to a registered DC scheme (in this case, in the form of life assurance premiums) would ordinarily trigger the loss of FP 2012. However, the same exemption for life assurance premiums that applies for EP also applies for FP 2012. FP 2012 will not be lost as long as the following conditions are met:

- The contributions are used to pay premiums under a policy of insurance, and that policy of insurance was made before 6 April 2006.
- There is no right to surrender any rights under the policy.
- There are no payments under the policy except on the individual's death.
- The policy is not varied significantly to either increase the prospective benefits or extend the term of the policy.

9.43 *Transitional protection*

In practice, it may be difficult to meet these conditions. The requirement for the policy to be the same one since 2006, not 2012 as might be expected, is a condition applying to the EP exemption. In any event, a re-broking of the policy is a significant variation. If this has not already occurred since 2006, it is something that is likely to occur in the future in relation to an employer's group life assurance scheme. Re-broking would therefore cause the loss of FP 2012 for anyone covered by the new insurance where it falls to be a DC arrangement under the scheme.

If death benefits continue to be provided under a hybrid arrangement where, until death occurs, there is the possibility of death benefits falling due on either a DB basis or a DC basis, the benefit accrual tests for both DB and DC arrangements need to be carried out.

Participation in a new arrangement – ie an arrangement that is new to the employee – will cause the loss of FP 2012 if it is part of a registered pension scheme. Therefore, putting new recruits into a registered pension scheme for life assurance will lose FP 2012 regardless of whether the scheme is DB or DC.

There has been a certain amount of confusion over the exact meaning of benefit accrual in relation to registered group life schemes. The following statement was made by HMRC on 30 March 2012 to clarify the position with regard to continuing life cover and whether this would be benefit accrual for the purpose of FP 2012:

> **'Fixed protection – lump sum death benefits paid on death in service**
>
> This announcement is to clarify HM Revenue Customs' (HMRC) interpretation of the tax rules for benefit accrual for those individuals with fixed protection in relation to lump sum death benefits and benefit accrual.
>
> **Lump sum death benefits and life insurance**
>
> HMRC is aware that there is concern about the views they have expressed in relation to the position where insurance has been taken out to cover the potential cost of paying lump sum death benefits and whether payment of insurance premiums on or after 6 April 2012 is benefit accrual for the purposes of fixed protection. Given the interest this issue has generated and in the light of the further information they have received from the pensions industry this note sets out and clarifies their revised position.
>
> Where a member who applies for fixed protection has a right to a defined benefits lump sum death benefit, as explained in the Registered Pensions Schemes Manual at RPSM11101532 the guidance sets out:
>
> "Whether or not an individual can continue to have death benefits (life cover) and keep fixed protection depends on the type of arrangement providing the death benefits. RPSM03109040 gives guidance on what type of benefit is provided by what type of arrangement.

Transitional protection **9.43**

If the death benefit promised is a defined benefit (and this is often the case in occupational pension schemes) continuing to provide death cover should not cause loss of fixed protection. This is because a death in service benefit is not considered to be part of a member's pension rights. So if a member continues to be provided with death in service benefits this will not be benefit accrual and so will not cause loss of fixed protection.

If the death benefit promised is other money purchase, cover may only continue with the member keeping fixed protection if it is provided by a policy established before 6 April 2006. The conditions at RPSM03109032 need to be met. Fixed protection will be lost where contributions are made to a policy set up on or after 6 April 2006."

HMRC's view is that increases in the benefit applying from 6 April 2012, whether for example as a result of a salary increase, a higher multiple of salary or both, cannot give rise to benefit accrual nor will the payment of contributions to fund the benefit.

HMRC has been told that in many cases pension schemes may take out an insurance policy to cover the potential cost of paying lump sum death benefits.

HMRC's view is that in such cases where the only lump sum death benefit being provided under an arrangement under the scheme rules is an amount equivalent to the proceeds of an insurance policy, ie there is no provision for a defined benefits lump sum death benefit, then the arrangement is clearly an "other money purchase arrangement" (for more detail see the Glossary definition of "other money purchase arrangement" at RPSM20000000). In addition, where the lump sum death benefit is expressed as being the greater of a defined benefit (an amount determined by reference to salary, service or some other factor) and the policy proceeds, then this will be a hybrid arrangement as depending on circumstances either a defined benefit or an other money purchase benefit will be payable. So in both cases, the payment of a premium on or after 6 April 2012 will result in benefit accrual and loss of fixed protection if the premium is a "relevant contribution" as defined by paragraph 14 of Schedule 36 to Finance Act 2004 by virtue of paragraph 14(11) of Schedule 18 to Finance Act 2011. See guidance at RPSM11101530.

However, HMRC is aware that there are a number of other types of insured death benefit lump sums. HMRC accepts that the following scenarios will not involve an other money purchase benefit and therefore not lead to benefit accrual and loss of fixed protection:

a. A Lump Sum Death Benefit (LSDB) of 4 × final salary is paid out of scheme funds. This benefit is a defined benefits lump sum death benefit. (For the purposes of these scenarios the defined benefits lump sum death benefit is assumed to be a lump sum equal to 4 × final salary, in practice the defined benefit may be different.)

9.43 *Transitional protection*

b. A LSDB is calculated as in a. above and is backed by an insurance policy where, if the policy proceeds exceed the LSDB, the excess is paid to, and retained within, the scheme.

c. A LSDB is calculated as in a. above and is backed by insurance policy with the scheme liable to make good any shortfall where the proceeds of the policy are insufficient to fully fund the cost of the LSDB.

d. A LSDB is calculated as in a. above and is backed by insurance policy. The policy will not pay out more than the LSDB but may contain restrictions which, if they apply, will result in an amount payable to the scheme (or payable directly to the beneficiary(ies) identified by the trustees) which is less than the unrestricted defined lump sum death benefit.

It has become clear from information provided to HMRC, that many policies contain such restrictions. They may for example apply when there is a "catastrophe" event or in the case of particular individuals who represent a greater risk. Where the LSDB paid to the beneficiaries after the restriction is applied can itself be expressed as a defined benefits LSDB, for example:

- it represents a percentage of the defined benefits LSDB that would have been provided in normal circumstances, or
- it is paid on a pro rata basis, or
- it is expressed as a lower amount, or
- the maximum paid under the policy is capped
- then HMRC accepts that the LSDB actually paid is a defined benefits LSDB.

The exact position will of course depend upon the restrictions that apply under a particular policy but provided the maximum LSDB that can be provided under the policy is the defined benefits LSDB of 4 × salary and the restricted LSDB is defined in a manner which satisfies either the definition of "defined benefits" at section 152(6) Finance Act 2004 or possibly "cash balance benefits" as defined at section 152(5) there will be no other money purchase elements to the benefits to be provided. For the avoidance of doubt where, under a group policy, there are restrictions applying to particular members covered under the policy but which do not apply in the case of the member(s) with fixed protection, then no account need be taken of those restrictions.

e. Where an individual has restricted benefits under one policy but a further policy is taken out by the scheme in respect of the individual to ensure that the maximum 4 × final salary LSDB is paid, the benefit will be a defined benefits LSDB subject to the top-up policy not itself being another money purchase arrangement because the entire proceeds will be paid out as a lump sum death benefit.

f. Where dependants' pension under a scheme's rules are insured, the insurance policy might, for example, make provision for a dependants' pension equal to say 30 per cent of the member's salary, but with the pension restricted to the "free-cover" divided by a specified multiple (say 30). So, if free-cover is £500,000, the max dependant's pension is £16,667. HMRC accepts that this is a defined benefit arrangement as a specified benefit (a pension) will be provided and that pension is calculated by reference to a factor rather than just the amount available for the provision of dependants' benefits.

What about people whose life cover has ceased because they believed the continuing payment of premiums on or after 6 April 2012 would lead to benefit accrual and loss of fixed protection?

In such cases, HMRC would not regard re-instatement of the life cover as being a new arrangement (which itself would lead to loss of fixed protection as it would not be made in "permitted circumstances") made for the member so long as:

- the cover is re-instated as soon as possible whether with the same or a new insurer, and

- the basis of the cover provided has not been increased in comparison to the cover previously provided

HMRC will update the guidance in the Registered Pension Schemes Manual in due course.

Death in service lump sums – refunds of contributions

HMRC is aware that it has been suggested that they may view a refund of contributions made on the death of a member as an other money purchase benefit.

For the avoidance of doubt, HMRC's view is that the payment of a refund of contributions on death is a defined benefit and that the lump sum is a defined benefits lump sum death benefit. Where the rules also provide for the refund to include an element of "interest" or growth to be paid, then provided that the scheme rules provide for the payment and it is expressed or can be expressed in percentage terms then this will not affect the defined benefits nature of the lump sum. The scheme rules may specify an annual percentage rate of "interest" or a rate in line with the average annual base rate of a bank etc or a rate to be determined by the scheme trustees in accordance with actuarial advice. All these examples are accepted as providing a defined benefit.'

The conditions for maintaining FP 2012 while participating in a registered pension scheme for death benefits are therefore quite detailed, and there is still much potential for confusion. There is also a danger that future actions in relation to the life cover arrangements will overlook those with FP 2012, thereby jeopardising it. For these reasons, the safer course of action for any

9.44 *Transitional protection*

employer seeking to provide life cover for employees with FP 2012 would seem to be to take out an EGLP (see **10.17** below).

Fixed protection 2014, and individual protection 2014

9.44 The further reduction to the LTA from 6 April 2014 has resulted in two new protections, FP 2014 and IP 2014. The latter is very different to the FP 2012 rules, whereas FP 2014 closely follows the FP 2012 rules.

FP 2014: FP 2014 was brought in by *FA 2013*, *s 48* and *Sch 22*, which restricted the level of the LTA from £1.5m to £1.25m from 6 April 2014. FP 2014 provides an individual with a personal LTA of £1.5m, whatever the current level of their pension savings.

FP 2014 was also made available to members of RNUKS, subject to their not having a pension input amount of greater than nil in the non-UK pension scheme in any tax year from 2014/15.

The rules of FP 2014 are similar to those which apply to FP 2012, meaning that protection could be lost by future events in the circumstances described above.

The conditions to be met for FP 2014 were that the individual:

- had one or more arrangements under a registered pension scheme on 6 April 2012;
- did not have PP;
- did not have EP; and
- did not have FP 2012.

FA 2013, *Pt 1* of *Sch 22* explains how benefit accrual can occur under different schemes and circumstances. Benefit accrual occurs at the end of the tax year where the pension input amount for a tax year is greater than nil.

Individuals must notify HMRC if they lose FP 2014, within 90 days of becoming aware of an event causing the loss. Failure to do so will result in penalties of up to £300 for failure to notify and daily penalties of up to £60 per day after the initial penalty is raised.

Application for FP 2014 had to be made to HMRC before 6 April 2014 (see the following HMRC Newsletters):

http://www.hmrc.gov.uk/pensionschemes/newsletter57.pdf
http://www.hmrc.gov.uk/pensionschemes/newsletter58.pdf
http://www.hmrc.gov.uk/pensionschemes/newsletter59.pdf
http://www.hmrc.gov.uk/pensionschemes/newsletter60.pdf
http://www.hmrc.gov.uk/pensionschemes/newsletter61.pdf
http://www.hmrc.gov.uk/pensionschemes/newsletter62.pdf
http://www.hmrc.gov.uk/pensionschemes/newsletter63.pdf

IP 2014: IP 2014 is a different form of individual protection from the LTA. IP 2014 provides an individual with an LTA of the greater of the value of their pension rights on 5 April 2014, up to an overall maximum of £1.5m, or the level of the standard LTA. IP 2014 is available to individuals with UK tax-relieved pension rights of more than £1.25m or who think they may have rights in excess of that amount by the time they take their pension benefits.

Unlike other forms of recent LTA protection, there is no restriction on the individual making future contributions or accruing further benefits. Nevertheless, if their LTA limit is exceeded, they will be subject to the LTA charge when they take their benefits. Individuals with IP 2014 may retain FP 2012 or FP 2014, as appropriate. However, IP 2014 will apply if they subsequently lose their fixed protection (see *FA 2014, Sch 6*).

IP 2014 will remain at the above level unless the standard LTA rises above this figure, in which case the individual's LTA would revert to the standard LTA. An individual who applied for FP2014 is still eligible to apply for IP2014, if applicable. There is an online tool to help individuals decide if they want to apply for IP2014.

Pension commencement lump sums under IP 2014 are limited to 25% of the individual's pension rights, subject to an overall cap of 25% of the personalised LTA. IP 2014 will cease if the monetary value of savings falls below £1.25m following a pension sharing order on divorce. However, if the pension debit reduces the value to a figure above £1.25m, IP 2014 will remain and the reduced level will apply from the date of the pension debit. The pension debit will be treated as reduced by 5% for each full tax year between 5 April 2014 and the date of the pension debit. Further information on IP 2014 is provided in HMRC's *'Pensions Individual Protection 2014: guidance note'*.

Applications may be made to HMRC until 5 April 2017. The application form is expected to be available online from August 2014.

HMRC's Pensions Newsletters 58, 61 and 63 describe the application of IP 2014 as at:

http://www.hmrc.gov.uk/pensionschemes/newsletter58.pdf;
http://www.hmrc.gov.uk/pensionschemes/newsletter61.pdf; and
http://www.hmrc.gov.uk/pensionschemes/newsletter63.

The above forms of protection are important considerations for the high earner, and scheme administrators and members should ensure that HMRC's protection certificates are not be inadvertently lost.

Examples reproduced from RPSM

9.45 The following examples and text are reproduced from HMRC's RPSM. They have been referred to earlier in this **Chapter** to help illustrate various aspects of the protections available from A-Day before further protections started to appear from 2011/12.. The examples appear here in their numerical order. The complete RPSM can be found on the HMRC website at *www.hmrc.gov.uk/manuals/rpsmmanual/index.htm*.

9.45 *Transitional protection*

RPSM03101040 (Crystallised rights: income drawdown):

> 'If the individual has "relevant existing pensions" that are being paid under income drawdown from
>
> - a retirement benefit scheme or
> - a deferred annuity contract (section 32 policy)
>
> the annual rate at which the pension is payable on 5 April 2006 is to be taken to be the maximum that could be drawn as income from the pension scheme or contract concerned – the actual drawings are not material.
>
> **Example 1**
>
> An individual is drawing a pension of £5,000 under drawdown, but the maximum annual rate of this pension is £10,000. The value of the crystallised rights in these circumstances is £250,000 (25 × £10,000 = £250,000).
>
> **Example 2**
>
> Alan had a fund of £1.6 million. He took a lump sum of £400,000 in January 2006. From the remaining fund of £1.2 million he takes a pension of £91,200 a year under income drawdown. This is the maximum pension that could have been taken under income drawdown. (Alan is assumed to be age 60 and gilt yields are assumed to be 4.5% per annum.)
>
> Alan's pension is therefore valued at £2,280,000 (25 × £91,200 = £2,280,000).
>
> There is no requirement to perform a valuation/review as at 5 April 2006 to determine the maximum amount of pension payable. The maximum amount determined by the most recent valuation/review may be used.
>
> The same principle applies in the case of an individual taking income withdrawal from a personal pension scheme. The crystallised value will be 25 times the maximum amount that could be taken as income drawdown on 5 April 2006. It is not 25 times the amount of income actually being drawn.'

RPSM03101551 (Retirement benefits scheme limit: preservation limit for retirement benefits schemes – Practice Notes published 1 October 1974):

> 'Following on from RPSM03101531 and RPSM03101550 if 5 April 2006 falls before an individual's normal retirement date in a retirement benefits scheme and the individual has employer sponsored money purchase rights in the scheme, the calculation of MPP should be carried out on the basis that preservation applies to the benefits.
>
> The relevant preservation calculation will be the one published in the IR 12 "Occupational Pension Schemes Practice Notes" at the time the scheme was approved.

Transitional protection 9.45

The following is a direct copy of the advice published in the version of IR 12 "Occupational Pension Schemes Practice Notes" published on 1 October 1974.

It applies to any schemes approved under s591 ICTA 1988 (previously s 20 FA 1970) before 1 May 1979.

PN 13.4

"A scheme of the type to which Regulation 5 of the Occupational Pension Schemes (Preservation of Benefit) (No 2) Regulations 1973 (SI 1973 No 1784) applies (whether or not in existence on 6 April 1974), i.e. a scheme providing benefits based on final remuneration but funded by means of a policy or policies with level annual premiums securing benefits based on current remuneration, may give a member leaving service the amount of deferred pension actually secured by premiums paid up to date of his withdrawal even if this is somewhat in excess of the amount calculated under N/NS × P formula. A money purchase scheme, or a scheme using earmarked policies (see paragraphs 18.10–18.20) must test leaving benefits against the N/NS × P formula unless

a. the member's earnings while a member of the scheme have not exceeded £5,000 in any year or

b. at the time of leaving he is less than 45 years of age or

c. such a restriction would infringe the preservation requirements of the Social Security Act 1973."

When calculating the limit above, final remuneration shall be determined by reference to the maximum amount of earnings allowed under the rules of the scheme for the purposes of calculating the maximum retirement benefits for that individual.'

RPSM03101560 (Retirement benefits scheme limit: preservation limit for retirement benefits schemes – Practice Notes published 1 May 1979):

'Following on from RPSM03101531, RPSM03101550 and RPSM03101551 if 5 April 2006 falls before an individual's normal retirement date in a retirement benefit scheme and the individual has employer sponsored money purchase rights in the scheme, the calculation of MPP should be carried out on the basis that preservation applies to the benefits.

The relevant preservation calculation will be the one published in the IR 12 "Occupational Pension Schemes Practice Notes" at the time the scheme was approved. The following is a direct copy of the advice published in the version of IR 12 "Occupational Pension Schemes Practice Notes" published on 1 May 1979.

It applies to any schemes approved under s591 ICTA 1988 (previously s 20 FA 1970) after 30 April 1979 and before 29 November 1991.

9.45 *Transitional protection*

PN 13.4

"Because of the preservation requirements of the Social Security Act 1973 it may not be possible for certain schemes to restrict the benefits of an early leaver by reference to the 1/60th of final remuneration or N/NS × P formula, above viz:

(a) schemes giving a benefit of a constant proportion of final or average earnings for each year of service, at an accrual rate greater than 1/60th (Memorandum No 18 paragraphs 111–121)

(b) money purchase schemes and insured level annual pension premium schemes set up before 6 April 1974 (ibid paragraphs 127 and 137)

(c) 'proceeds of policy' schemes (Memorandum No 78 paragraphs 251–259)

In such cases, the Inland Revenue limit will bite only if it is desired to give greater benefits than the minimum short service benefit.

Other schemes funded by level annual premium policies and securing benefits not exceeding the maximum approvable fraction of current remuneration may also give an early leaver the amount of deferred pension actually secured by premiums paid up to the date of his withdrawal, even if in excess of the amount calculated under the N/NS × P formula."

When calculating the limit above, final remuneration shall be determined by reference to the maximum amount of earnings allowed under the rules of the scheme for the purposes of calculating the maximum retirement benefits for that individual.'

RPSM03101570 (Retirement benefits scheme limit: preservation limit for retirement benefits schemes – Practice Notes effective from 29 November 1991):

'Following on from RPSM03101540, and RPSM03101550 to RPSM03101560 if 5 April 2006 falls before an individual's normal retirement date in a retirement benefit scheme and the individual has employer sponsored money purchase rights in the scheme, the calculation of MPP should be carried out on the basis that preservation applies to the benefits.

The relevant preservation calculation will be the one published in the IR 12 "Occupational Pensions Schemes Practice Notes" at the time the scheme was approved. The following is a direct copy of the advice published in the version of IR 12 "Occupational Pension Schemes Practice Notes" published on 1 September 1991.

It applies to any schemes approved under s 591 ICTA 1988 on or after 29 November 1991.

10.13
"The maximum benefits an approved money purchase scheme may provide at normal retirement date for a member (whether or not entitled to continued rights) who left pensionable service prior to that date, is a deferred pension (including the pension equivalent of any deferred lump sum benefits) of the greater of:

(a) 1/60th of final remuneration for each year of service (up to 40 years) increased in accordance with paragraph 10.12 [PN10.12 – at a fixed rate not exceeding 5% per annum compound, or by a greater percentage but restricted so as not to exceed the increase in the retail prices index during the period of deferment], and

(b) the total benefit the member could have expected to receive at normal retirement date calculated on the same basis as applies for incapacity (see paragraph 6.2) [PN6.2 – the fraction of final remuneration the employee could have received had he or she remained in service until normal retirement date] together with any statutory revaluation increases required by the relevant Social Security legislation.

NB A power of augmentation cannot be used to increase a member's benefit up to this limit: an increase in benefit up to the limits set out in paragraphs 7.4 and 7.36 is, however, permissible."

The following text was added to the end of paragraph 10.13 on 23 March 2001 (via the revised Practice Notes issued with Update 90).

"Where the member has a pension debit in relation to the scheme and does not fall within the administrative easement described in paragraph 7.7, the maximum benefits calculated in accordance with the requirements of this paragraph must be reduced by the pension debit (see paragraph 16.56)."

When calculating the limit above, final remuneration shall be determined by reference to the maximum amount of earnings allowed under the rules of the scheme for the purposes of calculating the maximum retirement benefits for that individual.'

RPSM03102030 (Protection from the lifetime allowance charge – taking benefits at different times):

'Where an individual takes benefits at different times the balance of the personal lifetime allowance will be indexed at the same rate that the standard lifetime allowance has been indexed.

Example

Jacob had £3 million of pension rights protected under primary protection on 5 April 2006, giving an additional lifetime allowance factor of 1.

He took benefits worth £1.8 million in 2011 when the standard lifetime allowance was £1.8 million. At that time, Jacob's primary

9.45 *Transitional protection*

protection was worth £3.6 million (standard lifetime allowance of £1.8 million plus additional lifetime allowance factor of £1.8 million). So Jacob used up 50% of his personal lifetime allowance.

In 2014 Jacob took the rest of his benefits that were worth £2 million. The standard lifetime allowance (SLA) in 2014 is say £1.5 million. Jacob's primary protection was then worth £3.6 million (£1.8 million plus a factor of 1). See RPSM03102020 for how Jacob's primary protection is calculated.

The amount of lifetime allowance used up by Jacob's previous benefit crystallisation is found by multiplying the amount of that BCE (£1.8 million) by the formula

SLA at time of current (2014) BCE/SLA at time of previous (2011) BCE

Where SLA is the standard lifetime allowance. So,

£1.8 million × (£1.5 million/£1.8 million) = £1.5 million.

Jacob has used up £1.5 million lifetime allowance so has £2.1 million available. In taking £2 million Jacob has no lifetime allowance charge to pay. This is because the amount taken is within the amount of protection still available to him.

In describing how the individual gets a lifetime allowance that is greater than the standard lifetime allowance, it has been assumed that the individual's rights when valued were within "HMRC limits". The valuation section of this guidance at RPSM03101510 explains how only rights valued on 5 April 2006 within "HMRC limits" can be taken into primary protection.'

RPSM03104590 (Relevant benefit accrual in defined benefits and cash balance arrangements: example):

'David is a member of a contracted-out defined benefits arrangement with an accrual rate of one sixtieth for each year of service. On 5 April 2006, David has 30 years' service and his pensionable earnings are £120,000. He takes benefits in April 2011. The arrangement uses the 20:1 valuation factor in s276 FA 2004.

Step 1

On 5 April 2006, David's rights are valued at £1.2 million (30/60 × £120,000 × 20).

Step 2

Calculate the 'appropriate limit' using the value from Step 1. Two calculations need to be done: the higher of the two is the "appropriate limit".

The first calculation is increasing £1.2 million by an indexation figure. The indexation figure is the highest figure obtained from a calculation over the period between 6 April 2006 and the date of the relevant event. The indexation figure is the highest of

- 5% annual compound interest over the period,
- $[RPI(2) - RPI(1)] / RPI(1)$

    where RPI(2) is the RPI for the month in which the first relevant event occurs and RPI(1) is the RPI for April 2006; or

- for contracted-out rights, the percentage rate specified in The Registered Pension Schemes (Uprating Percentages for Defined Benefits Arrangements and Enhanced Protection) Regulations 2006 – SI 2006/130.

Assume the highest figure is arrived at by using 5% compound for the five years between April 2006 and April 2011. Indexing £1.2 million in this way gives a figure of £1,531,538.

The second calculation is to use David's pensionable earnings in April 2011 and apply David's accrual rate under the arrangement to this. In this instance, the scheme rules would not apply an early retirement factor to David's pension rights when they come into payment in 2011. David's pensionable earnings are now £160,000. Assume that this pensionable earnings figure does not exceed the limit on post-commencement earnings. David's pre 6 April 2006 rights have a value of £1.6 million (30/60 × £160,000 × 20).

The amount of £1.6 million from the earnings re-calculation is higher than £1,531,400 figure from the indexation calculation. So the appropriate limit is £1.6 million.

Step 3

Compare the value of the benefit crystallisation event in April 2011 with the appropriate limit.

Scenario 1: The benefit crystallisation event in April 2011 is worth £1.75 million. Enhanced protection is lost but there is no lifetime allowance charge because the standard lifetime allowance is £1.8 million.

Scenario 2: The benefit crystallisation event in April 2011 is worth £2 million. Enhanced protection is lost and there is a lifetime allowance charge.'

RPSM03104600 (Example 1 of benefit increases after 5 April 2006 that are not relevant benefit accruals: low salary increases):

'The example here and on RPSM03104610 show where relevant benefit accrual as defined in paragraph 13, Schedule 36 FA 2004 has not occurred and consequently the individual has not lost enhanced protection.

9.45 *Transitional protection*

Example 1 Accrual after 5 April 2006, but low salary increases

Anthony had 30 years service on 5 April 2006. The scheme's accrual rate was 1/60th for each year of service. His final pensionable salary, as defined on that day in the scheme documentation, was £240,000. He therefore registered £2.4 million (£120,000 × 20) for enhanced protection.

Anthony remained an active member of the pension scheme for another five years until he reached normal retirement age. By this time, his final pensionable salary had grown to £252,000 giving a pension of £147,000 (35/60 × £252,000). The value of the benefit crystallisation event is £2.94 million (£147,000 × 20).

The test for relevant benefit accrual is whether the value of the benefit crystallisation event is greater than the value of the appropriate limit.

The appropriate limit is the greater of

- indexation of £2.4 million (× 5% compound, RPI or the percentage rate specified in The Registered Pension Schemes (Uprating Percentages for Defined Benefits Arrangements and Enhanced Protection) Regulations 2006 – SI 2006/130, and

- a recalculation of the pension accrued at 5 April 2006 reflecting current final pensionable salary and the scheme early retirement factor (where appropriate) for the current age and a valuation factor of 20.

For the purposes of this example it has been assumed that indexation at 5% compound gives a higher figure than the recalculation.

The value of the appropriate limit is £3,063,076 (£2.4 million indexed at 5%) which is more than the value of the benefit crystallisation event (£2.94 million). Therefore relevant benefit accrual has not occurred and enhanced protection is retained.'

RPSM03104610 (Example 2 of benefit increases after 5 April 2006 that are not relevant benefit accruals: early retirement factor applied):

'Early reduction factor where the member retires before normal retirement date

Matthew had 30 years' service on 5 April 2006. The scheme's accrual rate was 1/60th for each year of service. His final pensionable salary, as defined on that day in the scheme documentation, was £240,000. He therefore registered for enhanced protection.

He remained an active member of the pension scheme for another five years until age 55. His final salary grew to £300,000. The scheme operated a normal retirement age of 60. If the accrued pension had been taken as a deferred pension at age 60 the scheme would have paid £175,000 per annum (35/60 × £300,000). However Matthew wanted an immediate pension. The scheme applied its own early retirement factor of 4% per annum for each year that benefits were

Transitional protection **9.45**

taken before age 60. Matthew was therefore paid a pension of £140,000, which has a capital value of £2.8 million (£140,000 × 20).

The test for relevant benefit accrual as in example 1 in RPSM03104600 meant that a pension of £153,154 per annum (valued at £3,063,076) could have been paid without causing the loss of enhanced protection. Matthew retains enhanced protection.'

RPSM03105160 (Protection of lump sums with primary protection: taking benefits at more than one time – some lump sum benefits are not tax-free: example of a stand-alone and then a pension commencement lump sum payment):

'Sally has lump sum rights of £1 million on 5 April 2006 and has primary protection on pension rights of £5 million. She has rights in two arrangements. Her lump sum rights are payable by commuting pension rights.

She takes benefits on 23 April 2009, her 55th birthday, from the smaller of the two arrangements. The standard lifetime allowance in 2009–2010 is £1.65 million. The amounts of her protected pension and lump sum have increased in line with the increase in the standard lifetime allowance to £5.5 million and £1.1 million (each amount being multiplied by £1.65 million/£1.5 million).

As the smaller arrangement, a money purchase arrangement, is valued at £600,000 she chooses to take all her benefit as a stand-alone lump sum.

Sally takes benefits from her second arrangement in 2015–16 when the standard lifetime allowance is £1.5 million. The amounts of her protected pension and lump sum have increased to £6 million and £1.2 million – see RPSM03102020 to find out how these figures have been arrived at.

Sally has taken benefits previously so the amounts of benefits currently protected must be reduced by the value of the earlier benefits. The value of the earlier benefits must be increased in line with the increase in the standard lifetime allowance from its value when the benefits were taken to its current value. In this example, the standard lifetime allowance has reduced from £1.65 million to £1.5 million. However, the reduction has no impact because the figure of £1.8 million replaces the standard lifetime allowance since it is a lower amount. See RPSM03105155 for more details.

The value of the £600,000 stand-alone lump sum taken in 2009 is therefore £654,545 (£600,000 × 1.8/1.65).

Sally's available protected pension and lump sum are therefore £5,345,455 (£6 million – £654,545) and £545,455 (£1.2 million – £654,545) respectively.

Her second arrangement is a money purchase arrangement worth £8.3 million. She takes a pension commencement lump sum of

9.45 *Transitional protection*

£545,455 and uses the remainder of her protected pension rights, £4.8 million, to buy a lifetime annuity.

The residue of £2,954,545 in the arrangement (£8.3 million less protected pension rights of £5,345,455) is liable to the lifetime allowance charge. From this residue she takes a lifetime allowance excess lump sum of £1,329,545 after deduction of 55% tax (£1,625,000) under the lifetime allowance charge.'

RPSM03105170 (Protection of lump sums with primary protection: taking benefits at more than one time – some lump sum benefits are not tax-free: example 1):

'Jane has primary protection for her pension rights, and her lump sum rights on 5 April 2006 exceeded £375,000. She has already taken some benefits after 5 April 2006 under primary protection.

Her remaining rights are in a money purchase arrangement, which are valued at £1 million. Her available protected pension rights are valued at £600,000, which means her available personal lifetime allowance is £600,000. The amount of protected lump sum is £700,000 – her protected lump sum rights are greater than her available personal lifetime allowance.

Jane takes a pension commencement lump sum of £700,000, using up all of her available lifetime allowance. She takes the balance of the £1 million (£300,000), as a lifetime annuity. £600,000 of her pension commencement lump sum is free of income tax, but £100,000 is liable to the lifetime allowance charge under section 214 Finance Act 2004. So she receives £600,000 tax-free and a further lump sum of £45,000 after deduction of 55% tax under the lifetime allowance charge.

Jane cannot take all of her protected lump sum amount tax-free because the maximum amount of pension commencement lump sum exceeds the amount of her available lifetime allowance.

Because Jane took too little lump sum when she took her earlier benefits, the full aggregate lump sum available under protection was not paid entirely free of income tax.'

RPSM03105180 (Protection of lump sums with primary protection: taking benefits at more than one time, some lump sum benefits are not tax-free: example 2):

'Dean had registered pension rights of £3 million and lump sum rights of £800,000 by commutation under primary protection on 5 April 2006. £3 million was the equivalent of the standard lifetime allowance (£1.5 million) plus an additional factor of 1.

In January 2011, Dean took pension rights worth £3 million plus a lump sum of £600,000. In tax year 2010–2011 the standard lifetime allowance was £1.8 million. So Dean's personal lifetime allowance is £3.6 million (this being the standard lifetime allowance of £1.8

Transitional protection **9.45**

million at the time plus a factor of 1) and his maximum protected lump sum is £960,000 (£800,000 × £1.8 million/£1.5 million). Dean has now used up all of his personal lifetime allowance.

In 2013, Dean took further benefits including a lump sum, and paid a lifetime allowance charge on the whole of the benefits that he took.

Although Dean originally had a lump sum right of £800,000, he did not use this up whilst he had some personal lifetime allowance remaining. The result is that any lump sum taken after his personal lifetime allowance has been used up in full is not a pension commencement lump sum. The payment will be a lifetime allowance excess lump sum and so it is subject to the lifetime allowance charge.'

RPSM03105210 (Protection of lump sum rights with enhanced protection: example 1):

'Sally has uncrystallised lump sum rights of £400,000 and uncrystallised pension rights of £2 million on 5 April 2006. This gives (VULSR ÷ VUR) of 20%. She takes benefits from three schemes on different dates whilst retaining enhanced protection.

Sally takes benefits from the first scheme, which are worth £1 million, by taking unsecured pension (from 6 April 2011 called drawdown pension) using income withdrawal. She designates assets valued at £800,000 for the payment of her unsecured pension and takes a lump sum benefit of £200,000. This is the maximum permitted by (VULSR ÷ VUR) multiplied by the value of the funds designated for the payment of unsecured pension plus the lump sum – paragraph 29(2) of Schedule 36 Finance Act 2004. She cannot take the higher amount of 25% under the usual pension commencement lump sum rules. Sally's notification of enhanced protection has changed the maximum amount of lump sum she can be paid when she crystallises benefits.

Sally takes benefits from the second scheme worth £750,000 in the form of a lifetime annuity bought for £600,000 and a lump sum benefit of £150,000. This is the maximum permitted by (VULSR ÷ VUR) multiplied by the value of the annuity purchase price plus the lump sum – paragraph 29(2) of Schedule 36 Finance Act 2004.

Sally takes benefits from the third scheme (which is a defined benefits arrangement) as a scheme pension of £20,000 plus a lump sum benefit of £100,000. The scheme pension is valued at £400,000 (20 × the annual pension of £20,000). And the lump sum is the maximum permitted by (VULSR ÷ VUR) multiplied by the value of the scheme pension plus the lump sum – paragraph 29(2) of Schedule 36 Finance Act 2004.

If one of Sally's schemes paid her a lump sum of 15% of the combined value of her lump sum and pension benefits (because scheme rules did not permit a larger lump sum) her other schemes could not pay her a lump sum greater than 20% to make up the "shortfall".'

9.45 *Transitional protection*

The later developments and new protections have been described in detail in this **Chapter**. Additionally, FP 2012 can be found at RPSM11106000 onwards and FP 2014 at RPSM11106200 onwards.

CHECKLIST

- The pension tax regime which was introduced by *FA 2004* on A-Day differed from the introduction of previous tax regimes in one very important aspect: it was retrospective
- PP or EP was chosen, or both, it was necessary to value the rights that had accrued at 5 April 2006
- There were different methods of valuing rights for DC, DB, cash balance and hybrid schemes
- A formula is provided for valuing lump sum benefits
- PP and EP could be applied for at the same time
- PP is described, together with lump sum protections and death benefits
- EP is described, together with lump sum protections and death benefits
- The meaning of 'relevant benefit accrual' is given
- Permitted transfers are described
- Non-permissible transfers are described
- The conditions for FP 2012 are described, together with lump sum protections and death benefits
- The conditions for FP 2014 are described
- The conditions for the forthcoming IP 2014 are described
- RPSM extracts are provided for the earlier regimes of protections, the later developments and new protections have been described in detail in the **Chapter**.

Chapter 10

> **SIGNPOSTS**
> - There are various additional or alternative rewards for high earners
> - The recycling of tax-free lump sums is restricted
> - Master trust DC schemes can be attractive

Tax planning

INTRODUCTION

10.1 This **Chapter** highlights some of the general tax planning issues that members of registered pension schemes, advisers and employers may wish to consider.

Inevitably, the main areas of tax-planning and savings for an employer and members involve high earners. These matters are covered in **Parts Three** and **Five** below and, for overseas matters, in **Part Four** below.

PAYMENT OF CASH, AND ALTERNATIVES

10.2 The severe abatements of the AA and the LTA led to an increase in arrangements by employers to seek to reward their senior employees (especially those with DC pensions) by making a payment or payments in cash in lieu of pension contributions. Whereas this is a straightforward solution, and attractive to employees as it is immediate, the payment(s) will attract income tax and NICs.

Cash payment

Employers may wish to consider the attractions and the downsides of opting for making cash payments compared with making pension contributions. A cash payment will not benefit from tax-free investment growth, unless a suitable tax-efficient vehicle is found. Pension contributions would benefit from tax-free build up. However, a tax charge of 55% on excessive cash sums is incurred if the member's LTA is exhausted. Accordingly, employers may wish to seek guidance on the likely investment yields, and the cross-over position when the LTA is used up in full.

Where employers offer to pay their pension contributions as cash to employees who have exceeded their AA or LTA, it is not unusual to see the cash payment reduced for the effect of the NIC charge that arises on cash payment but not on an employer pension contribution payment. This achieves cost-neutrality for the employer but must be taken into account by the employee when deciding

10.3 *Tax planning*

whether it is better to receive a lower cash amount, subject to employer NICs and employee income tax and NICs, compared to a pension contribution that might be taxed at 55% above the LTA.

The above may lead some employers to consider additional or alternative rewards, as described in **Chapter 14** below.

Focus

- Inducement or incentive offers are vulnerable to attack by HMRC and are discouraged by the Pensions Regulator

---

Inducement/incentive offers

10.3 Inducement/incentive offers are payments by employers or registered pension schemes to incentivise scheme members into giving up certain rights in place of alternative provision or benefit enhancement. This can give rise to long-term savings on funding assumptions. However, care and specialist advice is essential if an employer is to consider making such an offer.

The HMRC position

10.4 HMRC's Employment/Income Manual at EIM15155 states:

'An employer/third party may offer to pay lump sums to employees and/or former employees who are members of the employer's registered pension scheme. In return the employee/former employee exchanges or surrenders their rights under the registered pension scheme, thereby reducing the employer's future liability for the scheme's funding. Such offers have been made in a number of circumstances.'

Back in January 2007, HMRC stated that the payment of cash sums 'in connection with the surrender or exchange of rights' are employment income, and are chargeable to IT, regardless of the age of the recipient or whether or not the recipient is retired, as they are deemed to fall within the meaning of relevant benefits payable from an EFRBS. It considered that the payment of a cash sum attracts NICs if it is deemed to be 'earnings'. Earnings 'paid to or for the benefit of the individual' (payments made direct from employer to individual) attract Class 1 NICs. Where payment is made by the employer into the registered scheme, it attracts neither Class 1 nor Class 1A NICs. However, HMRC stated that the above does not apply to payments that 'enhance the transfer value of the pension fund and which are included in the funds transferred between schemes'.

The Pensions Regulator position

10.5 The Pensions Regulator opted for the term 'incentive exercises', and its website guidance to trustees dated 19 July 2012 is summarised below:

- trustees should be consulted and engaged when an incentive exercise is proposed;
- trustees should start from a presumption that incentive exercises are not in most members' interests;
- trustees should take advice when an incentive exercise is proposed, to ensure they understand the extent of their legal obligations.

Despite the HMRC pronouncements above, the Regulator has since stated that trustees should presume that enhanced transfer exercises are not in member's interests. It stated: 'If a company is willing to encourage the transfer, the company's gain is likely to be the member's loss.' The draft *Pension Schemes Bill 2014/15* provides for regulations to be made which prohibit the practice of offering incentives to members to leave their DB schemes and transfer to alternative arrangements. The Regulator issued guidance on the matter, requiring members to be fully informed of the implications of transferring out and recommending that trustees should seek independent financial advice. It has stated that trustees should start from the presumption that such exercises and transfers are not in members' interests and should therefore approach any exercise cautiously and actively. The Regulator said trustees may decide to refuse to release data as a release would 'enable such an exercise to be run without their scrutiny'.

The Regulator's main guidance is summarised below:

- Any offer must be clear, fair and not misleading.
- Trustees should be actively involved and be sure that the selection, remuneration and broader commercial interests of advisers are aligned with members' interests.
- No pressure should be placed on members to make a decision to accept the offer.
- The Regulator points out that the Pensions Ombudsman can direct that compensation be made to the members.

The Regulator has updated its scheme returns to include questions on incentive exercises including enhanced transfer values and pension increase exchanges.

INHERITANCE TAX

10.6 In general, IHT charges are not incurred on the payment of benefits where registered pension scheme trustees have discretion over the payment of those lump sum death benefits. IHT exit and periodic charges would apply in unregistered pension schemes set up as discretionary trusts. However, *FA 2008* usefully extended IHT relief on savings to QROPS paid under discretionary trusts. Importantly, this was backdated to A-Day (*FA 2008, Sch 29, para 18*, which amended *IHTA 1984, s 58* concerning 'relevant property'). IHT relief also applies to QNUPS. However, in the Budget on 19 March 2014 the Chancellor stated that there will be consultation on whether to limit the IHT benefits currently afforded by QNUPS.

10.7 *Tax planning*

In a major reversal of policy, the abolition of ASP by *FA 2011, Sch 16*, removed the attaching IHT charges in various scenarios. The rules from 6 April 2011 are:

- IHT is not charged on drawdown funds which remain in a registered pension scheme. This applies even where the individual dies after reaching the age of 75.

- The existing IHT anti-avoidance charges in respect of registered pension schemes, QROPS and QNUPS, where the scheme member has not taken their retirement benefits/failed to buy an annuity, have been removed.

IHT charges continue to apply in circumstances where the scheme trustees have no discretion over the payment of lump sum death benefits and the deceased's estate has a right to the benefit. However, as long as the trustees of a registered pension scheme have discretion over the recipients of the lump sum death benefit, the benefit would not be subject to IHT, even where the trustees exercise their discretion to pay it to the estate.

Guidance can be found in HMRC's RPSM for pre- and post-April 2011 IHT rules, and in IHTM. Most IHT claims will arise in personal pension plans, as the member has more say in the scheme rules or policy conditions which are to be adopted. In occupational schemes, the rules tend to be more restrictive, offering less control to the member and generally the death benefits will be payable at the trustees' discretion so that no IHT liability arises.

RECYCLING TAX-FREE LUMP SUMS

10.7 The tax regime restricts the recycling of tax-free lump sums taken upon retirement. HMRC were concerned that members above normal minimum pension age could vest benefits, draw a tax-free lump sum and immediately re-invest it in a registered pension scheme. The lump sum contributions would obtain tax relief, and the member could then take another tax-free lump sum to enable the cycle to be repeated. It is important, therefore, to be aware that unacceptable arrangements have been blocked by the legislation, which removed the tax advantages relating to any lump sums artificially recycled.

When the recycling rule applies then all or part of the pension commencement lump sum is treated as an unauthorised member payment for tax purposes. Recipients of unauthorised member payments are liable for special stand-alone tax charges of either 40% or 55% of the payment depending on whether the amount of the lump sum in question that is deemed to be an unauthorised payment exceeds a set surcharge threshold of 25%. In addition the scheme may face a scheme sanction tax charge of at least 15% which its rules may allow it to recover from the member. So such a payment could become subject to tax charges totalling as much as 70% of the amount of the unauthorised payment.

An example of how the tax charge applies on re-cycling is given below:

Example

Brian takes a tax-free cash lump sum of £10,000 on 10 February 2013 intending to use it to pay significantly greater contributions to his registered

Tax planning 10.7

pension scheme. The amount is less than 1% of the LTA (£15,000 in 2012/13) and, as no other such lump sums were paid to Brian in the previous 12 months, the recycling legislation does not apply. However, on 1 January 2014 Brian takes another tax-free cash lump sum, this time of £8,750 to increase further significantly contributions to his registered pension scheme. Because he has received another tax-free cash lump sum within the previous 12 months, the amount of the later lump sum of £8,750 must be aggregated with the amount of that previous lump sum. The total of £18,750 exceeds 1% of the LTA (£15,000 for 2013/14) and so the recycling legislation is triggered.

As the amount of the significantly increased contribution of £8,750 exceeds 30% of the contribution that might have been expected (ie £8,750 @ 30% = £2,916), the whole of the second lump sum becomes an unauthorised payment and subject to a tax charge of 40% = £3,500.

However, HMRC state that the legislation is not intended to affect cases where an individual takes a tax-free lump sum as part of the normal course of taking pension benefits. It only applies to contributions which are greater than 30% of the lump sum. In such circumstances, the whole of the lump sum would be treated as an unauthorised payment and subject to the unauthorised payments tax charge. However, if it is less than 1% of the LTA, it is exempt.

HMRC provides the following example of situations where the recycling rule applies (see RPSM09208020 and RPSM04104980):

- using the pension commencement lump sum itself to make a contribution
- borrowing to facilitate recycling i.e. taking out a loan to provide the wherewithal to pay a contribution into a registered pension scheme with a pension commencement lump sum to be used to repay the that loan
- manufacturing salary sacrifice type arrangements as the means of making a contribution with the pension commencement lump sum replacing the sacrificed salary
- otherwise manufacturing employer contributions to facilitate recycling.

It also provides examples of when the recycling rule does not apply, viz:

- where the level of employee contribution payable increases following a change of employment
- where the basis on which contributions are paid is consistent (e.g. 5% of salary) but salary levels fluctuate
- where contributions do not increase substantially after adjusting for RPI increases to contributions last made some years ago
- where there is an increase in employer contributions for a reason unconnected with a pension commencement lump sum
- where an inheritance, a genuine windfall or a financial settlement is used to make significantly increased contributions

10.8 *Tax planning*

- where contributions are based on fluctuating profits from a self-employment.

HANCOCK ANNUITIES AND EFPOS

10.8 A Hancock annuity is an immediate annuity for a retiring employee. These products are still available as registered pension schemes, and they are subject to the LTA. Alternatively, an EFPOS (an acronym in an amendment to the *Social Security (Contributions) Regulations 2001, SI 2001/1004*)) could be considered. An EFPOS enjoys exemptions from NIC charges both on the employer contribution and the benefit paid from the scheme (as for an EFRBS), although it provides only a pension.

SCHEME PENSIONS

10.9 Scheme pensions can be more tax-efficient than drawdown or secured pensions, subject to meeting prescribed conditions. They are described in **Chapter 4** above.

INCREASES IN BENEFITS

10.10 Benefits may be increased under a discretionary power under the scheme provisions.

LOANS

10.11 Loans may be made, subject to the limits in **Chapter 5** below. Additionally:

- loans of up to 50% of fund value may be made by SSASs in the employer's workplace. This can be a significant aid to cash flow – the maximum level of employer-related investments for most other schemes is 5% only;

- SIPPS may invest in commercial property. If such schemes cannot meet mortgage repayments due to a failure to pay rental income, the scheme may by HMRC concession re-mortgage, subject to certain rules.

SCHEME ADMINISTRATION PAYMENTS

10.12 A scheme may make a scheme administration member payment without incurring a tax charge. It must be made at arm's length to a scheme member or former member in the course of administration or management of the scheme. Examples could include the payment of wages and a purchase of assets. The payments must be made in the ordinary course of business of the scheme. However, it is important to seek specialist advice as any element of bounty will lead to the payment as being treated as an unauthorised payment.

- A scheme may also make a scheme administration employer payment to a sponsoring employer or former employer. Examples can include the payment of wages or fees to persons who are involved in administration. Again, it must be made in the ordinary course of business of the scheme and at arm's length.

RE-ALLOCATIONS OF FUNDS OR ENTITLEMENTS TO BENEFITS

10.13 It is permitted to re-allocate funds or entitlements to benefits, either notionally or actually, within the same registered pension scheme. An example would be a re-allocation between members). However, it is it is important to seek specialist advice as HMRC would be very likely to challenge large re-allocations to non-employed family members.

Consideration may be given to *hybrid pension schemes*. They can be an attractive means for employers to share risk with their employees, but they are complex to administer. It is necessary to manage defined benefit entitlements as if they were a defined benefit scheme and manage defined contribution entitlements as if they were a defined contribution scheme. The Pensions Regulator publishes guidance entitled *'Hybrid scheme management'* on its website.

MASTER TRUSTS

10.14 Master trust DC schemes can be attractive. The ICAEW and the Pensions Regulator published a master trust voluntary framework document on 1 May 2014. It defines a master trust as

> 'an occupational trust-based pension scheme established by declaration of trust which is or has been promoted to provide benefits to employers which are not connected and where each employer group is not included in a separate section with its own trustees'.

It is intended to reassure members of such schemes and arrangements, and other larger DC schemes, that their schemes are being properly run, based on a set of control objectives. Master trusts should obtain annual independent assurance.

Master trusts are becoming more popular, particularly as a means of providing DC benefits for auto-enrolment.

CONTRACT-BASED SCHEMES

10.15 The Pensions Regulator publishes guidance on contract-based schemes. It is entitled *'Voluntary Employer Engagement in Work Place Contract-based Pension Schemes',* and it provides case studies.

On 26 June 2014 new legislation was put to parliament, and the government re-branded such schemes as DABs.

10.15 *Tax planning*

CHECKLIST

- Employers may seek to reward their senior employees by making a payment or payments in cash in lieu of pension contributions. This is a straightforward and immediate solution, but the payment(s) will attract income tax and NICs
- Additional or alternative rewards are described in **Chapter 14**
- Incentive offers may be considered by employers or registered pension schemes to incentivise scheme members into giving up certain rights. This can give rise to long-term savings on funding assumptions, but care and specialist advice is essential
- In general, IHT charges are not incurred on the payment of benefits where registered pension scheme trustees have discretion over the payment of those lump sum death benefits. The exemption also applies to QROPS and QNUPS
- There are restrictions on the recycling of tax-free lump sums taken upon retirement
- A Hancock annuity or an EFPOS could be considered for alternative pension provision
- Scheme pensions can be more tax-efficient than drawdown or secured pensions, subject to meeting prescribed conditions. They are described in **Chapter 4** below
- Benefits may be increased under a discretionary power under the scheme provisions
- Loans may be made, subject to the limits in **Chapter 5** below. There are concessions for SSASs and SIPPS
- A scheme may make a scheme administration member payment or a scheme administration employer payment
- It is permitted to re-allocate funds, or entitlements to benefits, either notionally or actually within the same registered pension scheme
- Master trust DC schemes can be attractive
- The Pensions Regulator publishes guidance on contract-based schemes

Part Three

High earners of registered pension schemes

Chapter 11

> **SIGNPOSTS**
> - Employer-financed retirement benefits schemes and employee benefit trusts have been under the scrutiny of HMRC
> - HMRC must be notified of the coming into operation of an employer-financed retirement benefits scheme
> - Disguised remuneration was introduced for certain activities, including certain payments to employer-financed retirement benefits schemes
> - Bonus sacrifices may be attractive
> - Flexible drawdown is available for DC schemes, and has been made more widely available

High earners of registered pensions schemes

INTRODUCTION

11.1 There have been considerable attacks on high earners in recent years. Some proposed provisions under the legislation were abandoned (as is the case for the SAAC) or repealed (for example, the HIERC), whilst new and far-reaching legislation has replaced them (for example, the disguised remuneration charges and severe cuts in the levels of the AA and the LTA).

In view of the new constraints which have been brought about by the cuts to the LTA and the AA, and the introduction of the concept of 'disguised remuneration', tax planning is becoming a major consideration for high earners. **Chapter 9** above of this book describes the transitional protections and anti-forestalling provisions which are available. **Chapter 12** below concerns IRPS; **Chapter 13** below explores the opportunities for overseas pension provision; **Chapter 14** below considers other forms of tax-efficient saving and **Chapter 15** below highlights the need for compliance, disclosure and the tax penalties which could be incurred by the unwary.

The remainder of this **Chapter** includes details of the rules applicable to EFRBS and unfunded schemes, and looks at the tax efficiency of bonus sacrifices and the flexible drawdown facility.

> **Focus**
> - EFRBS can be attractive top-up pensions vehicles, but HMRC has focussed on the potential use of EFRBS and EBTs as tax avoidance arrangements

11.2 *High earners of registered pensions schemes*

EMPLOYER-FINANCED RETIREMENT BENEFITS SCHEMES AND EBTs

11.2 EFRBS and employee benefit trusts (EBTs) have been popular for savers with high earnings levels for some time. However, they had both been in HMRC's spotlight as potential tax avoidance schemes, and some major changes have been made to HMRC practice and legislation. These are described below.

With effect from A-Day, FURBS were replaced by EFRBS. However, monies which had accrued up to A-Day retained most of their status, unless the FURBS opted to be registered pension schemes. In the main, FURBS entitlements are protected, subject to post A-Day indexation. In addition to *FA 2004, ss 245–249* and *Sch 36*, the following regulations made the relevant changes:

- *Employer-Financed Retirement Benefits (Excluded Benefits for Tax Purposes) Regulations 2006 (SI 2006/210)*;
- *Employer-Financed Retirement Benefits Schemes (Provision of Information) Regulations 2005 (SI 2005/3453)*;
- *Employer-Financed Retirement Benefits (Excluded Benefits for Tax Purposes) Regulations 2007 (SI 2007/3537)*; and
- *Employer-Financed Retirement Benefits (Excluded Benefits for Tax Purposes) (Amendment) Regulations 2011 (SI 2011/2281)*.

It is because of the valuable protections for pre A-Day accrual that the tax position for FURBS and UURBS is detailed below.

Background to FURBS and EFRBS

11.3 The main EFRBS rules are as follows:

- There was an extension to the persons who are responsible for certain actions under the *TMA 1970* beyond that of the scheme administrator to 'responsible persons' where assessments are due on certain payments or actions.

- Individuals will pay income tax on relevant benefits. Where the recipient is not an individual (for example, a company or club), the higher rate of tax is payable. (EIM15015 and EIM15055).

- Employers will not receive relief on contributions and administration expenses until benefits come into payment (*FA 2004, ss 245* and *246*, respectively).

- An employer's cost of insuring benefits against employer insolvency is chargeable to the member as a benefit-in-kind. The employer can claim the cost as an expense against profits at the time that it is paid.

- EFRBS trusts are taxable at the rate applicable to trusts/dividend trust rate/special rates for trustees' income, as applicable.

- Lump sum death benefits will be charged to IHT.
- There was to be no NIC charge on any benefits paid out of non-registered schemes provided they are within the limits of benefits that could be paid out of a registered pension scheme and all employer and connected employer relationship has ceased (but see 'disguised remuneration' later in this **Chapter** concerning certain payments).

HMRC guidance is difficult to find. The tax position for such schemes has to be gleaned largely from various sources and manuals relating primarily to:

- TSEM;
- EIM;
- company and employee tax offices;
- NICs;
- policy-holders taxation;
- the tax residence of trustees;
- foreign pensions;
- RPSM; and
- an ESC.

RPSM draws attention to the EIM for details of how a trust-based EFRBS is treated for tax purposes. This provides the following additional information:

- only 'relevant benefits' count as employment income *(ITEPA 2003, s 394)*;
- the charge on lump sums paid out may be reduced where prior employer contributions have been taxed and where the employee has made contributions; and
- a pension is charged separately as pension income under *ITEPA 2003 (Pt 9* charges pension income to tax).

In the above, 'relevant benefits' means any lump sum, gratuity or other benefit provided:

- on retirement or on death;
- in anticipation of retirement;
- after retirement or death in connection with past service;
- on or in anticipation of or in connection with any change in the nature of the employee's service; or
- by virtue of a pension sharing order or provision.

This includes a non-cash benefit, but not:

- pension income within *ITEPA 2003, Pt 9*; or
- benefits chargeable under *FA 2004, Sch 34*.

11.4 *High earners of registered pensions schemes*

Excluded benefits are benefits:

- in respect of ill-health or disablement of an employee during service;
- in respect of death by accident of an employee during service; or
- under a 'relevant life policy', which includes EGLP's (see **Chapter 14** below). (Further guidance on the meaning of 'relevant life policy' is available in HMRC's Insurance Policyholder Taxation Manual (IPTM).)

Guidance on how annuities, annual payments and non-cash receipts are dealt with is given at EIM15100.

Provision of information

11.4 The *Employer-Financed Retirement Benefits Schemes (Provision of Information) Regulations 2005 (SI 2005/3453)* state that HMRC must be notified of the coming into operation of an EFRBS on or before 31 January following the tax year in which it was set up. HMRC must also be informed of benefits provided from an EFRBS by 7 July following the tax year in which the benefits are paid. Notification may be made online.

Lists of the benefits should be sent to the HMRC office which deals with any PAYE scheme operated by the EFRBS. They will be treated as employment income in the hands of the employee or former employee, unless their overall value is no more than £100.

The relevant reporting individual is extended beyond the scheme administrator to 'responsible persons' under *TMA 1970*. The meaning of a 'responsible person' is contained in *ITEPA 2003, s 399A*.

The prescribed information is:

(a) the name, address and NI number of the recipient of the relevant benefit;

(b) the nature of the relevant benefit provided; and

(c) the amount of the relevant benefit calculated in accordance with *ITEPA 2003, s 398(2)*.

PRE A-DAY RULES

11.5 Prior to A-Day, the following rules applied to FURBS:

- *FA 1989* provided that only benefits granted under approved schemes had to be aggregated in calculating whether the benefit limits, including the earnings cap, had been reached. To compensate employees who were subject to the earnings cap, many employers chose to provide unapproved 'top-up' schemes for executives and high earners.
- Contributions were paid and accumulated, usually within a trust, until the benefits became payable.
- For most investment gains, capital gains tax was chargeable at the rate applicable to trusts (RAT).

High earners of registered pensions schemes **11.6**

- An employee was liable for income tax on the contributions paid by his employer in respect of him *(ITEPA 2003, s 386(1))*, so the employee was taxed when the employer made a payment to a scheme, even though the employee had not yet received any cash (separate contributions for the establishment and running costs of the scheme were not taxed). If a pension was paid, it was also taxable in the hands of the employee, even though the contributions had already been taxed *(ITEPA 2003, s 393(2))*. Conversely, lump sums were tax-free, meaning that FURBS invariably paid out, and will continue to pay out, their benefits in lump sum form.

- Contributions made to a FURBS by a company were deductible for CT purposes under *ICTA 1988, s 74* if the expenditure could be classified as an income expense. It was inadvisable for an employee to make contributions to a FURBS for two reasons. First, as there was no tax relief, it would be better for an employee to make voluntary contributions to an approved scheme. And, secondly, an employee's contributions could be regarded as providing funds for the purpose of a settlement. The income of the FURBS could then be treated as the employee's income and taxed at his highest marginal rate *(ICTA 1988, s 660A)*.

- An employer could decide to meet the employee's tax liability on contributions paid by the employer by 'grossing-up' the contributions. This would usually result in additional salary being paid, on which the employer would have to pay NI contributions. The grossed-up equivalent of the chargeable contribution and the tax figure was included on the employee's pay record.

- For schemes entered into on or after 1 December 1993, lump sums paid from FURBS were liable to tax if any of the scheme's income or gains had not been brought into the tax charge *(ITEPA 2003, s 395(3)–(4))*.

As stated above, unapproved schemes lost most of their attraction after A-Day under the new tax regime. Existing FURBS may enjoy the protection of a tax-free lump sum element, but only inclusive of indexation not fund yield, on values up to A-Day where such payments have qualified for relief either by virtue of the taxation of employer contributions on the member or the taxation of all income and gains under the fund. The normal IHT exemptions for discretionary distributions apply to pre A-Day assets in FURBS, but not post A-Day accrual, and future accrual will attract the full RAT.

Funding an EFRBS

11.6 Post A-Day there is a restriction of tax relief where an employer routes the funding of an EFRBS through a registered pension scheme under the *Registered Pension Schemes (Restriction of Employer's Relief) Regulations 2005 (SI 2005/3458)*.

Additionally, HMRC prevented the spreading rules for tax reliefs on contributions from being circumvented by routing them through a new

11.7 *High earners of registered pensions schemes*

company. *FA 2004, s 199A*, was inserted by *FA 2008, s 90*, for payments made on or after 10 October 2007 under binding obligations entered into on or after 9 October 2007, with effect from 10 October 2007.

HMRC Spotlight 5

11.7 HMRC's Spotlights were the first indications of its increasing vigilance over the tax affairs of EBTs and EFRBS.

HMRC Spotlight 5 concerned using trusts and similar entities to reward employees. It was the precursor of the introduction of disguised remuneration legislation and it stated as follows:

> 'HMRC are aware that companies have been seeking to reward employees without operating PAYE (Pay As You Earn)/NICs (National Insurance contributions) by making payments through trusts and other intermediaries that favour the employees or their families. The arrangements usually seek to secure a corporation tax deduction, as if the amounts were earnings at the time they are allocated, and also defer PAYE/NICs or avoid them altogether. HMRC's view is that at the time the funds are allocated to the employee or his/her beneficiaries, those funds become earnings on which PAYE and NICs are due and should be accounted for by the employer.
>
> In addition HMRC's view is that an inheritance tax charge may arise on the participators of a close company. Unless the participators are excluded beneficiaries and have not had funds applied for their benefit, such as the receipt of a loan, a charge to inheritance tax arises on participators of close companies at the time the funds are paid to the trustee by the close company. Relief is only available to the extent that a deduction is allowable to the company for the year in which the contribution is made. Later payments of earnings out of the trust that may trigger a deduction to the company would not qualify for relief.
>
> Participators affected by this may need to self assess a liability to inheritance tax. There is further technical advice on inheritance tax on contributions to employee benefit trusts available on the HMRC internet site.
>
> HMRC are actively challenging examples of such arrangements and considering legislative options to end further usage of these schemes.'

HMRC Spotlight 6

11.8 HMRC's Spotlight 6 concerned EFRBS. It stated:

> 'HMRC are aware of schemes where companies claim a corporation tax deduction for employer contributions to an EFRBS on the basis that either (a) the contribution to the EFRBS or (b) a subsequent transfer to a second EFRBS is a "qualifying benefit". This would

allow the company to secure a corporation tax deduction before any benefits are actually paid by the scheme to the employee. HMRC's view is that neither transaction involves the provision of a "qualifying benefit". Whilst it has been argued that there may be some ambiguity in the law around the meaning of the phrase "transfer of assets" since it does not state to whom the transfer is to be made, in HMRC's view the context resolves any ambiguity.

The law defines "qualifying benefits" and such benefits are plainly, from the context, benefits that if paid under the terms of an EFRBS might fall within the employment income charge. So in that context, a "transfer of assets" should be interpreted as a transfer that could give rise to such a charge. This will primarily mean a transfer of assets to the employee but also includes a transfer to a member of the employee's family. Neither an employer contribution to an EFRBS nor a transfer between EFRBS gives rise to a possible employment income tax charge on the employee. So there is no "qualifying benefit" entitling the employer to a deduction.'

Tax reliefs on EFRBS

11.9 Generally, tax relief for employers is available but it is deferred. Employers will receive relief on contributions and administration expenses when the benefits come into payment (*FA 2004, ss 245* and *246*, respectively). CGT is chargeable at full rate, and amounts held in the fund will not be included in the LTA. However, under *FA 2011* (see the following paragraphs), disguised remuneration may need to be taken into account.

The main sources of HMRC information are:

- EIM the main link sources commence at EIM15000;
- TSEM;
- ESC A10, as revised for disguised remuneration concerning lump sums; and
- Pensions Tax Simplification Newsletter No 21.

Further information is available from HMRC's Pensions Policy Team at FitzRoy House, Castle Meadow Road, Nottingham, NG2 1BD. Where a non-resident EFRBS and UK income are in point, information is available from HMRC Trusts & Estates, Non-Resident Trusts, Ferrers House, PO Box 38, Castle Meadow Road, Nottingham, NG2 1BB.

For pre 6 April 2011 EFRBS, HMRC published an updated version of its Frequently asked questions (FAQs) on EFRBS in November 2013. It offers a 'Resolution Opportunity' and it applies to contributions made by employers on or after 6 April 2006 and before 6 April 2011. It invites employers to discuss with it settlement of their EFRBS case by agreement without recourse to litigation.

HMRC's view is that, where contributions to the EFRBS (and subsequent allocation to a second EFRBS or sub-trust) were made with the intention of

11.10 *High earners of registered pensions schemes*

later providing 'relevant benefits' within the meaning of *ITEPA 2003, s 393B*, to beneficiaries, no CT deduction can arise until such time as relevant benefits are actually received by beneficiaries (ie in circumstances which trigger the charge to employment income under *ITEPA 2003, s 394*).

> **Focus**
>
> - The introduction of disguised remuneration rules had been unexpected. The rules are of great complexity and expert guidance is needed

Disguised remuneration

11.10 Disguised remuneration is the term used by HMRC, and now much of the pensions industry, for what is described in *FA 2011, Sch 2*, as 'employment income provided through third parties'. *Schedule 2* inserted a new *Part 7A* into *ITEPA 2003*. This was a major bombshell to EBT and EFRBS providers, and it seemed to fly in the face of the concept of EFRBS. The legislation applies to a wide range of tax avoidance devices, and there are exclusions which protect arrangements which are not tax avoidance arrangements, and benefits packages which are made available generally to the employer's workforce which are not accessible to specially selected individuals.

The first indication that such legislation was being drawn up was on 9 December 2010, on which date the draft *Finance (No 3) Bill 2010* was published, together with very detailed notes from government bodies. There followed three sets of HMRC Frequently Asked Questions (FAQs), several draft HMRC Guidance Notes and ministerial statements on the subject. HMRC's latest guidance is in its EIM as explained above.

Part 7A imposes PAYE and NIC charges on certain payments and deemed payments made by 'relevant arrangements' for the benefit of employees through a 'relevant third person'. The charges generally apply from 6 April 2011. They do not specifically apply to pension provision but to employers. Nevertheless, in the pensions field, they can have a significant impact on EFRBS.

Relevant third party

11.11 A 'relevant third party' effectively means payments to trust-based schemes, and excludes payments to other schemes/arrangements and the self-employed. However, not all payments are caught, and HMRC have stated that they think that few will be caught. This remains to be seen. The main principles follow.

Charging test

11.12 There is a charging test for making an asset available. This is intended to cover those circumstances where the employee could have benefited from the asset had the employee been the outright owner. The factors which may be taken into account include:

- where the employee can directly influence decisions about whether to sell or replace an asset; and
- where it is clear that the employee is likely to benefit from any eventual disposal proceeds of an asset (for example, because they will be paid back).

The tax charges

11.13 The charges are imposed on the sum of money involved or on the higher of the cost or market value where an asset is used to deliver the reward or recognition. In some cases, this value may be nil. However, transactions such as non-commercial loans or acquisitions will be targeted.

Anti-forestalling provisions

11.14 Anti-forestalling measures applied between 9 December 2010 and 5 April 2011 (inclusive). A tax charge arises on 6 April 2012 unless the sums have been repaid or relevant assets returned. The charges are to income tax where third party arrangements are used to provide a reward or recognition, or a loan, in connection with an employee's current, former or future employment. The amount will be taxed as employment income under PAYE and subject to NIC charges where earmarking for the employee concerned has taken place.

Also, charges may arise where there is a transfer from one unregistered scheme to another unregistered scheme and there is a payment to (or earmarking of sums and assets by) the receiving scheme, other than in respect of pre-6 April 2006 benefits where contributions were taxed at source.

Tax credits

11.15 If a *Part 7A* charge is incurred, there will be tax credits when the benefit becomes payable. Clearly, it will be necessary to keep full details of any charges throughout a member's lifetime until all benefits have been drawn. Members should be provided with records and reminded of the need to keep them in a safe place until needed.

Statutory terminology

11.16 The legislation brought in a welter of new terms and definitions. The key ones are described below.

Relevant arrangement – an arrangement for a person which is a means of providing, or is otherwise concerned (wholly or partly) with the provision of, rewards or recognition or loans in connection with that person's employment, or former or prospective employment.

11.17 *High earners of registered pensions schemes*

Relevant step – a step taken by a 'relevant third person' is where a person:

(a) pays a sum of money to a relevant person;
(b) transfers an asset to a relevant person;
(c) takes a step by virtue of which a relevant person acquires an asset in securities;
(d) makes available a sum of money or asset for use, or makes it available under an arrangement which permits its use:
   (i) as security for a loan made or to be made to a relevant person, or
   (ii) otherwise as security for the meeting of any liability, or the performance of any undertaking, which a relevant person has or will have, or
(e) grants to a relevant person a lease of any premises the effective duration of which is likely to exceed 21 years.

A relevant step is caught if it is reasonable to suppose that, in essence:

   (i) it is taken (wholly or partly) in pursuance of the relevant arrangement, or
   (ii) there is some other connection (direct or indirect) between the relevant step and the relevant arrangement.

Relevant third person –

(a) a person acting as a trustee,
(b) an employer acting as a trustee, or
(c) any person other than (a) or (b).

Main exemptions from charge

11.17 Most exclusions are in EIM45200 onwards and EIM45600 onwards, There are further exemptions in secondary legislation (the *Employment Income Provided Through Third Parties (Excluded Relevant Steps) Regulations (SI 2011/2696)*) which concern relevant steps arising or deriving from UK tax-relieved funds and relevant transfer funds.

The gateway test

11.18 *ITEPA 2003, Pt 7A,* only applies if the income comes through the *s 554A* gateway under *Part 7A*, and there is a relevant step taken by the third party under *s 554B* (effectively, earmarking). Even then, there may not be an incurred charge. HMRC TEMP 25 in the Employment Income Manual states that it is not intended to prevent the use of EFRBS but to prevent their use as a means of avoiding the tax-free allowances which apply to registered pension schemes or their use for purposes of tax avoidance. EIM45140 describes how undertakings given by employers etc in relation to retirement benefits will be treated.

The main exemptions and exclusions include:

- *Bona fide* salary sacrifice and bonus sacrifice schemes, unless they are blatant tax avoidance schemes. HMRC publish detailed guidance on how to make effective salary and bonus sacrifices, and will advise on the effectiveness of specific sacrifices on request.
- Existing earmarking, unless a loan is made to a relevant person or something is made available for use by such person as if it were his own.
- The self-employed.
- Employee contributions.
- Most transfers of sums and assets between non-UK pension schemes.
- A step taken after the employee's/member's death.
- Transfers of pre-6 April 2006 FURBS funds where the employer contribution was taxed on the member (EIM45645).
- Transfers to a scheme in relation to which a claim was accepted under *ITEPA 2003, s 390* (exception from charge on payments to non-approved pension schemes: non-domiciled employees with foreign employers) will not attract a charge.

Also, EIM45635 describes certain exemptions for pre-6 April 2011 lump sum rights.

The exemptions under *SI 2011/2696* concern 'relevant steps' arising or deriving from UK tax-relieved funds and 'relevant transfer funds'. These are in respect of sums or assets derived from:

- the UK tax-relieved fund of a relevant non-UK scheme;
- the relevant transfer fund created by a transfer from a registered pension scheme to a QROPS; or
- payments made by a registered pension scheme that have been subject to an unauthorised payments charge.

There are also exclusions for:

- employment income provided through third parties for commercial transactions, eg commercial loans through a third party (TEMP 31 in the EIM);
- commercial transactions other than loans (TEMP 32 in the EIM);
- employment income exemptions (TEMP 39 in the EIM);
- income arising out of earmarked sums or assets;
- a change of trustees; and
- income arising on contributions to a trust which is earmarked for particular employees or their families (for example, held within a sub-trust for a particular employee).

In view of the complexity of the legislation, and the ongoing uncertainty about its application, advisers and members will wish to seek specialist advice on transactions of the above nature.

11.19 *High earners of registered pensions schemes*

UNFUNDED SCHEMES

11.19 UURBS did not fall under the new tax regime from A-Day, unless they registered to do so by 7 July 2006. There were transitional protections for promises made under UURBS prior to that date.

Prior to A-Day, the following rules applied to UURBS:

- The only tax consequences arose, under *ICTA 1988, s 595*, when benefits were paid out. Payment could simply be reduced to take account of the tax charge. For an employee, all benefits were chargeable in full to income tax. The employer qualified for a deduction in respect of the benefit payments as a business expense. The result was a tax regime similar to that of a FURBS; the only difference is that there was no tax-free lump sum.

- The employee's pension was taxed as pension income at his highest marginal rate under *ITEPA 2003, Pt 9. Sections 393–394* also imposed a specific charge designed to catch lump sums and other benefits provided through UURBS that might otherwise escape income tax. If the lump sum was not paid to an individual, the administrator of the scheme would be liable to tax under *Case VI* of *Schedule D* at 40% (*ITEPA 2003, s 394(2)* and *(4)*). Authority for deducting this tax from the benefit payment had to be included in the governing documentation. The tax liability could not be mitigated by directly purchasing an annuity payable to the individual, as *ICTA 1988, s 657(2)(d)*, prevented such favourable treatment.

- Payments made to an employee under an UURBS were deductible for CT purposes under *ICTA 1988, s 74* as long as the payment was not excessive in relation to the employee's service. *FA 1989, s 76*, did not prevent a deduction, as the benefits were taxable in the hands of the employee (*s 76(2)(b)*). No deduction was allowed for book reserves; therefore, the CT deduction could only be claimed when the benefits were paid.

- If an UURBS was used to provide death benefits, which was likely to be calculated as a multiple of earnings, no IHT would be payable if the recipient was determined at the discretion of a third party, such as the employer or the trustees. This was because the payment would not form part of the employee's estate (*IHTA 1984, s 5*). The employee's estate had to be excluded from the class of potential beneficiaries for the avoidance of doubt. There would, however, probably be liability for income tax. The exemption contained in *ITEPA 2003, s 396(1)* did not apply, unless the lump sum benefit was insured, as the employee would not have paid sums that were assessable to tax to provide the benefit. If the death benefits were insured, the UURBS was treated as if it were funded, and income tax would have been payable on the insurance premiums. Income tax would not then be payable on receipt of the death benefit.

HMRC is currently been investigating unfunded schemes to ensure that they comply with the changing tax rules. They are attractive for the high earner as they are not bound by the AA and LTA limits, but they do not offer direct security of promise for the employee from the employer.

Some UURBS were developed in the past in an attempt to counter the problem of purely unfunded schemes not having assets to provide the benefits promised by the employer. In accordance with this promise, a reserve was accumulated in the balance sheet. Simultaneously, the company would buy assets that it secured by way of a charge with payment of the benefits. As long as the payment of the benefits was intended to come from company resources rather than the charged assets, purchase of the assets was not treated as funding. It is still possible to back a benefit (where appropriate) by an asset or security, but the member must pay a benefit-in-kind tax charge on the cost to the employer of providing security and/or underwriting.

Only 25% of a lump sum benefit may be paid (within limits) without also attracting PAYE and NIC charges. Payment may be made directly by the employer each year or be insured. Neither the lump sum nor the purchase price of an annuity will attract a benefit-in-kind income tax charge. The cost of insurance should be allowed as a deductible expense. Tax becomes payable when the benefit is paid.

BONUS WAIVERS

11.20 Bonus waivers are similar to salary sacrifices (see **Chapter 3** above). They were traditionally a means for members to increase their pension provision beyond the 15% limit on employee contributions which applied before A-Day. Also, they could be seen to be highly tax-efficient, by saving the employer and the employee from paying NICs and potentially taxation on the forgone salary. They are now becoming particularly attractive to the higher paid.

Again, in order to achieve an effective waiver, the employee has to waive his right to the bonus given up. Waivers must be in accordance with HMRC earnings guidelines (EIM42750).

Following a long consultative process, HMRC confirmed that salary sacrifices and bonus waivers are not caught by the disguised remuneration rules (described in **11.10–11.18** above) if they are *bona fide* and not tax avoidance schemes.

Statutory clearance from HMRC of the effectiveness of existing waivers can be obtained by writing to: HMRC Clearances Team, Alexander House, 21 Victoria Avenue, Southend-on-Sea, Essex, SS99 1BD; email hmrc.southendteam@hmrc.gsi.gov.uk.

The requirements for an effective bonus waiver

11.21 The effectiveness of a bonus waiver depends on: whether a bonus is discretionary or contractual; whether the whole or part of the bonus is waived; and the bonus waiver letter (which should be signed by the employee).

A waiver may be made to a contractual right to receive any bonus declared by the employer for the employee's benefit for the year, or a waiver of a specified amount or percentage by which any bonus declared exceeds the employee's contractual salary. The employer may, separately, pay an equivalent sum of money into the employer's pension scheme for the member.

11.22 *High earners of registered pensions schemes*

Such a waiver will amend the employee's contract of employment. The waiver must be before the employee's entitlement to the bonus arises.

The above criteria apply to a discretionary bonus; the bonus must still be waived before entitlement to it arises. *ITEPA 2003, ss 15(2)* and *18* refer.

EIM 42725 still contains the following example:

> 'A senior employee, who is not a director, is contractually entitled to a bonus each year. The amount of the bonus is based on the profits of the employing company.
>
> The company's year end is 31 January. Accounts for the year ended 31 January 2003 are finalised on 31 July 2003, enabling the amount of the bonus to be calculated. The employee is not entitled to payment of the bonus until 31 October 2003. The employee is informed on 31 August 2003 that the bonus will be £10,000.
>
> The letter informing the employee of the bonus asks the employee to give up her rights to the bonus as the company is now in a difficult financial position. The employee agrees to do this in a letter sent to the company on 30 September 2003.
>
> The employee is not liable to tax on the bonus as employment income because it was given up, on 30 September 2003, before it would have been treated as money earnings for employment income purposes, on 31 October 2003.
>
> If the bonus had been given up after 31 October 2003 the employee would have been liable to tax on the £10,000 as it would have been given up after it was treated as money earnings for employment income purposes.'

General observations

11.22 In either scenario above, the employer may offer an annual option to cancel the waiver for future years. The employer will also wish to reserve the right to withdraw the bonus waiver scheme at the end of its financial year, or on some other annual basis.

HMRC acknowledge that, in exceptional circumstances, an employee may be given the right to revert to the original income level. 'Exceptional circumstances' may include hardship or unexpected lifestyle event changes.

Focus
- The flexible drawdown income qualification has eased.

FLEXIBLE DRAWDOWN

11.23 Flexible drawdown is a drawdown facility under DC schemes which permits certain persons to access their funds as they wish. This facility is essentially for the wealthy/high earners, and it was brought in by *FA 2011, Sch 16*. Changes to the rules were made from 27 March 2014, as described below. Further changes are proposed from 6 April 2015, subject to consultation (see **4.14** above).

How it works

11.24 Flexible drawdown allows uncapped drawdown. It permits great flexibility in accessing benefits. There is no maximum on the amount of income which a person may draw down and there is no minimum limit. Drawings are subject to income tax under PAYE.

Conditions

11.25 The following conditions apply:

- In order to enter into this flexible drawdown, a person must evidence to the scheme administrator with effect from 27 March 2014 that they have entitlement to a minimum aggregate £12,000 per annum pension income from private and/or state sources *(FA 2014, s 41)*. This amount was previously set at £20,000.

- Any individual who has made contributions, or had contributions made on their behalf, to a DC scheme, or who is in active membership of any DB or cash balance scheme(s), must wait until the next tax year before they can enter into flexible drawdown.

- If the person makes any new pension savings, they will be liable to the AA charge on all pension input amounts.

- An application must be made to HMRC on the form on HMRC's website.

Regulations

11.26 The principal *Regulations* for a flexible drawdown declaration are the *Registered Pension Schemes (Prescribed Requirements of Flexible Drawdown Declaration) Regulations 2011 (SI 2011/1792)*. They prescribe the requirements for a 'valid declaration' that a member of a registered pension scheme or a dependant of a member meets 'the flexible drawdown conditions' set out in *FA 2004, ss 165(3B)* or *167(2B)*, as amended by *FA 2011, Sch 16, paras 10, 20* and *FA 2014, s 41*.

Regulation 2 sets out the prescribed requirements for a valid declaration. The declaration must be signed and dated by the member or dependant ('the member') and contain:

(a) the information specified below;

(b) a statement confirming that the flexible drawdown conditions are met;

(c) a statement confirming that the contents of the declaration are correct and complete to the best of the member's knowledge and belief, and

11.26 *High earners of registered pensions schemes*

(d) where *FA 2004, s 165(3A)* or *167(2A)* has previously applied to an arrangement relating to the member, a statement confirming that the declaration referred to in either of those subsections was accepted by the scheme administrator of the registered pension scheme under which the arrangement was made.

The specified information is:

(a) the member's full name;
(b) the member's sole or main address;
(c) the member's NI number (unless *reg 3* applies);
(d) details of each source of relevant income payable to the member for the tax year in respect of which the minimum income requirement is satisfied ('the declaration year'), including the name and address of the person responsible for making the payments of the relevant income; and
(e) the total amount of relevant pension income payable in respect of the source referred to in paragraph (d) for the declaration year.

Regulation 3 sets out the procedure to be followed if a scheme member or dependant wishes to make a valid declaration but does not qualify for a NI number.

CHECKLIST

- EFRBS and EBTs have long been popular for savers with high earnings levels. However they have both been in HMRC's spotlight as potential tax avoidance schemes
- With effect from A-Day, FURBS were replaced by EFRBS
- The post A-Day rules for EFRBS
- HMRC must be notified of the coming into operation of an EFRBS on or before 31 January following the tax year in which it was set up
- The pre A-Day rules and protections for FURBS are described
- HMRC's Spotlights on EBTs and EFRBS are reproduced
- Tax relief for employers is available, but it is deferred.
- Disguised remuneration is described. Note that the restriction on residential property was a bomb-shell to the SIPP industry
- Bonus sacrifices may be attractive for tax-planning for high earners
- Flexible drawdown is available for DC schemes, and the 'other pension income minimum requirement' has reduced

Chapter 12

> **SIGNPOSTS**
>
> - Investment-regulated pension schemes include old-style small self-administered schemes and self-invested personal pension schemes
>
> - Taxable property charges arise on investment in residential property and most tangible moveable property.
>
> - Taxable property charges are the unauthorised payment charge of 40% on the member, and a 40% scheme sanction charge on the scheme administrator, which may be reduced to 15% when the member has paid his or her liability. The member may also face a further 15% unauthorised payment surcharge, and payment may also trigger de-registration of the scheme by HMRC, resulting in a further charge on the scheme administrator of 40% of the scheme value
>
> - UK Real Estate Investment Trusts generally do not attract taxable property charges
>
> - There are exemptions for genuinely diverse commercial vehicles and certain activities

Investment-regulated pension schemes

INTRODUCTION

12.1 IRPS were introduced by *FA 2006, s 158* and *Sch 21*. SSASs and SIPPS fall within this category of scheme, as do certain other schemes which are described later. The Act brought in the concept of 'taxable property'. The main requirements were inserted into *FA 2004*, in the form of *Sch 29A*.

The first indication of this major policy reversal of a single tax regime was in the pre-Budget Report Technical Note dated 5 December 2005. It was stated that SIPPs 'will be prohibited from obtaining tax advantages when investing in residential property and certain other assets such as fine wines'.

This was a major shock to the pensions industry, particularly to SIPP providers. Some investors had made large deposits on buy-to-let property. The acquisition of taxable property acquisition would now attract prohibitive tax charges.

What is taxable property?

12.2 'Taxable property' means residential property and most tangible moveable property. Residential property can be in the UK or elsewhere and is a building or structure, including associated land that is used or suitable

12.3 *Investment-regulated pension schemes*

for use as a dwelling. 'Tangible moveable property' is things that you can touch and move; it includes assets such as art, antiques, jewellery, fine wine, classic cars and yachts. The provisions apply to taxable property that is held directly, and also to indirect holdings of property except through genuinely diverse commercial vehicles. (See *FA 2004, ss 174A, 185A* to *185I, 273ZA* and *Sch 29A*.)

Focus
- The taxable property charges can be prohibitive

What are the taxable property charges?

12.3 The taxable property charges are:

- an unauthorised payment charge at 40% on the member, and
- a 40% scheme sanction charge on the scheme administrator, which may be reduced to 15% when the member has paid his or her liability.

The member may also face a further 15% unauthorised payment surcharge, and payment may also trigger de-registration of the scheme by HMRC, resulting in a further charge on the scheme administrator of 40% of the scheme value.

There are transitional protections for investments which were already held at the date the changes were announced, and the following exemptions from charge apply, where:

- the scheme held an interest in such property on A-Day which it had acquired before that date, and which it was not prohibited from holding up to 5 April 2006;
- before A-Day the property was held by a person other than the scheme and the scheme was not prohibited from holding the interest it held in that person at that time; or
- the scheme, or a person in whom the scheme directly or indirectly held an interest, entered into a contract to acquire an interest in such property before 5 April 2006 and was not at that time prohibited from acquiring such an interest, but acquires the property on or after that date.

Focus
- The definition of an IRPS is provided

What is an IRPS?

12.4 A scheme, or arrangement, or a group of arrangements is an IRPS if:

- in the case of a scheme other than an occupational scheme, one or more members, or a person related to the member, is or was able to (directly or indirectly) influence or advise on investments for the purpose of the scheme under an arrangement for that member;

- in the case of an occupational scheme, a scheme with 50 or fewer members and at least one meets the following condition. The condition is that one or more of those members, or a person related to one of those members, is or was able to (directly or indirectly) direct influence or advise on investments held by the scheme;

- an arrangement, within an occupational scheme which is not an IRPS itself, has one or more members, or a person related to one of the members, who is or was able to (directly or indirectly) direct, influence or advise on investments which are linked to an arrangement relating to that member. The term 'linked' means that the sums or assets are held for the purpose of an arrangement under the scheme relating to that member, but not merely by virtue of apportionment of scheme assets.

In the above, the following expressions have the following meanings:

- *'related person'*: a person is related to a member if the member and the person are connected persons within the meaning of *CTA 2010, s 1122*, or the person acts on behalf of the member or a person connected to the member, within that meaning;

- *'held for the purposes of an arrangement'*: sums or assets which are held other than for administration or management of the scheme and would not otherwise be treated as held for the purpose of an arrangement. These sums or assets are to be treated as held for the purpose of an arrangement by reference to the respective rights under the scheme of the member to which the arrangement relates; and

- *'influence'*: there has been a relaxation in this area, With effect from 6 April 2006, the definition excludes schemes in which the individual members could not realistically be expected to influence scheme decisions to invest in taxable property. The change was made by *FA 2008, Sch 29*.

Focus
- Residential property is taxable property

Residential property

12.5 The following do not fall within the category of taxable property:

- where the property is occupied by an employee who is not a member of the pension scheme which owns the property and who is not connected to a member of the scheme, within the meaning of *CTA 2010, s 1122*;

- where the employee is not connected with the employer within the meaning of *CTA 2010, s 1122*, and

12.5 *Investment-regulated pension schemes*

- where the occupying employee is required to do so as a condition of their employment.

The following is also excluded from the meaning of taxable property:

- where the property is occupied by someone who is not a member of the pension scheme which owns the property and who is not connected to a member of the scheme within the meaning of *CTA 2010, s 1122*, and
- where it is used in connection with business premises held as a scheme investment.

Unhelpfully, there is no firm definition of tangible moveable property. RPSM07109120 gives a measure of guidance, stating

'These are things that you can touch and move. Examples are art, antiques, jewellery, fine wine, boats, classic and vintage cars, stamp collections, rare books'.

The following specific exemptions appear in the *Investment-regulated Pension Schemes (Exception of Tangible Moveable Property) Order 2006 (SI 2006/1959)*:

- gold bullion; and
- items with a market value of £6,000 or less which no member of the scheme or connected person has a right to use or occupy, and which the scheme does not hold an interest in directly, and which is held by a 'vehicle' (meaning a person described under *FA 2004, Sch 29A, para 20*) for the purpose of management or administration of that vehicle.

A scheme or person is deemed to hold taxable property directly if they alone or jointly or in common:

- hold the property or any rights, power or interest in or over the property;
- have a right to use or participate in arrangements relating to the use of the property itself or a description of property to which that property belongs;
- have the benefit of any obligation, restriction or condition affecting the value of any interest in, powers or rights over the property; or
- are entitled to receive payments determined by the value of the property or by the income from the property.

Where a scheme or person owns or jointly owns hotel accommodation in its entirety, the property is exempted (hotels, inns etc are regarded as commercial property and are therefore acceptable investments). Additionally, most property underlying certain insurance contracts is deemed not to be directly held taxable property.

A scheme or person is deemed to hold taxable property indirectly if it does not hold the property directly, and either alone, jointly or in common it:

- holds an interest in a person who holds the interest in the property directly; or

- holds an interest in a person who holds the interest in the property indirectly in accordance with the above condition.

An interest is deemed to exist where a person:

- holds an interest, right or power in or over that person; or
- lends money to that person to fund an acquisition of taxable property.

Similar provisions apply to schemes or persons holding an interest in a company, a collective investment scheme or a trust.

Focus
- Investment in UK REITS is generally permitted

UK Real Estate Investment Trusts

12.6 UK Real Estate Investment Trusts (UK-REITs) are described in *FA 2004, Pt 4*. Certain UK-REITs generally do not attract taxable property charges. UK-REITs are investment trusts which pool investors' money to buy a portfolio of commercial and residential properties. The properties are then let to companies and individuals. The rental income and profits from the sale of assets within the trusts are tax free.

The company must be resident in the UK and listed on a recognised Stock Exchange. It must withhold tax at the basic rate when making a distribution to shareholders out of its qualifying property income. This distribution is known as 'property income dividend' (PID).

Most of the profits of a UK-REIT must be distributed in the form of PIDs, and no single shareholder can own 10% or more of the shares if financial penalties are to be avoided.

An additional tax charge applies where any legal person, including an individual or a pension scheme, holds an interest of 10% or more in a UK-REIT where the company's interest in the holding is 10% or more (*FA 2004*, as amended by *FA 2007, s 52* and *Sch 17*).

What is deemed to be an acquisition and holding of taxable property?

12.7 The following rules apply, and are discussed further below.

Acquisition

12.8 A scheme or person is deemed to have acquired taxable property if it comes to hold an interest in such property:

- by an act of parties to a transaction;
- by an order of a court or other authority;

12.9 *Investment-regulated pension schemes*

- under any statutory provision; or
- by the operation of law.

The holding of an interest means where the interest is held by a person for the purposes of the pension scheme.

Direct holding

12.9 A scheme or person is deemed to hold taxable property directly if they alone or jointly or in common:

- hold the property or any rights, power or interest in or over the property;
- have a right to use or participate in arrangements relating to the use of the property itself or a description of property to which that property belongs;
- have the benefit of any obligation, restriction or condition affecting the value of any interest in, powers or rights over the property; or
- are entitled to receive payments determined by the value of the property or by the income from the property.

Where a scheme or person owns or jointly owns hotel accommodation in its entirety, the property is exempted (hotels, inns etc are regarded as commercial property and are therefore acceptable investments). Additionally, most property underlying certain insurance contracts is deemed not to be directly held taxable property.

Indirect holding

12.10 A scheme or person is deemed to hold taxable property indirectly if it does not hold the property directly and either alone, jointly or in common it:

- holds an interest in a person who holds the interest in the property directly; or
- holds an interest in a person who holds the interest in the property indirectly in accordance with the above condition.

An interest is deemed to exist where a person:

- holds an interest, right or power in or over that person; or
- lends money to that person to fund an acquisition of taxable property.

The second criteria is not met if the loan is an employer loan within the meaning of *FA 2004, s 179*, and the property is used for trading or administration purposes by the scheme's sponsoring employer, and it is not occupied or used by a member of the pension scheme or a connected person.

What is the meaning of the word 'interest'?

12.11 The following meanings apply, dependent upon whether the person in whom interest is held is a company, collective investment scheme or trust:

- Where the person in whom a scheme or person is deemed to hold an interest in an indirect holding under *FA 2004, Sch 29A, para 16* is a company, the scheme or person holds an interest if:
    - it holds or is entitled to or will become entitled to acquire shares or voting rights in the company;
    - it holds or is entitled to or will become entitled to acquire a right to receive or participate in distributions;
    - it is entitled to or will become entitled to secure that current or future income or assets of the company will be applied to its benefit; or
    - it controls the company alone or with others within the meaning of *ICTA 1988, s 416*.
- Where the person in whom a scheme or person is deemed to hold an interest in is a 'collective investment scheme', the scheme or person holds an interest if he or she or it is a participant in that collective investment scheme. *FSMA 2000, s 236*, defines collective investment schemes and their participants.
- Where the person in whom the scheme is deemed to hold an interest under *FA 2004, Sch 29A, paras 17, 18*, is a 'trust', the scheme holds an interest in that trust if:
    - the scheme has a 'relevant interest in the trust' (see below); and
    - the scheme, or a scheme member or person connected to a scheme member, has made a payment to the trust on or after acquisition of the above interest.
- Additionally, the scheme is deemed to hold an interest if:
    - a scheme member or person connected to a member holds a relevant interest in the trust; and
    - the scheme has made a payment to the trust on or after acquisition of the above interest.
- A person has a relevant interest in a trust if–
    - any property which may at any time be comprised in the trust or any derived property is, or will or may become, payable to or applicable for the benefit of the person in any circumstances; or
    - the person enjoys a benefit deriving directly or indirectly from any property which is comprised in the trust or any derived property.

However, a payment which is part of an arm's length transaction in return for property or a benefit, and which is not paid to enable a scheme member or person connected to a member to occupy or use any property, is disregarded for the above criteria.

- Where the person whom the scheme is deemed to hold an interest in is a trust, a person other than the pension scheme holds an interest in a trust if:

12.12 *Investment-regulated pension schemes*

- the person holds a relevant interest in the trust; and
- the person has made a payment to the trust on or after acquisition of the above interest.

However, a payment which is part of an arm's length transaction in return for property or a benefit, and which is not paid to enable a scheme member or person connected to a member to occupy or use any property, is disregarded for the above criteria.

The trust rules above are contained in *para 19*, but they do not apply to a unit trust scheme within *FSMA 2000, s 237(1)*.

Genuinely diverse commercial vehicles

12.12 There are exemptions for genuinely diverse commercial vehicles. These include collective schemes which provide an arm's length vehicle for investment in properties (see UK-REITs above). Rent must normally be paid, and it is taxable on the investor after costs, repairs and interest offsets. There is no CGT on the first £8,500 of annual profit on each title-holder, and taper relief applies on chargeable disposals. There are different capital gains rules for property which is rented out to holidaymakers and for furnished lettings.

Other diverse property vehicles

12.13 There are also exemptions for property held by a scheme directly or indirectly in certain other types of property investment vehicles, subject to certain conditions, where the pension scheme, and associates, directly or indirectly own 10% or less and there is no right to have private use of any taxable property. The vehicle must meet three conditions.

Condition 1

- the total value of assets held directly by the vehicle is at least £1 million; or
- the vehicle holds at least three assets which are residential property,

and, in either case, no one asset comprises more than 40% of the total assets.

Assets must be valued in accordance with generally accepted accounting practice; no account is to be taken of liabilities secured against or otherwise relating to assets (whether generally or specifically); and, where generally accepted accounting practice offers a choice of valuation between cost basis and fair value, fair value must be used.

Condition 2

If the vehicle is a company:

- it is resident in the UK and is not a close company, or
- it is not resident in the UK and would not be a close company if it were resident in the UK.

Condition 3

The vehicle does not have as its main purpose, or one of its main purposes, the direct or indirect holding of an animal(s) used for sporting purposes.

The pension scheme's interest in the vehicle must meet the following conditions.

The pension scheme:

- must not directly or indirectly hold an interest in the vehicle for the purposes of enabling a member of the pension scheme or a connected person of a member to occupy or use the property, and
- must meet either of the following conditions:
    (a) where the pension scheme is an occupational pension scheme, the pension scheme, together with any associated persons, must not hold directly or indirectly an interest in the vehicle that exceeds any one of the limits in the paragraph below, or
    (b) where the pension scheme is not an occupational pension scheme, no arrangement under the pension scheme, together with any associated persons, may hold directly or indirectly an interest in the vehicle that exceeds any one of the limits in the paragraph below.

The limits referred to in conditions (a) and (b) above are:

- 10% or more of the share capital or issued share capital of the vehicle;
- 10% or more of the voting rights in the vehicle;
- a right to receive 10% or more of the income of the vehicle;
- such an interest in the vehicle as gives an entitlement to 10% or more of the amounts distributed on a distribution in relation to the vehicle;
- such an interest in the vehicle as gives an entitlement to 10% or more of the assets of the vehicle on a winding up or in any other circumstances; and
- such an interest in the vehicle as gives rise to income and gains derived from a specific property.

These limits apply to indirect holdings of a vehicle as well. So, if a pension scheme holds 50% of company A, which in turn owns 15% of company B, the pension scheme's interest in company B will be 7.5%. The indirect holding in company B will therefore be less than 10%.

A pension scheme which is not an occupational pension scheme may have holdings in a vehicle through one or more arrangements for members that are not associated persons. In these circumstances, the tests of whether 10% or more of the vehicle is owned will apply separately for each arrangement. For the avoidance of doubt, where the same member has more than one arrangement, they must be considered jointly.

12.13 *Investment-regulated pension schemes*

HMRC published guidance entitled *"Offshore employment intermediaries"*, on 18 December 2013 together with a technical note and some frequently asked questions. Legislative changes are contained in the *FA 2014, Ch 2*. A quarterly return will need to be completed and, from April 2014, UK tax will be levied on the full employment income where the division of duties and remuneration between a UK and overseas contract is artificial and where tax is not payable on the overseas contract at a rate broadly comparable to UK tax rates.

CHECKLIST

- Investment-regulated pension schemes (IRPS) were introduced by *FA 2006, s 158* and *Sch 21*
- 'Taxable property' means residential property and most tangible moveable property.
- Taxable property charges are the unauthorised payment charge of 40% on the member, and a 40% scheme sanction charge on the scheme administrator, which may be reduced to 15% when the member has paid his or her liability. The member may also face a further 15% unauthorised payment surcharge, and payment may also trigger de-registration of the scheme by HMRC, resulting in a further charge on the scheme administrator of 40% of the scheme value
- The meaning of the term 'investment-regulated pension scheme' is provided
- Residential property and the exceptions that apply are described
- UK Real Estate Investment Trusts generally do not attract taxable property charges
- There are exemptions for genuinely diverse commercial vehicles
- There are exemptions for property held by a scheme directly or indirectly in certain types of property investment vehicles, subject to certain conditions

Part Four

Overseas considerations

Chapter 13

> **SIGNPOSTS**
>
> - Transfers may be made between UK registered pension schemes and QROPS without tax penalty
> - UK residents may also join a QROPS, subject to member payment charges on benefits which have previously received UK tax reliefs
> - The Government has been tightening the legislation and rules which apply to QROPS
> - Cross-border schemes can be particularly popular for the internationally mobile
> - The EC has been very active in issuing formal notices to member states which it considers to impose discriminatory treatment on other EU citizens and their pension schemes
> - OPS, ROPS, QROPS, QNUPS and QOPS are described

Overseas considerations

INTRODUCTION

13.1 The provisions of *FA 2004*, which had effect from A-Day, gave wide scope to make transfers to and from registered pension schemes. The IORPS Directive, and other changes in EU law, had a significant influence on the revisions to UK pensions legislation. In this **Chapter**, attention is given to overseas considerations in general, including transfers to and from overseas pension schemes (OPS).

Unfortunately, there had been some abuse of the wider transfer opportunities referred to above; and, as a result, HMRC issued a consultation document entitled *'Overseas Transfers of Pension Savings – Draft Guidance'* on 20 December 2011. Most of this weighty document presented few obstacles or changes for already fully compliant scheme managers and trustees, and it was of course in the main welcomed by them – but there were some issues which required reconsideration.

The HMRC initiative had almost certainly been brought about by those few abusers and misusers of 'pension scheme' provision, who have long been familiar to us as 'trust-busters' since pre A-Day days. This is now known as 'pensions liberation' (see **15.12** below) but is likely to re-named again by the Pensions Regulator.

The main concern is that the subsequent changes to UK law concerning overseas schemes could potentially impose double taxation charges on

13.2 *Overseas considerations*

UK residents, regardless of existing DTA's and the OECD Modeller for tax treaties. This could by-pass those robust and genuine pension scheme providers which do exist outside the UK and liaise regularly with HMRC. The matter is dealt with in greater detail in **13.36** below.

TAX AND PENSION RULES POST A-DAY

13.2 The major tax changes introduced by *FA 2004* have been modified since its enactment by regulations made thereunder and subsequent *Finance Acts*. Nevertheless, the provisions of the *Act* concerning overseas matters have, to date, remained largely in place. Additionally, *PA 2004* and subsequent legislation addressed the issue of international mobility of labour in connection with scheme membership and sponsorship. The interplay between the UK tax laws for overseas schemes, the UK pension laws for membership, transfers and the investment of such schemes and the related EU legislation are key factors for consideration when designing tax-efficient overseas pension provision. The IORPS Directive required the tax rules of Member States to become fully cross-border enabling. Accordingly, some detail is provided on such matters in this **Chapter**.

Many of the changes and relaxations relating to overseas matters will be of particular interest to high earners, who are more likely to be investors overseas, members of overseas schemes and/or the internationally mobile.

UK residents may save for their retirement provision through a non-UK employer (even one without a UK branch), and will be entitled to the same benefits as if they had saved with a UK registered pension scheme in respect of any assets which are transferred from a UK registered pension scheme to a QROPS. A QROPS may be based in the EU, EEA or elsewhere. On a wider field, there are real opportunities to meet the aims of the IORPS Directive in the area of occupational pension schemes for employees (whatever their residence status), of international companies and, where applicable, schemes and arrangements for the self-employed within cross-border scheme membership. UK tax charges and allowance ceilings apply to UK residents who transfer overseas or join overseas pension schemes, but such schemes can still be attractive for future planning and flexibility by providing modern-style, normally DC, retirement provision.

There had always been a dearth of providers of international schemes for the main workforces involved in multinational companies. Some companies do have long-established schemes in different jurisdictions, for example the motor industry and the oil industry. However, the different tax rules within various jurisdictions had made international benefit provision problematical, to say the least. The UK tax authorities had developed complicated laws with regard to international benefit provision over the years, in an attempt to deal with such situations, and there existed a minefield of transitional arrangements and grandfathering rules in order to make provision for such employees. Most of these obstacles were swept aside by *FA 2004* and by the IORPS Directive, ensuring the protection of members' benefits and widening the availability of tax reliefs. There are now structured reporting requirements of transfers and member benefit payments under undertakings to HMRC.

Overseas considerations **13.3**

> **Focus**
> - There is a welter of regulations for overseas schemes
> - Finance Acts have also included amendments to the *FA 2004* provisions

THE MAIN UK TAX LAW FOR OVERSEAS SCHEMES

13.3   The Government is constantly extending the legislation and rules which apply to QROPS. The main regulations which affect overseas schemes in general are listed below:

- the *Pension Schemes (Categories of Country and Requirements for Overseas Pension Schemes and Recognised Overseas Pension Schemes) Regulations 2006 (SI 2006/206)*.

  These *regulations* prescribe the requirements which must be met by a scheme in order to qualify as an overseas pension scheme under *FA 2004*. The *regulations* have been subject to further change. **Appendix 6** contains a marked-up consolidation version of these *Principal Regulations* which reflect the key changes in UK law which have affected these regulatory requirements.

- the *Pensions Schemes (Application of UK Provisions to Relevant Non-UK Schemes) Regulations 2006 (SI 2006/207)*.

  These *regulations* explain the method of calculation of tax on a payment made by a RNUKS in respect of a payment which is referable to a member's UK tax-relieved funds. They also contain provisions for HMRC to mitigate the charge to tax in appropriate circumstances.

- the *Pension Schemes (Information Requirements – Qualifying Overseas Pension Schemes, Qualifying Recognised Overseas Pension Schemes and Corresponding Relief) Regulations 2006 (SI 2006/208)*.

  These *regulations* describe the information which must be sent to HMRC for a QROPS and a QOPS to be recognised as such. They also describe the information which must be sent to HMRC in respect of an individual's contributions, and the 30-day rule which applies to the provision of information following the issue of a notice by HMRC. The UK does not restrict QROPS to EU and EEA Member States; they may be established on a wide international basis.

- the *Pension Schemes (Relevant Migrant Members) Regulations 2006 (SI 2006/212)*.

  These *regulations* describe the application of migrant member relief for a member of an OPS (an individual is a relevant migrant member if he meets the requirements of *FA 2004, Sch 33*).

- the *Registered Pension Schemes and Overseas Pension Schemes (Electronic Communication of Returns and Information) Regulations 2006 (SI 2006/570)*.

13.3 *Overseas considerations*

These *regulations* describe the electronic reporting and tax return rules for UK and overseas schemes.

- the *Registered Pension Schemes (Extension of Migrant Member Relief) Regulations 2006 (SI 2006/1957)*.

These *regulations* extend eligibility for migrant member relief to cases where a person was not resident in the UK at the time they joined a scheme, other than where:

   – a member's rights have been subject to one or more block transfers;
   – a series of block transfers have occurred; and
   – the scheme to which the member originally belonged is closed to new accruals for existing members and a further scheme for members of that scheme is set up.

- the *Pension Schemes (Categories of Country and Requirements for Overseas Pension Schemes and Recognised Overseas Pension Schemes) (Amendment) Regulations 2007 (SI 2007/1600)*.

These *regulations* amend Primary Condition 2 of the Principal Regulations and introduce a Schedule relating to Australian schemes (this is annotated in **Appendix 6**).

- the *Special Annual Allowance Charge (Application to Members of Currently-Relieved Non-UK Pension Schemes) Order 2009 (SI 2009/2031)*.

These *regulations* brought SAAC into legislation for RNUKS. SAAC was repealed in April 2011.

- the *Inheritance Tax (Qualifying Non-UK Pension Schemes) Regulations 2010 (SI 2010/51)*.

These *regulations* relate to IHT exemptions for QROPS, QNUPS and RNUKS retrospectively to A-Day for the purposes of the *IHTA 1984, s 271A*.

- the *Registered Pension Schemes etc (Information) (Prescribed Descriptions of Persons) Regulations 2010 (SI 2010/650)*

These *regulations* describe the circumstances in which HMRC will not require a copy of information to be sent to certain persons.

- the *Registered Pension Schemes and Overseas Pension Schemes (Miscellaneous Amendments) Regulations 2012 (SI 2012/884)*

These *regulations* contain very significant changes with effect from 6 April 2012. The *regulations* can be found in **Appendix 5** and their effect is described in **13.36** below.

- the *Pension Schemes (Categories of Country and Requirements for Overseas Pension Schemes and Recognised Overseas Pension Schemes) (Amendment) Regulations 2006 (SI 2012/1221)*.

These *regulations* excluded certain Guernsey pension vehicles from being ROPS for non-Guernsey residents. Their effect is described in **13.36** below.

- the *Pensions Schemes (Application of UK Provisions to Relevant Non-UK Schemes) (Amendment) Regulations 2012 (SI 2012/1795)*

    These *regulations* replaced 'unsecured pension' and 'ASP' with 'drawdown pensions' with retrospective effect from 6 April 2011.

- the *Registered Pension Schemes (Provision of Information) (Amendment) Regulations 2013 (SI 2013/1742)*

    These *regulations* made amendments to the registered pension scheme information requirements, which effectively are now largely extended to QROPS (see *SI 2013/2259* and *FA 2013* below).

- *FA 2013*

    This Act extended HMRC's information and inspection powers.

- the *Registered Pension Schemes and Overseas Pension Schemes (Miscellaneous Amendments) Regulations 2013 (SI 2013/2259)*

    These *regulations* further amended registered pension schemes and QROPS in respect of the information requirements.

Following the initial introduction of new procedures and restrictive tax changes to the *Primary Regulations* (see **13.36** below, **Appendix 5**, and **Appendix 6**) the list of QROPS on HMRC's website is updated twice monthly. It contains details of schemes that have consented to have their details published, meaning that not all QROPS will necessarily feature within it. Many of the listed QROPS are personal pension schemes/retirement annuities, and are being marketed solely for non-UK residents. HMRC have considered that some of these schemes have been used for pensions liberation purposes (see **15.12** below). For example, Singapore was removed from HMRC's list of acceptable providers following such a review and Guernsey is prevented from operating QROPS other than for Guernsey residents.

The QROPS notification form is APSS251 (see **7.15** above) The ever-changing reporting forms, together with descriptions of their purposes, are listed in **13.37** below. The scheme manager must send requisite notification and undertakings (quoting the appropriate reference numbers) to:

HM Revenue & Customs
Pension Schemes Services
FitzRoy House
Castle Meadow Road
Nottingham
NG2 1BD.

The scheme manager must quote their ID (where allocated) on all reports and forms. The QROPS Scheme Manager ID is a unique number that is allocated to each QROPS scheme manager within the new QROPS online filing system. HMRC has been writing to all QROPS scheme managers to

13.4 *Overseas considerations*

tell them their number. The IT system was available from December 2013 but there were delays in issuing the ID's. Further guidance on this matter can be found at HMRC's Newsletters 58 and 60 and are at *http://www.hmrc.gov.uk/pensionschemes/newsletter58.pdf* and *http://www.hmrc.gov.uk/pensionschemes/newsletter60.pdf* respectively.

ICTA 1988, s 615(3) schemes could continue after A-Day by virtue of *FA 2004, Ch 6, ss 245(5)* and *249(3)*. A wider class of overseas scheme is referred to in *ITEPA 2003, ss 647–654*, which repealed.the overlapping provisions in *s 615*.

Section 615 schemes can still be attractive to some foreign residents as they can enjoy virtually all of the tax advantages of registered pension schemes for UK employees. Relief on employer contributions is given on the principle of being made in pursuit of a trade or undertaking. Full commutation can be included. Tax exemption is given by virtue of Extra Statutory Concession A10 – which has been revised in order to take into account the disguised remuneration provisions of *ITEPA 2003*.

One advantage is that administration, trusteeship, asset management, auditing and actuarial functions can be carried out in parallel with the UK pension fund.

The main rules and provisions are summarised below:

- The scheme had to be established under irrevocable trusts with UK-based trustees and no pension could accrue while a member is in the UK.
- On winding up, the assets can be transferred into UK registered pension schemes.

ITEPA 2003 describes the meaning of 'foreign residence condition' etc, and provides that no liability to income tax arises on certain kinds of pensions if the condition is met. An individual is taken to be not resident in the UK only if:

- they make a claim to HMRC that they are not resident; and
- HMRC is satisfied that the person is not resident.

Generally, the EU's 'prudent person' principle should apply to investment decisions.

Focus

- The investment rules are flexible and follow the main principles of EU law
- DB schemes have tighter investment rules than DC

OTHER RELEVANT UK LEGISLATION

Investment regulations

13.4 The *Occupational Pension Schemes (Investment) Regulations 2005 (SI 2005/3378)* revoked the *Occupational Pension Schemes (Investment) Regulations 1996 (SI 1996/3127)*, and supplemented the changes to *PA 1995* which were made by *PA 2004*. The *Regulations* were primarily for the purpose of bringing in UK legislation to accord with the IORPS Directive. The most important parts of the IORPS Directive which were taken into consideration were:

- *Article 12* (to which *PA 1995, s 35* refers), concerning the need for a written statement of investment policy principles;
- *Article 18*, concerning the need for a prudent person approach to be applied as the underlying principle for capital investment; and
- various investment restrictions and requirements for sole and multiple employer schemes.

A summary of the main provisions is given below:

- Scheme assets must always be invested in the best interests of the members and beneficiaries.
- Assets must mainly consist of investments trading on regulated markets.
- Alternative investments must be kept at a prudent level.
- There must be diversity in the investment of assets (and special rules apply to derivatives and collective investment schemes).
- The investment powers and discretions under the scheme must ensure the security, quality, liquidity and profitability of the portfolio in its entirety.
- A statement of investment principles is required, and must be subjected to a triennial review.
- Trustees must always consider proper advice when advising on the suitability of a proposed investment.
- Specific requirements apply to borrowing, and there is a restriction in investment in the sponsor's undertaking to no more than 5% of the portfolio (20% where a group is concerned).
- The small scheme exemptions which already existed for small self-administered schemes (SSASs) in the UK (under *PA 1995* and the regulatory rules) were retained, and the exemptions under Article 5 of the IORPS Directive for schemes with fewer than 100 active or deferred members were adopted.

It is noteworthy that the exemptions for small schemes do not include the need for diversity of investments.

The *Occupational Pension Schemes (Investment) (Amendment) Regulations 2010 (SI 2010/2161)* brought certain investments by operators of a collective investment scheme within the meaning of employer-related investments (as defined by *SI 2005/3378, reg 11*) and removed transitional protection from schemes which applied immediately before 6 April 1997.

Trust and Retirement Benefits Regulations

13.5 The *Occupational Pension Schemes (Trust and Retirement Benefits Exemption) Regulations 2005 (SI 2005/2360)* prescribe the description of

13.6 *Overseas considerations*

schemes which are exempt from:

- the requirement in *PA 2004, s 252(2)* that trustees or managers of an occupational pension scheme with its main administration in the UK must not accept funding payments unless the scheme is established under irrevocable trust; and
- the requirement in *s 255(1)* that an occupational pension scheme with its main administration in the UK must be limited to retirement-benefit activities.

The effect is:

- *section 252(2)* transposes Article 8 of the IORPS Directive on the activities and supervision of IORPs (Article 8 requires legal separation of the assets of an occupational pension scheme and those of a sponsoring employer); and
- *section 255(1)* transposes Article 7 of the Directive (Article 7 requires that occupational pension schemes are limited to retirement-benefit activities).

Pensions Act 2004

13.6 *PA 2004* (like *FA 2004*) is a key statute which paved the way for wider membership of schemes. The Act set out the conditions that apply for a UK scheme to accept contributions from employers in other EU Member States and for UK employers to make contributions to an occupational pension scheme established in another EU Member State. In addition, the *regulations* in **13.7** below were made.

Focus

- Cross-border provisions can apply within the EU

Cross-border provision

13.7 The UK *Occupational Pension Schemes (Cross-border Activities) Regulations 2005 (SI 2005/3381)* make provision in connection with the carrying-out by the Pensions Regulator of its functions in relation to cross-border activity within the EU by occupational pension schemes and their trustees or managers, or by European pensions institutions. Minor amendments were made by:

- the *Occupational Pension Schemes (Cross-border Activities) (Amendment) Regulations 2006 (SI 2006/925)*; and
- the *Occupational and Personal Pension Schemes (Miscellaneous Amendments) Regulations 2007 (SI 2007/814)*.

European regulators have agreed service level agreements (SLAs) for the cross-border application process. In order to ensure these can be met, the Pensions Regulator's website states:

Overseas considerations **13.7**

'we strongly advise the trustees, employer or their advisers to contact us via customer support before completing any cross border application. This will ensure that all information and document requirements can be met. In the absence of such contact, the processing of any cross border application may be delayed.'

The provisions under the UK regulations concern:

- the meaning of 'European employer' and 'host Member State' under *PA 2004*, *Pt 7*;
- the information to be supplied to the Regulator when the trustees or managers of an occupational pension scheme make an application to the Regulator for a general authorisation to accept contributions from European employers;
- the conditions which must be met by an applicant for general authorisation before the Regulator may grant the application;
- the criteria to be applied by the Regulator in reaching any decision as to the revocation of a general authorisation;
- the information to be supplied to the Regulator when the trustees or managers of an occupational pension scheme make an application to the Regulator for approval in relation to a particular European employer;
- the conditions which must be met by an applicant for approval before the Regulator may grant an approval;
- the revocation of approvals and the criteria to be applied by the Regulator in reaching any decision as to the revocation of an approval;
- the modification of certain provisions of pensions legislation in their application to European members of occupational pension schemes which carry out cross-border activity;
- the circumstances in which the Regulator may issue a ring-fencing notice, and what such a notice may require of the trustees or managers of an occupational pension scheme;
- the requirements of the law relating to occupational pension schemes to be notified by the Regulator to the competent authorities of other Member States and complied with by European pensions institutions which accept contributions from UK employers; and
- the manner of applying to the Regulator for authorisation or approval.

Pension schemes located in one EU Member State need to apply for authorisation and approval to accept contributions from employers that employ members who are subject to the social and labour law of another EU Member State. The latest date for applications for existing schemes when the facility was introduced was 30 December 2005. UK schemes need authorisation and approval from the Pensions Regulator to operate cross-border within the EU.

The Regulator's website contains guidance on these matters, and states:

'This guidance sets out the application process for authorisation and approval.

13.7 Overseas considerations

As a trustee of an occupational pension scheme you need to decide whether you have to apply to the Pensions Regulator for authorisation and approval for your scheme to operate as an EU cross-border scheme. (References to trustees in this guidance include scheme managers where there are no scheme trustees.)

If you are an employer sponsoring an occupational pension scheme, you need to consider whether your scheme is operating as a cross-border scheme, and if it is likely to operate as an EU cross-border scheme in future.'

A flowchart to help decision-making is on the website. It is reproduced below for ease of reference:

'Does my scheme need authorisation and approval by the UK regulator?

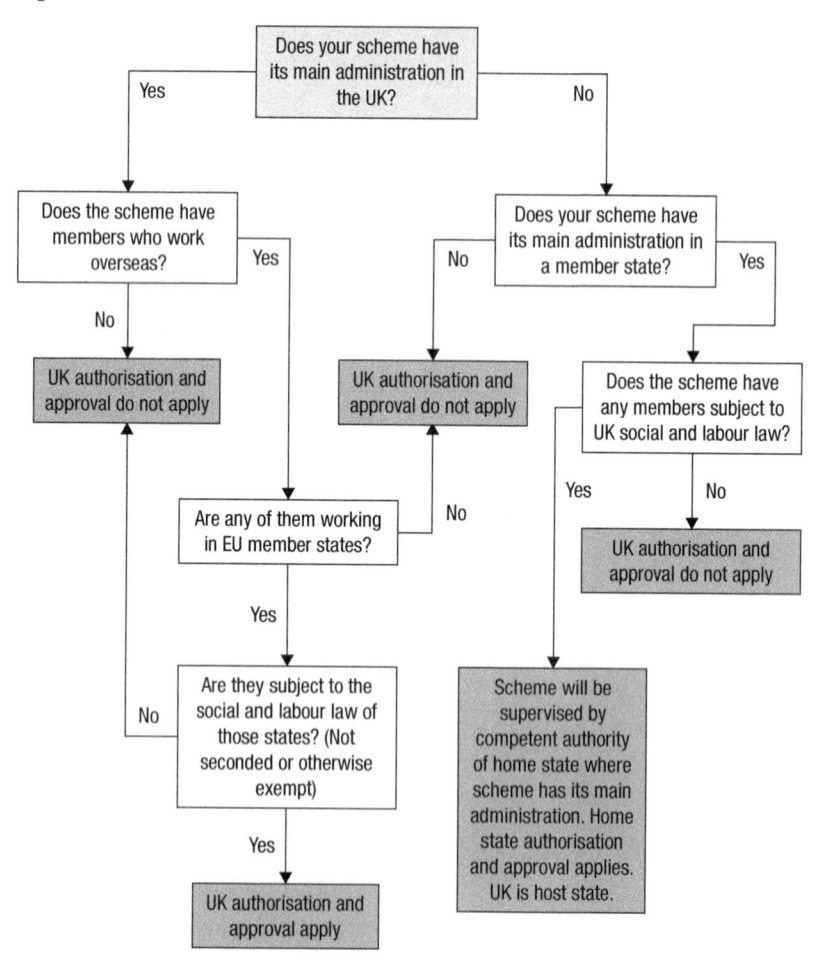

```
                    ┌─────────────────────────┐
                    │ Does your scheme have   │
         Yes        │ its main administration │        No
    ┌───────────────┤        in the UK?       ├───────────────┐
    │               └─────────────────────────┘               │
    ▼                                                         ▼
┌─────────────────┐                          ┌─────────────────────────┐
│ Does the scheme │                          │  Does your scheme have  │
│  have members   │    Yes                No │ its main administration │  Yes
│   who work      ├──────┐         ┌─────────┤   in a member state?    ├──────┐
│   overseas?     │      │         │         └─────────────────────────┘      │
└────────┬────────┘      │         │                                          │
         │ No            │         │                                          ▼
         ▼               │         ▼                          ┌─────────────────────────┐
┌─────────────────┐      │  ┌─────────────────┐               │    Does the scheme      │
│ UK authorisation│      │  │ UK authorisation│               │   have any members      │
│ and approval    │      │  │ and approval    │               │  subject to UK social   │
│ do not apply    │      │  │ do not apply    │               │    and labour law?      │
└─────────────────┘      │  └─────────────────┘               └───────┬─────────┬───────┘
         ▲               │         ▲                              Yes │         │ No
         │               ▼         │ No                               │         ▼
         │      ┌─────────────────┐                                   │ ┌─────────────────┐
         │      │ Are any of them │                                   │ │ UK authorisation│
         │      │ working in EU   ├───────────────────────────────────┘ │ and approval    │
         │      │ member states?  │                                     │ do not apply    │
         │      └────────┬────────┘                                     └─────────────────┘
         │               │ Yes
         │               ▼
         │      ┌─────────────────┐         ┌─────────────────┐
         │      │ Are they subject│         │  Scheme will be │
         │ No   │ to the social   │         │  supervised by  │
         └──────┤ and labour law  │         │ competent       │
                │ of those states?│         │ authority of    │
                │ (Not seconded   │         │ home state      │
                │ or otherwise    │         │ where scheme    │
                │ exempt)         │         │ has its main    │
                └────────┬────────┘         │ administration. │
                         │ Yes              │ Home state      │
                         ▼                  │ authorisation   │
                ┌─────────────────┐         │ and approval    │
                │ UK authorisation│         │ applies. UK is  │
                │ and approval    │         │ host state.     │
                │ apply           │         └─────────────────┘
                └─────────────────┘
```

The determining factors are the main administration of the scheme and the place of work of the member. If the scheme's main administration is in the UK and has members in another member state, it could still require authorisation and approval, even if the employer were in a third, non-EU country. If the scheme's main administration was in a non-EU country, it would not require authorisation and approval, even if it had members in both the UK and another EU member state (it would be a foreign scheme).'

The UK Government has traditionally opposed a number of EU pension reforms. For example, it had actively sought exemptions for schemes in wind-up from the draft portability directive and to enable a reduction in transfer values for underfunded schemes.

In a recent move, on 25 July 2014, the Government criticised the core ideal of the EC's approach to pension reform, noting that it pushed ahead with a revised IORPS Directive despite concerns that certain proposals were considered inadequate. It has even questioned whether the EC should be allowed to push ahead with the IORPS Directive at all, given that matters of pension regulation were for member states to decide. Practitioners will wish to track the situation for any relevant political developments in the future.

Contracting-out

13.8 The transfer of contracted-out rights overseas was simplified under the *Contracting-out, Protected Rights and Safeguarded Rights (Transfer Payment) Amendment Regulations 2005 (SI 2005/555)*. The requirement that the member must have permanently emigrated before a transfer of contracted-out or safeguarded pension rights was made to an OPS was removed.

Pension rights that include contracted-out rights can only be transferred to pension schemes eligible to hold such rights and recognised for the purposes of *FA 2004, s 169*. The receiving scheme administrator must obtain from the transferring scheme administrator the necessary transfer forms together with the details which apply to any transferring member in order to comply with the regulatory requirements.

BSP and S2P are to be replaced by a single-tier pension from 6 April 2016. Contracting-out was abolished with effect from 6 April 2012 for DC schemes. A DWP consultation entitled '*Occupational pension schemes: abolition of defined benefit contracting-out*' closed on 2 July 2014. It was accompanied by two sets of draft amending regulations. The majority of the provisions will come into force in April 2016. However, statutory override regulations are expected to come into force in autumn 2014.

Focus
- The EU keeps a watchful eye on the level of compliance with its Directives by member states

13.9 *Overseas considerations*

IORPS DIRECTIVE AND PORTABILITY DIRECTIVE

IORPS Directive

13.9 Below is a summary of the main aims of the IORPS Directive:

- to establish a framework for IORPs;
- to permit member states to decide on their own investment rules, subject to permitting investment up to 70% in shares and corporate bonds and at least 30% in currencies other than the currency of their future pension liabilities;
- to restrict portfolio self-investment in the sponsoring undertaking to 5% of the portfolio value (under the *EU Investment Services Directive*, this can be disapplied for schemes with fewer than 100 members);
- to achieve a high level of protection for future pensioners and beneficiaries, under prescribed rules of operation;
- to permit freedom to develop effective investment programmes and policy within prudent guidelines ('prudent person principle');
- to achieve greater investment security and diversity;
- to improve investment management, and the choice of managers approved by the member state;
- to ensure that schemes have effective liquidity on a needs basis;
- to rationalise tax problems encountered in differing states by pension schemes and arrangements;
- to allow flexibility in scheme design, whether by advance funding or pay-as-you-go schemes;
- to remove obstacles to effective management of pensions schemes across one member state to another (in compliance with the principle of a single integrated financial market, so avoiding an unnecessary multiplicity of managers around the EU);
- to control administration costs;
- to simplify or remove current restrictions and obstacles to integration;
- to ensure prudent calculation of benefits which are covered by sufficient assets;
- to enable member states to give supervisory powers to relevant authorities to monitor and supervise their IORPs to the required standard;
- to achieve mutual recognition of Member States' supervisory regimes to enable cross-border management ('home country control' principle);
- to permit a 'host' member state (where the sponsoring employer is located) to be able to request a 'home' member state (where the fund is located) to apply quantitative rules to assets held by cross-border schemes, provided the host member state applies the same, or stricter,

rules to its domestic funds – quantitative rules concern unlisted assets, assets issued by the sponsoring company, and assets held in a different denomination from that in which the scheme liabilities are expressed;

- to allow member states to permit a fund to offer survivor benefits and disability cover, particularly if requested by the employer and employee(s);
- to preserve any existing right to receive a lump sum without restrictions; and
- to give members the right to be informed about transfer rights on a change of employment.

Portability Directive

13.10 The draft *EU Portability Directive*, issued in October 2005, gave rise to much animated debate in the EU. The UK Government sought exemptions for schemes in wind-up and to enable a reduction in transfer values for underfunded schemes. It is to supplement *Directive 98/49/EC*, which already protects the supplementary pension rights of employed and self-employed workers who move within the EC, by providing such workers with increased rights.

The EC adopted the *Portability Directive* in June 2013. The *Directive* requires member states to implement minimum requirements for the acquisition and preservation of pension rights for people who go to work in another EU country. The agreement would see a vesting period for pension rights of three years for workers caught by the *Directive*. This is controversial as a number of member states apply a longer period for domestic workers.

Member states will have four years to apply the changes to national law.

EU warnings on tax discrimination

13.11 The EC has been very active in issuing formal notices to member states which it considers to impose discriminatory treatment on other EU citizens and their pension schemes. Examples have included:

- In November 2007 the ECJ said that it was illegal for the Dutch Government to tax dividends paid to foreign investors that domestic investors received tax-free. The case was brought by *Amurta*, a Portuguese company that lost 25% of its dividend payments from its investment in *Retailbox*, a Dutch company. *Retailbox's* Dutch investors were not charged the tax.
- On 1 February 2008 Germany and Estonia were requested requesting information on the different tax treatment of foreign pension funds in respect of dividends and interest. Those countries give full or partial tax exemption for their home schemes, but foreign schemes have to pay the full tax.

13.12 *Overseas considerations*

- Similar letters had already been sent to the Czech Republic, Denmark, Spain, Lithuania, the Netherlands, Poland, Portugal, Slovenia, Sweden, Italy and Finland in spring and summer 2007.

- The ECJ had already ruled against Denmark and Belgium in cases of perceived tax discrimination.

- The EC continues to report several other EU States over their dividend tax legislation, which it says discriminates against overseas pension funds.

- Proceedings against the Czech Republic, Estonia and Slovenia are now closed, following rectification of their tax laws. France and Spain are now similarly compliant.

The EC is seeking to stamp out tax discrimination in the EU in respect of pension contributions. In the UK both employee and employer contributions are allowable only if the UK scheme meets certain conditions, and such relief may not always be granted on contributions payable to certain overseas schemes. The UK rules are more restrictive than those of some other member states, and it has prevented certain jurisdictions from gaining QROPS status for their local pension schemes. The EC has already sent a formal request to the UK to change its original legislation, as it considered that the beneficial tax treatment of domestic pension schemes is incompatible with the freedoms mentioned in the EU Treaty. The EC required the UK to amend its legislation by extending the favourable tax treatment to contributions paid to schemes not fulfilling specific national requirements. The dispute is not yet fully resolved.

France and Spain have confirmed that they will give pension contributions paid to pension funds located in other member states the same tax treatment as contributions to their own domestic funds.

However, the IORPS Directive is not the only EU Directive which impacts on retirement provision for citizens of member states. There is a right to free movement of capital in the *Treaty on the Functioning of the European Union,* which states that:

- all restrictions on the movement of capital between Member States and between Member States and third countries shall be prohibited; and

- all restrictions on payments between Member States and between Member States and third countries shall be prohibited.

There is no doubt that the EC will continue to seek to drive out tax and retirement provision discrimination by members states in the future.

MIGRANT MEMBER RELIEF

13.12 The main effect of MMR under *FA 2004, Sch 33*, is that it replaced, and extended beyond, the corresponding relief which was available before A-Day. It is available for a migrant member who is a member of a QOPS (see **13.15** below). The individual's domicile does not have to be taken into account, and it does not matter where the scheme is established. Nevertheless, the scheme does have to be regulated in its country of origin and it must provide certain information to HMRC in respect of the member. The general effect was to widen considerably the number of people who may benefit from tax reliefs under the post A-Day tax regime.

A scheme may wish to notify HMRC of its status as a QOPS (see **13.17** below) if it has a member or members, and their employers, who wish to benefit from the tax reliefs which apply to relevant migrant members. The reporting criterion is in respect of BCEs, and the relevant form is APSS250 (see **13.37** below).

In order to understand how MMR works, it is necessary to be familiar with the terms which are used in the legislation. The main terms are as follows.

Relevant migrant member

13.13 This is a member who belongs to an OPS, who was not resident in the UK when they joined the scheme, and who was a member of the OPS at the beginning of their residence in the UK when they began to pay contributions. The member must also have received tax relief in respect of their contributions in their previous country/jurisdiction of residence, or received tax reliefs on contributions paid to the scheme in the country/jurisdiction of residence at any time in the previous 10 years.

Qualifying for migrant member relief

13.14 In order to be entitled to tax relief on contributions made to a QOPS, the member must have relevant UK earnings which are tax chargeable for the year in question, be resident in the UK when those contributions are made, and have notified the scheme manager of their intention to claim relief. Under *FA 2004, s 188*, employers may receive relief on their contributions to a QOPS if employees are entitled to MMR. *FA 2004, ss 196(2)–(6) and 200* contain the main provisions.

Qualifying overseas pension scheme and overseas pension scheme

13.15 In order to secure a scheme's status as a QOPS, the scheme manager must:

- notify HMRC of the scheme's status and provide any required evidence;
- undertake to inform HMRC if the scheme ceases to hold that status; and
- undertake to HMRC to comply with any prescribed BCE information requirements which may be necessary.

HMRC have the right to exclude an OPS from being treated as a qualifying scheme if it fails to meet such requirements.

13.15 *Overseas considerations*

MMR will be available where an individual:

- is resident in the UK but was not resident in the UK at the time they joined a QOPS;
- comes to the UK as a member of that scheme, and remains a member of the OPS;
- notifies the scheme manager that they intend to claim MMR;
- has earnings chargeable in the UK; and
- was eligible for tax relief on contributions to the OPS in the country in which they were resident immediately before coming to the UK, or meets such other conditions as may be prescribed by regulations.

The scheme must either be EC registered, or one that generally corresponds with a UK scheme, and must:

- notify HMRC that it is an OPS, providing supporting evidence if required;
- undertake to notify HMRC if it stops being an OPS;
- undertake to provide HMRC with certain information in accordance with regulations; and
- notify any member claiming MMR that it has undertaken to comply with the information requirements.

Employers may claim a deduction for contributions paid to a QOPS in respect of employees who are eligible for MMR.

The *Registered Pension Schemes (Extension of Migrant Member Relief) Regulations 2006 (SI 2006/1957)* extended eligibility for MMR to cases where a person was not resident in the UK at the time they joined a scheme, other than where:

- a member's rights have been subject to one or more block transfers;
- a series of block transfers have occurred; and
- the scheme to which the member originally belonged is closed to new accruals for existing members and a further scheme for members of that scheme is set up.

An OPS cannot be a registered pension scheme, and it must be established outside the UK. Normally, a scheme will be treated as established in the country where its registered office and main administration is, or, if there is no registered office, where its main administration is. The scheme's location of main administration is where the scheme's decisions are made. In the case of a trust-based scheme, that would normally be determined by reference to where the scheme trustees are resident.

An OPS must be regulated as a pension scheme in the country in which it is established, or, if there is no body by which it could be regulated, then certain conditions must be met. A scheme is regulated in a country or territory if it is subject there to supervision by the national authorities that are responsible for ensuring that pension schemes are administered soundly in order to protect members' interests. It must also be 'recognised for tax purposes' by the country or territory in which it is established. This means that it must meet the conditions of the *Principal Regulations*, as amended by *SI 2012/884* (see **Appendices 6** and **5** respectively). The impact of the recent changes is summarised in **13.36** below.

HMRC's residence guidance

13.16 HMRC has again updated and re-named its guidance on tax reliefs for residents and non-residents.

The main guidance on tax reliefs for residents and non-residents, HMRC guide HMRC6 entitled 'Residence, Domicile and the Remittance Basis', has been replaced by the following publications:

RDRI (1): Information Note: Changes to the Remittance Basis – published 28 May 2012

RDRI (2): Guidance Note: Statutory Residence Test – published August 2013

RDRI (3): Guidance Note: Overseas Workday Relief – published May 2013.

RDRI (1): states that the remittance basis was introduced for persons who:

- are not domiciled in the UK or not ordinarily resident in the UK;
- are UK resident in a tax year;
- make a claim to use the remittance basis in 2012–13 or in a later tax year; and
- have been resident in the UK in at least 12 of the 14 tax years before the year in which they make the claim.

OPS, ROPS, QROPS, QNUPS and QOPS

13.17 In order to be treated as a QROPS, a scheme must first qualify as a ROPS. A ROPS must, by nature, be an OPS. A brief description of all overseas schemes, as classified by HMRC, is given below.

OPS

RPSM14101030 states that, for a scheme to be an OPS, it cannot be a registered pension scheme and it must be established outside the UK. As described in the Principal Regulations (see **Appendix 6**) an OPS must be regulated as a pension scheme in the country in which it is established, or, if there is no body by which it could be regulated, then certain conditions must be met. Additionally, it must be 'recognised for tax purposes' by the country or territory in which it is established.

13.17 Overseas considerations

ROPS

A ROPS must comply with one of the two methods under the Principal Regulations (see **Appendix 6**).

- The scheme must:
- have undertaken to notify HMRC if the scheme ceases to be a ROPS; and
- be established in a member state of the EU, Norway, Liechtenstein or Iceland; or
- be established in a country or territory with which the UK has a DTA that contains exchange of information and non-discrimination provisions – see the list in RPSM14101046 (there is more information on the provisions of particular DTA's in HMRC's DTRM), or
- satisfy the requirement that, at the time of the recognised transfer, the rules of the scheme provide that:
  - at least 70% of the funds transferred will be designated by the scheme manager for the purpose of providing the member with an income for life,
  - the pension benefits (and any associated lump sum) payable to the member under the scheme, to the extent that they relate to the transfer, are payable no earlier than they would be if pension rule 1 in *FA 2004, s 165*, applied, and
  - membership of the scheme is open to persons resident in the country or territory in which it is established.

Pension rule 1 provides that no payment of pension may be made before the day on which the member reaches normal minimum pension age, unless the ill-health condition was met immediately before the member became entitled to a pension under the scheme. Guidance on the normal minimum pension age and on the ill-health condition is given at **4.33** above. See also **13.18** below, which contains the latest consolidated changes.

QROPS

The nature of a QROPS, and the application procedure in order to qualify as a QROPS, are described in **13.2** and **13.3** above respectively. The conditions in **13.18** or **13.19** below must be met, as appropriate.

QNUPS

The acronym QNUPS first appeared in the *Inheritance Tax (Qualifying Non-UK Pension Schemes) Regulations 2010 (2010/51)*. Such schemes are tax efficient in the matter of death benefits if they are properly constructed. However, transfers from registered pension schemes to QNUPS would not be recognised transfers unless the scheme is also a QROPS. A QNUPS must be a bona fide 'pension scheme within the meaning of *FA 2004, s 150(1)*. They escape many of the increasingly arduous reporting requirements for QROPS, but are currently under the watchful eye of HMRC.

QOPS

QOPS may be used to accommodate migrant members (see **13.12–14** above). The scheme must notify HMRC of its status on form APSS 250.

Overseas pensions schemes – first method of qualifying

13.18 The first method of qualifying is shown below, and the second method is shown in **13.19** below. They are a summarised consolidation of the application of the current Principal Regulations. **Appendix 6** tracks all the changes made since those regulations were first made.

1.(1) The *Regulations* came into force on 6 April 2006.

2.(1) In order to be an OPS the scheme must:

(a) satisfy the requirements in (2) and (3) below ; or

(b) be established (outside the UK) by an international organisation (see **11.19** below) for the purpose of providing benefits for, or in respect of, past service as an employee of the organisation and satisfy the requirements in **13.19** below.

(2) This para 2 is satisfied if:

(a) the scheme is an occupational pension scheme and there is, in the country or territory in which it is established, a body:

    (i) which regulates occupational pension schemes; and

    (ii) which regulates the scheme in question;

(b) the scheme is not an occupational pension scheme and there is in the country or territory in which it is established, a body:

    (i) which regulates pension schemes other than occupational pension schemes; and

    (ii) which regulates the scheme in question; or

(c) neither sub-para (a) or (b) is satisfied by reason only that no such regulatory body exists in the country or territory and:

    (i) the scheme is established in another member State, Norway, Iceland or Liechtenstein; or

    (ii) the scheme's rules provide that at least 70% of a member's UK tax-relieved scheme funds will be designated by the scheme manager for the purpose of providing that individual with an income for life, and the pension benefits payable to the member under the scheme (and any lump sum associated with those benefits) are payable no earlier than they would be if pension rule 1 in *FA 2004, s 165*, applied.

(3) This para is satisfied if the scheme is recognised for tax purposes.

A scheme is "recognised for tax purposes" under the tax legislation of a country or territory in which it is established if it meets the following conditions:

13.18 *Overseas considerations*

Condition 1

The scheme is open to persons resident in the country or territory in which it is established.

Condition 2

The scheme is established in a country or territory where there is a system of taxation of personal income under which tax relief is available in respect of pensions and :

(a) tax relief is not available to the member on contributions made to the scheme by the individual or, if the individual is an employee, by their employer, in respect of earnings to which benefits under the scheme relate;

(ab) the scheme is liable to taxation on its income and gains and is of a kind specified in *Schedule 1* to the *Principal Regulations*; or

(b) all or most of the benefits paid by the scheme to members who are not in serious ill-health are subject to taxation.

For the purposes of this condition 'tax relief' includes the grant of an exemption from tax.

Condition 3

The scheme is approved or recognised by, or registered with, the relevant tax authorities as a pension scheme in the country or territory in which it is established.

3.(1) ROPS, in addition to satisfying the requirements set out above – the pension scheme must satisfy:

(a) the requirement in para (6); and

(b) one or more of the following requirements:

　(i) the requirement that the scheme must be established in a country or territory mentioned in paragraph (2),

　(ii) the requirement in para (4),

　(iii) the requirement in para (5).

(2) The countries and territories referred to in para (1)(b)(i) are:

(a) the member States of the European Communities, other than the UK;

(b) Iceland, Liechtenstein and Norway; and

(c) any country or territory other than New Zealand in respect of which there is in force an Order in Council under *ICTA 1988, s 788*, giving effect in the UK to an agreement which contains provision about:

　(i) the exchange of information between the parties, and

　(ii) non-discrimination.

(3) For the purposes of para (2)(c)(ii) an agreement 'contains provision about non-discrimination' if it provides that the nationals of a Contracting State shall not be subjected in the territory of the other Contracting State to any taxation, or any requirement connected to such taxation, which is other than, or more burdensome than, the taxation and connected requirements to which the nationals of the other State are or may be subjected in the same circumstances.

(4) At the time of a transfer of sums or assets which would, subject to these *Regulations*, constitute a recognised transfer, a pension scheme must satisfy the condition in para (4A) and the rules of that scheme must provide that:

(a) at least 70% of the sums transferred will be designated by the scheme manager for the purpose of providing the member with an income for life;

(b) the pension benefits (and any lump sum associated with those benefits) payable to the member under the scheme, to the extent that they relate to the transfer, are payable no earlier than they would be if pension rule 1 in *FA 2004, s 165*, applied; and

(c) the scheme is open to persons resident in the country or territory in which it is established.

(4A) Where the pension scheme:

(a) is established in Guernsey, and

(b) is an exempt pension contract or an exempt pension trust within the meaning of *section 157E* of the *Income Tax (Guernsey) Law 1975* the scheme must not be open to non-residents of Guernsey

(5) At the time of a transfer of sums or assets which would, subject to the Principal Regulations, constitute a recognised transfer the scheme must be of a kind specified in *Sch 2* to the Principal Regulations (see **Appendix 6**).

(6) Where tax relief in respect of benefits paid from the scheme is available to a member of the scheme who is not resident in the country or territory in which the scheme is established, the same or substantially the same tax relief must:

(a) also be available to members of the scheme who are resident in the country or territory; and

(b) apply regardless of whether the member was resident in the country or territory:

   (i) when the member joined the scheme; or

   (ii) for any period of time when they were a member of the scheme.

(7) For the purposes of para (6) 'tax relief':

(a) is any tax relief that is available under the system of taxation of personal income in the country or territory in which the scheme is established; and

(b) includes the grant of an exemption from tax other than an exemption which applies by virtue of double taxation arrangements.

13.19 *Overseas considerations*

(8) In para (7)(b) 'DTA's' means arrangements made between the country or territory in which the scheme is established and another country or territory with a view to affording relief from double taxation.

QROPS second method of qualifying

13.19 In the case of an overseas pension scheme falling within **2**(1)(b) in **13.18** above, the scheme rules must provide that at least 70% of a member's UK tax-relieved scheme funds will be designated by the scheme manager for the purpose of providing the member with an income for life, and (b) the pension benefits payable to the member under the scheme (and any lump sum associated with those benefits) under the scheme must be payable no earlier than they would be if pension rule 1 in *FA 2004, s 165*, applied. (See also **3** in **13.18** above).

An 'international organisation' means an organisation to which *section 1* of the *International Organisations Act 1968* applies by virtue of an Order in Council under subsection (1) of that section.

RESIDENCY AND UNAUTHORISED PAYMENTS

13.20 Under *FA 2004*, an individual whose UK tax-relieved rights have been transferred to a QROPS can be liable to an unauthorised payments charge unless, when a payment is made to or in respect of the individual by the QROPS, they are not resident for purposes in the UK and had neither been UK resident in that UK tax year nor in any of the previous five tax years.

A QROPS did not have to report to HMRC a payment (or a deemed payment) if the member was not tax resident in the UK when the payment was made and had not been UK resident in that tax year or in any of the previous five tax years.

The rules described in **Appendix 4** and the *regulations* which are contained in **Appendix 5** changed some of the above rules from 6 April 2012 as described therein. They widened the information requirements and extended the five-year reporting rule to ten years. The key statutory changes are now listed in **13.36** below.

Employer contributions

13.21 Employer contributions to a QROPS are allowable under the normal rules of *Schedule D* for CT tax purposes. The contributions are subject to the provisions at *FA 2004, s 196*, which effectively applies the normal rules of calculating taxable profits. HMRC may apply the general commerciality test under *ITTOIA 2005* whereby expenses must be 'incurred wholly and exclusively for the purposes of the trade'.

Employers may deduct contributions from profits liable to tax once the relevant benefits are paid out.

The amount of an employer's contribution which has the benefit of tax relief in the UK does not affect the calculation of the proportion of the fund that is subject to UK tax rules. Regulations may deem certain payments to be authorised payments, and will also ensure those payments are subject to the authorised payments tax regime for registered pension schemes.

Employers making payments into approved occupational pension schemes will obtain tax relief only on the cash contributions made, not the amount shown in the company accounts.

Focus
- The reporting rules for QROPS have been greatly extended

PRINCIPAL REPORTING REGULATIONS

13.22 The *Pension Schemes (Information Requirements – Qualifying Overseas Pension Schemes, Qualifying Recognised Overseas Pension Schemes and Corresponding Relief) Regulations 2006 (SI 2006/208)* require reports of certain events to be made by QROPS administrators or managers. The relevant form is APSS253. If filed incorrectly through fraud or negligence, a penalty up to £3,000 may be levied. Late filing may result in a £300 fine, with £60 for each continuing day of late submission. Reports can be made throughout the year – HMRC will store information online for up to 22 months before submission. Nil returns are not required.

Reportable events pre 6 April 2012

13.23 The reporting requirements for overseas pension schemes prior to 6 April 2012 are described below. These were extended as from that date as described in the guidance in **Appendix 4**.

RPSM14101050 explained that the scheme manager of a ROPS/QROPS must have undertaken to comply with the information requirements for pre 6 April 2012 schemes. Reports were required in respect of payments out of members' funds which related to transfers from UK registered pension schemes or to migrant members. Member payment provisions only applied in relation to a payment made to or in respect of a relieved member or transfer member of a RNUKS if they:

- were resident in the UK when the payment is made (or treated as made); or
- although not resident in the UK at that time, had been resident in the UK earlier in the tax year in which the payment is made (or treated as made) or in any of the five tax years immediately preceding that tax year.

With effect from 6 April 2008, any day where an individual was present in the UK at midnight was counted as a day of presence in the UK for residence test purposes.

The manager of a QROPS that received a transfer from another OPS needed to check whether or not the transferring member had a UK tax-relieved fund or a

13.23 *Overseas considerations*

relevant transfer fund in the transferring scheme in order to establish if HMRC would have to be provided with information about payments made in respect of the individual. It would have been reasonable for the scheme manager to ask the individual to declare whether or not the transferred funds included any amounts that had received UK tax relief or had originated in a UK registered pension scheme.

The scheme manager could use form APSS253 to provide notification.

Where a non-pension payment such as a lump sum or a transfer was made, the scheme manager had to provide the information to HMRC by 31 January following the end of the tax year in which each payment was made. Where a pension payment was made, the scheme manager had to provide the information by 31 January following the end of the tax year in which the first payment was made, but it was only necessary to do this in respect of the first such payment to any individual.

Payments to members Relevant member payments	
Has the scheme made or been deemed to make a relevant member payment?	Reports are required. The information must be sent to HMRC by 31 January following the end of the tax year in which each payment is made.
Reporting payments to HMRC	
Form APSS253	The relevant information to be reported to HMRC is: • member's name and address; • member's date of birth; • member's NI number (if known); • date, amount and nature (pension, lump sum, transfer, annuity purchase) of the payment; • name of the QROPS; and • country or territory under the law of which that scheme is established and regulated. The information must be sent to HMRC by 31 January following the end of the tax year in which each payment is made.
Relevant migrant members and corresponding members	
Has a BCE taken place?	BCEs must be reported to HMRC.

Payments to members Relevant member payments	
Reporting BCEs to HMRC	The relevant information to be reported to HMRC is: • name and address of member where there has been a BCE in the tax year; and • date, amount and nature of the BCE. The information must be sent to HMRC by 31 January following the end of the tax year in which each payment is made.

Reportable events post 6 April 2012

13.24 The guidance in **13.23** above is finessed for all notifications from 6 April 2012 by the following:

- Form APSS251 is for use by a scheme manager to provide the required information and notifications. If it is later found that there were errors in that information (whether an inaccuracy, error or incorrect presumption) such that the scheme cannot meet the requirements to be a QROPS, then this will be considered to have always been the position – regardless of the issue of the QROPS reference. This will mean that any transfers that have been made to that scheme will not have been recognised transfers.

- If at any time after information has been supplied to HMRC, it becomes apparent to the scheme that:
  - something has changed and the change is a 'material change' in the information that establishes the scheme as a QROPS, or
  - that the information already supplied is incomplete or
  - the information already supplied contains a material inaccuracy, then

- form APSS251A is available for use by a scheme manager to provide details of changes where the QROPS status is retained, and form APSS251B is for use by a scheme manager to provide details of the changes where the QROPS status ceases (see **13.36** below for the changes that gave rise to these forms).

The information must be provided to HMRC

- within 30 days beginning on the day that the change occurred or the scheme manager became aware of the lack of completeness or inaccuracy, or
- by such other time as may be agreed between HMRC and the scheme manager.

13.25 *Overseas considerations*

Further guidance on this matter and other changes can be found at Newsletter 58, following the changes made under *FA 2013, s 53*, and regulations (see **13.36** below). The Newsletter is at *http://www.hmrc.gov.uk/pensionschemes/newsletter58.pdf*. The latest residence tests are to be found at the references in **13.16** above.

The current forms are listed in **13.37** below.

TRANSFERS

Reporting transfer payments

13.25 The administrator must report on APSS253 and APSS253 (Insert) to HMRC any transfer from their scheme to a QROPS using the online Event Report. The required information is:

- about the member
- the member's name, principal residential address and contact details – the member's date of birth;
    - the member's NI number or if they don't have one, their UTR with HMRC if they have one.
    - If the member isn't tax resident in the UK the date they ceased to be resident for tax purposes in the UK. If the member has neither a NI number nor a UTR the scheme manager should provide any reference number allocated by the tax authority of the country in which the member is tax resident.
- The name, address and contact details of the QROPS and the scheme manager.
- The date, amount and nature of the payment.
- If the payment is made to a pension scheme, the name and address of the receiving scheme, and if the scheme is a registered pension scheme or a QROPS the relevant Pension Scheme Tax Reference or QROPS number allocated by HMRC.
- If as a result of the payment there is no relevant transfer fund a statement to that effect.

Where the payment has been made following the member's death the following details for the recipient of the payment are needed:

- Payment to an individual
    - Name, principal residential address and date of birth.
    - NI number or if they don't have one, their UTR with HMRC if they have one. If the recipient isn't tax resident on the UK and has neither a NI nor a UTR and the scheme manager should provide any reference number allocated by the tax authority of the country in which the individual recipient is tax resident.

- Payment to someone other than an individual
  - the name and address

The provisions under which a scheme manager is treated as making a payment are in *FA 2004, ss 172–174A, Sch 28, para 2A* and *Sch 29, para 3A*. Guidance is provided in RPSM13104110 for post 6 April 2012 transactions and RPSM09100170 for pre 6 April 2012 transactions.

The pre 6 April 2012 guidance is at RPSM14101060. All QROPS scheme managers must now comply with the current information requirements.

The above details must be provided within 90 days beginning on the day on which the payment is made or treated as made; or by such other time as may be agreed between HMRC and the scheme manager.

Inheritance tax

13.26 When a member transfers from one pension scheme (say a registered pension scheme) to another (say a QROPS), then they have the right to determine the basis upon which the new death benefits under the receiving scheme are to be paid. That right is property and an asset of the member's estate in terms of *IHTA 1984, s 272*. So when they exercise that right by electing to have the death benefits paid on discretionary trusts outside their estate, then there is a loss to their estate in terms of *IHTA 1984, s 3(1)*. That loss and the consequent chargeable transfer is largely dependent on the member's state of health and life expectancy at the time of the transfer:

- If in normal health, then the value will be nominal – they would be expected to survive to take their full retirement benefits at which time the death benefits would lapse.
- If in ill health then the value could be substantive given the short period of time before a purchaser in the hypothetical open market would expect the death benefits to be paid out.

The transitional relieving provisions under *FA 2004, paras 56–58 of Sch 36*, apply and there is grandfathering of the IHT exemption for the pre-6 April 2006 fund on a transfer to a QROPS.

Transfer of rights to the payment of drawdown pension

13.27 It is possible, within the tax rules on authorised payments, for a drawdown pension (or an existing unsecured pension or ASP which remains in place) to be transferred to a QROPS. This also applies where no payments of pension were actually being drawn under the transferring scheme. All the sums and assets transferred must be held in an arrangement in the receiving scheme under which no other sums or assets are held at that time. In effect, it has to be dedicated for the purpose of the transfer.

The existing UK rules are all continued in the same way under the receiving scheme as if no transfer had taken place.

13.28 *Overseas considerations*

Transfers of pensions in payment, or rights where there is already an entitlement to benefits

13.28 RPSM14106060 states:

'**Additional provisions applying to transfer of crystallised rights to a qualifying recognised overseas pension scheme**

[Section 169(1B) to (1E), paragraph 17 of Schedule 32 and SI 2006/499]

Where a transfer takes place of already crystallised rights in a registered pension scheme to a qualifying recognised overseas pension scheme, a benefit crystallisation event 8 will occur. As a BCE 5B for a drawdown pension (before 6 April 2011, this would have been a BCE 1 for an unsecured pension) or a BCE 2 for a scheme pension will have applied at the original entitlement to benefits, overlap provisions will apply. This will have the effect that the amount crystallised (or an appropriate proportion) under the original BCE 1, 2 or 5B will be deducted from the amount crystallised under the BCE 8 occurring on transfer.

Unlike for a transfer of crystallised rights from a registered pension scheme to another registered pension scheme, where no further BCE occurs, a transfer to a qualifying recognised overseas pension scheme will produce a second BCE and so a further test against the lifetime allowance.

Following the transfer to the qualifying recognised overseas pension scheme, the receiving scheme will be required to provide benefits on a like for like basis as preceding the transfer. So the transfer of a scheme pension in payment, for example, should be continued in that form, and the conditions as set out in RPSM14106030 onwards should be followed. If any of those conditions are not met the member of the receiving scheme will be liable to an unauthorised payments charge by virtue of Schedule 34 (see RPSM13102020 onwards). That will be the case, in particular, if a lump sum is paid, the scheme pension is increased or the income withdrawal is speeded up (unless the member qualifies for flexible drawdown. See RPSM09103500 for more information about flexible drawdown.'

RPSM14106010 states:

'**Transfer of crystallised rights and scheme pension**

Section 169(1B) to (1E) & SI 2006 No. 499

It is possible within the tax rules on authorised payments to make a transfer from a registered pension scheme relating to a pension which is already in payment, or in the case of a drawdown pension fund (before 6 April 2011 either an unsecured or alternatively secured pension fund), where an entitlement to benefits has already arisen.

A pension in payment under a registered pension scheme is capable of being transferred to another registered pension scheme or a qualifying recognised overseas pension scheme and being regarded as a recognised transfer. This applies to any of the following

- member's scheme pension
- from 6 April 2011, member's drawdown pension
- until 6 April 2011, member's unsecured pension
- until 6 April 2011, member's alternatively secured pension
- dependant's scheme pension
- from 6 April 2011, dependant's drawdown pension
- until 6 April 2011, dependant's unsecured pension
- until 6 April 2011, dependant's alternatively secured pension.

If the provision of benefits derived from the transfer meet certain conditions, then the benefits paid from the transfer in the receiving registered pension scheme are capable of being within the pension rules and being authorised payments. Any failure to meet the conditions will result in the amount transferred being regarded as an unauthorised payment.

The conditions are set out in the Registered Pension Schemes (Transfer of Sums and Assets) Regulations 2006 (SI 2006/499) as amended.

To be regarded as a recognised transfer, a transfer must be "like for like". For example a transfer of a member's scheme pension must be applied as a member's scheme pension in the receiving scheme. If a transfer is not made like for like and instead it is applied as another form of pension, an unauthorised payment will arise.

The conditions are as set out below and RPSM14106020 for scheme pension (and dependants' scheme pension) and RPSM14106040 for drawdown pension (member and dependants) (before 6 April 2011 either an unsecured pension (member and dependants) or an alternatively secured pension [member and dependants]).

If it is applied as a scheme pension, then the scheme pension in the receiving scheme is treated for specific purposes as if it is a continuation of the original scheme pension and not as a new entitlement. This means that no BCE is deemed to arise at the transfer, and no entitlement to a pension commencement lump sum arises. A transfer on or after 6 April 2010 where the member is aged between 50 and 54 inclusive and who satisfied the normal minimum pension age test of 50 in the original scheme is treated as meeting normal minimum pension age of 55 in the receiving scheme. For measuring pension increases to see if a BCE 3 arises in future, the permitted margin (see RPSM11104350) will be measured from the start of the original scheme pension. And for a continuation of a "substantial reduction" test of the level of scheme pension or for

13.29 *Overseas considerations*

avoidance arrangements to increase the amount of tax-free lump sum (see RPSM09101590). And that a continuation of the measure of a pension protection lump sum death benefit (see RPSM10105150), or annuity protection lump sum death benefit (see RPSM10105160). So the protection lump sum concerned will be calculated by reference to the original scheme pension.

It will be permissible for any reduction which has taken place in the level of the original scheme pension before the transfer in accordance with the acceptable forms of reduction as set out in RPSM09101510 to continue to apply after the transfer. But it must be the case that, at the point of transfer, the level of the new scheme pension is not less than the rate of scheme pension immediately before the transfer. It will be acceptable, however, for reasonable administrative costs of the transfer to be deducted. It must also be the case that any guarantee period (see RPSM09101280) relating to the original scheme pension will continue to apply in the receiving scheme.

The conditions above will also apply where a transfer is made of a scheme pension paid by an insurance company as selected by the scheme administrator. This is where a transfer is made from one insurance company to another insurance company. The receiving insurance company will then be paying a scheme pension.

Further transfers of a scheme pension in payment may be made, but in such cases the conditions above will continue to apply by reference to the original scheme pension.

In addition to these conditions, some special provisions apply where a transfer of crystallised rights takes place from a registered pension scheme to a qualifying recognised overseas pension scheme (see RPSM14106060).'

Contracting-out transfers are permitted to QROPS that are eligible to hold such rights and recognised for the purposes of *FA 2004*. The scheme manager shall obtain from the transferring scheme administrator the necessary transfer forms together with the details which apply to any transferring member in order to comply with the regulatory requirements. The main legislative sources are contained in *PSA 1993, s 159* and *Pts III* and *IV*, in respect of any rights arising from contracting-out of SERPS or S2P in respect of a member.

TAX CHARGES, PENALTIES AND SANCTIONS

13.29 High levels of charges and surcharges can be incurred where payments are not regarded as authorised payments. These charges are known as 'member payment charges', and are described in *FA 2004, Sch 34*, and **Chapter 15** below. They also apply to payments made out of a registered pension scheme to a scheme which is, or is deemed to be, a RNUKS.

A RNUKS includes a scheme under which:

- MMR has been given;

- double taxation relief was received prior to A-Day;
- members have been exempted, under *ITEPA 2003, s 307*, from tax on pensions or death benefits at any time after A-Day whilst the scheme was an OPS; and
- there has been a relevant transfer from a UK registered pension scheme after 6 April 2006 whilst the scheme was a QROPS.

Member payment charges

13.30 Member payment charges include:

- the unauthorised payments charge;
- the unauthorised payments surcharge;
- a short service refund lump sum charge;
- a special lump sum death benefits charge; and
- charges on trivial commutation, winding-up lump sums and lump sum death benefits.

Under the *Pensions Schemes (Application of UK Provisions to Relevant Non-UK Schemes) Regulations 2006 (SI 2006/207)*, there are two methods to calculate the charge: the first is to calculate the member's tax relieved fund which is held under a RNUKS; and the second is to compute the amount of the member's relevant transfer fund under a RNUKS.

When the charge is incurred

13.31 A member will be subject to the charge if he was resident in the UK at the time the transfer was made or had been so in any of the preceding five years. The rate of tax payable is normally 40%. It is possible in some circumstances to mitigate the charge, if there is good reason to do so. The regulations relating to mitigation are:

- the *Registered Pension Schemes (Discharge of Liabilities under Sections 267 and 268 of the Finance Act 2004) Regulations 2005 (SI 2005/3452)*; and
- the *Pensions Schemes (Application of UK Provisions to Relevant Non-UK Schemes) Regulations 2006 (SI 2006/207)*, as amended.

Annual allowance and lifetime allowance charges

13.32 *FA 2004, Sch 34, paras 8–11*, provide formulae for calculating how the AA charge applies to currently relieved members of a current relieved RNUKS.

FA 2004, Sch 34, paras 13–19, describe how the LTA charge applies in similar circumstances.

13.33 *Overseas considerations*

Section 615 schemes

13.33 ICTA 1988, s 615,schemes,and the wider class of overseas scheme is referred to in *ITEPA 2003, ss 647–654*, may transfer assets UK registered pension schemes/QROPS on their cessation.

RPSM – international pages

13.34 A considerable amount of information appears in the RPSM's international pages. The headings cover a range of matters, including the following main issues. The following headings are summarised, and the comprehensive Manual will direct the reader to the stated subject matter.

'General principles of international enhancement.

International enhancement/non-residence factor:

- non-residence after 5 April 2006
- active membership period
- relevant overseas individual
- who is not a relevant overseas individual?
- pension scheme arrangements
- notifications procedure
- example of notifying HMRC
- separate notifications needed
- example of separate notifications
- notification and hybrid arrangements
- after HMRC notified
- benefit payment
- cash balance arrangement
- example for a cash balance arrangement
- cash balance arrangement: primary protection
- other money purchase arrangement
- example for other money purchase arrangement
- defined benefits arrangement
- example 1 for a defined benefits arrangement
- example 2 for a defined benefits arrangement
- non residence factor for defined benefit arrangements
- hybrid arrangement

Recognised overseas scheme transfer factor:

- post 5 April 2005 transfers
- not a relevant overseas individual

- benefit payment
- what happens after HMRC has been notified?

International enhancement/recognised overseas scheme transfer factor:

- how to calculate the factor
- examples of how to calculate the factor
- the relevant relievable amount
- cash balance arrangement relevant relievable amount
- example of relevant relievable amount for a cash balance arrangement
- other money purchase arrangement relevant relievable amount
- example of other money purchase arrangement relevant relievable amount
- defined benefits arrangement relevant relievable amount
- example 1 of defined benefits arrangement relevant relievable amount
- example 2 of defined benefits arrangement relevant relievable amount
- hybrid arrangement relevant relievable amount.'

RESIDENCE AND DOMICILE – NON-RESIDENT TRUSTS

13.35 HMRC's TSEM contains great detail on residency and non-residents trusts. The main contents are listed below. On the website they are followed by a list of questions and answers.

TSEM1002	Introduction to trusts
TSEM2000	Trust enquiries
TSEM3000	Trust income and gains
TSEM4000	Settlements legislation
TSEM5000	Trusts for particular purposes
TSEM6000	Legal background to trusts and estates
TSEM7000	Tax cases
TSEM7200	Deceased persons
TSEM8000	Trust Management Expenses
TSEM9000	Ownership and Income Tax
TSEMGlossary	Glossary
Appendix 1	HMRC Trustee Residence Guidance, including the OECD Tax Model Convention

13.36 *Overseas considerations*

Forms and guidance

- Procedure: Pre-transaction and post-transaction rulings under Clearances and Approvals 1
- HS261 – Foreign Tax Credit Relief: Capital Gains (2014)
- HS262 – Income and benefits from transfers of assets abroad and income from Non-Resident Trusts (2014)
- HS263 – Calculating foreign tax credit relief on income (2014)
- HS264 – Remittance basis (2014)
- HS270 – Trusts and settlements – income treated as the settlor's (2014)
- HS299 – Non-resident trusts and Capital Gains Tax (2014)
- HS301 – Beneficiaries receiving capital payments from non-resident trusts and the calculation of the increase in tax charge (2014)
- HS321 – Gains on Foreign Life Insurance Policies (2014)
- HS392 – Trust Management Expenses (TMEs) (2014)
- SA106 – Foreign (2014)
- SA106 Notes – Foreign Notes (2014)
- SA108 – Capital Gains Summary (2014)
- 50(FS) – Trust gains and capital payments year ended 5 April 2014.

SUMMARIES OF THE KEY RECENT CHANGES TO HMRC POLICY WITH REGARD TO QROPS

13.36 HMRC's document entitled *'Overseas Transfers of Pension Savings – Draft Guidance 20 December 2011'* (see **Appendix 4**) heralded a spate of changes to overseas pensions law and practice which is still ongoing.

A significant, and hotly disputed, change for QROPS was made by the *Registered Pensions Schemes and Overseas Pension Schemes (Miscellaneous Amendments) Regulations 2012 (SI 2012/884)* on 20 March 2012 and came into effect on 6 April 2012 (see **Appendix 5**). Transfers made to QROPS before 6 April 2012 could retain their status without penalty if the scheme lost its QROPS status from that date, but new transfers from UK registered pension schemes will be treated as unauthorised payments.

The regulations impose detailed reporting requirements on QROPS. They have their genesis in HMRC's perception of 'pensions liberation' by some schemes following the receipt of transfers from UK registered pension schemes (see **15.12** below), Transfers made in such circumstances will be deemed to be unauthorised payments

There is no doubt that some 'providers' of QROPS have marketed their schemes solely for the purpose of collapsing the fund, or paying unacceptable benefits out of previously UK tax-relieved funds, by placing reliance on the

Overseas considerations **13.36**

five-year absence rule. Any scheme manager who/which signs an APSS251 for such schemes is making a false statement, as it is in their knowledge that the scheme or arrangement has no intention of paying out pensions or complying with UK practice as undertaken in Part 3 of Form APSS251. Also, for such schemes, on form APSS251, ticking Part 2.3 was incorrect for offshore schemes without a regulatory body and ticking Part 2.7 for other countries. Therefore, some HMRC stance against these schemes was not entirely unexpected.

The main contentious issue in *SI 2012/884* concerns *regulation 4 (6)*, which requires that, where an exemption from tax in respect of benefits paid from the scheme is available to a member of a scheme who is not resident in the country or territory in which the scheme is established, the same exemption must also be available to a member who is resident in the country or territory, regardless of the member's residential status at the time of joining the scheme or during any later period of membership of the scheme. Some in the pensions industry feel that this condition is potentially in conflict with double taxation agreements, the OECD Modeller and EU anti-tax discrimination laws. Whereas, it seems unlikely that HMRC will relent, it is notable that the *Registered Pension Schemes and Overseas Pension Schemes (Miscellaneous Amendments) Regulations 2013 (SI 2013/2259)* has since disapplied the condition for overseas public service pension schemes, and those established outside the UK by an international organisation and falling within the *Principal Regulations*.

Of the remaining changes in these *regs*, the main one of interest is that *Sch 2* amended the information regulations *SI 2006/208* significantly, as follows:

- The principal residence and relevant member's NI number must be disclosed.
- There is a 10 year requirement from the date of transfer to be met if the member payment requirements are not to apply.
- The reporting date of 31 January is changed to 90 days from the date a payment is made or such other time as HMRC and the scheme manager may agree.
- Where a scheme ceases to be a QROPS, the scheme must provide the following information within 30 days:
  – the value of the relevant transferred sums or assets pertaining to each relevant transfer fund under the scheme; and
  – the name, principal residential address, date of birth and, if any, the National Insurance number of each member in respect of whom there is a relevant transfer fund under the scheme at the cessation date.
- Any changes to information already provided to HMRC must be notified to HMRC without undue delay.
- Where the scheme manager is a company, it must provide the names and addresses of the directors of the company to an officer of HMRC if required to do so in writing, and within such time as may be specified.

13.36 *Overseas considerations*

- A QROPS must provide to HMRC such of the information specified below as may be required in writing (this applies on a transfer to a QROPS from a registered pension scheme or QROPS:
  - the date of the transfer;
  - the name and address of any bank and details of any bank account which the scheme has used in relation to the transfer;
  - details of the sums or assets transferred;
  - where information is required from a scheme which is a transferee, the way that the sums or assets have been applied by the scheme;
  - where the transfer is from a RPS, the name and address of that scheme;
  - the name, principal residential address, date of birth and, if any, the NI number of the member who is connected with the sums or assets (where the member is a person to whom the member payment provisions do not apply by virtue of non-UK residence, the date that the member ceased to be resident in the UK);
  - the name and address of the body that regulates the scheme and the reference number, if any, issued to the scheme by the regulator;
  - the name and address of the tax authority that administers the scheme and the reference number, if any, issued to the scheme by the authority;
  - evidence to show that the scheme met at the time of the transfer and continues to meet the requirements specified in *SI 2006/206*; and
  - any other evidence relating to the transfer as may be required by HMRC.

- Additionally, if a scheme ceases to be a QROPS it must within 30 days beginning with the day on which the cessation takes place inform HMRC of:
  - the value at the cessation date of the relevant transferred sums or assets pertaining to each relevant transfer fund under the scheme; and
  - the name, principal residential address, date of birth and, if any, the national insurance number of each member in respect of whom there is a relevant transfer fund under the scheme at the cessation date.

Where:

(a) there is a material change affecting that information provided; or

(b) the information is incomplete or contains a material inaccuracy

the scheme must provide HMRC with details of the change, the complete information or correction of the inaccuracy without undue delay.

- 70% of the funds being transferred to schemes in New Zealand must be used to provide an income in retirement, unless the scheme is a Kiwisaver scheme, as defined in New Zealand's *Kiwisaver Act 2006*.

The *Pension Schemes (Categories of Country and Requirements for Overseas Pension Schemes and Recognised Overseas Pension Schemes) (Amendment) Regulations 2006 (SI 2012/1221)* excluded certain Guernsey pension vehicles under the *Income Tax (Guernsey) Law 1975, s 157E*, from being ROPS (and therefore QROPS) if they are open to non-residents of Guernsey.

The *Registered Pension Schemes (Provision of Information) (Amendment) Regulations 2013 (SI 2013/1742) SI 2013/1742* amended *SI 2006/567* to reflect the reduction to the LTA from £1.5m to £1.25m, and the AA from £50,000 to £40,000, with effect from tax year 2014/15. They also introduced FP 2014 and require the scheme administrator to provide HMRC with additional information where there is a recognised transfer to a QROPS. The scheme must notify HMRC, when a transfer is made to a QROPS and a member is no longer UK resident, of the date that their residency ceased.

The *Registered Pension Schemes and Overseas Pension Schemes (Miscellaneous Amendments) Regulations 2013 (SI 2013/2259)* made further changes to the information requirements, as shown below:

- A five yearly re-notification requirement on QROPS applies from 1 April 2015. HMRC will normally remind schemes 6 months before the due date (see also the re-issue and the re-notification dates listed later).

- Transitional provision is provided in respect of the requirements for the scheme administrator and member of a registered pension scheme to provide information in relation to transfers to QROPS which were in existence immediately before 6 April 2012 and which would have ceased to meet the necessary conditions for QROPS status as at 6 April 2012.

- Where a recognised transfer Is made to a QROPS, if the member is no longer resident in the UK, HMRC must be notified of the date that the residence ceased.

- The additional information requirements also apply to payments that are made, or treated as made, on or after 14 October 2013 and to former QROPS that ceased to be a QROPS on or after that date where such schemes have remaining relevant transfer funds.

FA 2013 revised *FA 2008, Sch 36*, so that for information and inspection powers the same rules in relation to inspection and requiring information apply to all pension matters whether the pension scheme is registered in the UK or is a QROPS or former QROPS. Under *s 52* of the *Act*, reporting requirements extend to all transfers of pension savings to a QROPS made free of tax. HMRC is empowered to make regulations setting out information requirements to require additional information from a new or existing QROPS; allow it to obtain information from a pension scheme that has been a QROPS; and to apply the penalties set out in *FA 2008, Sch 36, para 7*, to a failure by a former QROPS to comply with the new information requirements.

13.36 *Overseas considerations*

Under *s 53* of *FA 2013*, when HMRC issues a notice to require information or documents from a third party or a person who is not known, the same rules in relation to inspection and requiring information apply to all pension matters whether the pension scheme is registered in the UK or is a QROPS or former QROPS. There is also a provision that a notice requiring old documents in relation to a QROPS or former QROPS is extended to documents that originate up to 10 years before the date of the notice. A copy of such a notice must be given by HMRC to the scheme manager.

A QROPS that lost or gave up its status on or after 14 October 2013 must still provide certain information to HMRC when certain events occur. Regardless of when a scheme ceased to be a QROPS HMRC can issue an information notice either to the scheme manager or to anyone else using its powers at *FA 2008, Sch 36*.

A scheme that ceased to be a QROPS on or after 14 October 2013 still needs to report payments made by the scheme just as if the scheme was still a QROPS. Reports can be made using for APSS 253.

For schemes that ceased to be a QROPS on or after 14 October 2013. If at any time after any information has been supplied to HMRC, it becomes apparent to the scheme manager of that scheme that:

- there is a material change affecting the information, or
- the information is incomplete or contains a material inaccuracy

the scheme manager must provide HMRC with details of the change, the complete information or correction of the inaccuracy, as appropriate. The scheme manager can use form APSS 251A to provide details of the change.

The information must be provided to HMRC

- within 30 days beginning on the day that the change occurred or the scheme manager became aware of the lack of completeness or inaccuracy, or
- by such other time as may be agreed between HMRC and the scheme manager.

There is a cut-off point from which scheme managers of former QROPS no longer need to report changes to information. Scheme managers of former QROPS do not need to report changes to information if:

- There are no relevant transfer funds under the scheme; or
- The transfer to which the relevant information correction/change relates was made more than 10 years ago and the member is neither UK resident nor resident at any point earlier in the tax year or in any of the previous five tax years.

Additionally, for schemes that ceased to be a QROPS on or after 14 October 2013, HMRC can require the scheme manager of a former QROPS to provide information if that scheme received transfer whilst the scheme still had QROPS status and the transfer came from:

(a) A registered pension scheme; or

(b) Another QROPS where the transfer included rights that originated from a registered pension scheme.

This information must be provided:

- within 90 days beginning on the day the notice is given by HMRC, or
- by such other time as may be agreed between HMRC and the QROPS.

Regardless of when a scheme ceased to be a QROPS, HMRC can ask the scheme manager to provide information or produce documents using the powers at *FA 2008, Sch 3*. If the scheme manager does not comply with an information notice penalties will be due.

The member payment provisions do not apply to payments from a RNUK made to (or treated as made to), or in respect of, a relieved member of the scheme unless the payment is referable to that member's UK tax-relieved fund under the scheme.

From 1 April 2015 scheme managers will have to re-notify their scheme's ROPS status at certain intervals. This will normally be once every five years. The re-notification date for each QROPS will be set by the date of the letter sent by HMRC notifying the scheme manager of the QROPS reference number (the HMRC QROPS reference letter).

The required renewal or re-notification date will depend on if the HMRC QROPS reference letter was sent before April 2010 or on or after 1 April 2010. The re-notification date will be every five years following the date of the HMRC QROPS reference letter. So if the HMRC letter was dated 2 April 2010 the scheme manager must re-notify the QROPS status of their scheme on: 2 April 2015, by 2 April 2020 and so on.

A scheme where the HMRC QROPS reference letter was dated 15 June 2012 the scheme renewal deadlines will be:

15 June 2017

15 June 2022

15 June 2027 and so on.

Scheme managers can submit their re-notification up to six months before the re-notification deadline. So for the scheme with the HMRC QROPS reference letter dated 15 June 2012 the earliest the scheme manager can send in the re-notification is 16 December 2016 – six months before their renewal deadline of 15 June 2017.

FA 2014, s 45, provides a table for the calculation of the pension input amount for non-UK cash balance and DB arrangements.

FORMS

13.37 The forms listed in this paragraph are pertinent for overseas matters. They now overlap, as result of the recent legislation described in **13.36** above,

13.37 *Overseas considerations*

with most of the reporting requirements for UK registered pension schemes. Notably, forms APSS251 and APSS253 have been updated and new forms APSS262 and APSS263 created. The latest versions of APSS 262 and 263 were attached to Newsletter 58 and are at *http://www.hmrc.gov.uk/pensionschemes/newsletter58.pdf*. The latest versions of APSS 251; 251 Notes; 251A; 251B; 251B Insert; 253 and 253 Insert were attached to Newsletter 59 and are at *http://www.hmrc.gov.uk/pensionschemes/newsletter59.pdf*.

APSS262 was the first HMRC PSS form to become available as an i-form. In giving that form such priority, clearly indicates HMRC's increased vigilance over transfers to QROPS. It is accessible in Newsletter 63 at *http://www.hmrc.gov.uk/pensionschemes/newsletter63.pdf*.

Forms generally can be downloaded from the HMRC forms section. The scheme manager must quote their ID (where allocated) on all reports and forms (see **13.3** above).

The complete list is as follows:

Form number	Description
APSS250	Qualifying Overseas Pension Schemes
APSS251	Qualifying Recognised Overseas Pension Schemes
APSS251	Qualifying Recognised Overseas Pension Schemes Notes
APSS251A	Qualifying Recognised Overseas Pension Schemes – Change of details
APSS251B	Qualifying Recognised Overseas Pension Schemes – Change in status and notification of fund value
APSS251B	Qualifying Recognised Overseas Pension Schemes – Notification of fund value – insert
APSS252 (Insert)	Supplementary page for relevant migrant members
APSS253	Qualifying Recognised Overseas Pension Schemes – Payments in respect of qualifying members
APSS253 (Insert)	Qualifying Recognised Overseas Pension Schemes – Payments in respect of qualifying members – Additional page
APSS254	Election for a deemed BCE
APSS254 (Notes)	Election for a deemed BCE Completion notes
APSS262	Transferring UK tax-relieved assets to a QROPS (amended due to SI 2013/1742 – the new regulations for recognised transfers apply to transfer requests made by the member from 12 August 2013)
APSS263	Member information

FOREIGN PENSIONS OF UK RESIDENTS AND ANTI-AVOIDANCE

13.38 The following matters are relevant considerations generally for international tax-planning:

1. *FA 2011, s 72*, attempts to prevent individuals from taking advantage of a tax loophole. Notwithstanding the terms of a DTA with another territory, a payment of a pension or other similar remuneration may be taxed in the UK where:

- the payment arises in the other territory;
- it is received by an individual resident of the UK;
- the pension savings in respect of which the pension or other similar remuneration is paid have been transferred to a pension scheme in the other territory; and
- the main purpose or one of the main purposes of any person concerned with the transfer of pension savings in respect of which the payment is made was to take advantage of the double taxation arrangement in respect of that payment by means of that transfer.

In the event that tax is paid in the other jurisdiction, appropriate credit will be available against the UK tax chargeable.

The legislation had effect in relation to payments of pensions or other similar remuneration made on or after 6 April 2011.

2. British pensioners who live abroad will have to provide evidence that they are alive if they wish to keep their state pensions. At present, the DWP sends "life certificates" to individuals who have retired abroad, which they have to get countersigned. It is increasing the frequency with which the certificates are issued, although these new "push on life certificates" will only apply to countries such as France which do not automatically share the information with the UK.

3. In the future, non-UK residents will have to pay CGT on gains on UK residential properties that are not their primary residence. This will have impact on the investments of some pension schemes.

4. With effect from 5 December 2013, stamp duty for shares purchased in exchange traded funds was abolished in order to encourage those funds to locate in the UK.

5. The remittance basis ensures that individuals only pay UK tax on their foreign income when they remit it to the UK. From tax year 2012/13 a remittance basis charge of £50,000 applies if an individual:

- is not domiciled in the UK or not ordinarily resident in the UK
- is UK resident in a tax year

and makes a claim to use the remittance basis in 2012/13 or in a later tax year; and has been resident in the UK in at least 12 of the 14 tax years before the year in which they make the claim.

13.38 *Overseas considerations*

6. The pre April 2012 £30,000 remittance basis charge remains unchanged if an individual has been UK resident in at least seven of the previous nine tax years, but in less than 12 of the previous 14 tax years. They will not have to pay both charges in a tax year. The amount of the charge will be £30,000 or £50,000 depending on the length of their UK residence. Individuals using the remittance basis are not required to make any additional disclosures about their income and gains arising abroad. So long as they declare their remittances to the UK and pay UK tax on them, they will not be required to disclose information on the source of the remittances.

CHECKLIST

- The provisions of *FA 2004*, which had effect from A-Day, gave wide scope to make transfers to and from registered pension schemes

- *FA 2004* has been greatly modified since its enactment, but the provisions of the *Act* concerning overseas matters have, to date, remained largely in place

- UK residents may save for their retirement provision through a non-UK employer (even one without a UK branch)

- The Government is constantly extending the legislation and rules which apply to QROPS

- UK investment Regulations are primarily for the purpose of bringing in UK legislation to accord with the IORPS Directive

- Cross-border regulations make provision in connection with the carrying-out by the Pensions Regulator of its functions in relation to cross-border activity within the EU by occupational pension schemes. A flowchart is provided

- The purpose of the IORPS Directive is to establish a framework for IORPs

- The EU Portability Directive requires member states to implement minimum requirements for the acquisition and preservation of pension rights for people who go to work in another EU country

- The EC has been very active in issuing formal notices to member states which it considers to impose discriminatory treatment on other EU citizens and their pension schemes

- Migrant member relief is available to members who have relevant UK earnings, are resident in the UK when those contributions are made and have notified the scheme manager of their intention to claim relief. Under *FA 2004, s 188*, employers may receive relief on their contributions to a QOPS

- HMRC has produced updated residence guidance in its RDRI series publications

Overseas considerations **13.38**

- OPS, ROPS, QROPS, QNUPS and QOPS are described
- High levels of charges and surcharges can be incurred where payments are not regarded as authorised payments. These charges are known as 'member payment charges'
- *ICTA 1988, s 615*, schemes, and the wider class of overseas scheme is referred to in *ITEPA 2003, ss 647–654*, may transfer assets UK registered pension schemes/QROPS on their cessation
- A considerable amount of information appears in the RPSM's international pages
- HMRC's TSEM contains great detail on residency and non-residents trusts
- Summaries of the key recent changes to HMRC policy with regard to QROPS are provided, including HMRC's greatly extended information powers
- A list of overseas forms is provided

Part Five

Other forms of tax efficient provision for high earners and employers

Chapter 14

> **SIGNPOSTS**
>
> - There are various forms of retirement savings available to individuals in addition to the pension provision
> - Popular vehicles include SAYE, SIPS, EMIs, and new ISAs (NISAa)
> - Ex-gratia payments or golden handshakes must not be 'earnings' if tax or NIC liability is to be avoided

Other forms of tax-efficient provision for high earners and employers

INTRODUCTION

14.1 This **Chapter** highlights some of the tax planning issues that members of registered pension schemes, advisers and employers may want to consider. Many employers and savers are exploring alternative tax-efficient methods of saving due to the severe restriction of tax reliefs on pension saving.

Save-as you earn and share incentive plans

14.2 SIPs provide employees with tax and NIC advantages to employees when they buy or are given shares in the company they work for. Shares acquired or awarded under the plan are held on behalf of the scheme participant by the scheme trustees, who receive any dividends paid under the scheme. Cash dividends may be reinvested in further shares and are called 'dividend shares'. They are exempt from income tax under *ITTOIA 2005, s 770*.

SIPs are described in ERSM330000 and *ITEPA 2003, Ch 6* of *Pt 7* and *Sch 2*.

With effect from the tax year 2014/15, *FA 2014, s 49* increased the maximum value of free shares that can be awarded annually to an employee from £3,000 to £3,600. *ITEPA 2003, Sch 2*, is amended accordingly. The *section* also increases the maximum value of partnership shares that an employee can purchase annually from £1,500 to £1,800. The 10% maximum value of an employees' salary rule remains.

It is possible for companies to offer one, or a combination, of four types of shares:

1. Up to £3,600 of free shares in any tax year. If wished, the employer can link the award to employee-performance.

14.3 *Other forms of tax-efficient provision for high earners and employers*

2. Partnership shares can be bought back by employees from their gross pay. The monetary limit is £1,800.
3. Matching partnership shares can be bought by employees. They will be matched by their employer, giving them up to two free shares for every partnership share they buy.
4. Dividend shares can be paid to employees.

However, there is a potential tax charge under *ITTOIA 2005, ss 392 to 396* where:

- the trustees do not reinvest the dividends but pay over the cash dividend to the participant; or
- the dividend shares cease to be subject to the approved SIP.

Any amount not reinvested is taxed (and any entitlement to tax credit is determined) for the tax year in which the dividend is paid over to the scheme participant rather than the year in which it was originally paid. The scheme may only hold on to a cash dividend and carry it forward for three years from the date of payment.

The participant is treated as receiving a distribution in the year in which the shares cease to be subject to the SIP within three years of acquisition – this is a further distribution not a postponement of the original charge. The charge can be reduced if tax has been paid on capital receipts in respect of plan shares.

There are equivalent rules for SIPs involving shares in non-UK resident companies (*ITTOIA 2005, s 405*, refers).

FA 2014, Sch 8 amended the details of the operation of SIPS and the penalties that can apply.

Secondary legislation increases the limits on the maximum amount employees can save under SAYE schemes.

Enterprise management incentives

14.3 The use of EMIs as tax and NIC efficient share option vehicles for small, higher-risk companies has been on the increase for some time. There are no residence or incorporation conditions. The grant of the option is tax-free, and there will normally be no tax or NICs for the employee to pay when the option is exercised or NIC charge for the employer. Reliefs are available on exercise of options, provided that shares are bought at the market value they had on the day the option was granted.

EMIs were introduced by *FA 2000*. The main legislation is now to be found in *ITEPA 2003, Sch 5*. HMRC's guidance 'Enterprise Management Incentives: A guide for employees, employers and advisers' is replaced by the EMI guidance in ESSUM.

The following extracts are based on the current ESSUM guidance:

- EMI options can be granted by independent trading companies with gross assets not exceeding £30m.

Other forms of tax-efficient provision for high earners and employers **14.3**

- Options over shares with an unrestricted market value at the date of grant up to £250,000 (including any amount granted under an approved CSOP can be granted. The £250,000 limit applies from 16 June 2012; prior to that date, the individual limit was £120,000. There will normally be no income tax or NICs when the options are exercised.

- There is no approval process or clearance mechanism for EMI, but a simple requirement on companies to notify HMRC within 92 days of when an EMI option is granted. In addition there is also an annual reporting requirement. However, a company can request an advance assurance that it meets the qualifying conditions under the procedure described in ESSUM52020.

- In order for an option to be a qualifying option, it must be granted for genuine commercial reasons, to recruit or retain an employee in a company. An option does not qualify if it is granted as part of a scheme or arrangement the main purpose (or one of the main purposes) of which is to avoid tax.

- An employee may be granted qualifying options over shares with a total value of £250,000. This limit applies from 16 June 2012; prior to that date, the individual limit was £120,000.

- The shares under option include all EMI options granted by the employing company and any companies that are members of the same group of companies. The value of the shares under option is the value of the shares at the time the option was granted.

- Any options granted in excess of this limit are not qualifying options in so far as they relate to the excess. If an option is granted that exceeds £250,000 limit the option will be a qualifying option up to the individual limit and the excess will not be a qualifying option and so will not have any tax advantages.

- The individual limit includes the value of any CSOP options granted by the employing company and any companies that are members of the same group of companies. A CSOP option is an option to acquire shares granted under a scheme approved under *ITEPA 2003, Sch 4*. The maximum value of a CSOP option is £30,000. The value of the shares under option is the value of the shares at the time the option was granted.

- If the shares under option are quoted on the London Stock Exchange, the market value is based on the prices on the Stock Exchange's Daily Official List. If shares are not quoted on the London Stock Exchange, the company may offer its own valuation. In that case, HMRC may enquire into the valuation. Alternatively, the company can ask HMRC Shares and Assets Valuation to agree a valuation with them before the option is granted. This valuation will be in accordance with *TCGA 1992, Pt 8*.

- Once an employee has been granted EMI options, or EMI and CSOP options up to the £250,000 limit then no further EMI qualifying options can be granted until 3 years after the last of those options was granted,

14.4 *Other forms of tax-efficient provision for high earners and employers*

even if some options have been exercised or released. Once the 3 year limit has expired then further EMI options can be granted to the extent that any other EMI or CSOP options then held are below the £250,000 limit.

- The total unrestricted market value of shares under EMI options granted by the company cannot exceed £3m at any time. If an option is granted that causes this limit to be exceeded, the option is not a qualifying EMI option as to the excess. If more than one option is granted at the same time which causes the limit to be exceeded, the non-qualifying excess is divided amongst the options pro rata.

The granting of an EMI option in parallel with another EMI option is acceptable. This means granting two EMI options to the same person on the understanding that only one option can ever be exercised and that the other option falls away when the first option is exercised. This concept has been used, for example, to parallel discounted options with tough performance targets with non-discounted options that have no or more lenient targets. For the purpose of the EMI limits, only the maximum number of shares which may be acquired under either option need be counted; there is no need to take into account the value of both if only one can ever be exercised.

It is not a requirement that both options are granted at the same time, but it must be clearly stated within the terms of the second option that if either of the options is exercised the parallel option will cease to be capable of exercise.

In order for this arrangement to be acceptable, the grant of the second 'parallel' option must not change the terms of the first option which must remain capable of exercise, until it lapses or is given up. If the first option is exercised then the terms of the second option must provide that the second option will cease to be capable of exercise in these circumstances. Similarly, if the second option is exercised a condition of the exercise must be that the first option is either released or cancelled without consideration. Making such a provision in the terms of the second option will not be regarded as changing the terms of the first option.

Default retirement age

14.4 The default retirement age of 65 under the *Employment Equality (Age) Regulations 2006 (SI 2006/1031)* was abolished by the *Employment Equality (Repeal of Retirement Age Provisions) Regulations 2011 (SI 2011/106)* which started a six-month phasing out period from the start of April 2011. However, it should be noted that, in a recent landmark ruling by the Supreme Court, employers can continue to tell their staff the age they must leave so long as they give good reasons for doing so.

Overseas schemes

14.5 The ability to make transfers to and from registered pension schemes extends to QROPS. This can simplify administration procedures and result in cost-saving. It is therefore an attractive option for some, in particularly the internationally mobile and expatriates. The rules which apply are described in **Chapter 13** above.

EXCEPTED GROUP LIFE POLICIES

14.6 EGLPs can be an attractive alternative to providing death-in-service benefits through a registered pension scheme. They have similar tax advantages to a registered pension scheme but are not subject to the LTA. There is no benefit-in-kind income tax charge on the premiums paid, they can provide tax-free lump sum death benefits, and they can be efficient on IHT where a discretionary trust is in place. Employer contributions should be tax-relievable under the 'wholly and exclusively' test.

EGLPs are not subject to the punitive taxation that applies to EFRBS, and they are not subject to the disguised remuneration legislation introduced under *FA 2011*. There is no need to register an EGLP with HMRC and no need to comply with the new regime's reporting requirements. Since EGLPs sit outside the registered pension scheme tax regime, they could therefore be used to provide lump sum life cover for the following:

- Employees whose group life cover already exceeds their LTA.
- Employees whose group life cover, together with lump sum death benefits from other registered pension schemes, exceeds their LTA.
- Employees with EP or fixed protections (see **Chapter 9** above) where payment of the lump sum insured would jeopardise such protection.
- Employees with EP or fixed protections where payment of life assurance premiums would jeopardise such protection.
- Employees with PP where PP may not fully protect against a LTA charge.
- Employees with fixed protection where continuing membership of a registered group life assurance scheme could potentially jeopardise that protection if the life assurance scheme had not been established as a DB arrangement.
- New employees who have EP or fixed protection and would lose it if they became members of a registered pension scheme for life assurance benefits.
- Employees with EP or fixed protection where re-broking of the group life policy under a registered pension scheme would cause the loss of protection.

An EGLP must meet the conditions in *ITEPA 2003, ss 480–482*. This means it must be a group policy whose terms provide for the payment of benefits on the death of more than one individual and for those benefits to be paid on the death of each of those individuals. An EGLP must meet the four benefit conditions in s 481 and the three beneficiary conditions in *s 482*. The four benefit conditions are as follows:

- *Condition A*: a sum or other benefit of a capital nature is payable or arises:
  – on the death in any circumstances of each of the individuals insured under the policy who dies under an age specified in the policy that does not exceed 75, or

14.6 *Other forms of tax-efficient provision for high earners and employers*

- on the death, except in the same specified circumstances, of each of those individuals who dies under such an age.
- *Condition B*: the same method must be used for calculating the sums or other benefits of a capital nature payable or arising on each death, and any limitation on those sums or other benefits is the same in the case of any death.
- *Condition C*: the policy does not have, and is not capable of having, any surrender value, or if it does, the surrender value does not exceed the proportion of premiums already paid for an unexpired period of insurance up to the end of the policy term or, if earlier, the next premium due date.
- *Condition D*: no sums or other benefits may be paid or conferred under the policy, except as mentioned in condition A or C above.

The three beneficiary conditions are as follows:

- *Condition 1*: any sums payable or other benefits arising under the policy must (whether directly or indirectly) be paid to or for, or conferred on, or applied at the direction of:
    - an individual or charity beneficially entitled to them, or
    - a trustee or other person acting in a fiduciary capacity who will secure that the sums or other benefits are paid to or for, or conferred on, or applied in favour of, an individual or charity beneficially.
- *Condition 2*: no person who is, or is connected with, an individual whose life is insured under the policy may, as a result of a 'group membership right' relating to that individual, receive (directly or indirectly) any 'death benefit in respect of another individual' whose life is so insured.

  A 'death benefit in respect of an individual' means any sums or other benefits payable or arising under the policy on the individual's death or anything representing any such sums or benefits.

  A 'group membership right', in relation to an individual insured by a group life policy, means any right (including the right of any person to be considered by trustees in their exercise of a discretion) that is referable to that individual being one of the individuals whose lives are insured by the policy.

- *Condition 3*: tax avoidance is not the main purpose, or one of the main purposes, for which a person is at any time:
    - the holder, or one of the holders, of the policy, or
    - the person, or one of the persons, beneficially entitled under the policy.

  'Tax avoidance purpose' means any purpose that consists in securing a tax advantage, as defined in *ICTA 1988, s 840ZA*, now contained in *CTA 2010, s 1139*, whether for the holder of the policy or any other person.

From these conditions, it can be seen that the only sums payable must be lump sum death benefits or a refund of premium for an unexpired period of cover. The policy must not provide a benefit in the form of a survivor's pension.

Other forms of tax-efficient provision for high earners and employers 14.6

It is acceptable to insure the capitalised amount of a survivor's pension, but the benefit must be paid as a capital sum, not an income stream. The policy must not contain an investment element, and there should be no surrender value (other than a part refund of premiums on cancellation). An age 75 limit applies, and the same method must be used to calculate the lump sum death benefit in respect of each member covered. Any restriction on benefit must apply equally to each life assured.

Benefits may only be paid to individuals or nominated charities. A company sponsoring the scheme for its employees cannot be a beneficiary. Benefits must not be paid to another person covered by the same policy, ie an EGLP cannot be used for business protection purposes. However, it would be acceptable for another person covered under the policy to benefit upon the death of another member if that member were a spouse.

When putting an EGLP in place, it would be advisable to obtain confirmation of tax-effectiveness from the inspector of taxes.

There is a possibility of an IHT charge on the tenth anniversary of the trust. However, this would only occur if the proceeds of a claim had not been distributed by then or if the policy covered someone with very short life expectancy. The charge is a fraction of 6% of the trust value.

Tax treatment of an EGLP compared to a registered scheme can be summarised as follows:

Tax provision		**Registered pension scheme**	**Excepted group life policy**
Registered pension scheme tax regime	Premium counts towards AA	No[1]	No
	Benefits count towards LTA	Yes	No
	Jeopardy for enhanced and fixed protection	Yes	No
	Reporting requirements	Yes	No
	Unauthorised payment charges	Yes[2]	No
Income tax	Chargeable gain on proceeds	No	No
	Tax on lump sum benefit	No	No
	Benefit-in-kind charge on premium	No	No
CT	Premium allowable as an expense	Yes	Yes[3]
IHT	Proceeds form part of death estate	No	No
	Lifetime charge on settlement	No	No
	Ten year charge	No	No[4]
	Exit charge	No	No[5]

1. Unless treated by HMRC as a money purchase arrangement (this could apply if scheme rules simply express benefit to be paid as the proceeds of an insurance policy).

14.7 *Other forms of tax-efficient provision for high earners and employers*

2. Lump sums paid more than two years after the time when the trustees could reasonably be expected to know of the member's death would be unauthorised payments (death under age 75).
3. Confirmation of tax effectiveness should be obtained from the inspector of taxes.
4. Unless proceeds of a claim are not paid out by then or policy covers employee with very short life expectancy.
5. The rate will be nil where value in the trust at inception and at each tenth anniversary is nil.

A similar policy may be put in place where it covers only one employee, known as a 'relevant life policy'.

IN SPECIE PAYMENTS

14.7 Strictly speaking, *in specie* contributions as such are not permitted. The tax legislation requires contributions to be expressed as cash sums. The exception to this is that shares acquired under a SIPS or SAYE scheme may be treated as contributions if transferred within a certain timescale.

However, it is allowable for a member or employer to agree to pay a monetary contribution to a pension scheme and then to transfer an asset in settlement of that debt. The agreement to pay the contribution must be legally enforceable so that the scheme administrator can pursue the member or employer for payment. (see **3.4** and **3.32** above). The asset transferred should be a suitable investment for the pension scheme and should not constitute 'taxable property' (see **Chapter 12** above).

The value placed on the asset must be its open market value when ownership is transferred. In the case of property, its value must be determined by an independent valuation when the contracts are exchanged. In the case of quoted shares, their value is determined on the trade date.

The value placed on an asset by the person making the contribution may well be different from the value placed on it by the scheme administrator. HMRC require the value of the asset to match exactly the amount of the debt; so, if there is any discrepancy between these two amounts, the scheme administrator must either refund the excess or require a further payment. Instead of any excess being refunded, it may be possible to treat it as a further contribution. If the scheme administrator does not pursue any shortfall, it may be treated as an unauthorised payment.

In specie contributions attract tax relief in the same way as cash contributions. A member therefore has scope of up to 100% of earnings, and an employer may receive a deduction under the usual 'wholly and exclusively' rule, both of which are subject to the annual allowance.

As an *in specie* contribution is treated as a sale of the asset to the pension scheme, CGT and stamp duty charges apply as appropriate. However, once the asset is inside the pension scheme, any future gains are sheltered. The date used to value the asset is also the date used for CGT and stamp duty purposes.

Other forms of tax-efficient provision for high earners and employers **14.8**

Due to the timescales that can be involved in transferring certain assets, anyone contemplating an *in specie* contribution should consider what the implications would be if the transfer is delayed into a new tax year or contribution input period. It will be necessary to obtain independent valuations, which would extend the timescales further, so it may be preferable to start the process earlier in the tax year so that the contribution may be treated as falling within that tax year.

HMRC guidance on *in specie* contributions appears at RPSM05101045:

> 'As explained at RPSM05101020 contributions to a registered pension scheme must be a monetary amount. However, it is possible for a member to agree to pay a monetary contribution and then to settle this debt by way of a transfer of an asset or assets.
>
> For example, if a member wishes to pay a contribution he cannot do this by merely saying "take this asset and whatever it is worth that is my contribution".
>
> There must be
>
> - A clear obligation on the member to pay a contribution of a specified monetary sum, say, £10,000. This needs to create a recoverable debt obligation.
> - A separate agreement between the scheme trustees and the member to pass an asset to the scheme for consideration.
> - If the scheme agrees, the cash contribution debt may be paid by offset against the consideration payable for the asset. This is the scheme effectively agreeing to acquire the asset for its market value.
>
> If the asset market value is lower than the contribution debt the balance will be paid in cash.
>
> If the cash contribution debt is not created, then the transaction is the acquisition of an asset by the scheme not a contribution.
>
> If the contribution is being made to a registered pension scheme that operates relief at source (RAS) the amount of cash contribution specified should, if applicable, be the net amount after the individual exercises his right to deduct from the payment the basic rate RAS relief (see RPSM05101310). The basic rate relief will be recoverable by the scheme administrator in the normal way from HMRC and if appropriate the individual can claim higher rate relief via his self-assessment return.'

NEW INDIVIDUAL SAVINGS ACCOUNT

14.8 ISA have been popular for some years whereby providers may (for example) offer instant access, fixed rate bonds, or accounts with base rate guarantees. The ISA is a highly tax-efficient method of saving, either with cash or shares or a combination of both.

Cash ISAs give a better return on savings than a non-ISA account because the interest earned is free of UK income tax. For stocks and shares ISAs, the

14.9 *Other forms of tax-efficient provision for high earners and employers*

investments held are free of UK income and CGT – in relevant circumstances, tax is payable on any dividend income.

Although the savings limit is relatively modest for high earners, such persons will no doubt wish to ensure that they utilise this facility to the maximum permitted level. It is tax efficient to maximise ISA savings in combination with other benefits or rewards. The interest yield on ISAs has traditionally been most attractive.

Some share-based investments may be placed in ISAs, and shares in individual companies may be paid into a self-select ISA, which is usually managed by stockbrokers.

The ISA shares allowance is commonly placed in collective investment vehicles such as unit or investment trusts. Any profits made from share price increases do not attract capital gains tax, and all the tax on the bonds may be reclaimed.

A major relaxation in the ISA rules took place with effect from 1 July 2014. ISAs became a simpler product known as NISA. The overall annual subscription limit increased to £15,000 for 2014–15, replacing the individual ISA rate of £11,880, the stocks and shares rate of £5,940 and the junior rate of £3,840. Savers may pay this amount to a cash account, and investors will also have new rights to transfer their investments from a stocks and shares to a cash account. There is a wider range of securities (including certain retail bonds with less than five years before maturity) which can be invested. In addition, Core Capital Deferred Shares issued by building societies are now eligible to be held in a NISA, junior ISAs or CTFs.

The amount that can be subscribed to a child's Junior ISA or CTF in 2014–15 was increased to £4,000.

Benefits-in-kind

14.9 Benefits-in-kind are a popular means for a company to reward its employees. These awards can include accommodation, membership fees, school fees, company cars etc. The tax charges on the recipients are mitigated by certain allowances and exemptions. Additionally, provided that any expenditure is deemed to be for the furtherance of the company's trade or undertaking there will be tax reliefs available for the company.

Pension term assurance

14.10 Tax relief on pension contributions which are paid as premiums to pension term assurance policies was withdrawn by *FA 2007*. However, pre-6 December 2006 applications continued to benefit from tax relief.

HMRC's Helpsheet 347 states:

> 'You are not entitled to tax relief when you make personal term assurance contributions. Few payments are personal term assurance contributions. This helpsheet tells you whether or not any of your contributions are personal term assurance contributions.'

Other forms of tax-efficient provision for high earners and employers **14.11**

The restriction does not apply to member life assurance premiums under an occupational pension scheme if they are to a group policy and the other members covered by the policy are not connected with the individual paying the premiums (ie spouse, relative, civil partner). Additionally, life assurance which is paid by an employer for the benefit of his employees may continue.

Golden handshakes

14.11 Any ex-gratia payment or golden handshake must not be 'earnings' (see NIM02010) if tax or NIC liability is to be avoided. There must be no legal or contractual obligation on the employer to pay it. Even if the employee has no legal or contractual right to the payment it will still be earnings for NICs purposes if the payment can be held to derive from the employment.

CHECKLIST

- SAYE and SIPS can provide employees with tax and NIC advantages
- The use of EMIs as tax and NIC efficient share option vehicles for small, higher-risk companies has been on the increase for some time
- The default retirement age of 65 has been abolished. However, a recent landmark ruling by the Supreme Court means that employers can continue to tell their staff the age they must leave so long as they give good reasons for doing
- Transfers to QROPS can simplify administration procedures and result in cost-saving
- EGLPs can be an attractive alternative to providing death-in-service benefits through a registered pension scheme. They have similar tax advantages to a registered pension scheme but are not subject to the LTA
- It is allowable for a member or employer to agree to pay a monetary contribution to a pension scheme and then to transfer an asset in settlement of that debt
- New ISAs came into being on 1 July 2014. The overall annual subscription limit increased to £15,000 for 2014–15, replacing the individual ISA rate of £11,880, the stocks and shares rate of £5,940 and the junior rate of £3,840
- Benefits-in-kind remain a popular means for a company rewarding its employees
- Tax relief on pension contributions which are paid as premiums to pension term assurance policies was withdrawn by *FA 2007*
- Any ex-gratia payment or golden handshake must not be 'earnings' (see NIM02010) if tax or NIC liability is to be avoided

Part Six

Tax charges, penalties and disclosure of tax avoidance schemes

Chapter 15

> **SIGNPOSTS**
> - The various tax charges and penalties are described in this **Chapter**
> - Registered pension schemes must report unauthorised payments, and deemed unauthorised payments, to HMRC under Event Reports
> - Pension liberation will attract significant charges and a potential loss of registered pension scheme status
> - The UK's first general anti-abuse rule is described
> - The disclosure of tax avoidance schemes rules have extended

Tax charges, penalties and disclosure of tax avoidance schemes

INTRODUCTION

15.1 This **Chapter** describes the main requirements for tax compliance and DOTAS in respect of registered pension schemes and individuals, and for non-registered pension arrangements. Tax avoidance has not in the past been relevant to *bona fide* pension schemes, and that remains the case. However, HMRC consider that there are some providers of tax avoidance schemes who seek to achieve this through pension provision. This matter is dealt with later in this chapter under relevant headings.

For a general list of charges, penalties, the de-registration rules, the exemptions, and the right to appeal which can apply to registered pension schemes, see **15.2–15.17** below. The disclosure of tax avoidance schemes is explored in **15.18–15.25** below; and the tax charges which apply to different types of payments and schemes are discussed in **15.27–15.62** below.

SOURCES OF TAX CHARGES AND PENALTIES

15.2 The incurred tax charges, penalties and sanctions under the post A-Day pensions regime are codified. This is in keeping with the withdrawal of HMRC's discretionary powers in relation to tax-advantaged pension arrangements. The main charge under the current regime is the unauthorised payment tax charge of 40%, which can be imposed (according to circumstances) on the scheme member, the scheme administrator or the employer.

Traditionally, the tax charges which could apply to approved pension schemes had relied heavily on the provisions of *TMA 1970*. Whereas this is still an important, and relevant, statute, the *FA 2004* brought in new charges and

15.3 *Tax charges, penalties and disclosure of tax avoidance schemes*

compliance rules for registered pension schemes, and the legislation has been greatly extended in recent years. Nevertheless, the penalties and charges which existed at A-Day were, in the main, retained beyond that date. The relevant statute, in addition to the *FA 2004*, is therefore *TMA 1970*.

SUBJECT LIST OF TAX CHARGES AND PENALTIES

15.3 The following is a list of tax charges and penalties:

- benefit-in-kind charge;
- charge on deliberately winding up a scheme;
- de-registration of a scheme charge;
- penalties for failure to provide documents or required particulars;
- penalties for failure to provide information;
- penalties for submitting fraudulent or negligent statements;
- charges on liberated pension savings;
- charges on relevant non-UK scheme;
- charges on false or fraudulent information concerning the lifetime allowance; and
- charges on withholding information.

The above charges and penalties are described below. Further information concerning specific matters which are not covered below will be found under the relevant heading for each subject matter in this publication. For example:

- the AA charge, the LTA charge and the (now defunct) SAAC are described in **Chapter 3** above;
- permitted UK transfers are covered in **Chapter 6** above;
- taxable property is described in **Chapter 12** above;
- overseas transfers are covered in **Chapter 13** above; and
- the unauthorised payments reporting requirements, including those for excessive lump sums and the tax-free allowance charges, are in **Chapter 7** above.

The general charge on unauthorised payments of 40%; the unauthorised payments surcharge; the scheme sanction charge; the charges on value-shifting transactions and the charges on surplus repayments are described in **15.27** onwards.

ACCOUNTING FOR TAX BY SCHEME ADMINISTRATOR

15.4 Failure by a scheme administrator to make a return on form APSS302 (see **7.15** above) may attract a penalty under *FA 2004, s 260*. The form is to be used to make a return of income tax to which the scheme administrator is liable under *FA 2004, s 261, Pt 4*. The scheme administrator must complete, sign and date the declaration, even if the form is completed or submitted by a practitioner who has been authorised to act on their behalf. A separate return must be completed for each registered pension scheme for which they are a scheme administrator. Where funds are used to purchase, from an insurance company, an annuity or other insurance type contract from which benefits are paid, and the scheme administrator makes a payment from such a policy or contract on which a special lump sum death benefits charge arises, the scheme administrator is the person liable to that charge.

The form may also be used to amend information on a return that has already been submitted. Such errors may include:

- something which ought to have been included in the return for that quarter has not been so included;
- something which ought not to have been included in the return for that quarter has been so included; or
- some other error has occurred in the return for that quarter.

The amount of the penalty will depend on the amount of the tax which should have been paid and the number of people who have been omitted from the return. However, where fraud or negligence is concerned, additional penalties may be incurred under *s 260(6)*.

A failure to submit an AFT return (see **7.13** above) can incur the following penalties:

- a penalty of £100 where the return is made late;
- a daily penalty of £10 per day for a period of up to 90 days if the return is made more than 3 months late;
- a penalty of the greater of 5% of any liability to tax on the return and £300 where the failure continues for a period of 6 months from the first penalty date; and
- a further penalty of the greater of 5% of any liability to tax on the return and £300 where the failure continues for a period of 12 months from the first penalty date.

Higher penalties apply if, by failing to make a return for more than 12 months from the first penalty date, the scheme administrator deliberately withholds information which would enable or assist HMRC to assess the liability to tax. The penalty is the greater of 100% of the tax and £3,000 if the withholding of information is deliberate but not concealed.

PROTECTIONS FROM THE STANDARD LIFETIME ALLOWANCE

15.5 Although the date for application for enhanced protection has past, if any incorrect information or false documents or information is discovered

15.6 *Tax charges, penalties and disclosure of tax avoidance schemes*

to have been provided, *FA 2004, s 261* empowers HMRC to impose a penalty of up to 25% of the excess allowance claimed on the individual return. Where HMRC request evidence of an individual's registration for enhancements, failure to comply may incur a charge of up to £3,000 on the individual concerned (*s 262*).

If additional benefits accrue, and a member has claimed enhanced protection, HMRC must be notified. Failure to notify HMRC within 90 days of the recommencement of benefit accrual can incur a penalty on the individual of up to £3,000 under *FA 2004, s 263*. Penalties will also be incurred where an application for FP 2012 or FP 2014 is found to be incorrect or false.

GENERAL PENALTIES FOR NON-COMPLIANCE BY REGISTERED PENSION SCHEMES

Main principles

15.6 Registered pension schemes have to report unauthorised payments, and deemed unauthorised payments, to HMRC under Event Reports (see **7.3–7.11** above). Reports must be filed by 31 January following the end of the tax year in which the event occurred. An incorrect report will result in the scheme administrator incurring a penalty charge not exceeding £3,000. A failure to report will result in the scheme administrator incurring an initial penalty charge of £300, with penalties of £60 a day for continuing non-compliance. The same penalties apply where a company fails to report an unauthorised payment.

The penalties for failure by individuals to report an unauthorised payment on a tax return, or to declare liability if no return has been issued, or the late submission of a return, remain under the self-assessment rules. Unauthorised payments are described later in this chapter.

Fraudulent or negligent statements

15.7 Any individual who makes a fraudulent or negligent claim, representation or order to obtain tax reliefs, repayments or unauthorised payments may attract a penalty of £3,000 under *FA 2004, s 264(1)*. Any other persons who are implicated in the action may attract penalties of the same amount under *s 264(2)*.

Failure to provide information

15.8 *TMA 1970, s 98*, was amended to extend penalties in circumstances where there has been a failure to provide information, or false information has been provided.

A list of the main penalties that may apply to the scheme administrator is set out in the table below, Further detail is given under the relevant headings later in this **Chapter**.

Tax charges, penalties and disclosure of tax avoidance schemes 15.8

Section imposing penalty	Cause of penalty being imposed	Scale of penalty
FA 2004, s 257(1)	Failure to comply with a notice issued under *s 250* (pension scheme return)	Initial penalty £100
FA 2004, s 257(2)	Continuing failure to comply with a notice issued under *s 250* (pension scheme return)	Daily penalties up to £60 per day
FA 2004, s 257(4)	Fraudulent or negligent return or delivery of incorrect documents etc	Up to £3,000
FA 2004, s 258; *TMA 1970, s 98(1)(b)(i)*	Failure to supply event report required by regulations under *FA 2004, s 251(1)(a) or (4)*	Initial penalty up to £300
FA 2004, s 258; *TMA 1970, s 98(1)(b)(ii)*	Continuing failure to supply event report required by regulations under *FA 2004, s 251(1)(a) or (4)*	Daily penalties up to £60 per day
FA 2004, s 258; *TMA 1970, s 98(2)*	Fraudulent or negligent return or delivery of incorrect documents etc	Up to £3,000
FA 2004, s 258(2)	Failure to preserve documents as required by regulations made under *FA 2004, s 251(1)(b)*	Up to £3,000
FA 2004, s 261(3)	Producing an incorrect document or certificate or providing false information in connection with any matter registered in accordance with *SI 2006/131*	Up to 25% of the relevant excess
FA 2004, s 262	Failure to produce any document or certificate or to provide any information, when required to do so by *SI 2006/131*	Up to £3,000
FA 2004, s 263(2)	Failure to notify HMRC within 90 days of a relevant benefit accrual where *FA 2008, Sch 36, para 12* applies (enhanced protection)	Up to £3,000
FA 2004, s 264(1)	Making a false statement or representation to obtain a tax relief or repayment or to make an unauthorised payment	Up to £3,000

15.8 *Tax charges, penalties and disclosure of tax avoidance schemes*

Section imposing penalty	Cause of penalty being imposed	Scale of penalty
FA 2004, s 264(2)	Preparation of an incorrect document that may cause a registered pension scheme to make an unauthorised payment	Up to £3,000
FA 2004, s 265(3)	Winding up a registered pension scheme wholly or mainly for the purpose of facilitating the payment of winding-up lump sums or winding-up lump sum death benefits (or both) under the pension scheme	Up to £3,000 in respect of (a) each member to whom a winding-up lump sum is paid under the pension scheme, and (b) each member in respect of whom a winding-up lump sum death benefit is paid under the pension scheme
FA 2004, s 266(2)	Transfer to an insured scheme is not made to the administrator or insurance company of the receiving scheme	Up to £3,000
TMA 1970, s 95	Fraudulent overclaims for relief at source	Tax geared penalty
FA 2008, Sch 36	Failure to comply with a notice issued under *FA 2008, Sch 36*	RPSM12301730
FA 2008, Sch 36	Providing inaccurate information when complying with an information notice issued under *FA 2008, Sch 36*	RPSM12301730
FA 2009, Sch 55	Late filing or failure to file an accounting for tax return	RPSM12301340
FA 2009, Sch 56	Late payment or failure to pay tax due	RPSM12301330; RPSM12301340
FA 2007, Sch 24	Providing inaccurate information on an accounting for tax return	RPSM12301350

Additionally, failure to preserve documents can incur a penalty not exceeding £3,000 under *FA 2004, s 258(2)*.

Failure to comply with notices

15.9 Failure to comply with notices regarding documents or particulars may incur penalties under *FA 2004, s 259(1)*. The penalties will not exceed £300, plus an additional £60 per day for continuing failure. Where a person fraudulently or negligently produces incorrect documents or particulars, the penalty will not exceed £3,000 under *s 259(4)*.

Misdirection of transfer payments

15.10 It is a scheme administrator's duty to ensure that transfers to a registered pension scheme which invests in insurance policies are made to the appropriate person. Failure to do so can attract a penalty of up to £3,000 under *FA 2004, s 266*.

Winding-up lump sums

15.11 Any attempt to deliberately wind up the scheme for the purpose of providing lump sums to members or beneficiaries can attract a penalty on the administrator under *FA 2004, s 265*. The penalty will not exceed £3,000 in respect of each member to whom a lump sum has been paid. It is also important to note that the scheme may lose its registration and so suffer a 40% tax charge.

Pension liberation/trust-busting

15.12 Trust-busting, now referred to as pensions liberation, was normally deemed to have occurred where tax-free lump sums are paid to scheme members in excess of the amounts that are permitted under the existing approval terms, and members often had to pay 20% to 30% of the amount extracted in the form of commission. HMRC had stated that 'transfers are often arranged with offshore companies and bank accounts to a scheme in the name of a fictitious new employer'.

HMRC's Pensions Newsletters 57, 59, 60 and 61 describe its latest views on pensions liberation, see:

http://www.hmrc.gov.uk/pensionschemes/newsletter57; http://www. hmrc.gov.uk/pensionschemes/newsletter59.pdf; http://www.hmrc.gov.uk/ pensionschemes/newsletter60.pdf; http://www.hmrc.gov.uk/pensionschemes/ newsletter61.pdf.

Sadly, pensions liberation is still very much in evidence, and it has become a major concern recently. Typically, it involves encouraging members to access their pension savings before reaching the age of 55 and/or collapsing a pension scheme and paying out the proceeds in lump sum form. HMRC is being given extended powers s to identify and tackle pension schemes that are

15.13 *Tax charges, penalties and disclosure of tax avoidance schemes*

being used as, or are intended to be used as, liberation vehicles and to support future regulatory action by the Pensions Regulator. The Regulator may, as part of its intervention, appoint independent trustees or scheme administrators. The Regulator announced on 23 July 2014 that it is publishing real life tragedies and is considering, in yet another name change, re-branding pensions liberation schemes as 'pension scams'.

Liberated funds should be repatriated, *FA 2004, s 266*, provides relief from the charge if the member claims the relief within a year of the repatriation of the funds.

SCHEME DE-REGISTRATION

15.13 HMRC will only consider giving notice to the scheme administrator under *FA 2004, s 157* (ie to de-register a scheme under *s 158*), in extreme circumstances. For example, complex screenings from tax, and schemes which are set up to avoid, reduce or delay the payment of tax which is lawfully due, can bring about loss of registration. In other words, it is the administration of the scheme which counts, and a blatant lack of good faith will be heavily penalised. Specific examples may include:

- where unauthorised and deemed unauthorised and other payments incur the scheme sanction charge under *s 241*; and
- the amount exceeds the de-registration threshold in **15.14** below.

The de-registration charge under *s 242* is 40% of the value of the scheme immediately before it was de-registered.

The de-registration threshold

15.14 The de-registration threshold is breached when the total percentages of the fund used up by each scheme chargeable payments in any 12-month period is 25% or more.

The percentages of the fund used up by each scheme chargeable payments is calculated as follows:

$$\frac{\text{Scheme chargeable payment}}{\text{Value of scheme at that time}} \times \frac{100}{1}$$

The market value must be applied.

Right to appeal

15.15 There is a facility for the purpose of appealing against any HMRC action, and to seek an exoneration from any charges. The procedures are described in **7.20–7.22** above.

Focus

- Tax and NIC charges can be imposed under GAAR

GENERAL ANTI-ABUSE RULE

15.16 The UK's first general anti-abuse rule (GAAR) was brought into effect on 1 April 2013 by *FA 2013, Pt 5*. It is aimed primarily at the individual taxpayer, but it imposes a burden of proof on HMRC.

A designated HMRC officer may notify a taxpayer in writing where the officer considers that the taxpayer has obtained a tax advantage which should be counteracted. The taxpayer has 45 days from the day on which the notice is given to provide written representations in response to the notice to the designated officer.

NICA 2014 came into effect on 13 March 2014. *Sections 10* and *11* provide for the GAAR to also apply to NICs.

Focus

- There is a duty to disclose tax avoidance schemes. Tax and NIC charges can be imposed under DOTAS

DISCLOSURE OF TAX AVOIDANCE SCHEMES (DOTAS)

15.17 Tax avoidance schemes must be declared (*FA 2004, ss 306–319*). Mandatory disclosure by promoters of tax avoidance schemes came into effect on 1 August 2004. Since that time, HMRC has regularly extended the application of DOTAS, and that includes incursions into pension schemes which are not *bona fide* pension schemes, whether registered or non-registered. DOTAS requires scheme promoters to disclose information about a tax avoidance scheme that meets certain definitions within five days of it being made available to clients. The promoter is then issued with a scheme reference number (SRN) which must be passed on to clients. HMRC are empowered to investigate non-compliance and impose penalties for failing to disclose a scheme and for failing to pass on or report an SRN. The welter of regulations and changes in practice are described in **15.18–15.20** below.

FA 2004, Pt 7 relates to general tax avoidance. *Section 306* concerns notifiable arrangements and notifiable proposals under tax avoidance schemes. Such arrangements are those which fall within any description prescribed by the Treasury by regulations. They enable a person to gain a tax advantage by means of the main, or one of the main, benefits of the arrangement. A promoter is described in *s 307* as a person in relation to a notifiable proposal if, in the course of a trade, profession or business which involves the provision to other persons of services relating to taxation:

- he is to any extent responsible for the design of the proposed arrangements; or
- he makes the notifiable proposal available for implementation by other persons;

15.18 *Tax charges, penalties and disclosure of tax avoidance schemes*

In relation to notifiable arrangements, if he is a promoter in relation to a notifiable proposal which is implemented by those arrangements or if, in the course of a trade, profession or business which involves the provision to other persons of services relating to taxation, he is to any extent responsible for:

- the design of the arrangements; or
- the organisation or management of the arrangements.

A person is not to be treated as a promoter by reason of anything done in prescribed circumstances. Only those at the heart of the scheme or arrangement, who are capable of meeting its obligations, will be treated as the promoter.

The promoter must provide information to HMRC within a prescribed period after the date on which he makes a notifiable proposal, or the date on which he first becomes aware of any transaction forming part of the proposed arrangements (*s 308*). This applies to post-17 March 2004 relevant dates and transactions (*s 319*).

The duty falls on any client who enters into any transaction forming part of any notifiable arrangements in relation to which a promoter is resident outside the UK, and no promoter is resident in the UK (*s 309*). The duty extends to any other person who enters into any transaction forming part of any notifiable arrangements in similar circumstances (*s 310*). Sections 309 and 310 apply, by virtue of *s 319*, to post-22 April 2004 transactions.

Focus

- Specific regulations and statutes apply to promoters of tax avoidance arrangements

---

The Tax Avoidance Regulations

15.18 The list of DOTAS *Regulations* continues to grow at a great pace. They are summarised below.

The *Tax Avoidance Schemes (Promoters and Prescribed Circumstances) Regulations 2004 (SI 2004/1865)* concerned income tax, CT and CGT. Promoters of tax avoidance schemes must notify HMRC within a prescribed period of the earlier of:

- where a promoter makes schemes available for implementation by others, the date on which he does so; and
- for other promoters, the date on which they first become aware of any transaction forming part of the notifiable arrangements.

The *Tax Avoidance Schemes (Prescribed Descriptions of Arrangements) Regulations 2006 (SI 2006/1543)* made fresh provision for the disclosure of tax avoidance schemes in relation to income tax, CT and CGT. They replaced the *Tax Avoidance Schemes (Prescribed Descriptions of Arrangements)*

Tax charges, penalties and disclosure of tax avoidance schemes **15.18**

Regulations 2004 (SI 2004/1863), amended by *SI 2004/2429*. In particular, they prescribed the arrangements:

- which a promoter or (where he is obliged to report them) a user might wish to keep confidential from either HMRC or other promoters;
- for which a promoter might reasonably expect a premium fee;
- where:
    (a) the tax advantage arises, to more than an incidental degree, from the inclusion of a financial product;
    (b) a promoter or someone connected with him becomes a party to the financial product;
    (c) the price of the financial product differs significantly from what might reasonably be expected in the open market;
- which involve the use of standardised tax products;
- which are made available to more than one individual and are expected to generate losses to enable individuals to reduce their income tax or capital gains tax liability;
- which include a plant or machinery lease.

The *Tax Avoidance Schemes (Information) (Amendment) Regulations 2006 (SI 2006/1544)* (as amended) amended *Tax Avoidance Schemes (Information) Regulations 2004 (SI 2004/1864), reg 4* by providing that the period within which prescribed arrangements in connection with tax avoidance schemes are to be notified to HMRC under *FA 2004, s 310*, was 30 days from the date of the first transaction which formed part of the arrangements.

The *Tax Avoidance Schemes (Information) (Amendment) (No 2) Regulations 2007 (SI 2007/3103)* came into force on 20 November 2007 and inserted a new *reg 8B* into *SI 2004/1864*. The new *regulation* sets out the period after which a higher rate of penalty under *TMA 1970, s 98C(2B)* will apply where there is a failure to comply with the obligations under *FA 2004, s 308* following an order under *FA 2004, s 314A* (order to disclose) as follows:

> '8B. For the purposes of section 98C(2B) of the Taxes Management Act 1970 (higher rate of penalty after the making of an order under section 314A) the prescribed period is 10 days beginning with the date on which the order is made.'

The *Tax Avoidance Schemes (Information) (Amendment) Regulations 2008 (SI 2008/1947)* came into force on 1 November 2008 and:

– prescribed the information to be provided by a promoter to a client under *FA 2004, s 312* or by a client to other parties under *s 312A*;

– prescribed the period within which information prescribed under *s 312A* is to be delivered to the other parties as the period of 30 days beginning with the day on which the client first became aware of any transaction forming part of notifiable arrangements or proposed

15.18 Tax charges, penalties and disclosure of tax avoidance schemes

notifiable arrangements; or; if later, the day on which the prescribed information was notified to the client by the promoter under *s 312*; and

– exempted an employer from the duty to notify under *s 312A* if an employee of that employer received or expected to receive a tax advantage by reason of employment.

The *Tax Avoidance Schemes (Prescribed Descriptions of Arrangements) (Amendment) Regulations 2009 (SI 2009/2033)* came into effect on 1 September 2009 and brought certain pension schemes into the description of arrangements in the above regulations. The main change concerned the SAAC.

The *Tax Avoidance Schemes (Penalty) (Amendment) Regulations 2010 (SI 2010/2743)* revised the penalties due under DOTAS (see **15.21** below).

The *Tax Avoidance Schemes (Prescribed Descriptions of Arrangements) Regulations 2010 (SI 2010/2834)* came into effect on 1 January 2011 and brought certain pension schemes into the description of arrangements in the above regulations. The main changes were:

- change to the period to which confidentiality applies (where a promoter is involved) to any time following the event that triggers the disclosure, and including cases where a tax advantage is secured or might be secured;

- change to the period to which confidentiality applies (where no promoter is involved) to any time following the day on which any transaction forming part of the arrangements is entered into, and extending this rule to cover circumstances where a user may wish not to disclose in order to prevent HMRC obtaining information that might lead to an enquiry or inhibit repayment; and

- preventing the argument being used that, as the existence of the disclosure regime results in a premium fee not being obtainable, the scheme is not notifiable, and amending the description of premium fee so that it applies only if the fee is contingent upon the scheme working as a matter of law rather than upon other factors (eg it is an employment scheme where the fee is contingent upon the scheme being taken up by a certain number of employees).

The *National Insurance Contributions (Application of Part 7 of the Finance Act 2004) (Amendment) Regulations 2010 (SI 2010/2927)* extended the DOTAS regime to NICs.

The *Finance Act 2010, Schedule 17 (Appointed Day) Order 2010 (SI 2010/3019)* brought into effect the revised regime.

The *Tax Avoidance Schemes (Information) (Amendment) Regulations 2011 (SI 2011/171)* prescribed the information which is to be notified in relation to inheritance tax arrangements and the time limits within which that information is to be provided. This accommodated the *Inheritance Tax Avoidance Schemes (Prescribed Descriptions of Arrangements) Regulations 2011 (SI 2011/170)*.

The *Tax Avoidance Schemes (Information) Regulations 2012 (SI 2012/1836)* prescribe the information to be provided and the time limits for providing it. The *Information Regulations* consolidate earlier regulations which contained information powers. HMRC may specify the form and manner in which the information is to be provided.

The *National Insurance Contributions (Application of Part 7 of the Finance Act 2004) Regulations 2012 (SI 2012/1868)* extend DOTAS tax legislation to NICs (in some cases with modifications) to the extent that it applies to income tax.

The tax avoidance Finance Acts

15.19 The primary statutory sources of the revised DOTAS regime are described below.

FA 2010 brought in a number of measures altering the DOTAS regime. These were:

- changing the trigger point for disclosure of marketed schemes to ensure early disclosure of schemes;
- bringing in an information power to require persons who introduce scheme promoters to clients to identify who the promoter is;
- greater penalties for failure to comply with a disclosure obligation;
- a requirement for a promoter to provide HMRC with a periodic list of clients to whom they have issued SRNs; and
- revised and extended hallmarks.

Amendments were included in *FA 2010, s 56* and *Sch 17*, as follows:

- to bring forward the obligation to disclose a scheme to the time when the scheme is sufficiently developed for a description of it to be attractive to clients, and the promoter makes the existence of the scheme known to third parties who can make potential clients aware of the scheme;
- requiring promoters to supply HMRC within a prescribed period with the names and addresses of clients to whom an SRN has, or should have been, issued;
- requiring persons who introduce scheme promoters to clients to identify anyone who has provided the introducer with information about the scheme, within prescribed time limits; and
- increasing the daily penalty for failure to comply with a disclosure obligation to up to £5,000.

FA 2013, s 223, provided that, where HMRC suspects that a person other than the client is or is likely to be a party to tax avoidance arrangements, it may by written notice require the promoter to provide prescribed information in relation to any person other than the client whom the promoter might reasonably be expected to know is or is likely to be a party to the arrangements.

15.20 *Tax charges, penalties and disclosure of tax avoidance schemes*

FA 2014, ss 234–283, introduced new and extended rules to apply to promoters of tax avoidance schemes. These concern conduct notices; HMRC monitoring; appeals; duties of promoter to notify client and intermediaries of promoter's reference number; duties of those notified to notify others of promoter's reference number; duty of persons to notify Commissioners; Tribunal approval for use of power; ongoing duties to provide information by promoter and intermediaries; duty of person dealing with non-resident promoter etc.

HMRC's DOTAS publications

15.20 HMRC published DOTAS guidance in August 2011, with effect from 6 April 2011. It covers income tax, CT, CGT, NIC's, SDLT and IHT tax. It also describes:

- who is a promoter (*FA 2004, s 307*):
- who is an introducer (*FA 2004, s 307*);
- the 'benign' test (*SI 2004/1865, reg 4(1), (2)*);
- the 'non-adviser' test (*SI 2004/1865, reg 4(1), (3)*);
- the 'ignorance' test (*SI 2004/1865, reg 4(1), (4)*);
- who makes a scheme available for implementation by others; and
- various other matters, including flow charts for determining a 'hallmarked' scheme.

HMRC published a further guide entitled *'Disclosure of Tax Avoidance Schemes (DOTAS) Regime – the confidentiality and employment income hallmarks'* on 17 July 2013. The guide covered the confidentiality hallmark for promoters and the employment income hallmark on 'disguised remuneration' rules in *Pt 7A* of *ITEPA 2003*.

The disguised remuneration rules (see **15.60–15.68** below) further extended the DOTAS field.

FA 2014, s 284, describes the information powers which apply to DOTAS.

PENALTIES FOR NON-COMPLIANCE

15.21 Under *FA 2004, s 312*, the promoter had to provide information to the client within 30 days in relation to the arrangements. Penalties would be incurred for non-compliance (*TMA 1970, s 98C*). A penalty not exceeding £5,000 would be imposed on a promoter, with penalties of £600 a day for continuing non-compliance. Any person who was a party to the arrangement who failed to comply would be fined £100 per scheme, or £500 or £1,000 if he had previously failed to comply during the preceding period of 36 months on one or more occasion (respectively).

These penalties were subject to some change under the legislation described above.

Tax charges, penalties and disclosure of tax avoidance schemes **15.23**

The *Tax Avoidance Schemes (Information) (Amendment) (No 2) Regulations 2007 (SI 2007/3103)* prescribe the time after which the increased penalty applies when an order has been made under *s 314A*. It is 10 days from the date of the order.

The *Tax Avoidance Schemes (Penalty) Regulations 2007 (SI 2007/3104)*, in force from 20 November 2007:

- increased the penalty following the making of an order under *FA 2004, s 306A* so that the maximum daily penalty imposed under *TMA 1970, s 98C(1)* was increased to £5,000; and

- increased the penalty following the making of an order under *FA 2004, s 314A* so that the penalty imposed under *TMA 1970, s 98C(1)(b)* was increased to £5,000.

The *Tax Avoidance Schemes (Penalty) (Amendment) Regulations 2010 (SI 2010/2743)* introduced the daily maximum penalty of £5,000 to the new penalties under *FA 2010*.

FA 2010 further amended the penalty provisions of *TMA 1970, s 98C*, replacing the initial penalty of up to £5,000 with an initial daily penalty of up to £600 in cases of failure to comply with a disclosure obligation under *FA 2004, s 308, 309* or *310* (but not an ancillary information obligation under other sections in *Pt 7*).

DISCLOSURE FORMS

Pensions

15.22 Disclosures must be made on the forms available on the HMRC website. These apply for users where there is a UK promoter, an overseas promoter and where there is no external promoter. The forms are listed in **7.15** above. They are AAG1, AAG2, AAG3, AAG4 and continuation form AAG5.

Further notifiable arrangements

15.23 For disclosures in relation to schemes liable to be made in accordance with rules that existed prior to 1 August 2006, the following form(s) are used, as appropriate:

- AIU1 – for completion by promoters of notifiable arrangements;

- AIU2 – for completion by users of notifiable arrangements when an offshore promoter does not notify; and

- AIU3 – for completion by users of notifiable arrangements where there is no promoter, or the arrangements are promoted by a lawyer unable to make the full notification.

There is a continuation form AIU5.

15.24 *Tax charges, penalties and disclosure of tax avoidance schemes*

Notifying scheme reference numbers for income tax, capital gains tax, corporation tax and National Insurance contributions schemes

15.24 In most cases, the reference number of the arrangement or proposal should be entered in the box provided on the relevant return. However, there may be circumstances where a person is required to disclose a reference number for a notified arrangement or proposal but is unable to enter that number on a return. In these circumstances, the reference number of the notified arrangement or proposal should be disclosed on form AAG4 – Disclosure of Avoidance Scheme.

NON-DISCLOSURE

15.25 It is not necessary to disclose an arrangement if at least one of the following tests is failed:

Premium fee test

Both of the following factors must be present:

- the fee must be chargeable in relation to the tax avoidance element of the arrangements; and
- the fee must be attributable to, and contingent upon, obtaining a tax advantage.

Confidentiality test

The criterion is: Is there something about the tax avoidance scheme that the promoter would want to keep confidential?

Off-market terms test

This means that the promoter becomes a party to the financial product, such as being party to a loan, derivative or other financial product. The criterion is: Are the terms offered different from market rates?

The statutory rules are not only very wide, they are almost impossible to understand. The intended meanings of 'avoidance' and 'promoter' in the Act remain unclear, despite the amending regulations which are described above. HMRC's stance is becoming ever wider and more complex.

HMRC VISITS AND AUDITS

15.26 Audit programmes are conducted on the basis of random selection and risk assessment. Audits cover various matters including administration, contributions and valuation of assets, investments and benefits-in-kind, scheme payments, the calculation of the LTA etc. Non-compliance will incur penalties and sanctions, as will false claims for transitional protection and the making of payments that do not comply with existing protection.

AUTHORISED PAYMENTS, AND CHARGEABLE EVENTS

15.27 *FA 2004*, as amended, refers to 'authorised' and 'non-authorised' payments. However, such terms are, in strictness, misnomers. The removal of HMRC's discretionary powers meant that it is for registered pension schemes to make such payments as they deem appropriate. Tax charges and penalties are incurred on any payments which are, or are deemed to be, so chargeable under the governing legislation and codes of practice. Accordingly, in addition to the penalties described in **15.8** and **15.21** above, a description of authorised payments, and of tax chargeable payments, is given below. The special rules which apply to overseas schemes and overseas activities are described in **Chapter 13** above.

Details of tax-relievable benefits are given in **Chapter 4**. Authorised member payments are described in **15.28**, and authorised employer payments are described in **15.29** below. The general rules which apply to unauthorised payments are described in **15.30** below, the meaning of 'payments' is given in **15.31** below. Actual and 'deemed' unauthorised member payments are described in **15.32–15.39** below and the tax charges on unauthorised payments are described in **15.39–15.51** below. Thereafter, a summary of the charges which may be incurred by schemes on their other activities is provided. The permitted payment of small pension pots and trivial pensions in lump sum form, and new flexibilities for drawdown pensions, are described in **Chapter 3** above.

AUTHORISED MEMBER PAYMENTS

15.28 *FA 2004* describes five types of payment, under the provisions referred to below, which may be made to registered pension scheme members, or former members, which are classified as authorised member payments. Any other type of member payments will attract unauthorised payment charges. The authorised member payments are:

- lifetime pensions and pensions on death under *ss 165* and *167* respectively;
- lump sums and lump sum death benefits under *ss 166* and *168* respectively;
- recognised transfers under *s 169*;
- scheme administration member payments under *s 171*; and
- payments under various enactments, including:
  - the *Registered Pension Schemes (Authorised Member Payments) Regulations 2006 (SI 2006/137)*;
  - the *Registered Pension Schemes (Authorised Member Payments) (No 2) Regulations 2006 (SI 2006/571)*;
  - the *Taxation of Pension Schemes (Transitional Provisions) Order 2006 (SI 2006/572)*;

15.29 *Tax charges, penalties and disclosure of tax avoidance schemes*

- the *Registered Pension Schemes (Authorised Member Payments) Regulations 2007 (SI 2007/3532)*;
- the *Registered Pension Schemes (Authorised Payments) Regulations 2006 (SI 2006/209)*;
- the *Registered Pension Schemes (Authorised Payments – Arrears of Pension) Regulations 2006 (SI 2006/614)*;
- the *Registered Pension Schemes (Authorised Payments) (Transfers to the Pension Protection Fund) Regulations 2006 (SI 2006/134)*;
- the *Registered Pension Schemes (Meaning of Pension Commencement Lump Sum) Regulations 2006 (SI 2006/135)*; and
- the *Registered Pension Schemes (Authorised Payments) Regulations 2009 (SI 2009/1171)*
- the *Registered Pension Schemes (Authorised Payments) (Amendment) Regulations 2012 (SI 2012/552)*;
- The *Registered Pension Schemes (Authorised Payments) (Amendment) Regulations 2013 (SI 2012/1881)*.

Additionally, *FA 2008, Sch 29, para 1* inserted *s 164(2)* in the *FA 2004* in respect of authorised member payments, as follows:

'(2) Regulations under subsection (1)(f) may –

(a) provide that for the purposes of Part 9 of ITEPA 2003 all or part of a prescribed payment is to be treated as pension under a registered pension scheme, or as a lump sum of a prescribed description,

(b) provide that all or part of a prescribed payment is subject to the short service refund lump sum charge or the special lump sum death benefits charge,

(c) provide that a prescribed event in relation to a prescribed payment is to be treated for the purposes of the lifetime allowance charge as a benefit crystallisation event, and make provision as to the amount crystallised by that event,

(d) include provision having effect in relation to times before the regulations are made if that provision does not increase any person's liability to tax,

and "prescribed" means prescribed in regulations under subsection (1)(f).'

AUTHORISED EMPLOYER PAYMENTS

15.29 *FA 2004, s 175* describes six types of payment which may be made to a current or former employer of a registered pension scheme, as referred to below. The authorised employer payments are:

Tax charges, penalties and disclosure of tax avoidance schemes **15.30**

- public service scheme payments under *s 176*;
- authorised surplus payments under *s 177*;
- compensation payments under *s 178*;
- authorised employer loans under *s 179*;
- scheme administrator employment payments under *s 180*; and
- payments prescribed by legislation.

Unauthorised payments – general

15.30 *FA 2004, s 160* describes four types of unauthorised payment. The unauthorised payments are:

- a payment to a current or former member which is not an authorised payment;
- a deemed payment to or in respect of a current or former member which is specified as an unauthorised payment;
- a payment by an occupational pension scheme to a current or former sponsoring employer which is not an authorised payment; and
- a deemed payment by an occupational pension scheme to a current or former sponsoring employer in respect of value-shifting.

The categories can be further broken down to include the following:

- benefits taken before age 50 from A-Day and age 55 from 2010;
- cash lump sum benefits in excess of the permitted maximum;
- assignments or surrenders of pension;
- recycled cash lump sums;
- reductions or stopping of a pension, other than in certain circumstances;
- lump sum death benefits paid to a person not in existence at the death of a member;
- deceased member's rights used to increase the rights of a connected person;
- dependant's pension in excess of the member pension limit;
- transfers to non-registered pension schemes, other than in certain circumstances;
- unauthorised loans;
- winding-up lump sum death benefits paid to non-dependants;
- trivial commutation/small pension lump sums in excess of the permitted limits;
- payments to migrant members who have benefited from UK tax relief, other than in certain circumstances;

- debts payable by members to a scheme which are not on arm's-length terms (including debts payable by a person connected with the member);
- payments to a sponsoring employer out of a surplus which arises where a member surrenders his pension benefits (such a device can attract an income tax charge of up to 70%);
- value shifting of assets;
- non-commercial transactions;
- allocating an unallocated employer's contribution;
- taxable property held by an IRPS;
- acquisition of wasting assets;
- pension liberation;
- continued payment of pension after the member's death;
- death in service lump sum paid in breach of the rules more than 2 years after the scheme administrator was told the member had died;
- a scheme realises it incorrectly calculated the amount of the member's pension pot following a transfer of funds or purchase of an annuity and the balancing payment is made directly to the member.

Meaning of 'payments'

15.31 *FA 2004, s 161(2)*, describes payments as including transfers of assets or other money's worth. *Subsections (3) and (4) include:*

- a payment or benefit in respect of scheme assets;
- payments made to persons connected with the member or the sponsoring employer;
- payments made to persons who are not members or a sponsoring employer; and
- certain assets, increases in value or reductions in liability of a member or sponsoring employer or connected person,

even where the scheme or arrangement has wound up.

A 'connected person' has the meaning within *ITEPA 2003, s 554Z1*.

Unauthorised member payments

Actual and 'deemed' unauthorised member payments

15.32 Under *FA 2004*, an unauthorised member payment may be deemed to have been made whether or not money has been paid out. The main circumstances are described in **15.33–15.52** below.

Assignment of benefits or rights

15.33 Under *FA 2004, s 172*, an unauthorised payments charge based on the market value of the assigned benefits or rights of a member or dependant of that member, or any sums or assets assigned by such person under the scheme or arrangement, will fall on the member or, where deceased, the personal representative. It does not extend to assignments by spouses and civil partners.

Exclusions include assignments under pension-sharing orders and pensions payable under a death guarantee payment.

Surrender of benefits or rights

15.34 Under *FA 2004, s 172A*, an unauthorised payments charge based on the market value of the surrendered benefits or rights of a member or dependant of that member, or any sums or assets assigned by such person under the scheme or arrangement, will fall on the member or, where deceased, the personal representative. It does not extend to assignments by spouses and civil partners. Other exclusions include:

- surrenders under pension-sharing orders;
- a surrender to provide for a dependant after death;
- a transfer to another arrangement under the scheme relating to the member or a dependant of the member;
- a surrender to pay an authorised surplus payment;
- a surrender made as part of a retirement benefit activities compliance exercise; and
- a surrender permitted by regulations.

Increase in rights of a connected person on death

15.35 Prior to 6 April 2011, under *FA 2004, s 172B*, if a member's benefits were increased as a result of another member's death, an unauthorised payments charge based on the value of the increase fell on that member if he was a connected person within the meaning of *ITEPA 2003, s 554Z1*.

This applied where the deceased member's rights were uncrystallised, or unsecured or a dependant's unsecured pension.

Exclusions included:

- where, at the member's death, there were at least 20 scheme members and each had their benefit entitlements increased at the same rate;
- any transfer lump sum death benefit received from the deceased member;
- any pension or lump sum death benefit received from the deceased member; and
- any other sums specified in regulations.

15.36 *Tax charges, penalties and disclosure of tax avoidance schemes*

Under *FA 2004, s 172BA* (inserted by *FA 2007, Sch 19, para 13*) if, after the death of a member or dependant (and after 6 April 2007), another member became entitled to an ASP in relation to an entitlement of that member or dependant, an unauthorised payments charge based on the consideration that might be expected to be received for that benefit value of the increase fell on the other member or personal representative. The amount could be reduced by so much excess as arises from the other member becoming entitled to any pension or lump sum death benefit received from the deceased member. This restriction was removed by *FA 2004, Sch 16*. Additionally, *FA 2008, s 901, Sch 28*, introduced an additional restriction: it stipulated that tax-relieved pension savings which are diverted into IHT using scheme pensions and lifetime annuities in other circumstances than ASP were subject to unauthorised payment charges and IHT where appropriate. The charge applied to transfers and assignments after 10 October 2007 or increases in pension rights attributable to the death of a member when the member died on or after 6 April 2008. The charges did not apply where the pension scheme had at least 20 members whose rights were increased at the same rate because another member had died.

However, *FA 2011, Sch 16* repealed the IHT charges which related to ASP and unsecured pensions and most lump sums (see **4.12** above) and introduced replacement drawdown rules see **4.1–4.11**, and **11.23–11.26**, above). Full details of the pre 6 April 2011 rules were provided in the second edition of this book.

Increase in a member's benefits beyond the statutory limit

15.36 The charge falls under *FA 2004, s 172D*. It applies where:

- the scheme is an occupational pension scheme and the member and employer are connected, or the member and a person connected to the employer are connected (as described in *ITEPA 2003, s 554Z1*; and

- the pension arrangement is DB, or if it is a hybrid arrangement providing both DB and cash balance benefits.

Where the pension input amount for the input period (see **Chapter 3** above) exceeds the notional unconnected person input amount, the excess is taxed on the member as an unauthorised payment.

The notional unconnected person input amount is the notional pension input amount which would have applied if the member and employer had not been connected, or the member and a person connected to the employer had not been connected, as described in *ITEPA 2003, s 554Z1*.

Member use of assets

15.37 The charge falls under *FA 2004, s 173*. It applies where a scheme's assets are used to provide a benefit (other than a payment) to a person who is or has been a member of a pension scheme to:

Tax charges, penalties and disclosure of tax avoidance schemes **15.38**

- that person; or
- a member of the person's family or household, as defined in *ITEPA 2003, s 721*.

The cash equivalent of the benefit-in-kind is taxed on the member as an unauthorised payment.

If the benefit is provided by reason of an employment which is not an excluded employment, as defined in *ITEPA 2003, s 63(4)*, the charge does not arise.

If the benefit is provided by reason of an employment which is an excluded employment, as defined in *s 63(4)*, the charge only arises if:

- it would have been chargeable under *ITEPA 2003* if the employment was not an excluded employment;
- the scheme that holds the asset or benefit is an occupational pension scheme; and
- the person, or a member of the person's family or household, is a director of and holds a material interest (as described below) in a sponsoring employer.

A material interest is described in *ITEPA 2003, s 68*, meaning generally owning 5% of the share capital or having an entitlement to 5% of the assets.

The charge does not apply to taxable property held by an IRPS (see **Chapter 12** above).

Similar provisions apply to payments to a person's family or household following that person's death.

Value-shifting

15.38 The charge falls under *FA 2004, s 174*. It applies to:

- the creation, alteration, release or extinction of rights or powers relating to pension scheme assets or liabilities;
- the exercise, or failure to exercise, any powers, options or rights relating to such assets or liabilities; and
- the exercise, or failure to exercise, any power, option or right which is itself a scheme asset 'in a way which differs from that which might be expected if the parties to the transaction were at arm's length' for the benefit of a person who is or has been a member of a pension scheme.

Shifting value from the scheme to a member, or a person connected with the member, will result in the excess over 'that which might be expected if the parties to the transaction were at arm's length' being taxed on the member as an unauthorised payment.

Similar provisions apply to unauthorised employer payments under value-shifting by virtue of *FA 2004, s 181*.

Tax charges on unauthorised payments

15.39 The charges to tax, surcharges, penalties etc are codified. These charges are incurred when an action has taken place which is in breach of the legislation. The charges are summarised under appropriate headings below. Wasting assets (ie assets that have an anticipated life of less than 50 years, such as properties with less than 50-year leases, cars, racehorses, plant and machinery etc) will also be regarded as an unauthorised payment.

Payments by registered pension schemes which are not authorised by their rules or by legislation (see **15.29** above for descriptions of authorised payments) may incur an unauthorised payments charge on the amount paid out or the value of the excess payment or benefit. The tax is chargeable on the member, the recipient or the sponsoring employer, as appropriate.

An unauthorised payments charge arises where a payment (or a deemed payment) is made to or in respect of a current or former member, or a current or former sponsoring employer where the scheme is an occupational pension scheme, or to a connected party of either. Additionally:

- an unauthorised payment surcharge may become payable if the unauthorised payment exceeds certain limits;
- a scheme sanction charge is likely to arise on the scheme administrator where an unauthorised payment surcharge has become payable; and
- in some situations, a scheme sanction charge can arise on the scheme administrator even if no unauthorised payment surcharge has become payable.

There are some legislative reliefs under the legislation, which are described below.

Unauthorised payments charge

15.40 The charge is ring-fenced from other tax offsets, and is 40% on the amount paid out (*FA 2004, s 208*). The tax is chargeable on the member, the recipient if the member has died, or the recipient if it applies to an unauthorised employer payment. It applies whether or not the member, recipient or scheme administrator is UK resident. The amount on which the unauthorised payments charge is levied is the actual payment increased by any amount withheld to cover the scheme administrator's liability to pay the scheme sanction charge. However, any additional payment to the member representing all or part of the amount withheld is not an unauthorised payment if paid within a specified time.

Members can pay the charge on either by getting the scheme to pay the tax using the mandating procedure or by completing a self-assessment tax return. If the member wishes to use the mandating system, the scheme administrator will require the member to complete a mandate giving them authority to deduct the member's tax from the unauthorised payment and pay the tax to HMRC. The scheme administrator will thereafter pay any unauthorised payment less the tax to the member and remit the tax to HMRC.

Unauthorised payments surcharge

15.41 An unauthorised payments surcharge (*FA 2004, s 209*) may arise in addition to the unauthorised payment charge described above. This charge will be triggered if the unauthorised payment which is made to the member is 25% or more of the value of the member's uncrystallised and crystallised rights under the arrangements within the scheme. The value is described in *ss 211* and *212*. It applies whether or not the member, recipient or scheme administrator is UK resident.

The rate of the surcharge is 15% of the surchargeable unauthorised payment (*s 210*). Members must declare the surcharge on their tax returns unless they choose to opt for the mandating system. Similar provisions apply under *s 213* in respect of surchargeable unauthorised employer payments, based on the amount of the payment divided by the value of the total rights under the occupational scheme.

Period for measuring the charge threshold

15.42 The period over which the charge threshold is measured is described in *FA 2004, ss 210(3)* and *213(3)*, and it can straddle more than one tax return year.

Discharge from the unauthorised payments surcharge

15.43 *FA 2004, s 268* provides for individual persons and companies who are subject to the unauthorised payments surcharge to seek a discharge if 'in all the circumstances of the case, it would not be just and reasonable for the person to be liable'.

The time limit for applications, under the *Registered Pension Schemes (Discharge of Liabilities under Sections 267 and 268 of the Finance Act 2004) Regulations 2005 (SI 2005/3452)*, is:

- five years from 31 January following the end of the relevant tax year; or
- where HMRC have raised an assessment, within two years from its date of issue.

HMRC's decision can be appealed (see **7.20–7.22** above).

Declaration of liability for the unauthorised payments charge and the unauthorised payments surcharge

15.44 Individual persons and companies must declare any liability for the unauthorised payments charge and the unauthorised payments surcharge on their self-assessment returns, or by separate notification if no return has been received, subject to the mandating option described above. The *Registered Pension Schemes (Provision of Information) Regulations 2006 (SI 2006/567)*, as amended, require companies in receipt of unauthorised employer payments to send the details to their company tax office, and not to HMRC PSS.

Scheme sanction charge

15.45 A scheme sanction charge will fall on the administrator of any registered pension scheme which makes one or more scheme chargeable payments in the year. Under *FA 2004, s 239*, the rate of tax payable is 40% of the scheme chargeable payment. HMRC will issue a notice of assessment – the charge is not included in the quarterly AFT. It applies whether or not the liable person is UK resident.

The scheme administrator must pay the charge, although there may be some mitigation where other charges have already been incurred. The provisions which exempt members from charges, where they have been duped into making or receiving a chargeable payment, are followed through in the legislation for scheme administrators.

It is a requirement of the *FA 2004* that, in many circumstances, the administrator must be provided with information from the member (for example, the amount of the LTA which is available). If the administrator has been given false information, he may seek a discharge (see **15.48** below). An exception for payments made in error, and a reference to the exception in the case of false declarations, are referred to in **7.21** and **7.22** above in the context of the reporting requirements.

Payments which attract the scheme sanction charge

15.46 *FA 2004, s 241* defines scheme chargeable payments which attract the scheme sanction charge as:

- an incurred charge in respect of minimum unauthorised borrowing under *s 181A*;
- unauthorised payments other than payments exempted under *s 241(2)*;
- unauthorised borrowings under *s 183* or *185*; or
- income or gains from taxable property under *s 183A* or *185F* (see **Chapter 12** above).

Payments which are excluded from the scheme sanction charge

15.47 *FA 2004, s 241* excludes the following unauthorised payments from the scheme sanction charge:

- payments treated as made under *s 173* where the asset is not a wasting asset;
- compensation payments under *s 178* (a member's liability to a sponsoring employer in respect of a criminal, fraudulent or negligent act or omission by the member);
- payments made to comply with a court order or an order by a person or body with the power to order the making of that payment;

Tax charges, penalties and disclosure of tax avoidance schemes **15.49**

- payments made on the grounds that a court or any such person or body is likely to order (or would be, if it were asked to do so) the making of the payment;

- payments prescribed by the transitional provisions of the *Registered Pension Schemes (Unauthorised Payments by Existing Schemes) Regulations 2006 (SI 2006/365);*

and lump sums under *Sch 29, para 1(2)* which are not pension commencement lump sums (because they exceeded the permitted maximum) if the payment would not have been unauthorised if:

- for EP members, *paras 27* and *29* had not applied; or

- for non-EP members, *Sch 36, para 28* had not applied.

Relief from the scheme sanction charge

15.48 *FA 2004, s 266B* permits the scheme administrator to apply for relief from the scheme sanction charge in proportion to the amount of any unauthorised payment subsequently made good under a DWP restitution order.

Additionally, the Act provides for a discharge from liability if 'in all the circumstances of the case, it would not be just and reasonable for the scheme administrator to be liable'. In all other cases, the criterion is that 'the scheme administrator reasonably believed that the unauthorised payment was not an unauthorised payment'.

The time limit for applications, under the *Registered Pension Schemes (Discharge of Liabilities under Sections 267 and 268 of the Finance Act 2004) Regulations 2005 (SI 2005/3452)*, is:

- five years from 31 January following the end of the relevant tax year; or

- where HMRC have raised an assessment, within two years from its date of issue.

HMRC's decision can be appealed (see **7.20** above).

Reducing the scheme sanction charge

15.49 The scheme sanction charge is reduced from 40% in cases where the unauthorised payments charge has already been paid. The reduction is the lower of:

- 25% of the scheme chargeable payments on which the tax was paid, and

- the actual amount of tax paid on the unauthorised payment.

A concession is available where the scheme sanction charge is incurred on funds which have been liberated in the member's pension savings through no fault of the member. Where the funds are repatriated, *FA 2004, s 266*, relieves the scheme sanction charge. However, the scheme administrator must claim the relief within one year of the repatriation taking place.

15.50 *Tax charges, penalties and disclosure of tax avoidance schemes*

FA 2007, Sch 20, para 5 inserted *s 160(4A)* and *(4B)* into *FA 2004* in respect of unauthorised payments which are reduced by the amount of the scheme sanction charge, as follows:

> '(4A) If an unauthorised member payment or unauthorised employer payment made to or in respect of a person would have been greater but for a reduction made in respect of the whole, or any proportion, of the amount which the scheme administrator considers may be the amount of the liability to the scheme sanction charge in respect of it, it is to be regarded for the purposes of this Part as increased by the amount of the reduction.
>
> (4B) But if the amount, or that proportion of the amount, of that liability is in fact less than the amount of the reduction, a subsequent payment of an amount not exceeding the difference between that amount and the amount of the reduction made –
>
> (a) to or in respect of the same person, and
>
> (b) before the end of the period of two years beginning with the date on which the unauthorised member payment or unauthorised employer payment was made,
>
> is not to be regarded for the purposes of this Part as an unauthorised member payment or unauthorised employer payment.'

Release of scheme administrator from liability

15.50 The scheme administrator's tax liabilities are passed on at succession (*FA 2004, s 271*). However, if there is no successor, he retains that liability – but may apply to HMRC for a release from liability.

HMRC's decision can be appealed (see **7.20** above).

Surplus repayments

15.51 *FA 2004, ss 177* and *207*, provide that surplus monies may be paid to employers under governing scheme rules. There must be compliance with DWP rules and legislation. Although not strictly a penalty, an authorised surplus payment charge must be paid by a registered pension scheme which makes such a payment to a sponsoring employer. The tax chargeable is 35% of the amount of the surplus.

A surrender of pension rights made to fund an authorised surplus payment to a sponsoring employer, is not an authorised surplus payment. The surrender is to be treated as an unauthorised payment of the value of the rights surrendered. Additionally, it should be noted that any attempt by an employee to surrender their rights to any pension is unenforceable so there is no surplus that satisfies the requirements of *PA 1995, s 37* or *s 76*. Therefore, no authorised surplus payment can be made to the employer under the tax rules (see *http://www.hmrc.gov.uk/pensionschemes/surplus-avoidance-scheme.htm*).

A surrender of rights in favour of dependants will be treated as an unauthorised payment unless the new rights are provided under the same scheme under which the surrendered rights were held.

INVESTMENT-REGULATED PENSION SCHEMES

Taxable property

15.52 Potential tax charges will arise on investment in residential property and tangible moveable property by IRPS, as described in **Chapter 12** above. The charges fall under *FA 2004, ss 174A, 185A–185I, 273ZA* and *Sch 29A*.

EMPLOYER-FINANCED RETIREMENT BENEFITS SCHEMES AND EBTS

15.53 EFRBS and EBTs have been in HMRC's spotlight in recent years as potential tax avoidance schemes, and some major changes have been made to HMRC practice and legislation. The main charge which can be incurred by such schemes is for payment of 'disguised remuneration' – described in *FA 2011, Sch 2*, as 'employment income provided through third parties'. The very complex rules which apply are described in **Chapter 11** above.

THE SCHEME DE-REGISTRATION CHARGE

15.54 A scheme may be de-registered (*FA 2004, s 158(2)–(4)*) if it has failed to meet certain statutory requirements. This is an uncommon occurrence, and is most likely to be a result of pensions liberation or defaulting on large tax payments or providing false information. De-registration can also occur if there is no scheme administrator or no required information has been filed. In such circumstances HMRC will identify an appropriate person based on its reasonable judgment.

Under *s 242*, tax on de-registration is chargeable at 40% of the value of the whole fund, and it may be appealed within 30 days (see **7.20** above). The administrator is liable for the charge, regardless of that scheme administrator's residence or domicile status for UK tax purposes. If more than one person is the administrator, each person is jointly and severally liable for the tax due.

All tax reliefs on the scheme will be lost, and it will be regarded as an EFRBS unless it winds-up. Any life assurance business will cease to be pension business at the beginning of the company's period of account in which the scheme loses its registration status.

If there is an unauthorised payment, there is a tax charge either on the member or the sponsoring employer, as appropriate. Where the payment relates to a deceased member, the charge is on another person instead of the member. There may also be a tax charge on the scheme administrator.

HMRC gives the following example of de-registration (at RPSM02105030):

15.55 *Tax charges, penalties and disclosure of tax avoidance schemes*

'**Example**

Two scheme chargeable payments have been made within a 12-month period. The payments were of £14,000 and £10,000. The fund value at the time of the first payment comprised assets with a market value of £80,000 and cash of £20,000 giving a total value of £100,000.

The percentage of the scheme fund used up at the time of the first scheme chargeable payment is:

$$\frac{£14,000}{£100,000} \times \frac{100}{1} = 14\%$$

The fund was valued at £88,000 at the time of the second payment, which was £10,000:

$$\frac{£10,000}{£88,000} \times \frac{100}{1} = 11\%$$

Add together 14% and 11% and the aggregate is 25%. The de-regulation threshold is exceeded. This means there are grounds for HMRC to de-register the scheme.'

Recycling tax-free cash lump sums

15.55 *FA 2004, Sch 29, para 3A*, restricted the recycling of tax-free cash lump sums from A-Day. The concern was that the payment would obtain tax relief, and the member could then take another tax-free cash lump sum to enable the cycle to be repeated. Such arrangements are blocked by legislation which removed the tax advantages relating to any cash lump sums artificially recycled.

The legislation applies to contributions which are greater than 30% of the relevant cash lump sum made at the time a tax-free cash lump sum is paid. All or part of the pension commencement lump sum is treated as an unauthorised member payment.

Members must notify their scheme administrator when such an unauthorised payment is made and its amount.

THE TAX CHARGE ON BENEFITS IN KIND

15.56 A benefit-in-kind charge will be incurred where members or their relatives occupy residential property or enjoy the use of a pride in possession asset owned by a scheme at less than a commercial rent. The rate of tax is 40% of the value of the benefit in kind so enjoyed. The charge is payable by the member or any other recipient of the benefit regardless of their effective rate of tax.

EMPLOYER ASSET-BACKED PENSION CONTRIBUTIONS

15.57 Asset-backed contributions to DB which are not structured finance arrangements were banned from April 2012 by virtue *of FA 2012, s 48* and *Sch 13*. Such schemes acquire an asset from an employer with an employer contribution and receive an income stream for, say, 15 years from which time the property reverts to the employer. On 19 November 2013 the Pensions Regulator called for trustees to examine such schemes carefully, and it recommended that trustees explore less risky alternatives. It issued new guidance on its website on 18 December 2013.

TAX CHARGES FOR OVERSEAS SCHEMES

15.58 The tax charges which may be incurred by overseas schemes and their members are described in **Chapter 13** above, together with a detailed description of the complex rules which apply to QROPS.

CHECKLIST

- A comprehensive list of charges and penalties is provided. Greater detail is given under appropriate headings later in the Chapter
- A scheme administrator should make a return on form APSS302
- Penalties may apply on giving false information for primary protection, enhanced protection, fixed protection 2012, fixed protection 2014 and individual protection 2014. Registered pension schemes have to report unauthorised payments, and deemed unauthorised payments, to HMRC under Event Reports
- Any individual who makes a fraudulent or negligent claim, representation may attract a penalty of £3,000
- A failure by the scheme administrator to provide information, or false information, will attract the listed penalties
- Failure to comply with notices may incur penalties up to £300, plus an additional £60 per day for continuing failure. Where a person fraudulently or negligently produces incorrect documents or particulars, the penalty will not exceed £3,000
- Pension liberation will attract significant charges and a potential loss of registered pension scheme status
- The scheme de-registration threshold are described
- The UK's first general anti-abuse rule is described
- The disclosure of tax avoidance schemes rules are described, together with the required forms for completion
- The authorised payments are described

15.58 *Tax charges, penalties and disclosure of tax avoidance schemes*

- The unauthorised payments are described
- It is still permissible to refund surpluses
- Taxable property charges may be incurred
- Disguised remuneration charges may be incurred
- The scheme de-registration charge is described
- The recycling of tax-free cash lump sums rule is described
- The benefit-in-kind charge is described
- The employer-backed assets contributions rule is described
- The tax charges which may be incurred by overseas schemes and their members are described in **Chapter 13** above

Appendix 1

Benefit crystallisation events

A test must be made against the LTA under *Finance Act 2004, s 216* on any of the following BCEs. Post-75 events do not generally give rise to BCEs. The only sort of event that constitutes a BCE in relation to the individual after the individual has reached the age of 75 is an event that constitutes BCE 3.

From 6 April 2012, new capped and flexible drawdown provisions replaced the provisions that apply to new unsecured (drawdown) pensions. The term 'unsecured' was replaced by 'drawdown' as described in *Finance Act 2011, Sch 16, Pt 1, paras 2–5*. As unsecured pensions which were in payment as at 5 April 2012 can still be paid, reference is still made to them below. Later updates to the drawdown provisions, and the announcement of a new option to access funds, are described in **Chapter 4**.

EVENT 1

By the designation of sums or assets held for the purposes of a money purchase arrangement under any of the relevant pension schemes as available for the payment of pension to the individual.

The amount crystallised is the aggregate of the amount of the sums and the market value of the assets designated, where:

(a) immediately before the individual reaches the age of 75, there is under any of the relevant pension schemes a hybrid arrangement relating to the individual, and

(b) the benefits that may be provided to, or in respect of, the individual under the arrangement may, depending on the circumstances, be money purchase benefits or defined benefits

the event applies as if, at that time, the circumstances are such that the benefits to be provided are money purchase benefits (with the effect that the sums or assets held for the purposes of the arrangement are to be treated as having been designated as available for the provision of unsecured pension to the individual).

The amount crystallised is the greater of the amounts crystallised by the two BCEs.

This applies whenever funds are first designated under an arrangement as being available to provide a drawdown (before 6 April 2011, an unsecured) pension (and a drawdown (before 6 April 2011, an unsecured) pension fund is first created under the arrangement). It also happens at any later date

Appendix 1 *Benefit crystallisation events*

whenever all or part of any uncrystallised funds still held in that arrangement are absorbed into the drawdown (before 6 April 2011, unsecured) pension fund through additional fund designation.

A test will not be triggered where a review of drawdown (before 6 April 2011, unsecured) pension limits takes place at the three-year (previously five-year) review point or a pension sharing event occurs. It is only where new, uncrystallised funds are introduced to the drawdown (before 6 April 2011, unsecured) pension fund that a test will be triggered through BCE 1, or where a review is triggered through BCE 4 or BCE 2 due to an annuity purchase or provision of a scheme pension. In the latter case, there are rules to ensure that credit is given to any earlier amount crystallising through BCE 1 when calculating the amount crystallising through BCE 4 or BCE 2 (RPSM11104080).

BCE 1 only catches money purchase arrangements as only a money purchase arrangement can provide a drawdown (before 6 April 2011, an unsecured) pension (*FA 2004, s 165, 'pension rule 4'*).

EVENT 2

By the individual becoming entitled to a scheme pension under any of the relevant pension schemes.

The amount crystallised is $RVF \times P$.

If the scheme pension is funded (in whole or in part) by the surrender of sums or assets representing the whole or part of the individual's unsecured pension fund, the amount crystallised is to be reduced by the amount (or an appropriate proportion of the amount) previously crystallised on the designation of the sums or assets as available for the payment of unsecured pension.

Additionally, if:

(a) the individual becomes entitled before reaching normal minimum pension age to the payment of a lifetime annuity purchased under a money purchase arrangement under any of the relevant pension schemes, and

(b) the ill-health condition is not satisfied immediately before the individual becomes so entitled.

the event applies as if:

(a) the lifetime annuity were a scheme pension under the pension scheme; and

(b) the individual becomes entitled to it only on reaching normal minimum pension age.

EVENT 3

By the individual, having become so entitled, becoming entitled to payment of the scheme pension, otherwise than in excepted circumstances, at an increased

Benefit crystallisation events **Appendix 1**

annual rate which exceeds by more than the permitted margin the rate at which it was payable on the day on which the individual became entitled to it.

'Excepted circumstances' means:

(a) that at the time when the annual rate of the individual's pension is increased there are at least 50 pensioner members of the pension scheme; and

(b) all the scheme pensions being paid under the pension scheme to all the pensioner members of the pension scheme are at that time increased at the same rate.

The amount crystallised is RVF × XP.

If the individual became entitled to the pension on or after A-Day, the permitted margin is the amount by which the annual amount of the pension at the rate at which it was payable on the day on which the individual became entitled to it would be greater if it had been increased by whichever of calculation A and calculation B gives the greater amount.

Calculation A involves increasing that annual amount at the relevant annual percentage rate for the whole of the period:

(a) beginning with the month in which the individual became entitled to the pension; and

(b) ending with the month in which the individual becomes entitled to payment of the pension at the increased rate.

The relevant annual percentage rate is:

(a) in a case where the pension is paid under a pension scheme, or an arrangement under a pension scheme, in relation to which the relevant valuation factor is a number greater than 20, the annual rate agreed by HMRC and the scheme administrator; and

(b) otherwise, 5% per annum.

Calculation B involves increasing that annual amount by the relevant indexation percentage.

If the retail prices index for the month in which the individual becomes entitled to payment of the pension at the increased rate is higher than it was for the month in which the individual became entitled to the pension, the relevant indexation percentage is the percentage increase in the retail prices index.

If it is not, the relevant indexation percentage is 0%.

If the individual became entitled to the pension before A-Day, the permitted margin is the greater of:

(a) what would be the permitted margin at that time if the individual had become entitled to the pension on or after that date; and

(b) the amount by which the annual amount of the pension at the rate at which it was payable on the day on which the individual became entitled

Appendix 1 *Benefit crystallisation events*

to it would be greater if it had been increased for the whole of the specified period at the rate of P% per annum.

'P%' is the percentage by which, in accordance with the rules of the pension scheme immediately before A-Day, the annual rate of the pension is to be increased each year.

EVENT 4

By the individual becoming entitled to a lifetime annuity purchased under a money purchase arrangement under any of the relevant pension schemes.

The amount crystallised is the aggregate of the amount of such of the sums, and the market value of such of the assets, representing the individual's rights under the arrangement as are applied to purchase the lifetime annuity (and any related dependants' annuity).

If the lifetime annuity is purchased (in whole or in part) with sums or assets representing the whole or part of the individual's unsecured pension fund, the amount crystallised by the event is to be reduced by the amount (or an appropriate proportion of the amount) previously crystallised on the designation of the sums or assets as available for the payment of unsecured pension.

Additionally, if:

(a) the individual becomes entitled before reaching normal minimum pension age to the payment of a lifetime annuity purchased under a money purchase arrangement under any of the relevant pension schemes, and

(b) the ill-health condition is not satisfied immediately before the individual becomes so entitled

the event does not apply in relation to the lifetime annuity.

EVENT 5

By the individual reaching the age of 75 when prospectively entitled to a scheme pension or a lump sum (or both) under a defined benefit arrangement under any of the relevant pension schemes.

The amount crystallised is (RVF × DP) + DSLS.

RPSM11104640 explains why a money purchase arrangement is not covered by this Event, and covers where a member reaches age 75 before 6 April 2011 having previously designated funds as available to provide an unsecured pension under BCE 5A below and where all or part of the funds in the arrangement have not been crystallised (BCE 1).

Further circumstances are described in RPSM11104645; RPSM11104650; RPSM11104655; RPSM11104660; RPSM11104665; and RPSM11104670.

Where:

(a) immediately before the individual reaches the age of 75, there is under any of the relevant pension schemes a hybrid arrangement relating to the individual, and

(b) the benefits that may be provided to, or in respect of, the individual under the arrangement may, depending on the circumstances, be money purchase benefits or defined benefits

event 5 applies as if, at that time, the circumstances are such that the benefits to be provided are defined benefits.

The amount crystallised is the greater of the amounts crystallised by the two BCEs.

EVENT 5A

By the individual reaching the age of 75, having previously designated sums or assets under a money purchase arrangement for the provision of drawdown pension.

The amount crystallised is the aggregate of the amount of such of the sums, and the market value of such of the assets, representing the individual's drawdown pension under the arrangement less the aggregate of the amounts crystallised under BCE 1.

EVENT 5B

Where (on or after 6 April 2011) a member reaches the age of 75 under a money purchase arrangement in which there are remaining unused funds.

The funds are not caught through BCE 5 as they are no longer deemed to be designated into a drawdown pension fund. A LTA test is therefore not triggered through BCE 1. Instead, uncrystallised funds are now tested through BCE 5B.

For a money purchase arrangement, remaining unused funds means the amount of sums and assets held for the purposes of the arrangement which have not been designated by the member as available for the payment of drawdown pension and which have not been used to provide a scheme pension or a dependants' scheme pension.

For a cash balance arrangement, the actual level of the uncrystallised funds counting as remaining unused funds physically held in that arrangement at age 75 will not necessarily reflect the true value of the undrawn rights the member is entitled to under the arrangement at that time. RPSM11104645 describes the appropriate method of calculation.

EVENT 6

By the individual becoming entitled to a relevant lump sum under any of the relevant pension schemes.

Appendix 1 *Benefit crystallisation events*

RPSM11104710 describes the lump sums covered (a relevant lump sum); RPSM11104720 describes why a lifetime allowance excess lump sum is caught by this event; RPSM11104730 describes the effective date of the event; and RPSM11104740 calculates the crystallised value of the relevant lump sum paid. The amount crystallised is the amount of the lump sum (paid to the individual).

For the purposes of this event, a lump sum is a relevant lump sum if it is:

(a)   a pension commencement lump sum;

(b)   a serious ill-health lump sum; or

(c)   a LTA excess lump sum.

EVENT 7

By a person being paid a relevant lump sum death benefit in respect of the individual under any of the relevant pension schemes.

RPSM11104810 describes the lump sums covered (a relevant lump sum death benefit); and RPSM11104820 describes the effective date of crystallising and the amount crystallising.

The amount crystallised is the amount of the lump sum death benefit.

For the purposes of this event 7 a lump sum death benefit is a relevant lump sum death benefit if it is:

(a)   a defined benefits lump sum death benefit; or

(b)   an uncrystallised funds lump sum death benefit.

EVENT 8

By the transfer of sums or assets held for the purposes of, or representing accrued rights under, any of the relevant pension schemes so as to become held for the purposes of or to represent rights under a qualifying recognised overseas pension scheme in connection with the individual's membership of that pension scheme.

The amount crystallised is the aggregate of the amount of any sums transferred and the market value of any assets transferred.

For the purposes of this event:

(a)   Where any of the sums or assets transferred represent the whole or part of the individual's unsecured pension fund, the amount crystallised by the event is to be reduced by the amount (or the appropriate proportion of the amount) previously crystallised on the designation of the sums or assets as available for the payment of unsecured pension.

(b)   Where after the transfer a scheme pension to which the individual has become entitled before the transfer is to be payable out of sums or assets transferred, the amount crystallised by the event is to be reduced by the amount (or the appropriate proportion of the amount) previously crystallised in relation to the scheme pension.

EVENT 9

Certain prescribed authorised member payments. Currently, the making of the following prescribed authorised member payments constitutes a BCE 9.

Registered Pension Schemes (Authorised Payments) Regulations 2009 (SI 2009/1171), reg 16 can authorise a payment made after the death of a member, who died on or after 6 April 2006 but before reaching age 75, representing arrears of scheme pension that were due to be paid to that member before death, but were not so paid because entitlement to those pension instalments could not be established before the member's death. In order for such a payment to qualify under *reg 16*, the conditions specified in RPSM09108030 must be met.

The amount crystallised for the purpose of BCE 9 is the amount of the lump sum payment that represents the arrears of pension being paid. The BCE is deemed to occur immediately before the time of the member's death.

The terms used in the equations above have the following meanings:

- **P** is the amount of the pension which will be payable to the individual in the period of 12 months beginning with the day on which the individual becomes entitled to it (assuming that it remains payable throughout that period at the rate at which it is payable on that day).

  For the purposes of BCE 2 'P' is the amount of the pension which will be payable to the individual in the period of 12 months beginning with the day on which the individual becomes entitled to it (assuming that it remains payable throughout that period at the rate at which it is payable on that day). If the amount of the pension which will be payable will or may be reduced so as to reflect the amount of any tax to be paid by the scheme administrator, that reduction is to be left out of account in determining the amount of the pension which will be payable for such purposes.

- **RVF** is the relevant valuation factor for the purposes of BCEs 2, 3 and 5.

- **XP** is (subject to the above) the amount by which the increased annual rate of the pension exceeds the rate at which it was payable on the day on which the individual became entitled to it, as increased by the permitted margin.

- For the purposes of BCE 3 'XP' is (subject to the following paragraph) the amount by which:

  (a) the increased annual rate of the pension, exceeds

  (b) the rate at which it was payable on the day on which the individual became entitled to it, as increased by the permitted margin

  but if one or more BCEs has or have previously occurred by reason of the individual having become entitled to payment of the pension at an

Appendix 1 *Benefit crystallisation events*

increased rate, XP does not include the amount crystallised by that event or the aggregate of the amounts crystallised by those events.

- **DP** is the annual rate of the scheme pension to which the individual would be entitled if, on the date on which the individual reaches 75, the individual acquired an actual (rather than a prospective) right to receive it.
- For the purposes of BCE 5 'DP' is the annual rate of the scheme pension to which the individual would be entitled if, on the date on which the individual reaches 75, the individual acquired an actual (rather than a prospective) right to receive it.
- **DSLS** is so much of any lump sum to which the individual would be entitled (otherwise than by way of commutation of pension) as would be paid to the individual if, on that date, the individual acquired an actual (rather than a prospective) right to receive it.
- For the purposes of BCE 5 'DSLS' is the amount of any lump sum to which the individual would be entitled (otherwise than by way of commutation of pension) if, on that date, the individual acquired an actual (rather than a prospective) right to receive it.

RPSM11104860 describes the transfer to a QROPS and RPSM11104870 describes the process for testing the LTA.

Appendix 2

Glossary of terms

The references to sections and Schedules in this Glossary mean the *Finance Act 2004*, unless otherwise indicated.

'RPSM' means HMRC's Registered Pension Schemes Manual.

The Glossary to RPSM comprises HMRC's list of definitions.

The Manuals referred to below can be found on HMRC's list of Procedural Manuals on its website.

Accounting period	*ICTA 1988, s 834(1)*
Accounting for tax	HMRC's 'Completing a Pension Scheme Return, Accounting for Tax Return or Event Report'
Accounting return	*Section 260*
Acquiring an interest in property – for the purpose of the taxable property provisions	*Schedule 29A, paras 12, 27–29*
Active member (of a pension scheme)	*Section 151(2)*; RPSM
Active membership period (in ss 221–223)	*Section 221(4), (5)*
Alternatively secured pension	*Schedule 28, paras 12, 13*; RPSM
Alternatively secured pension fund	*Section 165* and *Schedule 28, para 11*; RPSM
Amount crystallised	*Section 216*
Annual allowance	*Section 228*; RPSM
Annual allowance charge	*Section 227(1)*; RPSM
Annual amount	RPSM
Annuity protection lump sum death benefit	*Schedule 29, para 16*; RPSM
Applicable amount limit	*Schedule 29, para 3*
Appropriate date	RPSM
Appropriate personal pension scheme	*PSA 1993*

Appendix 2 *Glossary of terms*

Appropriate portion	*Schedule 28, paras 16B(4), 16C(15)*
Arm's length bargain	RPSM
Arrangement	*Section 152(1)*; RPSM
Associated company	*ICTA 1988, s 716*; *SI 2006/567*
Authorised employer loan	*Section 179*
Authorised employer payment	RPSM
Authorised lump sums	*Section 204* and *Schedules 28, 31*
Authorised member payments	*Section 164*; RPSM
Authorised open-ended investment company	*FSMA 2000, s 262*; RPSM
Authorised pensions	*Section 204* and *Schedules 28, 31*
Authorised surplus payment	*Section 177*; *SI 2006/574*
Authorised surplus payments charge	*Section 208*
Available (in relation to a person's lifetime allowance)	*Section 219*
Bank	*ICTA 1988, s 840A(1)(b)*; RPSM
Basic rate	*ICTA 1988, s 832(1)*
Basic rate limit	*ICTA 1988, s 832(1)*
Basis amount	*Schedule 28, para 10*; RPSM
Benefit crystallisation event	*Section 216* and *Schedule 32*; *SI 2006/572*; RPSM
Benefit crystallisation events: supplementary	*Schedule 32*
Benefits (provided by pension scheme)	*Section 279(2)*
Block transfer	RPSM
Board of Inland Revenue	*Section 279(1)*
Borrowing (in Chapter 3)	*Section 163*
Building – for the purpose of the taxable property provisions	*Schedule 29A, para 7(2)*
Building society	*Building Societies Act 1986*; RPSM
Business Income Manual	HMRC's Business Income Manual
Capital gains tax	*TCGA 1992*
Capped drawdown	*FA 2011, Sch 16, paras 1–39*
Cash balance arrangement	*Sections 152(3), 230*; RPSM
Cash balance benefits	*Section 152(5)*

Glossary of terms **Appendix 2**

Category 1; category 2; category 3 (differing types of overseas recognised schemes)	*SI 2006/206*
Chargeable amount	RPSM
Chargeable gain	*ICTA 1988, s 832(1)*
Charity	*Section 279(1)*
Charity lump sum death benefit	RPSM
Codes of practice	The Pension Regulator's codes of practice on its website
Committee of European Insurance and Occupational Pension Supervisors	CEIOPS – replaced by the European Insurance and Occupational Pensions Authority
Company	*ICTA 1988, s 832(1)*
Compensation payment	*Section 178*
Connected	*ICTA 1988, s 839*
Consumer prices index	RPSM @ 'CPI'
Contracts of long-term insurance	*Section 278*
Contribution	*Sections 188(4)–(6) and 195*
Corporation tax	*CTA 2010*
Default retirement age	*Equal Rights Act 1996; Equal Rights Act 2010,* but phased out from 1 October 2011
Deferred member	RPSM
Defined benefits	*Section 152(7)*; RPSM
Defined contribution	See also 'money purchase'. This term is often used by the Pensions Regulator in preference to that alternative term
Defined benefits arrangement	*Sections 152(6), 234*; RPSM
Defined benefits lump sum death benefit	*Schedule 29, para 13*; RPSM
Department for Work and Pensions	The Government department which is responsible for welfare and pension policy
Dependant	*Schedule 28, para 15*; RPSM
Dependant's alternatively secured pension	*Schedule 28, paras 26, 27*; *FA 2007, Sch 19*; RPSM
Dependant's alternatively secured pension fund	*Schedule 2, para 25*; *FA 2007, Sch 19*; RPSM

Appendix 2 *Glossary of terms*

Dependant's unsecured pension	*Schedule 28, paras 20, 23, 24;* RPSM
Dependant's unsecured pension fund	*Schedule 28, para 22;* RPSM
Dependants' annuity	*Schedule 28, para 17;* RPSM
Dependants' scheme pension	*Schedule 28, para 16;* RPSM
Dependants' short-term annuity	*Schedule 28, para 20;* RPSM
De-registration	*Sections 157–159*
De-registration charge	*Section 242*
Director	*ICTA 1988, s 716; SI 2006/567*
Disclosure of tax avoidance schemes	*TSMA 1970, ss 309-319, Pt X, the Taxes Management Act 1970* – both as amended
Disguised remuneration	*ITEPA 2003, Pt 7A* (inserted by *FA 2011, Sch 2*)
Double taxation agreements	As listed on HMRC's website @ *www.hmrc.gov.uk/international/dta-intro-htm*
Drawdown arrangement	*FA 2011, Sch 16, Pt 1*
Drawdown pension	*FA 2004, s 165, Pension rule 5*
Drawdown pension year	*FA 2004, Sch 28, para 9* (inserted by *FA 2011, Sch 16, para 7*)
Electronic payment	*Section 255A*
Employee and employer (and employment)	*Section 279(1)*
Employee benefit trusts	BIM44535, *FA 2003, Sch 24; IHTA 1984, s 86*
Employer loan	*Schedule 30*
Employer-financed retirement benefits scheme	*Section 245; ITEPA 2003, s 393(a); SI 2005/3453;* RPSM
Employment income	*ITEPA 2003, s 7(2)*
Employment Income Manual	HMRC's Employment Income Manual
Enhanced lifetime allowance regulations	*Sections 256(2), 261, 262, 263*
Enhanced protection	*Schedule 36, paras 12–17*

Glossary of terms **Appendix 2**

Enhanced transfer value	NAPF's *'Incentive exercises for pensions – a code of good practice June 2012'* and regulatory sources including HMRC and the Pensions Regulator's websites
Entitled (in relation to a lump sum)	*Section 166(2)*
Entitled (in relation to a pension)	*Section 165(3)*
European Insurance and Occupational Pensions Authority	*EU Regulation 1094/2010* – the European Union financial regulatory institution that replaced the Committee of European Insurance and Occupational Pensions Supervisors (CEIOPS).
European Economic Area (EEA) investment portfolio manage	*FSMA 2000, Sch 3*; RPSM
European Insurance and Occupational Pensions Authority	*EU Regulation 1094/2010* – the European Union financial regulatory institution that replaced the Committee of European Insurance and Occupational Pensions Supervisors (CEIOPS)
Event report	*SI 2006/567*
Excepted circumstances	*FA 2005, Sch 32, para 10*; *FA 2004, Sch 28, para 16C(3)*
Exceptional circumstances amount	*Schedule 28, para 16C(13)*
Ex-spouse	RPSM
Financial Assistance Scheme	*PA 1995*, now administered by the Pension Protection Fund
Financial Conduct Authority	Together with the Prudential Regulation Authority, replaced the FSA in 2013
Financial Services Authority	Incorporated on 7 June 1985 as the Securities and Investments Board Ltd, which delegated some statutory regulatory powers to it under the *Financial Services Act 1986*. Replaced by the Financial Conduct Authority and the Prudential Regulation Authority in 2013, under the auspices of the Bank of England
Financial Services Compensation Scheme	*PA 1995*
Fixed protection 2012	*FA 2011, Sch 18, para 14*

Appendix 2 *Glossary of terms*

Fixed protection 2014	*FA 2014, s 48 and Pt 1 of Sch 22*
Flexible drawdown arrangement	*FA 2011, Sch 16, paras 1–39; FA 2004, ss 165(3A), 167(2A)*
Former civil partner	RPSM
Funded unapproved retirement benefit schemes	EIM 15000 et seq
FSAVCS	*ICTA 1988, s 592(1)(h)*; RPSM
GAD tables	RPSM
General anti-abuse rule	*FA 2013, Pt 5, Sch 43*
Government Actuary's Department	RPSM @ 'GAD
Guaranteed minimum pension	*PSA 1993*; RPSM
High income excess relief charge	*FA 2011, Sch 2*
Higher rate	*ICTA 1988, s 832(1)*
Holding an interest in a person – for the purpose of the taxable property provisions	*Schedule 29A, para 16(2)–(4)*
Holding an interest in property – for the purpose of the taxable property provisions	*Schedule 29A, para 13*
Holding directly an interest in a vehicle – for the purpose of the taxable property provisions	*Schedule 29A, para 20(3)*
Holding directly an interest in property – for the purpose of the taxable property provisions	*Schedule 29A, paras 14, 15*
Holding indirectly an interest in a vehicle – for the purpose of the taxable property provisions	*Schedule 29A, para 20(4)*
Holding indirectly an interest in property – for the purpose of the taxable property provisions	*Schedule 29A, para 16(1)*
Hybrid arrangement	*Sections 152(8), 23*, RPSM
Ill-health condition	*Schedule 28, para 1*
Individual (in *ss 215–219*)	*Section 214(5)*
Individual protection 2014	HMRC's website @ *www.pensions lifetime allowance: individual protection 2014 – gov.uk*, and *FA 2014*.
Inheritance tax	HMRC's Inheritance Tax Manual and the *Inheritance Tax Act 1984*, as amended

Glossary of terms **Appendix 2**

Initial member pension limit	*Schedule 28, para 16B(3)*
Inland Revenue	*Section 279(1)*
Institution for occupational retirement provision	*Directive 2003/41/EC of the European Parliament and the Council on the activities and supervision of institutions for occupational retirement provision*
Insurance company	*Section 275; FSMA 2000, Pt 4 and Schs 3, 15;* RPSM
Investment-regulated pension scheme – for the purpose of the taxable property provisions	*Schedule 29A, paras 1–3*
Investments (in relation to a pension scheme)	*Section 186(3), (4)*
Liability (in Chapter 3)	*Section 163*
Life Assurance Manual	HMRC's Life Assurance Manual
Life assurance premium contributions	*FA 2007, Sch 18*
Lifetime allowance (in relation to a person)	*Section 218;* RPSM
Lifetime allowance charge	*Sections 214(1), 267;* RPSM
Lifetime allowance enhancement factors	*Section 218(5)*
Lifetime allowance excess lump sum	*Schedule 29, para 11;* RPSM
Lifetime annuity (in Chapter 3)	*Schedule 28, para 3;* RPSM
Limited liability partnership	*Companies Act 2000* – a partnership in which the liability of the members is limited.
Loan (in Chapter 3)	*Section 162* and *Schedule 30*
Lump sum death benefit	*Section 168(1)*
Lump sum death benefit rule	*Section 168(2)*
Market value	*Section 278;* RPSM
Member (of a pension scheme)	*Section 151(1);* RPSM
Member payment charges	*Schedule 34, paras 1–7*
Member's alternatively secured pension fund	*Schedule 28, para 11*
Member's unsecured pension fund	*Schedule 28, para 8*
Migrant member relief	*Section 243*

Appendix 2 *Glossary of terms*

Minimum income requirement	*FA 2011, Sch 16, para 20; FA 2004, Sch 28, paras 24C–24G*
Money purchase	RPSM
Money purchase arrangement	*Sections 152(2), 233,* RPSM
Money purchase benefits	*Section 152(4);* RPSM
National Association of Pension Funds	Leading provider of representation and other services to those involved in designing, operating, advising and investing in all aspects of workplace pensions
National Insurance Manual	HMRC's National Insurance Manual
Net pay pension scheme	*Section 191(9)*
New dependants' scheme pension	*Section 169*
New scheme pension	*Section 169*
Nominated date	RPSM
Non-EEA annuity provider	*Section 275*
Non-group life policy	RPSM
Normal minimum pension age	*Section 279(1);* RPSM
Notional repayment amount	*SI 2005/3450*
Occupational pension scheme	*Section 150(5);* RPSM
Old arrangement	*Section 169*
Open-ended investment company	*The Open-Ended Investment Company Regulations 2001 (SI 2001/1228)*
Operative date	*SI 2005/3449*
Original dependants' scheme pension	*Section 169*
Original pension scheme	*Schedule 36, para 23(5)*
Original scheme pension	*Section 169*
Other money purchase arrangement	RPSM
Overseas arrangement active membership period	*Section 224(7), (8);* RPSM
Overseas pension scheme	*Section 150(7);* RPSM
Pay As You Earn	*ITEPA 2003 and the Income Tax (Pay as You Earn) Regulations 2003 (SI 2003/2682),* as amended
Payment (in Chapter 3)	*Section 161*

Glossary of terms **Appendix 2**

Payments (made by pension scheme)	*Section 279(2)*
Pension	*Section 165(2)*
Pension commencement lump sum	*Schedule 29, paras 1–3*; *SI 2006/135*; RPSM
Pension commencement lump sum: applicable amount	*Schedule 29, para 3*
Pension commencement lump sum: deduction from applicable amount in case of scheme pension	*Schedule 29, para 3(8)*
Pension credit and pension debit	*WRPA 1999, s 279(1)*; *FA 1999, Sch 10*; RPSM
Pension credit member	RPSM
Pension death benefit rules	*Section 167*
Pension input amount	*Section 229*; RPSM
Pension input period	*Section 238*; RPSM
Pension Protection Fund	*PA 1995* – a statutory fund, run by the Board of the Pension Protection Fund established under the provisions of *PA 2004*
Pension protection lump sum death benefit	*Schedule 29, para 14*; RPSM
Pension scheme	*Section 150(1)*; RPSM
Pension scheme (in *ss 215–219*)	*Section 214(5)*
Pension sharing event	*Schedule 28, para 24(8A)*
Pension sharing order	*WRPA 1999, s 28(1)*; *SI 1999/3147* in Northern Ireland; RPSM
Pension sharing order or provision	*Section 279(1)*; RPSM
Pension year	RPSM
Pensioner member (of a pension scheme)	*Section 151(3)*; RPSM
Period of account	*ICTA 1988, s 832(1)*
Permitted margin	*Schedule 32, para 11*; *Schedule 28, para 16C(7)*
Permitted maximum	*Section 172C*
Personal pension scheme	RPSM
Personal representatives	*Section 279(1)*; RPSM
Power to split schemes	*Section 274A*
Prescribed occupation	*SI 2005/3451*; RPSM

Appendix 2 *Glossary of terms*

Prescribed person	*ITEPA 2003, s 399A*; *SI 2005/3453*
Prescribed rate of interest	*Section 179*; *SI 2005/3449*
Prescribed scheme	*SI 2005/3451*; RPSM
Primary protection	*Schedule 36, paras 7–11*
Property investment LLP	*ICTA 1988, s 842B*; RPSM
Protected pension age	*Schedule 36, paras 2, 23*
Protected rights	RPSM
Public service pension scheme	*Section 150(3)*; RPSM
Public service scheme payment	*Section 176*
Qualifying overseas pension scheme	*Schedule 33, para 3*; RPSM
Qualifying recognised overseas pension scheme	*Section 169(2)*; RPSM
Real Estate Investment Trust	*CTA 2010*, as amended
Recognised European Economic Area (EEA) collective investment scheme	*FSMA 2000, s 235*; RPSM
Recognised for tax purposes	*SI 2006/208*
Recognised overseas pension scheme	*Section 150(8)*; RPSM
Recognised overseas scheme arrangement	*Section 224(2), (3)*
Recognised transfer(s)	*Section 169*; RPSM
Recycled pension commencement lump sum	*Schedule 29, para 3A*
Reference date	SI 2005/3449
Refund of excess contributions lump sum	RPSM
Registered pension scheme	*Section 150(2)*; RPSM
Registered Pension Schemes Manual	HMRC's list of Procedural Manuals
Registered pension scheme return	*Section 250*; RPSM
Registration	*Section 153*
Related dependant's annuity	*Schedule 29, para 3(4A)*
Relevant administrator	RPSM
Relevant annual percentage rate	*FA 2005, Sch 32, para 11*
Relevant annuity	*SI 2006/129*; RPSM
Relevant associated persons	*Section 278*

Glossary of terms **Appendix 2**

Relevant benefits	*ITEPA 2003, s 393(a)*; *SI 2005/3453*
Relevant commencement date	RPSM
Relevant consolidated contribution	RPSM
Relevant existing pension	*Schedule 28, para 16C(5)*
Relevant lump sum	*FA 2005, Sch 32, para 15*
Relevant lump sum death benefit	*FA 2005, Sch 32, para 16*; *SI 2006/567*
Relevant member	*SI 2006/208*
Relevant migrant member	*Schedule 33, paras 3, 4*
Relevant non-UK scheme	*Schedule 34, para 1*
Relevant overseas individual	*Sections 178, 221(3)*; RPSM
Relevant pension schemes	*FA 2005, Sch 32, para 1*
Relevant UK earnings	*Section 189(2)*; RPSM
Relevant UK individual	*Section 189*; RPSM
Relevant uncrystallised funds	*Schedule 28, para 8*
Relevant valuation factor	*Section 276*
Relief at source	*Section 192*
Relievable pension contributions	*Section 188(2), (3)*; RPSM
Reportable event	*Section 251*; *SI 2006/567*
Residential property – for the purpose of the taxable property provisions	*Schedule 29A, paras 7(1), 8 and 9*
Responsible person	*ITEPA 2003, s 399A*; *SI 2005/3453*; *SI 2005/3455*
Retail prices index/RPI	*Section 279(1)*; RPSM
Retirement annuity contract	RPSM
Retirement benefit scheme	*ICTA 1988, Pt XIV, Ch I*; RPSM
Save As You Earn	A HMRC approved savings-related share scheme where you can buy shares for a fixed price
Scheme administration employer payments	*Section 180*; RPSM
Scheme administration member payments	*Section 171*; RPSM
Scheme administrator	*Section 270* (but see also *sections 271–274*); RPSM
Scheme chargeable payment	*Section 241*; RPSM

Appendix 2 *Glossary of terms*

Scheme manager	*Section 169(3)*
Scheme pension	*Schedule 28, para 2*; RPSM
Scheme sanction charge	*Sections 239(1), 268*
Scheme-held taxable property	*Section 185B(3)*
Section 9(2B) rights	*PSA 1993, s 9(2B)*; RPSM
Secured pension	RPSM
Self-invested personal pension scheme	Joint Office Memorandum 101, issued by the (then) Inland Revenue in 1989, and *FA 2004*
Serious ill-health lump sum	*Schedule 29, para 4*
Short service refund lump sum	*Schedule 29, para 5*; RPSM
Short service refund lump sum charge	*Section 205(1)*
Short-term annuity	*Schedule 28, para 6*; RPSM
Small self-administered scheme	*FA 1973*
Special annual allowance charge	*FA 2009, s 72, Sch 35*
Special Compliance Office	HMRC'S Special Compliance Office
Special lump sum death benefits charge	*Section 206(1)*
Split approval	*Section 274A*
Split scheme	*SI 2006/569*
Split scheme administrator	*SI 2006/569*
Sponsoring employer	*Section 150(6)*
Stand-alone lump sum	*SI 2006/2004*; RPSM
Standard lifetime allowance	*Section 218(2), (3)*; RPSM
State second pension	*SSPA 1975*
Sums and assets held for the purposes of an arrangement	*Section 279(3)*
Sums and assets held for the purposes of an arrangement (for the purpose of the taxable property provisions)	*Schedule 29A, para 5*
Tangible moveable property	*Section 29A*
Tax year	*Section 279(1)*
Taxable property (for the purpose of the taxable property provisions)	*Schedule 29A, paras 6, 10* and *11*
Taxable property provisions	*Schedule 29A, para 1(3)*

Glossary of terms **Appendix 2**

Total income	*ICTA 1988, s 835*
Total pension input amount	*Section 229*; RPSM
Transfer lump sum death benefit (NB abolished by *FA 2007, Sch 19*)	*Schedule 29, para 19*; RPSM
Transferee pension scheme	*Schedule 36, paras 22, 23(5)*
Trivial commutation lump sum	*Schedule 29, paras 7–9*; RPSM
Trivial commutation lump sum death benefit	*Schedule 29, para 20*; RPSM
Trusts, Settlements and Estates Manual	HMRC's Trusts, Settlements and Estates Manual
Unauthorised borrowing	*Section 182*
Unauthorised employer payment	*Section 160(4)*; RPSM
Unauthorised member payment	*Section 160(2)*; RPSM
Unauthorised payment	*Section 160(5)*
Unauthorised payments charge	*Section 208(1)*; RPSM
Unauthorised payments surcharge	*Sections 209(1), 268*; RPSM
Uncrystallised funds	RPSM
Uncrystallised funds lump sum death benefit	*Schedule 29, para 15*; RPSM
Unfunded unapproved retirement benefit scheme	EIM 15000 et seq
Unit trust scheme manager	*FSMA 2000, Pt 4 or Sch 4*; RPSM
Unsecured pension	RPSM
Unsecured pension fund	RPSM
Unsecured pension fund lump sum death benefit	*Schedule 29, para 17*; RPSM
Unsecured pension years etc	*Schedule 28, paras 10, 24*
Untraceable member	RPSM
Unvested funds	RPSM
Unvested funds lump sum death benefit	RPSM
Valuation assumptions (in relation to a person)	*Section 277*; RPSM
Value shifting	*Sections 174, 181*
Value added tax	HMRC's VAT Manual

Appendix 2 *Glossary of terms*

Vehicle (in the taxable property provisions)	In the context of tangible moveable property, a person described under *Schedule 29A, para 20(2)* for the purpose of management or administration of that vehicle
Winding-up lump sum	*Schedule 29, para 10*; RPSM
Winding-up lump sum death benefit	*Schedule 29, para 21*; RPSM
Working day	*SI 2005/3449*

Appendix 3

The main features of the pre A-Day tax regime

CONTINUED RIGHTS

A large number of differing tax regimes were in place before A-Day. The most significant changes, and complications, were introduced in 1987 and 1989, under the *Finance (No 2) Act 1987* as regards (principally) pension and lump sum accrual, and the *Finance Act 1989* (*FA 1989*) as regards (principally) the application of the earnings cap for pension purposes.

In order to protect the interests of existing member entitlements at the dates of change, transitional protection was given in the form of protected rights. The different member classifications which existed were generally referred to as follows:

(a) 'pre-1987 continued rights members';

(b) '1987 continued rights members'; and

(c) '1989 members'.

Controlling directors

Special restrictions were placed on the calculation and payment of pension benefits for controlling directors, which were more closely regulated than those of other members. A controlling director was, broadly, a director who alone or with a number of associates (eg close family members or family trusts) owned or controlled 20% or more of the ordinary share capital of the employer company.

Final remuneration

The definition of final remuneration was a key feature of the pre-A-Day means of testing benefits against HMRC limits. The main meaning is summarised below:

Final remuneration could be no greater than either:

(a) the highest remuneration for any one of the five years prior to cessation of pensionable service, comprising basic pay for that year plus a three or more year average of fluctuating emoluments (unless received for a

Appendix 3 *The main features of the pre A-Day tax regime*

shorter period for averaging purposes) expiring at the end of that year. Such fluctuating earnings could include profit-related pay (whether or not relieved from tax), benefits in kind, overtime, bonuses and commissions etc, which were assessable to income tax under Schedule E. They could be increased by the rise in RPI to the end of the basic pay year; or

(b) the yearly average of total emoluments for any three or more consecutive years ending not more than ten years before cessation of pensionable service;

Provided that:

- 'golden handshakes' and income from share options/gains etc (except where the shares or rights were obtained before 17 March 1987) were excluded;
- method (b) had to apply to controlling directors, not method (a);
- method (b) would apply to employees whose income exceeded £100,000 in any year subsequent to 5 April 1987, unless the employee chose a figure of £100,000 to apply;
- final remuneration or other remuneration which related to a year other than the last year in pensionable service could be increased by the rise in RPI to the date of cessation of service, except that any increase given on benefits for pre-1987 continued rights members had always to be applied to the aggregate total benefits;
- final remuneration should not exceed the earnings cap other than for pre-1987 continued rights members or 1987 continued rights members;
- the final remuneration to be used for the purpose of calculating the maximum lump sum for a 1987 continued rights member should not exceed £100,000;
- a member in receipt of much reduced income due to incapacity lasting more than ten years prior to his cessation of pensionable service could have final remuneration calculated under (a) or (b) above as at the cessation of normal pay and increased in line with RPI to the date of cessation of pensionable service;
- an early retirement pension payable by the employer was excluded from final remuneration;
- there was a concession in the method of calculation of remuneration for the 4 × lump sum death benefit described above. Any one of the following methods could be used:
    - the annual basic rate of pay at date of death;
    - method (a) above, plus a three-year average of fluctuating emoluments to date of death; or
    - the total emoluments, including fluctuating emoluments, paid in any 12 months in the three years prior to date of death.

Full commutation

Full commutation of pension was permitted where the aggregate value of pension benefits was 'trivial' (ie did not exceed £260 pa) and accorded with both the preservation requirements and the contracting-out requirements. Protected rights could not be commuted into lump sum form.

Full commutation of pension was also permitted in exceptional circumstances of serious ill-health, where the member's expectation of life was 'unquestionably very short'. A tax charge arose on excess monies over basic limits.

Retained benefits

Schemes which provided benefits in excess of 1/60ths × final pensionable salary × years of service, had to take retained benefits from other approved schemes into account in testing against the permitted maximum benefits.

Small self-administered schemes (SSASs) and self-invested personal pension schemes (SIPPS)

Special restrictions were placed on the permitted investment rules as applied to SSASs and SIPPS. HMRC also required a pensioner trustee to be in place at all times in order to ensure compliance with the governing rules.

Pre-1987 continued rights members

Maximum pension

The maximum rate of pension build-up was in accordance with the table set out below:

Years of service completed before normal retirement date	Maximum pension fraction of final remuneration
1–5	1/60th for each year
6	8/60ths
7	16/60ths
8	24/60ths
9	32/60ths
10 or more	40/60ths

For such members, immediate pension benefits could be taken on or after normal retirement date (NRD) even where the member remained in service, but, generally, scheme rules would require pensions to be taken not later than age 75. A retirement pension under an approved scheme could not normally come into payment before actual retirement or leaving service.

Appendix 3 *The main features of the pre A-Day tax regime*

Maximum lump sum

As with pension, commutation could either be on a basic or on an accelerated scale. The basic scale was 3/80ths of a member's final remuneration for each year of service up to a maximum of 40. Accordingly, the maximum commutation permitted after 40 years on the basic scale was 1.5 × final pensionable pay. An enhanced scale was permitted over 20 years (with lesser broadly proportionate amounts for service of less than 20 years), when again commutation of 1.5 × final remuneration was permitted:

Years of service to NRD	80ths of final remuneration
1–8	3 for each year
9	30
10	36
11	42
12	48
13	54
14	63
15	72
16	81
17	90
18	99
19	108
20 or more	120

Leaving service

A deferred pension equal to the ordinary early retirement pension based on final remuneration at date of leaving service and revalued in deferment. This was commutable within normal limits on retirement.

Early retirement

In accordance with HMRC's practice on discretionary approval, retirement on pension was permitted at any time after age 50.

A ratio of completed service to potential service was applied, calculated in accordance with the following formula:

$N/NS \times P$

where:

- P is the maximum pension approvable based on the employee's service to normal retirement date based on final remuneration to the date of retirement;

The main features of the pre A-Day tax regime **Appendix 3**

- N is the number of years of actual service completed, with a maximum of 40 years; and
- NS is the number of years actually completed plus the number of years of potential service to normal retirement date, again limited to 40.

The maximum pension available was the maximum fraction of final remuneration which the employee could have attained had he remained in service until normal retirement date, but based on his final remuneration as at the date of leaving service.

Late retirement

Scheme rules could make provision for pension and lump sum benefits to continue to accrue in respect of pensionable service after normal retirement date. Pensionable service completed after normal retirement date could count to the actual date of retirement, and actuarial increases or increases in proportion to the rise in the cost of living were available. However, where the employee had less than 40 years' service, a pension of no more than two-thirds of final remuneration at the date of actual retirement was permitted. Where the employee had more than 40 years' service, an additional five years of pensionable service could be earned, giving a total pension of 45/60ths for an employee with 45 years' pensionable service.

Death-in-service cash sum

4 × final remuneration, or actual remuneration plus a refund of employee's contributions (with interest).

Death-in-service pension

2/3 × the maximum potential pension which could have been provided for the member at normal retirement date. This could be paid to a surviving spouse. In addition, pensions could be paid to the dependants of the member. The maximum aggregate benefit payable to a surviving spouse and dependants, or all dependants, was the member's own maximum pension as described above. In the absence of a surviving spouse the maximum pension payable to one dependant is the same as may be paid to a surviving spouse.

Death after retirement pension

2/3 × the maximum pension which could have been provided for the member at actual retirement, increased in line with RPI (no commuted lump sum was available). This could be paid to the surviving spouse. In addition to this benefit, or a lesser amount of benefit, pensions could be paid to the dependants of the member. The maximum aggregate benefit payable to a surviving spouse and dependants, or all dependants, was the member's own maximum pension as described above. In the absence of a surviving spouse the maximum pension payable to one dependant was the same as could be paid to a surviving spouse.

Appendix 3 *The main features of the pre A-Day tax regime*

AVCs

The additional benefits purchased had to be paid in pension form, except that a commutation lump sum could be paid (subject to the overall limits) if the employee had entered into the AVC arrangement prior to 8 April 1987.

Surplus AVCs could be repaid to the employee after tax had been deducted which equated to a tax credit at the basic rate only.

1987 continued rights members

Maximum pension

The maximum rate of pension build-up was 1/30th of final remuneration for each year of pensionable service up to a maximum of 20 years. Accordingly, a pension of two-thirds of final remuneration could only be built up over 20 years, as opposed to 10 for a pre-1987 continued rights member.

Maximum lump sum

Additional restrictions were imposed in order to peg the maximum rate of permitted accelerated accrual to the maximum permitted rate of accrual for pension purposes, again over a maximum 20-year period as follows:

(a) if the member's pension benefits were calculated on an N/60ths basis, there could be no enhanced lump sum and the member would be entitled only to a basic-rate lump sum, ie of 3/80ths of final remuneration for each year of service up to a maximum of 40;

(b) if there was an enhanced pension entitlement (limited to 1/30th of final remuneration for each year of pensionable service up to a maximum of 20), one took the percentage difference between the basic and the maximum permitted rate of pension accrual. The basic lump sum entitlement on the 3N/80ths basis was then increased by that same percentage.

Remuneration in excess of the 'permitted maximum', which for such members was £100,000, could not be brought into account in determining the maximum lump sum which could be produced by commutation.

Leaving service

Scheme rules could make similar provision for a deferred pension to be paid as applied to pre-1987 continued rights members.

Early retirement

Scheme rules could make similar provision for pension and lump sum benefits to be paid before normal retirement date as applied to pre-1987 continued rights members.

Late retirement

Scheme rules could make similar provision for pension and lump sum benefits to continue to accrue as applied to pre-1987 continued rights members.

Death-in-service cash sum

4 × final remuneration, or actual remuneration plus a refund of employee's contributions (with interest).

Death-in-service pension

Scheme rules could make similar provision for pension as applied to pre-1987 continued rights members.

Death after retirement pension

Scheme rules could make similar provision for benefits as applied to pre-1987 continued rights members.

AVCs

Scheme rules could make similar provision for AVCs as applied to pre-1987 continued rights members.

1989 members

Maximum pension

2/3 × final remuneration after 20 years' service. If service was less than 20 years, 1/30 × final remuneration for each year of service.

Maximum lump sum

Further lump sum restrictions applied to limit the permitted accelerated rate of commutation. They applied to members who joined a scheme established before 14 March 1989 on or after 1 June 1989 and to all members of schemes established after 14 March 1989. For such members, the permitted basis of commutation was 3/80ths for each year of pensionable service or a higher alternative maximum of 2¼ × the initial pension payable under the scheme. This initial pension was the pre-commutation pension payable for the first year (including pension arising from additional voluntary contributions), ignoring changes in that year and on the assumption that the employee would survive for that year, ignoring also any surrender of pension to provide benefits for survivors.

Scheme rules could make provision for pension and lump sum benefits to continue to accrue in respect of pensionable service after normal retirement date, ie deferred benefits. Where a member was entitled to continued rights (meaning pre-17 March 1987 or pre-1 June 1989 continued rights), pensionable service completed after normal retirement date could count to the actual date of retirement, and actuarial increases or increases in proportion to the rise in

Appendix 3 *The main features of the pre A-Day tax regime*

the cost of living were available. However, where the employee had less than 40 years' service, a pension of no more than two-thirds of final remuneration at the date of actual retirement was permitted. Where the employee had more than 40 years' service, an additional five years of pensionable service could be earned, giving a total pension of 45/60ths for an employee with 45 years' pensionable service.

Leaving service

The permitted benefits were:

(a) a deferred pension equal to the ordinary early retirement pension based on final remuneration at date of leaving service and revalued in deferment;

(b) a deferred lump sum of 2¼ × initial annual rate of actual pension (before commutation or allocation).

Early retirement benefits

The permitted benefits were:

(a) a pension of 1/30 × final remuneration × years of service, subject to a maximum pension of 2/3 × final remuneration;

(b) a lump sum of 2¼ × initial annual rate of actual pension (before commutation or allocation).

Late retirement

The position was as follows:

(a) maximum pension could not exceed 1/30th of final pensionable pay for each year of pensionable service to a maximum of 20 years, with the date of actual retirement being substituted for normal retirement date;

(b) benefits had to commence payment prior to age 75. No part of any pension benefit (pension or lump sum) could be paid before actual retirement or leaving service except guaranteed minimum pensions which had to be payable at state pension age, subject to permitted deferral in the case of a late retiree remaining in pensionable service.

Death-in-service cash sum

4 × final remuneration, or actual remuneration plus a refund of employee's contributions (with interest).

Death-in-service pension

Scheme rules could make similar provision for pension as applied to pre-1987 continued rights members.

Scheme rules could make similar provision for benefits as applied to pre-1987 continued rights members.

Appendix 4

Overseas Transfers of Pension Savings

HMRC Draft Guidance: 20 December 2011

INTRODUCTION

On 6 December 2011 draft secondary legislation to make changes to the system for transfers of pension savings to qualifying recognised overseas pension schemes (QROPS) was published for an 8 week consultation.

This document contains the draft guidance in relation to the changes to the system for transfers of pension savings to QROPS that is the subject of an 8 week consultation.

Once the regulations take effect the guidance will be incorporated into the Registered Pension Schemes Manual which is available on the HM Revenue & Customs website.

To aid ease of reading a 'qualifying recognised overseas pension scheme' is referred to throughout this guidance as a QROPS.

THIS GUIDANCE APPLIES WITH EFFECT FROM 6 APRIL 2012

For guidance applicable before 6 April 2012 see RPSM14101020.

OVERVIEW OF CHANGES

- Summary of what the changes are:
    - firm up the tests to be an overseas pension scheme to make the rules work as always originally intended.
    - new member information and signed acknowledgement to be provided to the RPS pre transfer out of RPS
    - revised timeframe for an RPS to report a transfer to a QROPS as well as additional information to be provided and a switch to reporting via a paper form
    - changes to the period in which a QROPS has to report information on payments to HMRC

Appendix 4 *Overseas Transfers of Pension Savings*

- payments by QROPS to be reported within 60 days on new paper form
- When changes take effect:
  - The changes come into effect on 6 April 2012 although there are a couple of transitional aspects

The key changes for affected parties to be aware of are:

- New overseas schemes seeking to attract transfers of UK tax-relieved funds:
  - A revised Form APSS251 is available for schemes to notify HMRC that they meet the requirements to be a recognised overseas pension scheme. This information will be required for any notifications dealt with by HMRC after 5 April 2012.
  - The new reporting process will be applicable to any payments made or treated as made by these schemes.
- Existing overseas schemes that have already notified HMRC that they meet the requirements to be a recognised overseas pension scheme:
  - These schemes will need to ensure that they meet Conditions 3 and 4 of the requirements to be considered an overseas pension scheme. Any scheme that is established in New Zealand will also need to look at the revision that has been made to the definition of a recognised overseas pension scheme.
  - There is a new reporting requirement for a scheme that ceases to be a QROPS after 5 April 2012.
  - The revised reporting requirements are applicable to any payments made from a QROPS after 5 April 2012.
  - There is a new obligation to notify HMRC of any material changes to information that has been provided to HMRC previously in relation to the information requirements.
- Registered Pension Schemes:
  - Need member information before transfer. Need to report transfer within 30 days on APSS262. Transfer made on or before 5.April 2012 report online on 'old' basis.
- Changes for members:
  - for transfer requests made/effected from 6 April 2012 will need to provide information and signed statements. Form APSS263 or similar.

BACKGROUND AND SUMMARY TAX POSITION ON A TRANSFER TO A QROPS

A transfer is the moving of an individual's accrued pension rights from one scheme to another. The pension tax legislation specifies which transfers may be made without adverse tax consequences. These transfers are known as 'recognised transfers' and are a type of authorised member payment. To be an authorised member payment transfers must be made to either a registered pension scheme or a QROPS.

A transfer from a registered pension scheme to a non-UK pension scheme that is not a QROPS is not a recognised transfer. If a transfer is not a recognised transfer, it will be an unauthorised payment and generate unauthorised payment charges and scheme sanction charge. For further information see RPSM14102020.

SUMMARY TAX POSITION ON TRANSFER TO A QUALIFYING RECOGNISED OVERSEAS PENSION SCHEME

TAX RELIEF

The transfer is not a contribution so no UK tax relief is due in respect of it. The transfer is merely re-locating the pension rights represented by UK tax-relieved contributions to a different pension scheme.

ANNUAL ALLOWANCE

The transfer is treated in the same way as a transfer from a registered pension scheme to another registered pension scheme. See RPSM14101010 (of relevance only to the transferring registered pension scheme).

LIFETIME ALLOWANCE

The transfer is a benefit crystallisation event for the purpose of the member's lifetime allowance (see RPSM11100010 onwards). The amount crystallised is the amount of the transfer. If the transfer results in the member's lifetime allowance being exceeded, the rate of tax chargeable is 25%.

The taking of benefits relating to the transferred amount from a QROPS is not a benefit crystallisation event for the purposes of the individual's lifetime allowance.

MEMBER PAYMENT CHARGE

Any future payment from the overseas scheme which is a type of payment which would not have been authorised from a UK registered scheme will potentially give rise to a member payment charge under *Schedule 34 Finance Act 2004* on a resident or recently resident individual (for more details see RPSM13102110).

INHERITANCE TAX

When a member transfers from one pension scheme (here a UK registered scheme) to another (here a QROPS) then he has the right to determine the basis upon which the new death benefits under the transferee scheme are to be paid. That 'right' is property and an asset of the member's estate in terms of *section 272 Inheritance Tax Act 1984*. So when he exercises that right by electing to have the death benefits paid on discretionary trusts outside his estate then there is a loss to his estate in terms of *section 3(1) Inheritance Tax Act 1984*. That loss and the consequent chargeable transfer is largely dependent on the member's state of health and life expectancy at the time of the transfer. If in normal health then the value will be nominal – he would be expected to survive to take his full retirement benefits at which time the death benefits would lapse. If in ill health then the value could be substantive given the short period of time before a purchaser in the hypothetical open market would expect the death benefits to be paid out.

The transitional relieving provisions under *paragraphs 56–58* of *Schedule 36* to *Finance Act 2004* apply and there is grandfathering of the IHT exemption for the pre-6 April 2006 fund on a transfer to a QROPS.

WHAT MAKES A SCHEME A QROPS?

There are 4 tests that a scheme must meet in order to be a QROPS. It must be:

1 A pension scheme

2 An overseas pension scheme as defined by the legislation,

3 A recognised overseas pension scheme, and

4 A qualifying recognised overseas pension scheme.

If a scheme is not designed to provide benefits in respect of retirement, ill-health, death or similar circumstances then it's unlikely to be a pension scheme so won't be a QROPS.

If a pension scheme fails the level 2 test (i.e. it is not an overseas pension scheme) it is not necessary to see if it meets the level 3 test it is not a QROPS. Similarly if a scheme meets the level 2 test but then fails to meet the level 3 recognised overseas pension scheme test it cannot be a QROPS.

Tests 2–4 are covered in more detail later in this guidance.

RELEVANCE OF QROPS STATUS FOR UK TAX PURPOSES

QROPS status does not confer on an overseas scheme the UK tax exemptions to which a registered pension scheme is entitled. In particular, it does not affect the scheme's liability to UK tax on any income it has from UK property.

If a QROPS invests in an unauthorised unit trust any gains accruing to that unit trust remain chargeable if the overseas scheme is exempt from capital gains tax or corporation tax on such gains only by reason of its residence.

QROPS status does not directly affect every aspect of the pension scheme and is principally of relevance to the transfer of UK tax-relieved pension savings and to the treatment of payments from such schemes. For example there is no change to UK tax treatment of pension income from a QROPS it is treated in the same way as a pension from any other pension scheme outside of the UK.

OVERSEAS PENSION SCHEME

For a scheme to be classed as an overseas pension scheme under *section 150(7) Finance Act 2004*, it:

- cannot be a registered pension scheme,
- must be established outside the United Kingdom.

Normally, a scheme will be treated as established in the country where its registered office and main administration is, or, if there is no registered office, where its main administration is. The scheme's location of main administration is where the scheme's decisions are made. In the case of a trust-based scheme that would normally be determined by reference to where the scheme trustees are resident as that is where the decision- making responsibilities in respect of the scheme will lie. It should be noted that the country in which a scheme is established may change if the location of the main administration and decision-making changes. In such a case, the scheme manager would have to revisit whether the scheme still met the requirements to be an overseas pension scheme.

For a scheme to be classed as an overseas pension scheme it must also meet the following requirements that are prescribed under the *Pension Schemes (Categories of Country and Requirements for Overseas Pension Schemes and Recognised Overseas Pension Schemes) Regulations 2006 [SI 2006/206]*, as amended:

- it must meet the 'regulation requirements' test.
- it must meet the 'tax recognition test' by the country or territory in which it is established. This means that it must meet the tax recognition conditions 1–4 set out below

Exceptionally, if it is a scheme established by an international organisation it must meet the conditions set out in the paragraph below headed 'Established by an International Organisation' instead of meeting the above conditions.

An overseas pension scheme can be an occupational pension scheme (including a public sector scheme), a personal pension scheme or a social security scheme.

THE 'REGULATION REQUIREMENTS'

The requirements set out below look at whether there is a body in the other country which regulates pension schemes. There is a distinction between regulation of a pension scheme and regulation of, say, pension providers or trustee companies. The test is aimed at identifying a regulator in the other country that oversees legislation/guidelines that impact on the operation of the pension scheme to ensure that pension schemes are administered soundly in order to protect members' interests. Regulation tends to vary from country to

Appendix 4 *Overseas Transfers of Pension Savings*

country but such regulation might extend to submitting accounts, investment guidelines, rules on trustees, etc. In considering this test, HMRC would expect the scheme to be fully subject to the regulation in that country that covers these aspects.

Dependent on the country or territory in which a scheme is established, it may be necessary to identify whether the scheme is an occupational pension scheme or some other type of pension scheme. An occupational pension scheme is a scheme established by an employer and in order to provide benefits for its own employees although it may also admit other types of member. For example it may also admit employees of other companies within the same group.

The regulation test is met if one of the following requirements is satisfied:

Requirement (a)

(1) the scheme is an occupational pension scheme,
(2) there is in the country or territory in which it is established a body which regulates occupational pension schemes and
(3) the scheme is regulated by that body.

Requirement (b)

(1) the scheme is not an occupational pension scheme
(2) there is in the country or territory in which it is established a body which regulates pension schemes other than occupational pension schemes and
(3) it is regulated by that body.

This requirement needs to be satisfied if there is a regulator for any other type of pension scheme (other than occupational pension schemes) in the other country. If, for whatever reason, a pension scheme does not come within the remit of that regulator then this requirement cannot be met.

Requirement (a) or (b) here relates to the relevant pension regulator body of the relevant country or territory that regulates the scheme. This is not the same as the tax authorities test at condition 3 of the tax recognition test described later.

Requirement (c)

Neither requirement (a) or (b) is met by reason only that no such pension regulatory body exists in the country or territory and, either,

(1) the scheme is established in a Member State of the European Union or in Norway, Iceland or Liechtenstein, or
(2) the scheme's rules provide that at least 70% of a member's UK tax-relieved scheme funds will be designated by the scheme manager for the purpose of providing the member with an income for life. The pension benefits payable to the member (and any associated lump sum) must be

payable no earlier than they would be if pension rule 1 in section 165 Finance Act 2004 applied.

In many cases, 'UK tax-relieved scheme funds' will simply mean the sums and assets that have been transferred from the UK registered pension scheme to the QROPS. The term has a definition that extends to all UK tax-relieved pension savings - the sum of the member's UK tax-relieved fund and their relevant transfer fund. Those terms are explained in RPSM13102150 and in RPSM13102170.

Pension rule 1 in section 165 Finance Act 2004 provides that no payment of pension may be made before the day on which the member reaches normal minimum pension age, unless the ill-health condition was met immediately before the member became entitled to a pension under the scheme. Guidance on the normal minimum pension age is provided at RPSM08100010 to RPSM08100030, and there is guidance on the ill-health condition in RPSM08100070.

<u>A scheme cannot ignore Regulation Requirements (a) and (b) and opt to meet (c)</u>

Requirement (c) is only provided for use in a situation where the country or territory in which the scheme is established does not regulate schemes of its type, whether an occupational pension scheme or not an occupational pension scheme. For example, if a scheme is an occupational pension scheme established in a country where there is regulation of occupational pension schemes then in order to be able to be an overseas pension scheme it must be so regulated. If it is not the scheme does not meet the Regulation Requirement test so cannot be an Overseas Pension Scheme so it cannot be a QROPS.

THE 'TAX RECOGNITION' REQUIREMENT

The pension scheme needs to be 'recognised for tax purposes' under the tax legislation of the country or territory in which it is established.

<u>This requirement is met if all the following 4 conditions are met.</u>

Condition 1

The scheme must be open to persons resident in the country or territory in which it is established.

HMRC's view of this condition is that membership of the scheme should be genuinely available to residents of the country or territory in which it is established. If there are membership criteria, it would be of concern if these only applied to residents of the country of establishment.

Condition 2

The scheme is established in a country or territory where there is a system of taxation of personal income under which tax relief is available in respect of pensions, and test (a), (b) or (c) is met.

Appendix 4   *Overseas Transfers of Pension Savings*

(a) tax relief is not available to the member on contributions made to the scheme by that individual or, if the individual is an employee, by their employer in respect of earnings to which benefits under the scheme relate, or

(b) the scheme is liable to taxation on its income and gains, and is a complying superannuation plan as defined in section 995–1 (definitions) of the Income Tax Assessment Act 1997 of Australia, or

(c) all or most of the benefits paid by the scheme to members who are not in serious ill-health are subject to taxation.

For the purposes of this condition tax relief includes the grant of an exemption from tax.

If the tax regime of the country or territory does not tax personal income then schemes based in that country or territory will not meet the requirements of condition 2. Such schemes cannot meet the necessary requirements to be an overseas pension scheme and consequently cannot be a QROPS.

It is necessary for the country or territory as part of its tax regime for taxing personal income to give some tax relief incentive in respect of pensions. The tax relief that is referred to here (and which is considered under (a) and (c) above) must be specifically in respect of pension savings. Given the regulation requirement, see paragraph above headed "The 'Regulation Requirements'", and the other conditions, it follows that the test cannot be met by some other form of tax-advantaged saving product in the other country that is not a pension scheme but is simply capable of being used to pay out pension savings on retirement.

Looking at the treatment of contributions to or benefits from the scheme in the country or territory where the scheme is established, at least one of the following statements must be true:

- tax relief is not available to the member on contributions made to the scheme by them or by their employer, or

- all or most of the benefits paid by the scheme to members (who are not in serious ill-health) are subject to taxation.

So tax relief or an exemption from tax either applies at the point money goes into the scheme as a contribution or the point it leaves as a benefit payment. It cannot be exempt at both of these points. Either the contribution into the scheme or most of the benefit payments out of it (excepting serious ill health benefits) must be taxable.

HMRC provides a form APSS251 for the purposes of an overseas scheme to notify that it meets the requirements to be a QROPS. It is necessary to state on form APSS 251 which sections of the tax legislation provide either for the tax relief on contributions or for the taxation of benefits paid.

Condition 2(b) is only applicable to Australian schemes. A scheme must be a complying superannuation plan as defined in *section 995–1*(definitions) of the *Income Tax Assessment Act 1997* of Australia.

Any serious ill-health provision under the pension tax regime of the country or territory in which the scheme is established must reflect the provision applying in respect of a member of a registered pension scheme under *paragraph 4(1) (a)* of *Schedule 29* to *Finance Act 2004*. The provision does not have to apply the same conditions as are set out in RPSM08100080, but the approach must be fundamentally similar in order for the requirement at (c) to be met.

Condition 3

The scheme is approved or recognised by, or registered with, the relevant tax authorities as a pension scheme in the country or territory in which it is established.

This requirement relates to the relevant tax authorities of the relevant country or territory that recognise the scheme and is not the same as the pension regulator body that applies to the Regulation Requirements test, see the page above headed 'The Regulation Requirements'.

This condition is based on the other country or territory needing to have some sort of mechanism for identifying the pension schemes that can qualify for the tax relief that is available in the tax system as referred to at condition 2. The words 'approved', 'recognised' and 'registered' should be read accordingly. In the United Kingdom, tax reliefs are available in respect of 'registered' pension schemes. In other countries, the tax legislation may use the concept of approval or some other form of recognition.

The scheme will satisfy condition 3 if it is accepted by the tax authority of the country in which it is established as being of a type that can qualify for the tax reliefs available there.

Condition 4

Where an exemption from tax in respect of benefits paid from the scheme is available to members of the scheme who are not resident in the country or territory in which the scheme is established, the exemption must,

(a) also be available to members of the scheme who are resident in the country or territory; and

(b) apply regardless of whether the member was resident in the country or territory,

    (i) when the member joined the scheme; or

    (ii) for any period of time when they were a member of the scheme.

For the purposes of this condition "exemption" means any exemption available under the system of taxation of personal income in the country or territory in which the scheme is established. It does not refer to an exemption that applies by virtue of double taxation arrangements i.e. an arrangement made between 2 countries to afford relief from double taxation.

If the country's tax regime does not meet these conditions then schemes based in that country will not be able to be a recognised overseas pension scheme.

Appendix 4 *Overseas Transfers of Pension Savings*

If there is no exemption from tax available to members who are not residents in the country or territory where the scheme is established then condition 4 will be met. For example, if the country taxes benefits paid out of schemes established there regardless of residence and there is no exemption provided for non-residents elsewhere in the tax legislation, the condition is met. For the purposes of this condition, any exemption provided due to a double taxation agreement is ignored.

If there is an exemption then it must apply equally to residents and non-residents of that country. There must also be no qualification around whether residents receive the exemption.

Example:

Country X does not tax benefits paid out of a scheme established in Country X if they are paid to a non-resident. It is also possible for residents of Country X to claim exemption from tax on such benefits provided they did not contribute to the scheme in any period in which they were resident in Country X. As the exemption in relation to residents is qualified, condition 4 cannot be met. The scheme cannot be a QROPS.

Established by an International Organisation

There are separate rules to meeting the definition of an overseas pension scheme if the scheme is established outside the United Kingdom by an international organisation.

An international organisation means an organisation to which *section 1* of the *International Organisations Act 1968* applies by virtue of an Order in Council under subsection (1) of that section. This category includes the United Nations and the European Union. (International organisation in this context does not extend to multinational companies that operate or have subsidiaries in several countries).

A scheme established by an international organisation for the purpose of providing benefits for, or in respect of, past service as an employee of the organisation must meet the following conditions:

(1) its rules must provide that at least 70% of a member's UK tax-relieved scheme funds will be designated by the scheme manager for the purpose of providing the member with an income for life, and

(2) the pension benefits payable to the member under the scheme (and any lump sum associated with those benefits) must be payable no earlier than they would be if pension rule 1 in *section 165 Finance Act 2004* applied.

"UK tax-relieved scheme funds" means the sum of the member's UK tax-relieved fund and their relevant transfer fund. Those terms are explained in RPSM13102150 and in RPSM13102170.

Overseas Transfers of Pension Savings **Appendix 4**

Pension rule 1 in *section 165 Finance Act 2004* provides that no payment of pension may be made before the day on which the member reaches normal minimum pension age, unless the ill-health condition was met immediately before the member became entitled to a pension under the scheme. Guidance on the normal minimum pension age is provided at RPSM08100010 to RPSM08100030, and there is guidance on the ill-health condition in RPSM08100070.

Recognised overseas pension scheme

Under *section 150(8) Finance Act 2004* a recognised overseas pension scheme is an overseas pension scheme that meets the following requirements prescribed under the *Pension Schemes (Categories of Country and Requirements for Overseas Pension Schemes and Recognised Overseas Pension Schemes) Regulations 2006 [SI 2006/206]*.

It must:

(a) be established in a Member State of the European Union, Norway, Liechtenstein or Iceland, or

(b) be established in a country or territory, other than New Zealand, with which the UK has a Double Taxation Agreement that contains exchange of information and non- discrimination provisions, or

(c) satisfy the requirement that, at the time of the recognised transfer, the rules of the scheme provide that:

1. at least 70% of the funds transferred will be designated by the scheme manager for the purpose of providing the member with an income for life,

2. the pension benefits (and any associated lump sum) payable to the member under the scheme, to the extent that they relate to the transfer, are payable no earlier than they would be if pension rule 1 in section 165 applied, and

3. membership of the scheme is open to persons resident in the country or territory in which it is established, or

(d) satisfy the requirement that, at the time of the recognised transfer the transfer is made to a pension scheme which is a *KiwiSaver* scheme as defined in section 4(1) (interpretation) of the *KiwiSaver Act 2006* of New Zealand.

Pension rule 1 in *section 165 Finance Act 2004* provides that no payment of pension may be made before the day on which the member reaches normal minimum pension age, unless the ill-health condition was met immediately before the member became entitled to a pension under the scheme. Guidance on the normal minimum pension age is provided at RPSM08100010 to RPSM08100030, and there is guidance on the ill-health condition in RPSM08100070.

Appendix 4 *Overseas Transfers of Pension Savings*

Qualifying recognised overseas pension scheme

A scheme that meets the requirements to be a recognised overseas pension scheme can be a QROPS if the scheme manager gives HMRC certain undertakings. This includes an undertaking to comply with prescribed information requirements found in the *Pension Schemes (Information Requirements – Qualifying Overseas Pension Schemes, Qualifying Recognised Overseas Pensions Schemes and Corresponding Relief) Regulations 2006 [SI 2006/208]* as amended.

The scheme manager is the persons or persons administering or responsible for the management of the pension scheme.

The scheme manager must:

- notify HMRC that the scheme is a recognised overseas pension scheme, and have provided evidence of that if required,
- inform HMRC of the name of the country or territory in which the scheme is established. If the scheme qualifies as a recognised overseas pension scheme under the requirement described at paragraph (c) in the paragraph above headed "Recognised overseas pension scheme" evidence of this qualification must be supplied. The form APSS251 asks for a set of the scheme rules as part of this evidence,
- provide any other evidence required by HMRC,
- undertake to notify HMRC if the scheme ceases to be a recognised overseas pension scheme, and
- undertake to provide HMRC with certain information on making payments in respect of certain scheme members. The paragraph below headed 'What information an accepted QROPS has to give to HMRC' gives more detail on this.

In addition, the scheme must not have ceased to be a QROPS as a result of HMRC notifying the scheme manager that it is excluded from being one, see paragraph below headed "Exclusion of a scheme".

Submitting a QROPS notification

The guidance in RPSM14101050 applies where HMRC deals with the notification prior to 6 April 2012. This guidance applies to all other notifications.

The scheme manager must send the required notification and undertakings to

HM Revenue & Customs
Pension Schemes Services FitzRoy House
Castle Meadow Road Nottingham
NG2 1BD
United Kingdom

Form APSS251 is for use by a scheme manager to provide the required information and notifications. There is a set of APSS251 notes available to help fill in this form.

Overseas Transfers of Pension Savings **Appendix 4**

On receipt of APSS251, HMRC may ask the scheme manager for more evidence or information before deciding whether to issue the scheme with a QROPS reference number. The QROPS reference is used for administrative purposes by HMRC in its dealings with the scheme.

In many cases the issue of a QROPS reference will be done on the basis of the information that the scheme has provided to HMRC on the Form APSS251 stating that it meets the requirements to be a QROPS. If it transpires that there are errors in that information such that the scheme cannot meet the requirements to be a QROPS, this will be considered to have always been the position regardless of the issue of the QROPS reference.

Changes to information supplied

If, at any time after information has been supplied to HMRC, it becomes apparent to the scheme that there is a material change to that information, the information is incomplete or it contains a material inaccuracy the scheme must provide to HMRC details of the change, the complete information or correction of the inaccuracy without undue delay.

QROPS LIST

When completing Form APSS 251 the scheme manager indicates whether or not the name of the scheme can be published on the HMRC internet site. The published list is provided as a means for UK registered pension scheme administrators and overseas pension scheme managers to verify that a scheme has notified HMRC that it meets the conditions to be a QROPS. The list is not intended for use for any other purpose and is not intended to give assurance that HMRC has checked all the information provided by any named scheme. The list is updated twice a month by Pension Schemes Services (PSS). A scheme's name will be removed from the list as a matter of urgency if it ceases to be a QROPS. If HMRC has concerns about the scheme's status at any time, the scheme's name may be removed whilst HMRC carries out further checks.

Administrators and members of registered pension schemes need to bear in mind that:

- not all QROPS will necessarily feature within the list,
- the list is not to be taken as a recommendation for a particular scheme or product,
- publication on the list should not be seen as confirmation by HMRC that it has verified all the information supplied by the scheme in its QROPS application, and
- if a scheme has been included on the list in circumstances where it should not have been included e.g. because it did not satisfy the conditions to be a recognised overseas pension scheme, any transfer will potentially not be a recognised transfer. As such, the transfer could give rise to an unauthorised payments charge and unauthorised payments surcharge

Appendix 4 *Overseas Transfers of Pension Savings*

liability for the member and to a scheme sanction charge liability for the scheme administrator (see RPSM14102020 and RPSM14101055).

If your scheme is on the published list, the UK scheme administrator will know that your scheme has notified HMRC that it meets the requirements to be a QROPS. If it is not on the list, we can only confirm to them that your scheme has sent such a notification if we have your written permission to do so.

Due to HMRC confidentiality rules, PSS will not be able to answer queries about the QROPS status of an unlisted overseas pension scheme unless it has received written authorisation from the manager of that scheme to disclose this information to a named person. The letter or form providing authorisation must be signed by the manager of the overseas scheme in order for PSS to answer the query.

Administrators of registered pension schemes can phone the PSS helpline to:

- ask if, since the last list was published, an overseas pension scheme has been noted for inclusion on the next publication of the list. PSS will not be able to answer such an enquiry if it is waiting to find out if the scheme is prepared to go on the published list, and

- check if the omission from the latest published list of a scheme that had been included previously was deliberate.

REMOVAL FROM QROPS PUBLISHED LIST

There are a number of reasons why a pension scheme might no longer appear on the published list. Due to confidentiality rules HMRC cannot say why a particular scheme is no longer included unless it receives written authorisation from the scheme manager to divulge information to a named individual.

The following is an overview of the main reasons why a scheme may no longer appear and of the implications of each scenario on transfers to the scheme:

- a QROPS has asked to be removed from the list but it is still a QROPS.

    Transfers to the scheme made before and after removal from the published list will be recognised transfers under section 169. They will not give rise to an unauthorised payments charge (or an unauthorised payments surcharge) on the member or to a scheme sanction charge on the administrator.

- a scheme was eligible to be a QROPS when it originally notified HMRC but no longer has that status. For example, the scheme might no longer meet the requirements to be a recognised overseas pension scheme or HMRC could have excluded the scheme from being a QROPS.

- Transfers to the scheme made before withdrawal of its QROPS status will be recognised transfers so they will not give rise to an unauthorised payments charge (or a surcharge) on the member or to a scheme sanction charge on the administrator. Transfers made after the date on which the scheme ceased to be a recognised overseas pension scheme or it was excluded will not be recognised transfers. These transfers will give rise

Overseas Transfers of Pension Savings **Appendix 4**

to an unauthorised payments charge (and surcharge) on the member and to a scheme sanction charge on the administrator (see RPSM04104500, RPSM04104600 and RPSM04104800).

- HMRC has temporarily suspended the QROPS listing, see paragraph below headed 'Temporary suspension of QROPS listing from HMRC published list'.

- HMRC has discovered that a scheme's original notification that it was a recognised overseas pension scheme was incorrect.

Transfers made to the scheme will not be recognised transfers because the scheme will not, as a fact, have been a QROPS at any time. They will give rise to an unauthorised payments charge (and surcharge) on the member and to a scheme sanction charge on the administrator.

Where the scheme administrator has relied in good faith on the fact that the overseas scheme is included on the latest published QROPS list when making a transfer to it this should provide just and reasonable grounds for HMRC to discharge their liability to the scheme sanction charge if the scheme is subsequently withdrawn from the list by HMRC (see RPSM04104870).

This is on the basis that the administrator is expected to have carried out reasonable checks. Before making an overseas transfer the administrator should have checked the published QROPS list, and in particular must have done so no more than one day before the transfer was made. The administrator should keep in their file a printout of the page from the list including the QROPS from the day before the transfer (and also retain a copy of the overseas scheme's QROPS reference notification letter if this has also been obtained).

There may still be an unauthorised payments charge/surcharge liability for the member in these circumstances (see RPSM04104510 and RPSM04104780). Enforcement of those charges will depend on the particular facts and circumstances of each individual case.

EXCLUSION OF A SCHEME

A scheme may be excluded from being a QROPS under *section 169(5)* if HMRC decides that there has been a significant failure to comply with any information requirements such that it is inappropriate for transfers from registered pension schemes to the recognised overseas pension scheme to be recognised transfers. A failure will be significant if a substantial amount of information has not been provided or if the failure to provide information is likely to result in serious prejudice to the assessment or collection of tax.

HMRC must notify the person or persons appearing to be the scheme manager that the scheme has been excluded. The scheme manager can appeal against an exclusion decision. Pages at RPSM12102000 onwards explain the appeals process including the possibility of a HMRC review of the decision. It is also possible for HMRC to decide that a scheme is no longer excluded.

If a scheme is excluded from being a QROPS it can no longer receive a recognised transfer under *section 169 Finance Act 2004*.

Appendix 4 *Overseas Transfers of Pension Savings*

TEMPORARY SUSPENSION OF QROPS LISTING FROM HMRC PUBLISHED LIST

HMRC may temporarily remove a scheme from the published list in certain circumstances. For example, if it has concerns about the scheme's operation or is unable to contact the scheme. This will not necessarily mean that the scheme has been excluded by HMRC from being a QROPS but the scheme will be removed from the published list until we have completed our review. Dependent on the circumstances of the case, the outcome of that review could be:

- The scheme is reinstated to the list
- The scheme is found not to meet the requirements to be a recognised overseas pension scheme from a point in time
- The scheme is excluded from being a QROPS.

The implications for transfers to the scheme will be as set out in the section above headed, "Removal from QROPS published list".

PROCESS OF TRANSFERRING FROM REGISTERED PENSION SCHEME TO QROPS

Can a transfer be made to any QROPS?

UK scheme administrators and members should be aware that a transfer may not be permissible even though an overseas pension scheme is a QROPS. QROPS status has significance for UK tax purposes only. Whether or not a transfer to a QROPS can be made will depend also on the scheme being able to accept a transfer under the legislation of the country in which it is established. In particular, it is HMRC Pension Scheme Service's (PSS) understanding that transfers to US "qualified" retirement plans, including individual retirement arrangements (IRAs), cannot be made as such plans are not permitted to accept a transfer of funds from a UK registered pension scheme. UK scheme administrators and members should contact the relevant overseas authority for confirmation, not PSS.

What form can a transfer take – cash or assets or both?

Transfers are valued in cash terms.

Although most transfers will be in the form of cash, a transfer can also be made by way of insurance policies, or other assets, or as a combination of these.

If a transfer involves an asset (for example, a property or a holding of company shares) being transferred between pension schemes, that asset must be valued in cash terms by an appropriately qualified independent person before being transferred.

When do the new member requirements and registered pension scheme transfer procedures apply?

The requirements and procedures explained below apply to recognised transfers which are requested by the member after 5 April 2012.

A transfer requested before 6 April 2012 has to be reported in the electronic Event Report, see RPSM14101070.

Member requirements

When arranging a transfer the member will have to complete any forms and provide such information as is required by the administrators of the schemes involved. This is to enable the scheme to make the transfer, ensure that the member receives the benefits to which they are entitled and to pay the correct amount of tax due where appropriate.

When transferring to a QROPS the member will need to advise the administrator of the UK scheme whether they have sufficient lifetime allowance to cover the amount transferred.

This is because such a transfer counts as a benefit crystallisation event. Failure to confirm that they have sufficient lifetime allowance may result in a lifetime allowance charge being payable in relation to the amount transferred.

Where the member asks for a transfer to a QROPS they must, when requested by the scheme administrator, provide information and make a written and signed member acknowledgement to the scheme administrator containing the following:

Information

The member's:

(a) Name

(b) Date of birth,

(c) Principal residential address and, where that address is not in the United Kingdom, the member's last principal residential address in the UK,

(d) National insurance number or, where applicable, confirmation in writing that the member does not qualify for a national insurance number,

(e) Telephone number, if any, which the member provides for use by the scheme administrator or HMRC in relation to the scheme,

(f) The name and address of the QROPS and the country or territory under the law of which the QROPS is established and regulated.

Acknowledgement

The member must sign a statement to confirm they acknowledge that they are aware that a transfer other than a recognised transfer to a qualifying

Appendix 4 *Overseas Transfers of Pension Savings*

recognised overseas pension scheme of sums and assets held for the purposes of, or representing accrued rights under, an arrangement under a registered pension scheme,

(a) gives rise to a liability under *section 208* (unauthorised payments charge), and

(b) may give rise to a liability under *section 209* (unauthorised payments surcharge).

For more information on these tax charges see RPSM04104010.

The precise manner in which this information and the acknowledgement can be made to the scheme administrator is not dictated and most schemes will produce their own paperwork for this purpose. However as the member's signature is required for the acknowledgement it will need to be done in a paper document. HMRC has made available Form APSS263 which can be used for this purpose as well as APSS 263 notes to help fill in this form.

The information and the signed acknowledgement must be provided by the member to the scheme within 2 months from the date the member requests the scheme transfer.

If the transfer to a QROPS goes ahead and the scheme administrator calculates that the member has sufficient lifetime allowance available for the transfer they will advise the member of the amount of lifetime allowance that the transfer overseas will use up. The member should keep this information for possible future reference as they will need to take it into account if they were to take benefits from a registered pension scheme.

If the transfer to a QROPS goes ahead and the scheme administrator calculates that the member does not have sufficient lifetime allowance available they will work out how much tax by way of lifetime allowance charge is payable and deduct it from the amount being transferred overseas.

What a registered pension scheme has to do before making the transfer

Before making an overseas transfer the UK scheme administrator should have checked the published QROPS list, and in particular must have done so no more than one day before the transfer was made, see guidance above starting at paragraph headed 'QROPS List'.

In the paragraph above headed 'Member requirements', there are details of the information that a member should pass to the scheme administrator prior to a transfer taking place. The scheme administrator is expected to send the member details of these requirements within 30 days from the date the member requests the transfer.

A transfer from a registered pension scheme to a QROPS is a benefit crystallisation event 8(BCE). The amount of the transfer value will be the amount crystallised for lifetime allowance purposes. The scheme administrator needs to calculate whether the member has sufficient lifetime allowance left to cover this amount. If the member does not have sufficient lifetime allowance available to cover the amount to be transferred, there will be a lifetime allowance charge (see RPSM11105000).

What a registered pension scheme has to do after making the transfer

These transfers are not included within the scheme annual Event Report. Transfers should be reported to HMRC on form APSS262 within 30 days of the date of the transfer. The scheme administrator must submit a paper Form APSS 262 and cannot do this electronically or via Pension Schemes Online. HMRC has provided APSS 262 notes to help fill in this form.

The information required on Form APSS 262 is, in addition to the member's name and national insurance number, the following:

(a) The member's principal residential address and, where that address is not within the United Kingdom, the member's last principal residential address in the UK.

(b) The member's date of birth.

(c) The member's telephone number, if any, which the member has provided to the scheme administrator for use by HMRC in relation to the scheme.

(d) The member acknowledgement.

(e) The date of the recognised transfer.

(f) The amount of the sums transferred, if any.

(g) A description and valuation of each type of asset transferred, if any, including the value of any unquoted shares, quoted shares and real property.

(h) The name and address of the QROPS to which the sums or assets have been transferred.

(i) The country or territory under the law of which the QROPS is established and regulated.

(j) The name, address, business telephone number and, where available, the electronic mail address of the manager of the QROPS.

The completed APSS262 must be provided to HMRC within 30 days beginning on the relevant transfer date.

QROPS THAT RECEIVES A TRANSFER FROM ANOTHER OVERSEAS PENSION SCHEME

The scheme manager of a QROPS that receives a transfer from another overseas pension scheme will need to check whether or not the transferring member has a UK tax-relieved fund (see RPSM13102150) or a relevant

Appendix 4   *Overseas Transfers of Pension Savings*

transfer fund in the transferring scheme. This is in order to establish if HMRC will have to be provided with information about payments made in respect of the individual. It would be reasonable for the scheme manager to ask the individual to declare whether or not the transferred funds include any amounts that have received UK tax relief or have originated in a UK registered pension scheme. If the answer is 'yes' more detailed information will need to be obtained by the QROPS scheme manager to establish if the individual will have a relevant transfer fund in their receiving scheme.

INFORMATION THAT A QROPS MUST AUTOMATICALLY GIVE TO HMRC

The scheme manager of a recognised overseas pension scheme must have undertaken to comply with the information requirements imposed under *the Pension Schemes (Information Requirements – Qualifying Overseas Pension Schemes, Qualifying Recognised Overseas Pensions Schemes and Corresponding Relief) Regulations 2006 [SI 2006/208]* if the scheme is to be a QROPS.

Cessation Information – The scheme manager must undertake to inform HMRC if it ceases to be a recognised overseas pension scheme.

A scheme which ceases to be a QROPS must provide to an officer of HMRC:

(a) the value at the cessation date of the relevant transferred sums and assets pertaining to each relevant transfer fund under the scheme; and

(b) the name, principal residential address, date of birth and, if any, the national insurance number of each member in respect of whom there is a relevant transfer fund at the cessation date.

This information must be provided within 30 days beginning with the day on which the cessation takes place (the cessation date).

Payment Information – The scheme manager must notify HMRC when they make a payment, or are treated under certain provisions as making a payment, in respect of a relevant member. However, the scheme manager does not have to notify HMRC if:

- the payment is made 10 years after the day of the transfer that created the relevant transfer fund and
- the relevant member is a person to whom the member payment provisions do not apply under paragraph 2 of Schedule 34 (see RPSM13102120).

The member payment provisions do not apply unless:

- the member is resident in the UK when the payment is made (or treated as made), or
- although not resident at that time, has been resident in the UK earlier in the tax year the payment is made or in any of the 5 tax years immediately preceding that tax year.

Overseas Transfers of Pension Savings **Appendix 4**

In the United Kingdom a tax year runs from 6 April to the following 5 April. A payment includes a transfer from the scheme.

The provisions under which a scheme manager is treated as making a payment are *sections 172* to *174A*, *paragraph 2A* of *Schedule 28* and *paragraph 3A* of *Schedule 29* to *Finance Act 2004*. Guidance on those deemed payments is provided in RPSM09100170. A payment to a transfer member has to be notified to HMRC regardless of whether or not it is more than 10 years after the day of transfer if it is deemed to have been made from their taxable asset transfer fund (see RPSM13102180).

A relevant member is one in respect of whom there is a relevant transfer fund within the meaning in *paragraph 4(2)* of *Schedule 34* to *Finance Act 2004*. Broadly speaking, a member will have a relevant transfer fund within the scheme if they have transferred sums or assets into it that relate to UK tax-relieved contributions. That includes transfers from registered pension schemes and certain transfers from non-UK schemes that are not registered pension schemes. Further details are provided at RPSM13102170.

Where a non-pension payment such as a lump sum or a transfer is made a notification is needed in respect of each payment. Where a pension payment is made it is only necessary to send a notification of the first such payment to any individual.

The scheme manager must provide HMRC with the following information:

(a)   the name and principal residential address of the relevant member, and

(b)   the date, amount and nature of the payment.

This information must be provided within 60 days beginning on the day;

- on which the payment is made or treated as made; or
- by such other time as may be agreed between HMRC and the scheme manager.

HMRC provides a form APSS253 for the purposes of reporting these payments as well as APSS253 notes to help fill in the form.

Does QROPS complete old or new Form APSS253?

For a payment made or treated as made on or before 5 April 2012 a report should be made on the old process using old Forms APSS 253 and 253 (insert) together with their APSS 253 notes. Reports for the tax year 2011/12 have to be submitted by 31 January 2013, see RPSM14101070.

For each payment made or treated as made on or after 6 April 2012 the new process applies. Reports on new Forms APSS 253 and 253 (insert) should be made within 60 days. There are completion notes APSS 253 notes to help scheme manager do this.

Changes to information supplied

If at any time after any information has been supplied to HMRC it becomes apparent to the QROPS that there is a material change affecting the information

Appendix 4 *Overseas Transfers of Pension Savings*

or that the information is incomplete or contains a material inaccuracy the QROPS must provide to HMRC details of the change, the complete information or correction of the inaccuracy without undue delay.

OTHER INFORMATION THAT A QROPS MAY NEED TO PROVIDE TO HMRC

The previous section dealt with information that a QROPS must automatically supply to HMRC when specific events happen. There are other circumstances in which the trigger for the supply of information is a request for that information from HMRC.

The information requirements state that the following information must be provided in response to a written notice from HMRC:

1. Where the scheme manager is a company the names and addresses of the directors of the company.

This information must be provided by the time specified in the HMRC notice requiring it.

2. Where there has been a transfer to a QROPS from a registered pension scheme or another QROPS, of sums and assets which have been held for the purposes of, or representing accrued rights under, a registered pension scheme.

- (a) The date of the transfer to the QROPS.
- (b) The name and address of any bank and details of any bank account which the QROPS has used in relation to the transfer.
- (c) Details of the sums and assets and how they have been applied.
- (d) Where the transfer is from a registered pension scheme the name and address of that scheme.
- (e) The name, principal residential address, date of birth and the national insurance number, if any, of the member who is connected with the sums and assets.
- (f) Where the member is a person to whom the member payment provisions do not apply by virtue of *paragraph 2 of Schedule 34 to Finance Act 2004*, the date that the member ceased to be resident in the United Kingdom.
- (g) The name and address of the body that regulates the QROPS and the reference number, if any, issued to the QROPS by that regulator.
- (h) The name and address of the tax authority which administers the taxation of the QROPS and the reference number, if any, issued to the QROPS by that tax authority.
- (i) Evidence to show that the QROPS met at the time of the transfer or continues to meet the requirements specified in *regulations 2 and 3 of the Pension Schemes (Categories of Country and*

Overseas Transfers of Pension Savings **Appendix 4**

Requirements for Overseas Pension Schemes and Recognised Overseas Pension Schemes) Regulations 2006 [SI 2006/206].

(j) Any other evidence relating to the transfer.

This information must be provided within 60 days beginning on the day;

- on which the requirement is notified by the officer of HMRC; or
- by such other time as may be agreed between HMRC and the QROPS

Changes to information supplied

If at any time after any information has been supplied to HMRC it becomes apparent to the QROPS that there is a material change affecting the information or that the information is incomplete or contains a material inaccuracy the QROPS must provide to HMRC details of the change, the complete information or correction of the inaccuracy without undue delay.

Appendix 5

The Registered Pension Schemes and Overseas Pension Schemes (Miscellaneous Amendments) Regulations

SI 2012/884

INCOME TAX

The Registered Pension Schemes and Overseas Pension Schemes (Miscellaneous Amendments) Regulations 2012

Made	*20th March 2012*
Laid before the House of Commons	*21st March 2012*
Coming into force	*6th April 2012*

The Commissioners for Her Majesty's Revenue and Customs, in exercise of the powers conferred by sections 132 and 133(2) of the Finance Act 1999(**a**), sections 135 and 136 of the Finance Act 2002(**b**) and sections 150(7) and (8), 169(4) and 251(1) and (4) of, and paragraph 5(2) of Schedule 33 and paragraph 51(4) of Schedule 36 to, the Finance Act 2004(**3**)(**c**) and now exercisable by them(**d**), make the following Regulations:

Citation, commencement and interpretation

1. (1) These Regulations may be cited as the Registered Pension Schemes and Overseas Pension Schemes (Miscellaneous Amendments) Regulations 2012 and shall come into force on 6th April 2012.

(a) 1999 c 16; section 132 was amended by the Communications Act 2003 (c 21), Schedule 17, paragraph 156 and by SI 2011/1043, article 6.
(b) 2002 c 23; section 135 was amended by the Commissioners of Revenue and Customs Act 2005 (c 11), Schedule 4, paragraphs 94 and 95, by the Finance Act 2007 (c 3), section 93 and by SI 2011/1043, article 6.
(c) 2004 c 12. Section 150 was amended by SI 2007/1388, Schedule 1, paragraphs 106 and 108. Section 169 was amended by the Finance Act 2005 (c 7), Schedule 10, paragraphs 1 and 36 and by the Finance Act 2011 (c 11), Schedule 16, paragraphs 62 and 66. Section 251 was amended by the Finance Act 2005, Schedule 10, paragraphs 1 and 47 and by the Finance Act 2010 (c 13), section 49. Schedule 33 was amended by the Finance Act 2005, Schedule 10, paragraphs 1 and 46, by the Finance Act 2006 (c 25), Schedule 23, paragraphs 1 and 32 and by SI 2009/56, Schedule 1, paragraphs 419 and 435. Schedule 36 was amended by the Finance Act 2005, Schedule 10, paragraphs 1 and 55.
(d) The functions of the Commissioners of Inland Revenue were transferred to the Commissioners for Her Majesty's Revenue and Customs by section 5(1) of the Commissioners for Revenue and Customs Act 2005. Section 50(1) of that Act provides that, in so far as it is appropriate in consequence of section 5, a reference, however expressed, to the Commissioners of Inland Revenue is to be read as a reference to the Commissioners for Her Majesty's Revenue and Customs.

(2) The amendments made by—

(a) regulations 7 and 8(1) to (5), (7) and (8) have effect in respect of information relating to payments that are made, or are treated as made, on or after 6th April 2012; and

(b) regulations 11 and 12 have effect in relation to recognised transfers which are requested by the member on or after 6th April 2012.

Amendments to the Pension Schemes (Categories of Country and Requirements for Overseas Pension Schemes and Recognised Overseas Pension Schemes) Regulations 2006

2. The Pension Schemes (Categories of Country and Requirements for Overseas Pension Schemes and Recognised Overseas Pension Schemes) Regulations 2006(5) are amended as follows.

3. (1) Regulation 2 (requirements of an overseas pension scheme) is amended as follows.

In paragraph (3)—

(a) for 'primary conditions and also meets one of Conditions A and B' substitute 'following conditions';

(b) for the italic cross headings '*Primary condition 1*', '*Primary condition 2*' and '*Condition A*' substitute respectively the italic cross headings '*Condition 1*', '*Condition 2*' and '*Condition 3*';

(c) in condition 2 (as amended by sub-paragraph (b)) in sub-paragraph (ab) for 'the Schedule' substitute 'Schedule 1'; and

(d) omit condition B.

4. In regulation 3 (recognised overseas pension schemes: prescribed countries or territories and prescribed conditions)—

(a) in paragraph (1) for 'the pension scheme must' to the end substitute—

'the pension scheme must satisfy—

(a) the requirement in paragraph (6); and

(b) one or more of the following requirements—

(i) the requirement that the scheme must be established in a country or territory mentioned in paragraph (2),

(ii) the requirement in paragraph (4),

(iii) the requirement in paragraph (5).';

(b) in paragraph (2)—

(i) for 'paragraph (1)(a)' substitute 'paragraph (1)(b)(i)';

(ii) in sub-paragraph (c) after 'any country or territory' insert ', other than New Zealand,';

(c) in paragraph (4) omit 'The requirement is that,'; and

Appendix 5 *SI 2012/884*

(d)　after paragraph (4) insert—

'(5) At the time of a transfer of sums or assets which would, subject to these Regulations, constitute a recognised transfer the scheme must be of a kind specified in Schedule 2 to these Regulations.

(6) Where tax relief in respect of benefits paid from the scheme is available to a member of the scheme who is not resident in the country or territory in which the scheme is established, the same or substantially the same tax relief must—

(a)　also be available to members of the scheme who are resident in the country or territory; and

(b)　apply regardless of whether the member was resident in the country or territory—

(i)　when the member joined the scheme; or

(ii)　for any period of time when they were a member of the scheme.

(7) For the purposes of paragraph (6) 'tax relief'—

(a)　is any tax relief that is available under the system of taxation of personal income in the country or territory in which the scheme is established; and

(b)　includes the grant of an exemption from tax other than an exemption which applies by virtue of double taxation arrangements.

(8) In paragraph (7)(b) 'double taxation arrangements' means arrangements made between the country or territory in which the scheme is established and another country or territory with a view to affording relief from double taxation.'.

5. In the Schedule (specified schemes), for the heading 'Schedule' substitute the heading 'Schedule 1'.

6. After Schedule 1 (as amended by regulation 5) insert—

'SCHEDULE 2　　　　　　　　　　　Regulation 3(5)

Specified Schemes

A pension scheme which is a KiwiSaver scheme as defined in section 4(1) (interpretation) of the KiwiSaver Act 2006 of New Zealand.'.

Amendments to the Pension Schemes (Information Requirements – Qualifying Overseas Pension Schemes, Qualifying Recognised Overseas Pensions Schemes and Corresponding Relief) Regulations 2006

7. The Pension Schemes (Information Requirements – Qualifying Overseas Pension Schemes, Qualifying Recognised Overseas Pensions Schemes and Corresponding Relief) Regulations 2006(6) are amended as follows.

8. (1) Regulation 3 (information – qualifying recognised overseas pension schemes) is amended as follows.

(2) In paragraph (2)(a)—

(a)   after 'name and' insert 'principal residential'; and

(b)   at the end omit 'and'.

(3) After paragraph (2)(a) insert—

'(aa) the relevant member's national insurance number, if any; and'.

(4) In paragraph (3) for 'the relevant member' to the end substitute—

'the following conditions are met—

(a)   at the date of the payment more than ten years has elapsed beginning with the date on which the relevant transfer fund in respect of the relevant member came into existence; and

(b)   the relevant member to whom the payment is made or treated as made is a person to whom the member payment provisions do not apply (see paragraph 2 of Schedule 34).'.

(5) In paragraph (5) for 'provided by 31st January' to the end substitute—

'provided—

(a)   within 90 days beginning with the day on which the payment is made or is treated as made; or

(b)   by such other time as may be agreed between an officer of Revenue and Customs and the scheme manager.'.

(6) After paragraph (5) insert—

'(5A) Where the scheme manager is a company it must provide the names and addresses of the directors of the company to an officer of Revenue and Customs if required to do so in writing, and within such time as may be specified, by the officer.'.

(7) In paragraph (6) in the definition of 'relevant member' omit from 'within the meaning' to the end.

(8) After paragraph (6) insert—

'(7) For the purposes of this regulation and regulation 3B 'relevant transfer fund' has the meaning given in paragraph 4(2) of Schedule 34.'.

9. After regulation 3 insert—

'Information – transfer of sums or assets to a qualifying recognised overseas pension scheme

3A. (1) For the purposes of section 169(4), where paragraph (2) applies a qualifying recognised overseas pension scheme ('the scheme') mentioned in that paragraph must provide to an officer

Appendix 5 SI 2012/884

of Revenue and Customs such of the information specified in paragraph (3) as may be required in writing by the officer.

(2) This paragraph applies where there is a transfer to a qualifying recognised overseas pension scheme of sums or assets which have at any time been held for the purposes of, or representing accrued rights under, a registered pension scheme from—

(a) a registered pension scheme; or

(b) another qualifying recognised overseas pension scheme.

(3) The information is—

(a) the date of the transfer;

(b) the name and address of any bank and details of any bank account which the scheme has used in relation to the transfer;

(c) details of the sums or assets transferred;

(d) where information is required from a scheme which is a transferee, the way that the sums or assets have been applied by the scheme;

(e) where the transfer is from a registered pension scheme, the name and address of that scheme;

(f) the name, principal residential address, date of birth and, if any, the national insurance number of the member who is connected with the sums or assets;

(g) where the member referred to in sub-paragraph (f) is a person to whom the member payment provisions do not apply by virtue of paragraph 2 of Schedule 34, the date that the member ceased to be resident in the United Kingdom;

(h) the name and address of the body that regulates the scheme and the reference number, if any, issued to the scheme by the regulator;

(i) the name and address of the tax authority that administers the scheme and the reference number, if any, issued to the scheme by the authority;

(j) evidence to show that the scheme met at the time of the transfer and continues to meet the requirements specified in regulations 2 and 3 of the Pension Schemes Categories of Country and Requirements for Overseas Pension Schemes and Recognised Overseas Pension Schemes) Regulations 2006; and

(k) any other evidence relating to the transfer as may be required by the officer of Revenue and Customs.

(4) Information required in accordance with paragraph (1) must be provided—

(a) within 90 days beginning with the day on which the requirement is notified by the officer of Revenue and Customs; or

(b) by such other time as may be agreed between the officer and the scheme manager.

Information – cessation of qualifying recognised overseas pension scheme

3B. For the purposes of section 169(4), a pension scheme which ceases to be a qualifying recognised overseas pension scheme must within 30 days beginning with the day on which the cessation takes place ('the cessation date') provide to an officer of Revenue and Customs—

(a) the value at the cessation date of the relevant transferred sums or assets pertaining to each relevant transfer fund under the scheme; and

(b) the name, principal residential address, date of birth and, if any, the national insurance number of each member in respect of whom there is a relevant transfer fund under the scheme at the cessation date.

Information – changes, completion or correction

3C. For the purposes of section 169(4), if at any time after a pension scheme has provided an officer of Revenue and Customs with information in accordance with regulation 3, 3A or 3B it becomes apparent to the scheme that—

(a) there is a material change affecting that information; or

(b) the information is incomplete or contains a material inaccuracy,

the scheme must provide to an officer of Revenue and Customs details of the change, the complete information or correction of the inaccuracy without undue delay.'.

10 In regulation 4 (notice in cases of serious prejudice to proper assessment or collection of tax)—

(a) in paragraph 1(a) for 'these Regulations' substitute 'regulation 2'; and

(b) in paragraph (2) for 'regulations 2 and 3' substitute 'regulation 2'.

Amendments to the Registered Pension Schemes (Provision of Information) Regulations 2006

11. The Registered Pension Schemes (Provision of Information) Regulations 2006(**7**) are amended as follows.

12. In regulation 3 (provision of information by scheme administrator to the Commissioners)—

(a) in paragraph (1), in entry 9 in the table (transfers to qualifying recognised overseas pension schemes)—

Appendix 5   SI 2012/884

(i) in the first column after 'qualifying recognised overseas pension scheme' insert '('QROPS')';

(ii) in the second column for entries (a) to (d) substitute—

'(a) the member's principal residential address and, where that address is not in the United Kingdom, the member's last principal residential address in the United Kingdom;

(a) the member's date of birth;

(b) the member's telephone number, if any, which the member has provided to the scheme administrator for use by the Commissioners in relation to the scheme;

(c) the acknowledgement mentioned in regulation 11BA(2)(b);

(d) the date of the recognised transfer;

(e) in the case of a transfer of sums, the amount of the sums;

(f) in the case of a transfer of assets, a description and valuation of each type of asset transferred including the value of any unquoted shares, quoted shares and real property;

(g) the name and address of the QROPS to which the sums or assets have been transferred;

(h) the country or territory under the law of which the QROPS is established and regulated; and

(i) the name, address, business telephone number and, where available, the electronic mail address of the manager of the QROPS.'.

(b) in paragraph (6)(b) after 'qualification in' insert 'paragraph (7) and'; and

(c) after paragraph (6) insert—

'(7) An event report in respect of reportable event 9 must be delivered within 60 days beginning with the day of the transfer to which it relates.'.

13. After regulation 11B (information provided by members to scheme administrators: pension commencement lump sums)(a) insert—

'Information provided by members to scheme administrators: recognised transfers

11BA. (1) Paragraph (2) applies where a member of a registered pension scheme makes a request to the scheme administrator to make a recognised transfer ('transfer request') in respect of a qualifying recognised overseas pension scheme.

(2) The member must provide to the scheme administrator—

(a) the member's—

  (i) name;

  (ii) date of birth;

  (iii) principal residential address and, where that address is not in the United Kingdom, the member's last principal residential address in the United Kingdom;

  (iv) national insurance number or, where applicable, confirmation in writing that the member does not qualify for a national insurance number;

  (v) telephone number, if any, which the member provides for use by the scheme administrator or the Commissioners in relation to the scheme;

  (vi) the name and address of the qualifying recognised overseas pension scheme;

  (vii) the country or territory under the law of which the qualifying recognised overseas pension scheme is established and regulated; and

(b) the member's acknowledgement in writing that the member is aware that a transfer other than a recognised transfer to a qualifying recognised overseas pension scheme of sums or assets held for the purposes of, or representing accrued rights under, an arrangement under a registered pension scheme—

  (i) gives rise to a liability under section 208 (unauthorised payments charge); and

  (ii) may give rise to a liability under section 209 (unauthorised payments surcharge).

(3) The information specified in paragraph (2) must be provided within 60 days beginning with the day of the transfer request.

(4) The scheme administrator must send the member notification of the requirements specified in this regulation within 30 days beginning with the day of the transfer request.'.

14. In regulation 11C(1) (information provided by individuals to scheme administrator: national insurance number)(**a**) after 'event report' insert ', other than an event report in respect of reportable event 9,'.

Amendments to the Registered Pension Schemes and Overseas Pension Schemes (Electronic Communication of Returns and Information) Regulations 2006

15. (1) The Registered Pension Schemes and Overseas Pension Schemes (Electronic Communication of Returns and Information) Regulations 2006(**b**) are amended as follows.

Appendix 5 *SI 2012/884*

(2) In Schedule 1 (information which must be supplied to Revenue and Customs by an approved method of electronic communications)—

(a) in the entry beginning with 'A return under section 254', after the words 'that return' insert—

', which does not relate to a currently-relieved non-UK pension scheme'; and

(b) for 'An event report under' substitute 'An event report in respect of a reportable event specified in entries 1 to 8A and 10 to 21 in the table in paragraph (1) of'.

(3) In Schedule 2 (information which may be supplied either to or by Revenue and Customs by an approved method of electronic communications)—

(a) after the entry beginning 'A notice under section 250' insert—

'An amendment to a return under section 250 by the scheme administrator'; and

(b) after the entry beginning 'A certificate by Revenue and Customs under the ELA Regulations' insert—

'An amendment to an event report in respect of a reportable event specified in entries 1 to 8A and 10 to 21 in the table in paragraph (1) of regulation 3 of the Registered Pension Schemes (Provision of Information) Regulations 2006 (provision of information by scheme administrator to the Commissioners).'.

(a) Regulation 11C was inserted by SI 2011/301.
(b) SI 2006/570; amended by SI 2009/56, 2010/652 and 2011/702.

Appendix 6

Annotated copy showing revisions to SI 2006/206

Note: deleted wording is marked as struck out, inserted wording is underlined

INCOME TAX

The Pension Schemes (Categories of Country and Requirements for Overseas Pension Schemes and Recognised Overseas Pension Schemes) Regulations 2006

Made	*1st February 2006*
Laid before the House of Commons	*2nd February 2006*
Coming into force	*6th April 2006*

The Commissioners for Her Majesty's Revenue and Customs, in exercise of the powers conferred by section 150(7) and (8) of the Finance Act 2004, and now exercisable by them, make the following Regulations:

Citation, commencement and interpretation

1.—(1) These Regulations may be cited as the Pension Schemes (Categories of Country and Requirements for Overseas Pension Schemes and Recognised Overseas Pension Schemes) Regulations 2006 and shall come into force on 6th April 2006.

(2) In these Regulations a reference, without more, to a numbered section or Schedule is a reference to the section of, or Schedule to, the Finance Act 2004 which is so numbered.

Requirements of an overseas pension scheme

2.—(1) For the purposes of section 150(7) (meaning of overseas pension scheme) an overseas pension scheme must—

(a) satisfy the requirements in paragraphs (2) and (3); or

(b) be established (outside the United Kingdom) by an international organisation for the purpose of providing benefits for, or in respect of, past service as an employee of the organisation and satisfy the requirements in paragraph (4).

413

Appendix 6 *Annotated copy showing revisions to SI 2006/206*

(2) This paragraph is satisfied if—

(a) the scheme is an occupational pension scheme and there is, in the country or territory in which it is established, a body—

  (i) which regulates occupational pension schemes; and

  (ii) which regulates the scheme in question;

(b) the scheme is not an occupational pension scheme and there is in the country or territory in which it is established, a body—

  (i) which regulates pension schemes other than occupational pension schemes; and

  (ii) which regulates the scheme in question; or

(c) neither sub-paragraph (a) or (b) is satisfied by reason only that no such regulatory body exists in the country or territory and—

  (i) the scheme is established in another member State, Norway, Iceland or Liechtenstein; or

  (ii) the scheme's rules provide that at least 70% of a member's UK tax-relieved scheme funds will be designated by the scheme manager for the purpose of providing that individual with an income for life, and the pension benefits payable to the member under the scheme (and any lump sum associated with those benefits) are payable no earlier than they would be if pension rule 1 in section 165 applied.

(3) This paragraph is satisfied if the scheme is recognised for tax purposes.

A scheme is "recognised for tax purposes" under the tax legislation of a country or territory in which it is established if it meets the following conditions:

~~Primary~~ *Condition 1*

The scheme is open to persons resident in the country or territory in which it is established.

~~Primary~~ *Condition 2*

The scheme is established in a country or territory where there is a system of taxation of personal income under which tax relief is available in respect of pensions and —

(a) tax relief is not available to the member on contributions made to the scheme by the individual or, if the individual is an employee, by their employer, in respect of earnings to which benefits under the scheme relate; ~~or~~

(ab) the scheme is liable to taxation on its income and gains and is of a kind specified in Schedule 1 to these Regulations; or

(b) all or most of the benefits paid by the scheme to members who are not in serious ill-health are subject to taxation.

Annotated copy showing revisions to SI 2006/206 **Appendix 6**

For the purposes of this condition "tax relief" includes the grant of an exemption from tax.

Condition 3

The scheme is approved or recognised by, or registered with, the relevant tax authorities as a pension scheme in the country or territory in which it is established.

~~*Condition B*~~

~~If no system exists for the approval or recognition by, or registration with, relevant tax authorities of pension schemes in the country or territory in which it is established—~~

~~(a)   it must be resident there; and~~

~~(b)   its rules must provide that—~~

~~(i)   at least 70% of a member's UK tax-relieved scheme funds will be designated by the scheme manager for the purpose of providing the member with an income for life,~~

~~and~~

~~(ii)   the pension benefits payable to the member under the scheme (and any lump sum associated with those benefits) must be payable no earlier than they would be if pension rule 1 in section 165 applied.~~

(4) In the case of an overseas pension scheme falling within paragraph (1)(b) the requirements are that—

(a)   the scheme rules must provide that at least 70% of a member's UK tax-relieved scheme funds will be designated by the scheme manager for the purpose of providing the member with an income for life, and

(b)   the pension benefits payable to the member under the scheme (and any lump sum associated with those benefits) under the scheme must be payable no earlier than they would be if pension rule 1 in section 165 applied.

(5) In this regulation—

"international organisation" means an organisation to which section 1 of the International Organisations Act 1968 applies by virtue of an Order in Council under subsection (1) of that section;

"occupational pension scheme" has the meaning given by section 150(5); and

"UK tax-relieved scheme funds" means, in relation to a member, the sum of the member's UK tax-relieved fund and his relevant transfer fund, as defined respectively by regulations 2 and 3 of the Pension Schemes (Application of UK Provisions to Relevant Non-UK Schemes) Regulations 2006.

Appendix 6 *Annotated copy showing revisions to SI 2006/206*

Recognised overseas pension schemes: prescribed countries or territories and prescribed requirements

3.—(1) For the purposes of section 150(8) (recognised overseas pension schemes), in addition to satisfying the requirements set out in regulation 2 above – the pension scheme must <u>satisfy—</u>

<u>(a)   the requirement in paragraph (6); and</u>

<u>(b)   one or more of the following requirements—</u>

<u>   (i)   the requirement that the scheme must be established in a country or territory mentioned in paragraph (2),</u>

<u>   (ii)   the requirement in paragraph (4),</u>

<u>   (iii)   the requirement in paragraph (5).</u>

~~(a)   be established in a country or territory mentioned in paragraph (2); or~~

~~(b)   satisfy the requirement in paragraph (4).~~

(2) The countries and territories referred to in paragraph (1)(<u>b</u>)(i) are—

(a)   the member States of the European Communities, other than the United Kingdom;

(b)   Iceland, Liechtenstein and Norway; and

(c)   any country or territory <u>other than New Zealand</u> in respect of which there is in force an Order in Council under section 788 of the Income and Corporation Taxes Act 1988 giving effect in the United Kingdom to an agreement which contains provision about—

   (i)   the exchange of information between the parties, and

   (ii)   non-discrimination.

(3) For the purposes of paragraph (2)(c)(ii) an agreement "contains provision about non-discrimination" if it provides that the nationals of a Contracting State shall not be subjected in the territory of the other Contracting State to any taxation, or any requirement connected to such taxation, which is other than, or more burdensome than, the taxation and connected requirements to which the nationals of the other State are or may be subjected in the same circumstances.

~~(4) The requirement is that, at the time of a transfer of sums or assets which would, subject to these Regulations, constitute a recognised transfer, the rules of the scheme must provide that—~~

~~(a)   at least 70% of the sums transferred will be designated by the scheme manager for the purpose of providing the member with an income for life;~~

~~(b)   the pension benefits (and any lump sum associated with those benefits) payable to the member under the scheme, to the extent that they relate to the transfer, are payable no earlier than they would be if pension rule 1 in section 165 applied; and~~

416

Annotated copy showing revisions to SI 2006/206 **Appendix 6**

(c) ~~the scheme is open to persons resident in the country or territory in which it is established.~~

(4) At the time of a transfer of sums or assets which would, subject to these Regulations, constitute a recognised transfer, a pension scheme must satisfy the condition in paragraph (4A) and the rules of that scheme must provide that—

(a) at least 70% of the sums transferred will be designated by the scheme manager for the purpose of providing the member with an income for life;

(b) the pension benefits (and any lump sum associated with those benefits) payable to the member under the scheme, to the extent that they relate to the transfer, are payable no earlier than they would be if pension rule 1 in section 165 applied; and

(c) the scheme is open to persons resident in the country or territory in which it is established.

(4A) Where the pension scheme—

(a) is established in Guernsey, and

(b) is an exempt pension contract or an exempt pension trust within the meaning of section 157E of the Income Tax (Guernsey) Law, 1975 the scheme must not be open to non-residents of Guernsey

(5) At the time of a transfer of sums or assets which would, subject to these Regulations, constitute a recognised transfer the scheme must be of a kind specified in Schedule 2 to these Regulations.

(6) Where tax relief in respect of benefits paid from the scheme is available to a member of the scheme who is not resident in the country or territory in which the scheme is established, the same or substantially the same tax relief must—

(a) also be available to members of the scheme who are resident in the country or territory; and

(b) apply regardless of whether the member was resident in the country or territory—

(i) when the member joined the scheme; or

(ii) or any period of time when they were a member of the scheme.

(7) For the purposes of paragraph (6) "tax relief"—

(a) is any tax relief that is available under the system of taxation of personal income in the country or territory in which the scheme is established; and

(b) includes the grant of an exemption from tax other than an exemption which applies by virtue of double taxation arrangements.

Appendix 6 *Annotated copy showing revisions to SI 2006/206*

(8) In paragraph (7)(b) "double taxation arrangements" means arrangements made between the country or territory in which the scheme is established and another country or territory with a view to affording relief from double taxation.

SCHEDULE 1 Specified Schemes

A complying superannuation plan as defined in section 995-1 (definitions) of the Income Tax Assessment Act 1997 of Australia

(1) The Income Tax Assessment Act 1997 of Australia was amended by the Tax Law Amendment (Simplified Superannuation) Act 2007 of Australia. The terms used in the definition of "complying superannuation plan" are further defined in the Superannuation Industry (Supervision) Act 1993 of Australia and the Retirement Savings Accounts Act 1997 of Australia.

SCHEDULE 2 Specified Schemes

A pension scheme which is a KiwiSaver scheme as defined in section 4(1) (interpretation) of the KiwiSaver Act 2006 of New Zealand.

Index

[*all references are to paragraph numbers and appendices*]

Accounting
  scheme administrator, and, 15.4
  tax reports, and, 7.13
A-Day
  See also **Pre-A-Day tax regime**
  generally, 1.1
  transitional protection, and, 9.1
Additional voluntary contributions (AVCs)
  lump sum benefits, and, 4.17
Administrator of annuities in payment
  reporting, and, 7.8
Alternatively secured pensions (ASPs)
  current position, 4.9
  generally, 4.7
Annual allowance
  employer contributions
    generally, 3.34
    testing against lifetime allowance, 3.35
  member contributions
    exemptions, 3.14
    generally, 3.13
    provision of information, 3.15
  overview, 1.8
Annual allowance charges
  generally, 3.39
  QROPS
    generally, 13.32
    RPSM international pages, 13.34
    section 615 schemes, 13.33
Annuities
  investment rules, and, 5.10
Anti-avoidance
  foreign pensions of UK residents, and, 13.38
Anti-forestalling
  disguised remuneration, and, 11.14
  employer contributions, and, 3.34
Appeals
  decisions, against, 7.20
  scheme de-registration, and, 15.15
Asset-backed pension contributions
  generally, 15.57

Audit requirements
  record keeping, and, 7.16
Authorised employer payments
  generally, 15.29
  introduction, 15.27
Authorised member payments
  generally, 15.28
  introduction, 15.27
Authorised payments
  See also **Benefits**
  charges to tax, and
    employer payments, 15.29
    introduction, 15.27
    member payments, 15.28
  introduction, 4.1
  lump sum death benefit rules, 4.40–4.45
  lump sum rules, 4.16–4.36
  pension death benefit rules, 4.37–4.39
  pension rules, 4.2–4.15

Benefit accrual
  enhanced protection, and, 9.29
  fixed protection, and
    cash balance arrangements, 9.38
    defined benefit arrangements, 9.38
    hybrid arrangements, 9.39
    introduction, 9.36
    money purchase arrangements, 9.37
Benefit crystallisation events
  employer contributions, and, 3.36
  generally, 4.49
  introduction, 4.1
  relevant events, App 10
Benefits
  alternatively secured pensions
    current position, 4.9
    generally, 4.7
  authorised payments
    introduction, 4.1
    lump sum death benefit rules, 4.40–4.45

Index

Benefits – *contd*
  authorised payments – *contd*
    lump sum rules, 4.16–4.36
    pension death benefit rules, 4.37–4.39
    pension rules, 4.2–4.15
  benefit crystallisation events
    generally, 4.49
    introduction, 4.1
    relevant events, App 1
  capped drawdown (from 6 April 2011)
    access, 4.11
    generally, 4.10
    inheritance tax, 4.12
  capped drawdown (from 27 March 2013), 4.13
  capped drawdown (from 27 March 2014), 4.14
  charity lump sum death benefit, 4.45
  children's pensions, 4.39
  collective defined benefit schemes, 4.50
  crystallisation events
    generally, 4.49
    introduction, 4.1
  death benefit rules
    lump sum, 4.40–4.45
    pension, 4.37–4.39
  drawdown pension
    access, 4.12
    background, 4.7–4.10
    conditions, 4.14
    generally, 4.11
    inheritance tax, 4.13
    job shifting, 4.15
  flexible drawdown
    conditions, 11.25
    generally, 11.23
    operation, 11.24
    regulations, 11.26
  funeral grant, 4.44
  introduction, 4.1
  lifetime annuity
    compulsory insurance, 4.6
    generally, 4.5
  lump sum death benefit rules
    charity, 4.45
    defined benefit arrangements, 4.41
    funeral grant, 4.44
    general rules, 4.40
    money purchase arrangements, 4.42
    trivial commutation lump sum, 4.43

Benefits – *contd*
  lump sum rules
    AVCs, 4.17
    block transfers, 4.24
    excessive lump sums, 4.32
    interaction between protected sum and overall limit, 4.27
    overall limit, 4.19–4.20
    payment of protected sums, 4.25
    pension commencement lump sum, 4.16
    protected lump sums, 4.21
    serious ill-health lump sum, 4.30
    short-service refund lump sum, 4.28–4.29
    stand-alone lump sum, 4.26
    trivial commutation lump sum, 4.31
    two or more schemes relating to the same employment, 4.18
    valuing rights at 5 April 2006, 4.22–4.23
  overview, 1.10
  pension ages
    normal minimum pension age, 4.33
    occupational pension schemes, 4.36
    personal pension schemes, 4.35
    protected low retirement age, 4.34
  pension death benefit rules
    children's pensions, 4.39
    general rules, 4.37
    meaning of 'dependant', 4.38
  pension rules
    compulsory insurance, 4.6
    drawdown, 4.7–4.15
    effect of reduction of pension, 4.4
    introduction, 4.2
    lifetime annuity, 4.5–4.6
    scheme pension, 4.3–4.4
  pension sharing
    post-A-Day pension credit, 4.47
    post-A-Day pension debit, 4.48
    pre-A-Day pension debit and credit, 4.46
  scheme pension
    effect of reduction of pension, 4.4
    generally, 4.3
  trivial commutation lump sum
    death benefit rules, 4.43
    general rules, 4.31
  unauthorised payments, 4.1
  unsecured pensions
    current position, 4.8
    generally, 4.7

Index

Benefits in kind
  high earners, and, 14.9
  tax charge, and, 15.56
Block transfers
  lump sum benefits, and, 4.24
Bonus waivers
  generally, 11.20
  observations, 11.22
  requirements, 11.21
Borrowing
  investment rules, and, 5.7

Capped drawdown
  from 6 April 2011
    access, 4.11
    generally, 4.10
    inheritance tax, 4.12
  from 27 March 2013, 4.13
  from 27 March 2014, 4.14
Carry forward provisions
  conditions, 3.21
  generally, 3.20
  timing, 3.22
Cash balance schemes
  rights not yet in payment, and, 9.8
Cash payments
  tax planning, and, 10.2–10.3
Category A, B and C transactions
  investment rules, and, 5.19
Charity lump sum death benefit
  generally, 4.45
Children's pensions
  benefits, and, 4.39
Claim-based relief
  member contributions, and, 3.10
Collective defined benefit schemes
  generally, 4.50
Commencement lump sums
  AVCs, 4.17
  generally, 4.16
  overall limit, 4.19–4.20
  two or more schemes relating to the same employment, 4.18
Compensation payments
  member contributions, and, 3.12
Completion notes
  registration of schemes, and, 2.5
Compliance
  overview, 1.16
Compulsory insurance
  lifetime annuity, and, 4.6
Confidentiality test
  disclosure of tax avoidance schemes, and, 15.25

Contract-based schemes
  tax planning, and, 10.15
Contracting out
  QROPS, and, 13.8
Contributions
  employer contributions
    deductible expenses, 3.25
    deficiency payments, 3.30
    general principles, 3.23
    in specie contributions, 3.32
    investment business employers, 3.26
    levy payments, 3.31
    life assurance company employers, 3.27
    reduced annual allowance, 3.34–3.35
    restrictions on tax relief, 3.33
    salary sacrifice, 3.42
    scheme administrator responsibilities, 3.36–3.37
    spreading rules, 3.28–3.29
  member contributions
    carry forward provisions, 3.20–3.22
    compensation payments, 3.12
    general principles, 3.2
    in specie contributions, 3.4
    life assurance premiums, 3.6
    methods of giving relief, 3.7–3.10
    non-relievable contributions, 3.5
    pension input amounts, 3.19
    pension input periods, 3.16–3.18
    public service pension schemes, 3.11
    reduced annual allowance, 3.13–3.15
    tax relievable contributions, 3.3
  overview, 8.2
  third party contributions, 3.2
Creation of new arrangements
  enhanced protection, and, 9.28
  fixed protection, and, 9.41

Death benefits
  enhanced protection, and
    normal protection, 9.25
    protected life cover, 9.26
  lump sums, and
    charity, 4.45
    defined benefit arrangements, 4.41
    funeral grant, 4.44
    general rules, 4.40
    money purchase arrangements, 4.42
    trivial commutation lump sum, 4.43

421

Index

Death benefits – *contd*
  pensions, and
    children's pensions, 4.39
    general rules, 4.37
    meaning of 'dependant', 4.38
  primary protection, and
    normal protection, 9.18
    protected life cover, 9.19
Debts
  investment rules, and, 5.8
Deductible expenses
  employer contributions, and, 3.25
Default retirement age
  high earners, and, 14.4
Deficiency payments
  employer contributions, and, 3.30
Defined benefit arrangements
  lump sum death benefits, and, 4.41
  valuing pre-A-Day rights, and, 9.9
Dependants
  pension death benefits, and, 4.38
De-registration
  appeals, 15.15
  charge, 15.54
  generally, 15.13
  threshold, 15.14
Discharge from liability
  administrators, and, 7.21
Disclosure of information
  regulations, 7.23
Disclosure of tax avoidance schemes (DOTAS)
  confidentiality test, 15.25
  disguised remuneration, 15.20
  forms
    further notifiable arrangements, 15.23
    pensions, 15.22
    scheme reference numbers, 15.24
  generally, 15.17
  information
    generally, 15.20
    penalties for non-compliance, 15.21
  HMRC audits, 15.26
  HMRC guidance, 15.17
  HMRC visits, 15.26
  non-disclosure, 15.25
  off-market terms test, 15.25
  overview, 8.13
  penalties for non-compliance, 15.21
  premium fee test, 15.25
  prescribed circumstances, 15.18
  prescribed descriptions of arrangements, 15.18

Disclosure of tax avoidance schemes (DOTAS) – *contd*
  promoters, 15.18
  revised regime, 15.19
  scheme reference numbers, 15.24
Disguised remuneration
  anti-forestalling provisions, 11.14
  charging test, 11.12
  disclosure of tax avoidance schemes, and, 15.20
  exemptions from charge, 11.17
  gateway test, 11.18
  generally, 11.10
  meaning, 11.10
  overview, 1.1
  relevant third party, 11.11
  salary sacrifice, and, 3.42
  tax charges, 11.13
  tax credits, 11.15
  terminology, 11.16
Disposals of assets whilst retaining ability to use
  investment rules, and, 5.17
Documentation
  registration of schemes, and, 2.13
Domicile
  QROPS, and, 13.35
DOTAS
  confidentiality test, 15.25
  disguised remuneration, 15.20
  forms
    further notifiable arrangements, 15.23
    pensions, 15.22
    scheme reference numbers, 15.24
  generally, 15.17
  information
    generally, 15.20
    penalties for non-compliance, 15.21
  HMRC audits, 15.26
  HMRC guidance, 15.17
  HMRC visits, 15.26
  non-disclosure, 15.25
  off-market terms test, 15.25
  overview, 8.13
  penalties for non-compliance, 15.21
  premium fee test, 15.25
  prescribed circumstances, 15.18
  prescribed descriptions of arrangements, 15.18
  promoters, 15.18
  revised regime, 15.19
  scheme reference numbers, 15.24

Index

Drawdown pension
background
ASP rules, 4.9
introduction, 4.7
unsecured pension rules, 4.8
capped drawdown (from 6 April 2011)
access, 4.11
generally, 4.10
inheritance tax, 4.12
capped drawdown (from 27 March 2013), 4.13
capped drawdown (from 27 March 2014), 4.14
flexible drawdown
conditions, 11.25
generally, 11.23
operation, 11.24
regulations, 11.26
inheritance tax, 4.12
job shifting, 4.15

EBTs
generally, 11.2
HMRC Spotlight, 11.7
introduction, 15.53

EFPOS
tax planning, and, 10.8

EFRBS
background, 11.3
disguised remuneration, and
anti-forestalling provisions, 11.14
charging test, 11.12
exemptions from charge, 11.17
gateway test, 11.18
generally, 11.10
meaning, 11.10
relevant third party, 11.11
tax charges, 11.13
tax credits, 11.15
terminology, 11.16
funding, 11.6
generally, 11.2
HMRC Spotlights, 11.7–11.8
introduction, 15.53
overview, 1.17
provision of information, 11.4
reporting, and, 7.19
tax reliefs, 11.9

Eligibility
overview, 1.7

Employer asset-backed pension contributions
generally, 15.57

Employer contributions
amount, 3.23
annual allowance
generally, 3.34
testing against lifetime allowance, 3.35
anti-forestalling, 3.34
benefit crystallisation events, and, 3.36
deductible expenses, 3.25
deficiency payments, 3.30
disguised remuneration, and, 3.42
general principles, 3.23
in specie contributions, 3.32
investment businesses, and, 3.26
levy payments, 3.31
life assurance companies, and, 3.27
lifetime allowance, and
examples, 3.37
generally, 3.35
member contributions, and, 3.5
reduced annual allowance, 3.34–3.35
restrictions on tax relief, 3.33
salary sacrifice, 3.42
scheme administrator responsibilities, 3.36–3.37
spreading rules
accounting period, 3.29
generally, 3.28
tax relievable contributions, 3.24
transitional protection, and, 3.34

Employee benefit trusts (EBTs)
generally, 11.2
HMRC Spotlight, 11.7
introduction, 15.53

Employer-financed retirement benefit schemes (EFRBS)
background, 11.3
disguised remuneration, and
anti-forestalling provisions, 11.14
charging test, 11.12
exemptions from charge, 11.17
gateway test, 11.18
generally, 11.10
meaning, 11.10
relevant third party, 11.11
tax charges, 11.13
tax credits, 11.15
terminology, 11.16
funding, 11.6
generally, 11.2
HMRC Spotlights, 11.7–11.8
introduction, 15.53
overview, 1.17

423

Index

Employer-financed retirement benefit schemes (EFRBS) – *contd*
   provision of information, 11.4
   reporting, and, 7.19
   tax reliefs, 11.9
Employer companies
   reporting, and, 7.9
Employer loans
   investment rules, and, 5.5
Employer shares
   investment rules, and, 5.6
Enhanced protection
   background, 9.1
   creation of new arrangements, 9.28
   death benefits
      normal protection, 9.25
      protected life cover, 9.26
   generally, 9.20
   impermissible transfers, 9.30
   introduction, 9.2
   loss of
      impermissible transfers, 9.30
      introduction, 9.28
      permitted transfers, 9.31
      relevant benefit accrual, 9.29
   method, 9.20
   lump sum benefits greater than £375,000, 9.24
   pension benefits, 9.23
   permitted transfers, 9.31
   protected life cover
      defined benefit arrangements, 9.27
      money purchase arrangements, 9.26
   registration, 9.22
   relevant benefit accrual, 9.29
   surrender of relevant excess, 9.21
   tax charges, and, 15.5
   voluntary surrender, 9.28
Enhanced transfer values
   HMRC, 10.4
   introduction, 10.3
   Pensions Regulator, 10.5
Enterprise management incentives (EMIs)
   high earners, and, 14.3
Errors
   pension payment, and, 7.22
Establisher
   registration of schemes, and, 2.2
Excepted group life policies (EGLPs)
   high earners, and, 14.6
Excessive lump sums
   benefits, and, 4.32

Exoneration
   liability of administrators, and, 7.21
Failure to comply with notices
   penalties, and, 15.9
Failure to provide information
   penalties, and, 15.8
Finance Acts
   overview, 1.4
Financial service regulation
   investment rules, and, 5.26
Fixed protection (2012)
   background, 9.32
   benefit accrual
      cash balance arrangements, 9.38
      defined benefit arrangements, 9.38
      hybrid arrangements, 9.39
      introduction, 9.36
      money purchase arrangements, 9.37
   conditions, 9.33
   creation of new arrangements, 9.41
   effect, 9.34
   generally, 9.32–9.43
   impermissible transfers, 9.40
   introduction, 9.2
   life cover, 9.43
   loss of
      benefit accrual, 9.36–9.39
      creation of new arrangements, 9.41
      impermissible transfers, 9.40
      introduction, 9.35
   new arrangements, 9.41
   overview, 9.1
   payment of protected lump sum, 9.42
   tax charges, and, 15.5
   transfers, 9.40
Fixed protection (2014)
   generally, 9.44
Flexible drawdown
   conditions, 11.25
   generally, 11.23
   operation, 11.24
   regulations, 11.26
Forms
   disclosure of tax avoidance schemes, and
      further notifiable arrangements, 15.23
      pensions, 15.22
      scheme reference numbers, 15.24
   QROPS, and, 13.37
   registration of schemes, and, 2.5
Fraudulent statements
   penalties, and, 15.7

424

Fund assets
  investment yield, 3.38
Funded unapproved retirement benefit schemes (FURBS)
  background, 11.3
  generally, 11.2
  rules, 11.5
Funeral grants
  benefits, and, 4.44
Futures-derived income
  investment rules, and, 5.15

General anti-abuse rule
  generally, 15.16
Glossary of terms
  general, App 2
Golden handshakes
  high earners, and, 14.11
Goode Report
  background to pensions regime, 1.3

Hancock annuities
  tax planning, and, 10.8
High earners
  benefits in kind, 14.9
  bonus waivers
    generally, 11.20
    observations, 11.22
    requirements, 11.21
  default retirement age, 14.4
  disguised remuneration, and
    anti-forestalling provisions, 11.14
    charging test, 11.12
    exemptions from charge, 11.17
    gateway test, 11.18
    generally, 11.10
    meaning, 11.10
    relevant third party, 11.11
    tax charges, 11.13
    tax credits, 11.15
    terminology, 11.16
  enhanced protection
    background, 9.1
    creation of new arrangements, 9.28
    death benefits, 9.25–9.27
    generally, 9.20
    impermissible transfers, 9.30
    introduction, 9.2
    loss of, 9.28–9.31
    method, 9.20
    lump sum benefits greater than £375,000, 9.24
    pension benefits, 9.23
    permitted transfers, 9.31

High earners – *contd*
  enhanced protection – *contd*
    protected life cover, 9.26–9.27
    registration, 9.22
    relevant benefit accrual, 9.29
    surrender of relevant excess, 9.21
    voluntary surrender, 9.28
  enterprise management incentives, 14.3
  excepted group life policies, 14.6
  fixed protection (2012)
    background, 9.32
    benefit accrual, 9.36–9.39
    conditions, 9.33
    creation of new arrangements, 9.41
    effect, 9.34
    generally, 9.32–9.43
    impermissible transfers, 9.40
    introduction, 9.2
    life cover, 9.43
    loss of, 9.35–9.41
    new arrangements, 9.41
    overview, 9.1
    payment of protected lump sum, 9.42
    transfers, 9.40
  fixed protection (2014), 9.44
  flexible drawdown
    conditions, 11.25
    generally, 11.23
    operation, 11.24
    regulations, 11.26
  golden handshakes, 14.11
  high income excess relief charge, 9.32
  in specie payments, 14.7
  individual protection (2014), 9.44
  member protection
    background, 9.1
    enhanced protection, 9.20–9.31
    examples from RPSM, 9.4–9.13
    fixed protection (2012), 9.32–9.43
    fixed protection (2014), 9.44
    introduction, 9.2
    primary protection, 9.14–9.19
  new ISAs, 14.8
  overseas schemes, 14.5
  overview, 8.10
  pension term assurance, 14.10
  primary protection
    background, 9.1
    death benefits, 9.18–9.19
    generally, 9.14

Index

High earners – *contd*
  primary protection – *contd*
    introduction, 9.2
    lump sum benefits greater than £375,000, 9.17
    method, 9.14
    pension benefits, 9.16
    protected life cover, 9.19
    registration, 9.15
  registered pension schemes, of
    bonus waivers, 11.20–11.22
    disguised remuneration, 11.10–11.18
    EFRBS, 11.2–11.9
    flexible drawdown, 11.23–11.26
    introduction, 11.1
    unfunded schemes, 11.19
  rights in payment, 9.12
  rights not yet in payment
    cash balance arrangements, 9.8
    defined benefit arrangements, 9.9
    HMRC limits, 9.11
    hybrid arrangements, 9.10
    introduction, 9.6
    money purchase arrangements, 9.7
  RPSM examples
    generally, 9.45
    introduction, 9.4
    lump sum rights, 9.13
    rights in payment, 9.12
    rights not yet in payment, 9.6–9.11
    valuing pre-A-Day rights, 9.5–9.13
  save-as-you-earn schemes, 14.2
  scheme protection
    background, 9.1
    introduction, 9.3
  share incentive plans, 14.2
  tax considerations, 8.10
  transitional protection
    enhanced protection, 9.20–9.31
    examples from RPSM, 9.4–9.13, 9.45
    fixed protection (2012), 9.32–9.43
    fixed protection (2014), 9.44
    introduction, 9.1
    member protection, 9.2
    primary protection, 9.14–9.19
    scheme protection, 9.3
  valuing pre-A-Day rights
    introduction, 9.5
    lump sum rights, 9.13
    rights in payment, 9.12
    rights not yet in payment, 9.6–9.11

High income excess relief charge
  transitional protection, and, 9.32
HMRC audits
  disclosure of tax avoidance schemes, and, 15.26
HMRC guidance
  disclosure of tax avoidance schemes, and, 15.17
HMRC Registered Pension Schemes Manual
  examples, 9.45
  overview, 1.19
  tax reliefs, and, 3.1
  transitional protection, and
    generally, 9.45
    introduction, 9.4
    lump sum rights, 9.13
    rights in payment, 9.12
    rights not yet in payment, 9.6–9.11
    valuing pre-A-Day rights, 9.5–9.13
HMRC/Treasury Simplification Team reports
  background to pensions regime, 1.3
HMRC visits
  disclosure of tax avoidance schemes, and, 15.26
Hybrid arrangements
  valuing pre-A-Day rights, and, 9.10

In specie contributions
  employer contributions, and, 3.32
  high earners, and, 14.7
  member contributions, and, 3.4
Incentive payments
  HMRC, 10.4
  introduction, 10.3
  Pensions Regulator, 10.5
Increases in benefits
  tax planning, and, 10.10
Individual savings account (ISAs)
  high earners, and, 14.8
Inheritance tax
  drawdown pension, and, 4.13
  overview, 8.6
  tax planning, and, 10.6
Insurance company
  reporting to personal representative on death, and, 7.10
Investment businesses
  employer contributions, and, 3.26
Investment-regulated pension schemes (IRPS)
  acquisitions, 12.8
  direct holding of taxable property, 12.9

Index

Investment-regulated pension schemes (IRPS) – *contd*
generally, 12.1
genuinely diverse commercial vehicles, 12.12
holding of taxable property
  direct, 12.9
  indirect, 12.10
  introduction, 12.7
indirect holding of taxable property, 12.10
'interest', 12.11
meaning, 12.4
other diverse property vehicle4s, 12.13
REITs, 12.6
residential property, 12.5
scheme sanction charge, 12.3
taxable property, 12.2, 15.52
taxable property charges, 12.3
unauthorised payment charge, 12.3
Investment rules
annuities, 5.10
borrowing, 5.7
category A, B and C transactions, 5.19
debts, 5.8
disposals of assets whilst retaining ability to use, 5.17
employer loans, 5.5
employer shares, 5.6
financial service regulation, 5.26
futures and options-derived income, 5.15
introduction, 5.1
IORPS Directive (2003/41/EC), 5.2
land and buildings, 5.2
liquidity, 5.18
loans
  employers, to, 5.5
  members, to, 5.3
  third parties, to, 5.4
market value, 5.20
member loans, 5.3
member use of assets, 5.22
non-commercial use of assets by member or associate, 5.12
non-income producing assets, 5.23
occupational pension schemes, 5.2
overview, 1.12
Pension Regulator's DC Code, 5.27
permitted transactions, 5.2
property investment limited liability partnerships, 5.14
QROPS, and, 13.4
quoted shares, 5.2

Investment rules – *contd*
residential property, 5.16
shares, 5.2
stock-lending fees, 5.15
tax considerations, 8.5
third party investments, 5.9
trading income, 5.11
underwriting commissions, 5.13
value shifting, 5.21
waivers of debt, 5.24
wasting assets, 5.25
IORPS Directive (2003/41/EC)
generally, 13.9
introduction, 13.1
investment rules, and, 5.2
transfers, and, 6.1

Job shifting
drawdown pension, and, 4.15

Land and buildings
investment rules, and, 5.2
Levy payments
employer contributions, and, 3.31
Life assurance companies
employer contributions, and, 3.27
Life assurance premiums
member contributions, and, 3.6
Life insurance
enhanced protection, and
  defined benefit arrangements, 9.27
  money purchase arrangements, 9.26
fixed protection, and, 9.43
primary protection, and, 9.19
Lifetime allowance
employer contributions, and
  examples, 3.37
  generally, 3.35
overview, 1.8
transfers, and, 6.2
Lifetime allowance charge
generally, 3.41
QROPS
  generally, 13.32
  RPSM international pages, 13.34
  section 615 schemes, 13.33
Lifetime annuity
compulsory insurance, 4.6
generally, 4.5
Liquidity
investment rules, and, 5.18
Loans
employers, to, 5.5
members, to, 5.3

Index

Loans – *contd*
  tax planning, and, 10.11
  third parties, to, 5.4
Lump sum death benefits
  charity, 4.45
  defined benefit arrangements, 4.41
  funeral grant, 4.44
  general rules, 4.40
  money purchase arrangements, 4.42
  trivial commutation lump sum, 4.43
Lump sums
  AVCs, from, 4.17
  block transfers, 4.24
  commencement lump sum
    AVCs, 4.17
    generally, 4.16
    overall limit, 4.19–4.20
    two or more schemes relating to the same employment, 4.18
  enhanced protection, and, 9.24
  excessive lump sums, 4.32
  interaction between protected sum and overall limit, 4.27
  overall limit
    amendments effective from 6 April 2011, 4.20
    generally, 4.19
  overview, 8.4
  pension commencement lump sum
    AVCs, 4.17
    generally, 4.16
    overall limit, 4.19–4.20
    two or more schemes relating to the same employment, 4.18
  primary protection, and, 9.17
  protected lump sums
    block transfers, 4.24
    excessive lump sums, 4.32
    generally, 4.21
    interaction with overall limit, 4.27
    payment, 4.25
    scheme administration member payment, 4.29
    serious ill-health lump sum, 4.30
    short service refund lump sum, 4.28
    trivial commutation lump sum, 4.31
    valuing rights at 5 April 2006, 4.22–4.23
  serious ill-health lump sum, 4.30
  short-service refund lump sum, 4.28–4.29
  stand-alone lump sum, 4.26
  trivial commutation lump sum, 4.31

Lump sums – *contd*
  two or more schemes relating to the same employment, 4.18
  transitional protection, and
    enhanced protection, 9.24
    primary protection, 9.17
  valuing rights at 5 April 2006
    generally, 4.22
    two or more schemes relating to the same employment, 4.23

Maintenance of schemes
  forms and completion notes, 2.6
Market value
  investment rules, and, 5.20
Master trusts
  tax planning, and, 10.14
Member contributions
  annual allowance
    exemptions, 3.14
    generally, 3.13
    provision of information, 3.15
  carry forward provisions
    conditions, 3.21
    generally, 3.20
    timing, 3.22
  claim-based relief, 3.10
  compensation payments, 3.12
  employer contributions, and, 3.5
  general principles, 3.2
  in specie contributions, 3.4
  life assurance premiums, 3.6
  methods of giving relief
    claim-based, 3.10
    introduction, 3.7
    net pay arrangement, 3.9
    relief at source, 3.8
  net pay arrangements, 3.9
  non-relievable contributions
    employer contributions, 3.5
    generally, 3.5
    life assurance premiums, 3.6
  pension credit rights, and, 3.2
  pension input amounts, 3.19
  pension input periods
    changing end dates, 3.17
    generally, 3.16
    transitional, 3.18
  public service pension schemes, 3.11
  relevant UK earnings, 3.3
  'relievable pension contribution', 3.9
  relief at source, 3.8
  SAYE option scheme shares, and, 3.2
  share incentive scheme shares, and, 3.2

Member contributions – *contd*
　tax relievable contributions, 3.3
　transfer of shares, and, 3.2
Member control over assets
　registration of schemes, and, 2.2
Member loans
　investment rules, and, 5.3
Member payment charges
　generally, 13.30
Member protection
　background, 9.1
　enhanced protection
　　background, 9.1
　　creation of new arrangements, 9.28
　　death benefits, 9.25–9.27
　　generally, 9.20
　　impermissible transfers, 9.30
　　introduction, 9.2
　　loss of, 9.28–9.31
　　method, 9.20
　　lump sum benefits greater than £375,000, 9.24
　　pension benefits, 9.23
　　permitted transfers, 9.31
　　protected life cover, 9.26–9.27
　　registration, 9.22
　　relevant benefit accrual, 9.29
　　surrender of relevant excess, 9.21
　　voluntary surrender, 9.28
　examples from RPSM
　　generally, 9.45
　　introduction, 9.4
　　lump sum rights, 9.13
　　rights in payment, 9.12
　　rights not yet in payment, 9.6–9.11
　　valuing pre-A-Day rights, 9.5–9.13
　fixed protection (2012)
　　background, 9.32
　　benefit accrual, 9.36–9.39
　　conditions, 9.33
　　creation of new arrangements, 9.41
　　effect, 9.34
　　generally, 9.32–9.43
　　impermissible transfers, 9.40
　　introduction, 9.2
　　life cover, 9.43
　　loss of, 9.35–9.41
　　new arrangements, 9.41
　　overview, 9.1
　　payment of protected lump sum, 9.42
　　transfers, 9.40
　fixed protection (2014), 9.44
　individual protection (2014), 9.44

Member protection – *contd*
　introduction, 9.2
　overview, 9.1
　primary protection
　　background, 9.1
　　death benefits, 9.18–9.19
　　generally, 9.14
　　introduction, 9.2
　　lump sum benefits greater than £375,000, 9.17
　　method, 9.14
　　pension benefits, 9.16
　　protected life cover, 9.19
　　registration, 9.15
　　rights in payment, 9.12
　　rights not yet in payment
　　　cash balance arrangements, 9.8
　　　defined benefit arrangements, 9.9
　　　HMRC limits, 9.11
　　　hybrid arrangements, 9.10
　　　introduction, 9.6
　　　money purchase arrangements, 9.7
　　RPSM examples
　　　generally, 9.45
　　　introduction, 9.4
　　　lump sum rights, 9.13
　　　rights in payment, 9.12
　　　rights not yet in payment, 9.6–9.11
　　　valuing pre-A-Day rights, 9.5–9.13
　　valuing pre-A-Day rights
　　　introduction, 9.5
　　　lump sum rights, 9.13
　　　rights in payment, 9.12
　　　rights not yet in payment, 9.6–9.11
Member use of assets
　investment rules, and, 5.22
Membership
　registration of schemes, and, 2.17
Migrant member relief
　eligibility, 13.14
　employer contributions, 13.21
　HMRC Guide, 13.16
　introduction, 13.12
　qualifying overseas pension schemes (QOPS), 13.15
　recognised overseas pension schemes (ROPS), 13.17–13.19
　relevant migrant member, 13.13
　residency, 13.20
　unauthorised payments, 13.20
Misdirection of transfer payments
　penalties, and, 15.10
Modification powers
　registration of schemes, and, 2.14

Index

Money purchase arrangements
  lump sum death benefits, and, 4.42
  valuing pre-A-Day rights, and, 9.7
Myners Report
  background to pensions regime, 1.3

National insurance contributions (NIC)
  overview, 8.2
Negligent statements
  penalties, and, 15.7
Net pay arrangements
  member contributions, and, 3.9
New ISAs
  high earners, and, 14.8
Non-commercial use of assets by member or associate
  investment rules, and, 5.12
Non-compliance penalties
  failure to comply with notices, 15.9
  failure to provide information, 15.8
  fraudulent statements, 15.7
  main principles, 15.6
  misdirection of transfer payments, 15.10
  negligent statements, 15.7
  pension liberation, 15.12
  trust-busting, 15.12
  winding up lump sums, 15.11
Non-income producing assets
  investment rules, and, 5.23
Non-registered schemes
  overview, 1.17
Non-relievable contributions
  employer contributions, 3.5
  generally, 3.5
  life assurance premiums, 3.6
Non-resident trusts
  QROPS, and, 13.35
Non-UK based scheme
  registration of schemes, and, 2.12
Notification of changes
  registration of schemes, and, 2.15

Occupational pension schemes
  investment rules, and, 5.2
  pension age, and, 4.36
Off-market terms test
  disclosure of tax avoidance schemes, and, 15.25
Online applications
  registration of schemes, and, 2.1

Opting out
  registration of schemes, and effect, 2.9
  generally, 2.8
Options-derived income
  investment rules, and, 5.15
Outline reporting
  record keeping, and, 7.15
Overseas issues
  anti-avoidance, 13.38
  contracting out, 13.8
  development of tax and pension rules, 13.2
  domicile, 13.35
  forms, 13.37
  high earners, and, 14.5
  HMRC draft guidance, App 4
  introduction, 13.1
  investment regulations, 13.4
  IORPS Directive (2003/41/EC)
    generally, 13.9
    introduction, 13.1
  migrant member relief
    eligibility, 13.14
    employer contributions, 13.21
    HMRC Guide, 13.16
    introduction, 13.12
    qualifying overseas pension schemes (QOPS), 13.15
    recognised overseas pension schemes (ROPS), 13.17–13.19
    relevant migrant member, 13.13
    residency, 13.20
    unauthorised payments, 13.20
  new regulations, 13.36
  non-resident trusts, 13.35
  overview, 1.18
  Pensions Acts
    cross-border provision, 13.7
    introduction, 13.6
  Portability Directive, 13.10
  protected rights transfer payment regulations, 13.8
  reporting requirements
    administrator's undertaking to HMRC, 13.24
    generally, 13.22
    manager's undertaking to HMRC, 13.24
    reportable events, 13.23
  residence, 13.35
  tax charges, penalties and sanctions
    annual allowance charge, 13.32–13.34

Overseas issues – *contd*
  tax charges, penalties and sanctions – *contd*
    generally, 13.29
    lifetime allowance charge, 13.32–13.34
    member payment charges, 13.30
    overview, 15.58
    timing, 13.31
  tax considerations, 8.11
  tax discrimination warnings, 13.11
  transfers
    inheritance tax, 13.26
    member payment, 13.26
    pensions in payment, of, 13.28
    reporting payments, 13.25
    rights to payment of drawdown pension, to, 13.27
    rights where there is already an entitlement to benefits, of, 13.28
  trust and retirement benefits regulations, 13.5
  UK tax law, 13.3

Payments in error
  reporting, and, 7.22

Penalties
  non-compliance by registered schemes, for
    failure to comply with notices, 15.9
    failure to provide information, 15.8
    fraudulent statements, 15.7
    main principles, 15.6
    misdirection of transfer payments, 15.10
    negligent statements, 15.7
    pension liberation, 15.12
    trust-busting, 15.12
    winding up lump sums, 15.11
  sources, 15.2
  subject list, 15.3

Pension ages
  normal minimum pension age, 4.33
  occupational pension schemes, 4.36
  personal pension schemes, 4.35
  protected low retirement age, 4.34

Pension benefits
  capped drawdown (from 6 April 2011)
    access, 4.11
    generally, 4.10
    inheritance tax, 4.12
  capped drawdown (from 27 March 2013), 4.13

Pension benefits – *contd*
  capped drawdown (from 27 March 2014), 4.14
  compulsory insurance, 4.6
  drawdown pension
    background, 4.7–4.9
    capped drawdown (from 6 April 2011), 4.10–4.12
    capped drawdown (from 27 March 2013), 4.13
    capped drawdown (from 27 March 2014), 4.14
    flexible drawdown, 11.23–11.26
    job shifting, 4.15
  effect of reduction of pension, 4.4
  enhanced protection, and, 9.23
  flexible drawdown
    conditions, 11.25
    generally, 11.23
    operation, 11.24
    regulations, 11.26
  introduction, 4.2
  lifetime annuity
    compulsory insurance, 4.6
    generally, 4.5
  primary protection, and, 9.16
  reduction of pension, 4.4
  scheme pension
    effect of reduction of pension, 4.4
    generally, 4.3
  transitional protection, and
    enhanced protection, 9.23
    primary protection, 9.16
  unsecured pensions
    current position, 4.8
    generally, 4.7

Pension commencement lump sums
  AVCs, 4.17
  generally, 4.16
  overall limit, 4.19–4.20
  two or more schemes relating to the same employment, 4.18

Pension credit rights
  member contributions, and, 3.2

Pension death benefits
  children's pensions, 4.39
  general rules, 4.37
  meaning of 'dependant', 4.38

Pension input amounts
  member contributions, and, 3.19

Pension input periods
  changing end dates, 3.17
  generally, 3.16
  transitional, 3.18

Index

Pension liberation
penalties, and, 15.12
Pension Scheme Tax Reference (PSTR)
registration of schemes, and, 2.1
Pension sharing
post-A-Day pension credit, 4.47
post-A-Day pension debit, 4.48
pre-A-Day pension debit and credit, 4.46
Pension term assurance
high earners, and, 14.10
Pensions regime
A-Day, 1.1
annual allowance, 1.8
background, 1.2–1.3
benefits, 1.10
compliance, 1.16
disguised remuneration, 1.1
EFRBS , 1.17
eligibility, 1.7
Finance Acts, 1.4
HMRC Registered Pension Schemes Manual, 1.19
introduction, 1.1
investments, 1.12
legislation
  Finance Acts, 1.4
  Tax Law Rewrites, 1.5
lifetime allowance, 1.8
non-registered schemes, 1.17
overseas issues, 1.18
registration, 1.14
reporting, 1.15
self-assessment, 1.15
summary, 1.6–1.19
Tax Law Rewrites, 1.5
tax relievable allowances, 1.8
transferability of member rights, 1.11
transitional protection, 1.13
unauthorised member payments, 1.16
Pensions Regulator
codes of practice, and, 3.43
investment rules, and, 5.27
registration of schemes, and, 2.2
Personal pension schemes
pension age, and, 4.35
Personal representatives
reporting, and, 7.11
Pickering Report
background to pensions regime, 1.3
Portability Directive (draft)
QROPS, and, 13.10
transfers, and, 6.1

Pre-A-Day tax regime
main features, App 3
pension sharing, 4.46
valuing rights
  introduction, 9.5
  lump sum rights, 9.13
  rights in payment, 9.12
  rights not yet in payment, 9.6–9.11
Premium fee test
disclosure of tax avoidance schemes, and, 15.25
Primary protection
background, 9.1
death benefits
  normal protection, 9.18
  protected life cover, 9.19
generally, 9.14
introduction, 9.2
lump sum benefits greater than £375,000, 9.17
method, 9.14
pension benefits, 9.16
protected life cover, 9.19
registration, 9.15
Promoters
disclosure of tax avoidance schemes, and, 15.18
Property investment limited liability partnerships
investment rules, and, 5.14
Protected lump sums
block transfers, 4.24
excessive lump sums, 4.32
generally, 4.21
interaction with overall limit, 4.27
payment, 4.25
scheme administration member payment, 4.29
serious ill-health lump sum, 4.30
short service refund lump sum, 4.28
trivial commutation lump sum, 4.31
valuing rights at 5 April 2006, 4.22–4.23
Protected rights transfer payment regulations
QROPS, and, 13.8
Providers
registration of schemes, and, 2.16
Public service pension schemes
member contributions, and, 3.11

Qualifying recognised overseas pension schemes (QROPS)
contracting out, 13.8

Index

Qualifying recognised overseas pension schemes (QROPS) – *contd*
development of tax and pension rules, 13.2
domicile, 13.35
forms, 13.37
HMRC draft guidance, App 4
introduction, 13.1
investment regulations, 13.4
IORPS Directive (2003/41/EC)
 generally, 13.9
 introduction, 13.1
migrant member relief
 eligibility, 13.14
 employer contributions, 13.21
 HMRC Guide, 13.16
 introduction, 13.12
 qualifying overseas pension schemes (QOPS), 13.15
 recognised overseas pension schemes (ROPS), 13.17–13.19
 relevant migrant member, 13.13
 residency, 13.20
 unauthorised payments, 13.20
new regulations, 13.36
non-resident trusts, 13.35
overview, 1.18
Pensions Acts
 cross-border provision, 13.7
 introduction, 13.6
Portability Directive, 13.10
protected rights transfer payment regulations, 13.8
reporting requirements
 administrator's undertaking to HMRC, 13.24
 generally, 13.22
 manager's undertaking to HMRC, 13.24
 reportable events, 13.23
residence, 13.35
tax charges, penalties and sanctions
 annual allowance charge, 13.32–13.34
 generally, 13.29
 lifetime allowance charge, 13.32–13.34
 member payment charges, 13.30
 timing, 13.31
tax discrimination warnings, 13.11
transfers
 inheritance tax, 13.26
 member payment, 13.26
 pensions in payment, of, 13.28

Qualifying recognised overseas pension schemes (QROPS) – *contd*
transfers – *contd*
 reporting payments, 13.25
 rights to payment of drawdown pension, to, 13.27
 rights where there is already an entitlement to benefits, of, 13.28
trust and retirement benefits regulations, 13.5
UK tax law, 13.3
Quoted shares
investment rules, and, 5.2

Real estate investment trusts (REITs)
tax planning, and, 12.6
Reallocations of funds or entitlements to benefits
tax planning, and, 10.13
Record keeping
accounting for tax reports, 7.13
audit requirements, 7.16
introduction, 7.12
outline reporting, 7.15
registered pension scheme return, 7.14
Recycling tax-free lump sums
tax planning, and, 10.7, 15.55
Registered Pension Schemes Manual (RPSM)
overview, 1.19
scheme protection, and, 9.45
tax reliefs, and, 3.1
transitional protection, and
 introduction, 9.4
 lump sum rights, 9.13
 rights in payment, 9.12
 rights not yet in payment, 9.6–9.11
 scheme protection, 9.45
 valuing pre-A-Day rights, 9.5–9.13
Registered pension scheme return
record keeping, and, 7.14
Registration of pension schemes
adhering companies, 2.18
applications, 2.5
completion notes, 2.5
core information, 2.2
documentation, 2.13
establisher, 2.2
forms, 2.5
introduction, 2.1
legal structure, 2.2
loss of approval before 6 April 2006, 2.11

Index

Registration of pension schemes – *contd*
member control over assets, 2.2
membership, 2.17
modification powers, 2.14
non-UK based scheme, 2.12
notification of changes, 2.15
online applications, 2.1
opting out
  effect, 2.9
  generally, 2.8
overview, 1.14
Pension Scheme Tax Reference (PSTR), 2.1
Pensions Regulator, with, 2.2
providers, 2.16
rejection, 2.7
relief at source (RAS), 2.2
scheme administrator
  generally, 2.3
  introduction, 2.2
scheme documentation, 2.13
scheme practitioner, 2.4
stakeholder plans, 2.2
state second pension (S2P), and, 2.2
withdrawal, 2.10

Relevant benefit accrual
enhanced protection, and, 9.29
fixed protection, and
  cash balance arrangements, 9.38
  defined benefit arrangements, 9.38
  hybrid arrangements, 9.39
  introduction, 9.36
  money purchase arrangements, 9.37

Relief at source (RAS)
registration of schemes, and, 2.2

'Relievable pension contribution'
member contributions, and, 3.9

Reporting
accounting for tax reports, 7.13
administrator of annuities in payment, by, 7.8
administrator, by
  administrator, to, 7.6
  HMRC, to, 7.3
  member, to, 7.4
  personal representative, to, 7.7
appealing against decisions, 7.20
audit requirements, 7.16
discharge of administrators from liability, 7.21
disclosure of information regulation, 7.23
EFRBS, 7.19

Reporting – *contd*
employer company, by, 7.9
errors in payment, 7.22
event reports
  administrator of annuities in payment, by, 7.8
  administrator to administrator, by, 7.6
  administrator to HMRC, by, 7.3
  administrator to member, by, 7.4
  administrator to personal representative, by, 7.7
  employer company, by, 7.9
  insurance company to personal representative on death, by, 7.10
  member to administrator, by, 7.5
  personal representative to HMRC, by, 7.11
exoneration of administrators, 7.21
insurance company to personal representative on death, by, 7.10
introduction, 7.1
legislative provision, 7.2
member to administrator, by, 7.5
outline reporting, 7.15
overview, 1.15
payments in error, 7.22
personal representative to HMRC, by, 7.11
QROPS, and
  administrator's undertaking to HMRC, 13.24
  generally, 13.22
  manager's undertaking to HMRC, 13.24
  reportable events, 13.23
record keeping
  accounting for tax reports, 7.13
  audit requirements, 7.16
  introduction, 7.12
  outline reporting, 7.15
  registered pension scheme return, 7.14
registered pension scheme return, 7.14
self-assessment
  members, by, 7.18
  pension schemes, by, 7.17
tax avoidance, 7.24
transfers, and, 6.9

Residence
QROPS, and, 13.35

Residential property
investment rules, and, 5.16

Rights in payment
generally, 9.12
Rights not yet in payment
cash balance arrangements, 9.8
defined benefit arrangements, 9.9
HMRC limits, 9.11
hybrid arrangements, 9.10
introduction, 9.6
money purchase arrangements, 9.7

Salary sacrifice
generally, 3.42
Sandler Review
background to pensions regime, 1.3
Save-as-you-earn schemes
high earners, and, 14.2
SAYE option scheme shares
member contributions, and, 3.2
Scheme administration payments
tax planning, and, 10.12
Scheme administrator
employer contributions, and, 3.36–3.37
registration of schemes, and
generally, 2.3
introduction, 2.2
reporting, and
administrator, to, 7.6
annuities in payment, of, 7.8
HMRC, to, 7.3
member, to, 7.4
personal representative, to, 7.7
Scheme de-registration
appeals, 15.15
charge, 15.54
generally, 15.13
threshold, 15.14
Scheme documentation
registration of schemes, and, 2.13
Scheme pension
effect of reduction of pension, 4.4
generally, 4.4
tax planning, and, 10.9
Scheme practitioner
registration of schemes, and, 2.4
Scheme protection
background, 9.1
introduction, 9.3
Scheme reference numbers
disclosure of tax avoidance schemes, and, 15.24
Scheme sanction charge
generally, 15.45
introduction, 15.39

Scheme sanction charge – *contd*
payments excluded, 15.47
payments which attract, 15.46
reduction, 15.49
release of scheme administrator from liability, 15.50
relief, 15.48
surplus repayments, 15.51
Self-assessment
members, by, 7.18
overview, 1.15
pension schemes, by, 7.17
Serious ill-health lump sum
benefits, and, 4.30
Share incentive plans (SIPs)
high earners, and, 14.2
Share incentive scheme shares
member contributions, and, 3.2
Shares
investment rules, and, 5.2
Short-service refund lump sum
benefits, and, 4.28–4.29
Special annual allowance charge
generally, 3.40
Spreading rules
accounting period, 3.29
generally, 3.28
Stakeholder plans
registration of schemes, and, 2.2
Stand-alone lump sum
benefits, and, 4.26
State second pension (S2P)
registration of schemes, and, 2.2
Stock-lending fees
investment rules, and, 5.15
Surrender of relevant excess
enhanced protection, and, 9.21

Tax avoidance
reporting, and, 7.24
Tax charges
annual allowance charge, 3.39
authorised payments, and
employer payments, 15.29
introduction, 15.27
member payments, 15.28
benefits in kind, on, 15.56
contributions, and
annual allowance charge, 3.39
lifetime allowance charge, 3.41
special annual allowance charge, 3.40
disguised remuneration, and, 11.13
introduction, 15.1

Index

Tax charges – *contd*
　lifetime allowance charge, 3.41
　overview, 8.13
　QROPS, and
　　annual allowance charge, 13.32–13.34
　　generally, 13.29
　　lifetime allowance charge, 13.32–13.34
　　member payment charges, 13.30
　　overview, 15.58
　　timing, 13.31
　scheme sanction charge
　　generally, 15.45
　　introduction, 15.39
　　payments excluded, 15.47
　　payments which attract, 15.46
　　reduction, 15.49
　　release of scheme administrator from liability, 15.50
　　relief, 15.48
　　surplus repayments, 15.51
　sources, 15.2
　special annual allowance charge, 3.40
　subject list, 15.3
　unauthorised payments
　　actual unauthorised member payments, 15.32
　　assignment of benefits and rights, 15.33
　　charge, 15.40
　　deemed unauthorised member payments, 15.32
　　generally, 15.30
　　increase in member's benefits beyond the statutory limit, 15.36
　　increase in rights of connected person on death, 15.35
　　member use of assets, 15.37
　　'payments', 15.31
　　relevant charges, 15.39–15.51
　　scheme sanction charge, 15.45–15.51
　　surcharge, 15.41–15.44
　　surrender of benefits and rights, 15.34
　　types, 15.30
　　value-shifting, 15.38
　unauthorised payments charge
　　declaration of liability, 15.44
　　generally, 15.40
　　introduction, 15.39

Tax charges – *contd*
　unauthorised payments surcharge
　　declaration of liability, 15.44
　　discharge, 15.43
　　generally, 15.41
　　introduction, 15.39
　　period for measuring the threshold, 15.42
　VAT, 3.44
Tax credits
　disguised remuneration, and, 11.15
Tax discrimination
　QROPS, and, 13.11
Tax Law Rewrites
　overview, 1.5
Tax planning
　See also **High earners**
　cash payments, 10.2–10.3
　considerations
　　contributions, 8.2
　　DOTAS, 8.13
　　high earners, 8.10
　　income tax, 8.2
　　inheritance tax, 8.6
　　introduction, 8.1
　　investments, 8.5
　　lump sums, 8.4
　　NICs, 8.2
　　other forms of savings, 8.12
　　overseas issues, 8.11
　　pensions, 8.3
　　tax charges, 8.13
　　transitional protections, 8.7
　contract-based schemes, 10.15
　EFPOS, 10.8
　Hancock annuities, 10.8
　incentive payments
　　HMRC, 10.4
　　introduction, 10.3
　　Pensions Regulator, 10.5
　increases in benefits, 10.10
　inheritance tax, 10.6
　introduction, 10.1
　investment-regulated pension schemes (IRPS)
　　acquisitions, 12.8
　　direct holding of taxable property, 12.9
　　generally, 12.1
　　genuinely diverse commercial vehicles, 12.12
　　holding of taxable property, 12.9–12.10

436

Index

Tax planning – *contd*
  investment-regulated pension schemes (IRPS) – *contd*
    indirect holding of taxable property, 12.10
    'interest', 12.11
    meaning, 12.4
    other diverse property vehicle4s, 12.13
    REITs, 12.6
    residential property, 12.5
    scheme sanction charge, 12.3
    taxable property, 12.2, 15.52
    taxable property charges, 12.3
    unauthorised payment charge, 12.3
  loans, 10.11
  master trusts, 10.14
  real estate investment trusts (REITs), 12.6
  reallocations of funds or entitlements to benefits, 10.13
  recycling tax-free lump sums, 10.7
  scheme administration payments, 10.12
  scheme pensions, 10.9
  transitional protection
    enhanced protection, 9.20–9.31
    examples from RPSM, 9.4–9.13, 9.45
    fixed protection (2012), 9.32–9.43
    fixed protection (2014), 9.44
    introduction, 9.1
    member protection, 9.2
    primary protection, 9.14–9.19
    scheme protection, 9.3

Tax reliefs
  annual allowance (employer contributions)
    generally, 3.34
    testing against lifetime allowance, 3.35
  annual allowance (member contributions)
    exemptions, 3.14
    generally, 3.13
    provision of information, 3.15
  carry forward provisions
    conditions, 3.21
    generally, 3.20
    timing, 3.22
  claim-based method, 3.10
  compensation payments, 3.12
  deficiency payments, 3.30

Tax reliefs – *contd*
  employer contributions
    deductible expenses, 3.25
    deficiency payments, 3.30
    general principles, 3.23
    in specie contributions, 3.32
    investment business employers, 3.26
    levy payments, 3.31
    life assurance company employers, 3.27
    reduced annual allowance, 3.34–3.35
    restrictions on tax relief, 3.33
    salary sacrifice, 3.42
    scheme administrator responsibilities, 3.36–3.37
    spreading rules, 3.28–3.29
    tax relievable contributions, 3.24
  fund assets and yield, 3.38
  in specie contributions
    employer contributions, 3.32
    member contributions, 3.4
  introduction, 3.1
  investment business employers, 3.26
  levy payments, 3.31
  life assurance company employers, 3.27
  life assurance premiums, 3.6
  member contributions
    carry forward provisions, 3.20–3.22
    compensation payments, 3.12
    general principles, 3.2
    in specie contributions, 3.4
    life assurance premiums, 3.6
    methods of giving relief, 3.7–3.10
    non-relievable contributions, 3.5
    pension input amounts, 3.19
    pension input periods, 3.16–3.18
    public service pension schemes, 3.11
    reduced annual allowance, 3.13–3.15
    tax relievable contributions, 3.3
  methods of giving
    claim-based, 3.10
    introduction, 3.7
    net pay arrangement, 3.9
    relief at source, 3.8
  net pay arrangement, 3.9
  non-relievable contributions, 3.5
  overview, 1.8
  pension input amounts, 3.19

437

Index

Tax reliefs – *contd*
  pension input periods
    changing end dates, 3.17
    generally, 3.16
    transitional, 3.18
  public service pension schemes, 3.11
  reduced annual allowance (employer contributions)
    generally, 3.34
    testing against lifetime allowance, 3.35
  reduced annual allowance (member contributions)
    exemptions, 3.14
    generally, 3.13
    provision of information, 3.15
  refunds to employer, and, 3.45
  relief at source, 3.8
  relievable contributions, 3.3
  retirement annuity contracts, 3.10
  salary sacrifice, 3.42
  scheme administrator responsibilities
    generally, 3.36
    lifetime allowance example, 3.37
  spreading rules
    accounting period, 3.29
    generally, 3.28
  tax relievable contributions
    employer contributions, 3.24
    member contributions, 3.3
    third party contributions, 3.2
Third party investments
  investment rules, and, 5.9
Trading income
  investment rules, and, 5.115
Transfer of shares
  member contributions, and, 3.2
Transfers
  introduction, 6.1
  lifetime allowance, and, 6.2
  loss of protection, 6.6
  non-registered pension schemes, from, 6.5
  non-registered pension schemes, to, 6.4
  overview, 1.11
  payment, in, 6.7
  permitted transfers, 6.2
  QROPS, and
    inheritance tax, 13.26
    member payment, 13.26
    pensions in payment, of, 13.28
    reporting payments, 13.25

Transfers – *contd*
  QROPS, and – *contd*
    rights to payment of drawdown pension, to, 13.27
    rights where there is already an entitlement to benefits, of, 13.28
  'recognised transfer', 6.2
  registered pension schemes, between, 6.3
  registered pension schemes, from, 6.4
  registered pension schemes, to, 6.5
  reporting to HMRC, 6.9
  requirement to receive, 6.8
  response time to request for confirmation of status of receiving scheme, 6.10
Transitional protection
  employer contributions, and, 3.34
  enhanced protection
    background, 9.1
    creation of new arrangements, 9.28
    death benefits, 9.25–9.27
    generally, 9.20
    impermissible transfers, 9.30
    introduction, 9.2
    loss of, 9.28–9.31
    method, 9.20
    lump sum benefits greater than £375,000, 9.24
    pension benefits, 9.23
    permitted transfers, 9.31
    protected life cover, 9.26–9.27
    registration, 9.22
    relevant benefit accrual, 9.29
    surrender of relevant excess, 9.21
    voluntary surrender, 9.28
  fixed protection (2012)
    background, 9.32
    benefit accrual, 9.36–9.39
    conditions, 9.33
    creation of new arrangements, 9.41
    effect, 9.34
    generally, 9.32–9.43
    impermissible transfers, 9.40
    introduction, 9.2
    life cover, 9.43
    loss of, 9.35–9.41
    new arrangements, 9.41
    overview, 9.1
    payment of protected lump sum, 9.42
    transfers, 9.40
  fixed protection (2014), 9.44

438

Index

Transitional protection – *contd*
individual protection (2014), 9.44
introduction, 9.1
lump sum rights, 9.13
member protection
  background, 9.1
  enhanced protection, 9.20–9.31
  examples from RPSM, 9.4–9.13
  fixed protection (2012), 9.32–9.43
  fixed protection (2014), 9.44
  individual protection (2014), 9.44
  introduction, 9.2
  primary protection, 9.14–9.19
overview, 1.13
primary protection
  background, 9.1
  death benefits, 9.18–9.19
  generally, 9.14
  introduction, 9.2
  lump sum benefits greater than £375,000, 9.17
  method, 9.14
  pension benefits, 9.16
  protected life cover, 9.19
  registration, 9.15
rights in payment, 9.12
rights not yet in payment
  cash balance arrangements, 9.8
  defined benefit arrangements, 9.9
  HMRC limits, 9.11
  hybrid arrangements, 9.10
  introduction, 9.6
  money purchase arrangements, 9.7
RPSM examples
  introduction, 9.4
  lump sum rights, 9.13
  rights in payment, 9.12
  rights not yet in payment, 9.6–9.11
  valuing pre-A-Day rights, 9.5–9.13
scheme protection
  background, 9.1
  introduction, 9.3
tax considerations, 8.7
valuing pre-A-Day rights
  introduction, 9.5
  lump sum rights, 9.13
  rights in payment, 9.12
  rights not yet in payment, 9.6–9.11

Trivial commutation lump sums
death benefit rules, 4.43
general rules, 4.31

Trust and retirement benefits regulations
QROPS, and, 13.5

Trust-busting
penalties, and, 15.12

Unauthorised payments
actual unauthorised member payments, 15.32
assignment of benefits and rights, 15.33
charge
  declaration of liability, 15.44
  generally, 15.40
  introduction, 15.39
  overview, 12.3
deemed unauthorised member payments, 15.32
generally, 15.30
increase in member's benefits beyond the statutory limit, 15.36
increase in rights of connected person on death, 15.35
member use of assets, 15.37
overview, 1.16
'payments', 15.31
relevant charges
  general charge, 15.40
  scheme sanction charge, 15.45–15.51
  surcharge, 15.41–15.44
scheme sanction charge
  generally, 15.45
  introduction, 15.39
  payments excluded, 15.47
  payments which attract, 15.46
  reduction, 15.49
  release of scheme administrator from liability, 15.50
  relief, 15.48
  surplus repayments, 15.51
surcharge
  declaration of liability, 15.44
  discharge, 15.43
  generally, 15.41
  introduction, 15.39
  period for measuring the threshold, 15.42
surrender of benefits and rights, 15.34
tax charges
  declaration of liability, 15.44
  generally, 15.40
  introduction, 15.39
  overview, 12.3
types, 15.30
value-shifting, 15.38

Index

Unauthorised payments charge
  declaration of liability, 15.44
  generally, 15.40
  introduction, 15.39
Unauthorised payments surcharge
  declaration of liability, 15.44
  discharge, 15.43
  generally, 15.41
  introduction, 15.39
  period for measuring the threshold, 15.42
Underwriting commissions
  investment rules, and, 5.13
Unfunded unapproved retirement benefit schemes (UURBS)
  generally, 11.19
Unsecured pensions
  current position, 4.7
  generally, 4.8
UURBS
  generally, 11.19

Value shifting
  investment rules, and, 5.21
Valuing pre-A-Day rights
  introduction, 9.5
  lump sum rights, 9.13
  rights in payment, 9.12
  rights not yet in payment
    cash balance arrangements, 9.8
    defined benefit arrangements, 9.9
    HMRC limits, 9.11
    hybrid arrangements, 9.10
    introduction, 9.6
    money purchase arrangements, 9.7
VAT
  generally, 3.44
Voluntary surrender
  enhanced protection, and, 9.28

Waivers of debt
  investment rules, and, 5.24
Wasting assets
  investment rules, and, 5.2
Trust-busting
  penalties, and, 15.12
Winding up lump sums
  penalties, and, 15.11